PENGUIN  CLASSICS

MONODIES
AND
ON THE RELICS OF SAINTS

GUIBERT OF NOGENT (ca. 1060–ca. 1125), a French monk and one of the most familiar personalities from all the Middle Ages, was born in northern France, where he suffered an unhappy childhood before being elected abbot of Nogent. Despite his relatively slender record of accomplishment, a series of professional missteps, and a general disregard from his peers, he has emerged as one of the most original thinkers of the twelfth century—a century particularly rich in innovative thought and brilliant minds—and one of our most valuable sources for understanding medieval politics, culture, literature, and sensibility. His autobiography, *Monodies*, is considered his crowning achievement.

JOSEPH MCALHANY is an associate professor of classics and the director of the Great Ideas program at Carthage College in Kenosha, Wisconsin.

JAY RUBENSTEIN—a MacArthur Fellow and Rhodes scholar—is an associate professor of medieval history at the University of Tennessee–Knoxville. His extensive publications in the fields of medieval cultural and intellectual history include *Armies of Heaven: The First Crusade and the Quest for Apocalypse* and *Guibert of Nogent: Portrait of a Medieval Mind*, the first comprehensive study of Guibert's life and thought in over a century.

GUIBERT OF NOGENT

Monodies
and
On the Relics of Saints

THE AUTOBIOGRAPHY AND A
MANIFESTO OF A FRENCH
MONK FROM THE TIME
OF THE CRUSADES

Translated by
JOSEPH MCALHANY
and
JAY RUBENSTEIN

Introduction and Notes by
JAY RUBENSTEIN

PENGUIN BOOKS

PENGUIN BOOKS

Published by the Penguin Group
Penguin Group (USA) Inc., 375 Hudson Street, New York, New York 10014, U.S.A.
Penguin Group (Canada), 90 Eglinton Avenue East, Suite 700, Toronto,
Ontario, Canada M4P 2Y3 (a division of Pearson Penguin Canada Inc.)
Penguin Books Ltd, 80 Strand, London WC2R 0RL, England
Penguin Ireland, 25 St Stephen's Green, Dublin 2, Ireland (a division of Penguin Books Ltd)
Penguin Group (Australia), 250 Camberwell Road, Camberwell,
Victoria 3124, Australia (a division of Pearson Australia Group Pty Ltd)
Penguin Books India Pvt Ltd, 11 Community Centre, Panchsheel Park, New Delhi - 110 017, India
Penguin Group (NZ), 67 Apollo Drive, Rosedale, Auckland 0632,
New Zealand (a division of Pearson New Zealand Ltd)
Penguin Books (South Africa) (Pty) Ltd, 24 Sturdee Avenue,
Rosebank, Johannesburg 2196, South Africa

Penguin Books Ltd, Registered Offices:
80 Strand, London WC2R 0RL, England

This translation published in Penguin Books 2011

Map illustration by Cartographic Services Laboratory,
Department of Geography, University of Tennessee, Knoxville.

LIBRARY OF CONGRESS CATALOGING IN PUBLICATION DATA
Guibert, Abbot of Nogent-sous-Coucy, 1053–ca. 1124.
[De vita sua. English]
Monodies ; and, On the relics of saints : the autobiography and a manifesto of a French monk
from the time of the crusades / Guibert of Nogent ; translated by Joseph McAlhany
and Jay Rubenstein ; introduction and notes by Jay Rubenstein.
p.   cm.—(Penguin classics)
Includes bibliographical references and index.
ISBN 978-0-14-310630-2
1. Guibert, Abbot of Nogent-sous-Coucy, 1053–ca. 1124. 2. Abbots—France—Biography. 3. Relics.
4. Jesus Christ—Relics. 5. Abbaye de Saint-Médard (Soissons, France) I. McAlhany, Joseph.
II. Rubenstein, Jay, 1967– III. Guibert, Abbot of Nogent-sous-Coucy, 1053–ca. 1124.
De pignoribus sanctorum. English. IV. Title. V. Title: On the relics of saints.
BX4705.G698A3 2011
271'.102—dc23   2011030054

Set in Sabon Lt Std

146122990

Contents

Introduction

Guibert of Nogent:
His Book and His Demons

No one would call the years 1060 to 1125 in France the "Age of Guibert," but Guibert of Nogent has probably done more than anyone else to shape our understanding of medieval Europe at that time. By any standard measure of achievement, he led a quiet and undistinguished life. For about thirty years he lived as a monk at the monastery of Saint-Germer de Fly before being elected abbot of Nogent-sous-Coucy. He studied for a time with St. Anselm of Bec, one of the Middle Ages' greatest philosophical and theological minds. Under Anselm's influence, he composed two lengthy books of biblical exegesis, one on Genesis and another on the minor Old Testament prophets. He also wrote a history of the First Crusade and several shorter theological treatises, all of which achieved at least limited circulation and a small readership. Some of these texts may even have played a part in shaping the thought of better-known monastic writers such as Bernard of Clairvaux. But Guibert himself was quickly forgotten, leaving barely a trace on the historical record, outside his own writings.

The two texts included in this volume—his autobiographical memoir, *Monodies* (1115), and his treatise *On the Relics of Saints* (1119)—were, in terms of circulation, his least successful books. No medieval exemplar of the *Monodies* survives—it reaches us in its entirety in a single seventeenth-century copy. *On the Relics of Saints* appears in only one twelfth-century manuscript, mostly written in Guibert's own hand;[1] from the available evidence, it never circulated beyond the walls of Guibert's own church. But in terms of content, these books are among the most strikingly original achievements from all the

Middle Ages, comparable to Anselm of Bec's demonstration of God's existence in the *Proslogion*, or to Bernard of Clairvaux's monumental series of sermons on the Song of Songs.

Guibert did not engage with great issues in the same ways as did his more successful contemporaries. His goals were more mundane: he would withdraw into his own mind and ponder the wonders of everyday life, including, in particular, the development of his own personality. He sought not to understand all creation but only the small corner of it that he inhabited—a turbulent, violent, irksome, and beautiful world undergoing such profound changes that some have called it the age of "the discovery of the individual."[2] And we find perhaps our best and most mesmerizing guide to this world in the voice of Guibert of Nogent.

Guibert's narrative and argumentative paths are not always easy to follow. Like all great writers, Guibert had his own sense of how to tell a story, his own particular vocabulary, and his own theories about the workings of the world, the shape of history, and the nature of evil. In his writings—and in these two books in particular—he put those theories to the test. What makes Guibert especially engaging as a narrator is that he does not claim to have found all the answers. He knows how human psychology ought to work, but he also willingly acknowledges the significant gaps that exist between his beliefs and earthly and heavenly realities.

Nearly nine centuries after his death, Guibert remains a distinctive voice, capable of moving, infuriating, and disturbing audiences. His books speak for themselves, but this introduction, it is hoped, will prepare readers to experience Guibert's world.

MEMORIES, MEMOIRS, AND MONODIES

The *Monodies* was an unusual project, as indicated by its title alone, likely as unfamiliar to Guibert's audience as it is to us. "Monody" is a technical term from Greek drama, referring to a sad song, sung on stage by a single singer. As its name implies, therefore, the *Monodies* is a deeply personal work. It is also astonishingly original. Put in the starkest terms: Around AD 400, Augustine of Hippo wrote his *Confessions*, which, in modern parlance, is an autobiography. Taking the form of a prayer to God, it describes his birth, his family, his childhood, his early career, and his eventual conversion to Christianity. After Augustine's mother's death, the text takes a radically metaphysical turn, abandoning the world of events and becoming instead a meditation on sensory perception and, eventually, on the meaning of scripture and Creation. The next person to attempt a similar project was Guibert of Nogent. Completed in 1115, the *Monodies* was the first fully realized autobiography in more than seven hundred years.

Like Augustine, Guibert begins with the story of his birth and family. He describes his childhood, his education, his early career as a monk at the church of Saint-Germer de Fly outside of Beauvais, and his eventual election as abbot at Nogent, a newly founded church community midway between the cities of Laon and Soissons. After his promotion, which represents for Guibert a conversion of sorts, his book, like Augustine's, takes a sharp turn. Rather than look inward to meditate upon the soul and upon God, however, Guibert shifts his gaze outward to explore the world around him, in all its imperfect, frightening detail.

The obvious question for readers of the *Monodies* is, "Why did Guibert write this book?" Or perhaps, more appropriately, "What *enabled* Guibert to write this book?" The need to tell one's story, to leave a mark on the world through putting words on parchment or paper, is perhaps universal among writers. And the Early Middle Ages do not lack examples of authors and historians who regularly insert themselves into the stories they were telling. But to make one's life the subject of a book, to fashion one's memories and emotions into a coherent narrative, represents another kind of creativity. Why then did this obscure abbot—who during his life achieved little fame outside of a small circle of readers in northern France—feel that his life story was one worth telling, and why did his story take this particularly unusual form?

To review the details of Guibert's life, he was born around 1060 near Beauvais.[3] His father was a younger son in the lesser nobility of the region. But the background to this birth, Guibert feels, is also important. For during the first seven years of his parents' marriage, they were unable to consummate their relationship. (He must have heard these stories from his mother, conversations that surely caused him no small discomfort.) With the help of friendly witchcraft, the couple finally did have sex and had at least three sons, Guibert the youngest of them. His father, Evrard, died when Guibert was still a child, too young for him to have formed any real impressions of the man to compare with stories his mother told. Now widowed and under pressure from her husband's family to remarry, his mother, whom he never names, instead established an independent life for herself and hired a teacher to help raise her obviously gifted youngest son. The teacher's name was, appropriately, Solomon, though as Guibert presents him, the man had no Solomonic wisdom and no real skills as a pedagogue, save for a quick whip hand. Eventually both mother and surrogate father abandoned Guibert to take up clerical lives, the mother as an anchoress outside the church of Saint-Germer de Fly, and Solomon as a monk within church walls. At this point Guibert flirted with the idea of a career as a knight, but eventually he, too, followed his mother to Saint-Germer, living for a time as a student inside the monastery before finally joining Solomon as a monk.

It was an unremarkable beginning to what would prove an undistinguished ecclesiastical career. For a time it seemed that Guibert would never move beyond his first church. Despite family connections in the area, and a concerted effort by his relatives to buy him a prestigious office, no one was interested in his talents. Eventually he learned to view failure as a blessing. His desire for promotion, he decided, had been an insidious form of temptation. It was far safer to embrace a life of obscurity and quiet contemplation. But just as he had begun to resign himself to this sort of life, he learned to his great surprise that a group of monks he had never heard of had elected him to the abbacy of Notre-Dame de Nogent, a small, recent foundation built in the shadow of the imposing castle at Coucy, about seventy miles from his home at Saint-Germer. The transition to leadership proved difficult. Within three years his monks had driven him out of his office because of circumstances to which he refers in his *Monodies* but never explains. One year later, in 1108, under equally obscure circumstances, he returned, carrying with him an elegant, learned, and at times ecstatic chronicle of the First Crusade, titled *The Deeds of God Through the Franks*, which he dedicated to the bishop of Soissons.

Five years later, apparently well settled at Nogent but amenable to the possibility of further promotion, Guibert dedicated a work of biblical exegesis to the bishop of Laon—his *Moral Commentary on Genesis*. It is a text he had been working on for almost a quarter of a century, and it holds the keys to his entire system of thought, as he in fact tells us in his memoirs. In *Monodies* 1.17, he describes his first meetings with Anselm, initially prior and then abbot of the Norman monastery of Bec. Anselm was in the habit of visiting Saint-Germer de Fly, beginning sometime in the 1070s. The reasons for these visits are unclear, but Anselm lavished so much attention upon young Guibert—or so Guibert tells us—that you would have thought their lessons alone justified his time there.

> By dividing the mind into a three- or four-part scheme, he taught me to treat all the transactions of the internal mystery under the categories of affection, will, reason, and intellect. Many people, including myself, thought the first two (affection and will) were one and the same, but he clearly defined the distinction between them and showed that they were not identical. However, there are clear arguments to prove that when either the fourth (intellect) or third (reason) is present, then the first two are the same.

Guibert went on, he says, to apply these ideas to scriptural passages, particularly to his commentary on Genesis.

This brief description establishes clear signposts for interpreting the *Moral Commentary on Genesis*. It does not, however, do full justice to the originality of Guibert's work. The *Moral Commentary on Genesis* is, first, a purely tropological analysis. That is, Guibert examines scripture exclusively for lessons that Christians could apply to their everyday lives. Through tradition, exegetes approached the Bible on four levels: the literal (what do the words actually mean?), the allegorical (what do the words tell us about the development of Christian ecclesiastical practice?), the tropological (what do the words teach about how to live a Christian life?), and the anagogical (what do the words reveal about the last days?). Guibert, in his decision to emphasize the moral or tropological meanings, was very much in step with his age, and perhaps even at its forefront. The twelfth century would prove to be the great era of moral commentary, illustrated most vividly in the impassioned sermons of Bernard of Clairvaux on the Song of Songs, but characteristic of uncounted lesser-known works as well.

Guibert's own readings, however, are far more systematic than those of the moral exegetes who succeeded him. In Guibert's analysis, every character in Genesis becomes the embodiment of a psychological faculty—usually affection, will, reason, or intellect. More startlingly, the characters of Genesis and the mental faculties they represent together form a single mind, and their interactions a single story. It is, to be precise and to use Guibert's own phrasing, "a mystical narrative." Most usually, one of the patriarchs (Abraham, Isaac, or Jacob) embodies Reason. The patriarchs' wives usually symbolize the Will, and their children act as Affection. If the mind is in its proper working order, with the patriarch or Reason in charge, it will enjoy peace and riches. If Reason surrenders its authority (as when, for example, Abraham has his wife, Sarah, pretend to be his sister, thus acting as if she is not subservient to him as a wife but rather shares an equality of blood), disorder is introduced, and the Christian mind falls into sin. The pattern repeats itself throughout Genesis, until the story of Joseph, the son of Jacob. Joseph embodies a new intellectual function: Intellect, or Understanding. Clarifying some of the obscurity from the *Monodies*, Guibert tells us that Joseph represents a part of the mind, developed through spiritual exercises such that the Christian is now capable of focusing entirely on the divine. Guibert's name for this faculty, *intellectus*, recalls St. Anselm's famous dictum from the *Proslogion* (which Anselm was writing at precisely the time he would have met Guibert): *fides quaerens intellectum*, or "faith seeking understanding." The "Understanding" that Anselm found was the ontological argument, a logical path that explained the necessity of God's existence. To paraphrase: "If that than which nothing greater can be thought exists in the mind, it must also exist in reality and can only be God." What Guibert sought in his moral commentaries was the prize that had probably eluded Anselm's overly refined logic—continuous monastic contemplation and the concomitant unbroken vision of God.

That structure of personal development (initial conversion born out of fear, spiritual growth, and contemplative bliss) is the same model that informs Guibert's *Monodies*, or at least the first book of the *Monodies*. Guibert the child is rootless Affection. His mother is a stern Will, but she, like Guibert, lacks a strong Reason, or virtuous husband or patriarch, to guide her. When her husband dies, as Guibert structures his story, his teacher, Solomon, almost immediately replaces him in the narrative. The character Solomon is a more fitting model for Reason, but he lacks true understanding, imparting to Guibert lessons that he himself cannot grasp. When Solomon and Guibert's mother both abandon him for Saint-Germer, Guibert surrenders himself to sin. Affection is in control of the mind and predictably falls deeply into sin—though the sins in fact seem mild. Essentially, Guibert begins sleeping late and wearing foppish clothes. He also starts training to be a knight. Reason and will—Solomon and his mother—however, soon reassert their authority and call young Guibert to Saint-Germer. Upon visiting the church, he realizes that he intensely desires to become a monk. After overcoming a few final temptations—namely, his ambitions first to win fame through writing lewd poetry and then to achieve great honor by attaining higher office—Guibert at last attains something like internal peace and contemplative joy.

It is no wonder that psychohistorians in the 1970s found

much to like about the *Monodies*. As is readily apparent from even this brief description, Guibert was something of a psychological theorist. Like some of his modern counterparts, he divided the mind into three faculties, and a comparison between "affection, will, and reason" and "id, ego, and superego" would not be inappropriate. In book 1 of the *Monodies*, Guibert applies his theory to his life, using not only his moral vocabulary but also his ideas about the structure of Christian conversion to explain his reactions to the world around him as he sought to locate his place in God's plan for humanity. In this insight we have also answered the important questions raised earlier: Guibert was able to write an autobiography because he had developed a theory about human psychology, and he shaped the *Monodies* according to the dictates of this theory.

After making the advance in virtue that Guibert describes in *Monodies* 1.19, the next step in the progress of the ideal Christian life would be to take on the role of Joseph and to achieve, if only on occasion, a sense of contemplative peace and a foretaste of paradise, a glimpse of the vision of God. This is the goal that all contemplatives seek and one that, in this world, they never attain to perfection. The final image of Genesis is of Joseph being buried in Egypt, the land of the pharaohs. According to Guibert's exegesis, Joseph in his grave is a Christian intellect focused upon God but surrounded by all the worst temptations of the world, never truly freed until it has attained an actual place in heaven. In the language of Pope Gregory the Great (ca. 540–604), such burdens are a sacrifice of humility, an unfortunate necessity in this life.[4] Guibert's own sacrifice of humility came in the form of his election as abbot. But he also lived through some of the most turbulent events in French history, social upheavals that he could not explain but that he documents in great detail in the third book of his *Monodies*.

As he turns his attention first to Nogent, in book 2 of the *Monodies*, and then to Laon and Soissons in book 3, Guibert himself disappears for great stretches of his narrative. In his place, we meet a panoply of bizarre and intriguing characters who together provide readers with a dynamic and variegated overview of France in the early twelfth century. There is Gaudry, the astonishingly venal and profane bishop of Laon; Jean of Soissons, the delightfully irreverent count who attends church services only to admire pretty women and who often threatens to convert to Judaism; Sibylle de Porcien, the promiscuous and sadistic wife of Enguerrand de Boves; the illiterate heretics Clement and Evrard; and, most memorable of all, Thomas of Marle, the castellan son of Enguerrand whose cruelty earned him the reputation during his life of being the worst man who had ever lived. Thomas is emblematic of France's castellan class, men who asserted independent rule over tiny pockets of territory, based largely on an ability to use their primitive castles as safe houses from which to terrify the populace. These castellans exercised judicial authority with a random brutality, inflicting on subjects who displeased them such penalties that blinding and castration seemed the least of them. It is not apparent from the *Monodies*, but the early twelfth century was the swan song of castellans such as Thomas. A more assertive French monarchy had begun working aggressively to bring these turbulent men to heel. In Guibert's analysis, however, the king most responsible for starting this process, Louis VI, is just as greedy and inconstant as the men he would seek to dominate.

It is a toxic mix of personality and ambition that together leads to the most memorable and historically significant event that Guibert describes: the communal revolt at Laon, about twenty miles from Nogent. Laon was one of many cities in twelfth-century France whose citizens struggled to gain a charter of liberties—to establish a commune. *Communio* is a name that Guibert finds ironic. The ultimate effect of the institution, as he saw it, was to break down traditional lines of community. But from the perspective of the citizens, or burghers, of Laon, their goal was much more constructive and conservative. They wished only to free themselves, in exchange for a lump sum, from the arbitrary customs, dues, and punishments imposed upon them by the clergy and the nobility (and in Laon, the bishop exercised both comital and ecclesiastical duties). In an urban world with a rapidly expanding monetary economy, the ordinary townsmen could not afford to become embroiled in the feuds typical of the aristocracy. The emergence of the commune in Laon, therefore, was a sign of the social dynamism and expansion that characterized Guibert's world. But to Guibert, "commune" seemed only another sign of the sinfulness and decay that was pulling his society apart, making his job as spiritual pastor that much more difficult.

The revolt occurred with astonishing abruptness in April 1112. Its causes remain a subject for debate. As is usually the case with Guibert, he doesn't give easy answers. He presents, rather, a dizzying array of explanations—economic, social, and theological—and all but challenges his readers to come up with their own theories. Or perhaps he is only being evasive, or is simply unable to admit his own responsibility for what happened. Without the incompetent and unprincipled Gaudry as bishop of Laon, the revolt might never have occurred, and Guibert had had several occasions to stop the bishop. In 1106, for example, Guibert spoke before Pope Pascal II and the papal curia in the city of Langres, defending the election of Gaudry as bishop of Laon, despite his evident unsuitability for office. In 1111, after the murder of Gerard de Quierzy in the cathedral of Laon by Gaudry's henchmen, Guibert preached a sermon of reconciliation and purification to the people. In light of the riot that occurred a few months later, the sermon failed. Finally, in the same year, Guibert listened in shock as Bishop Gaudry excommunicated not the murderers but the people who had tried to punish the murderers. When offered the chance to express his complaints publicly, Guibert fell silent. Offered many opportunities to intervene—to condemn the villains in the story or to pacify an angry populace—Guibert failed on each occasion. He must have recognized as much, but of all the shortcomings painfully apparent in his memoirs, of all the demons that haunt his world, this is surely the one that troubled him the most and the one that he was never able to acknowledge.

ON THE RELICS OF SAINTS

The other text in this book is more polemical than the *Monodies*, but it is equally personal, and, like the *Monodies*, its structure reflects Guibert's fundamental beliefs about moral theology. The topic of *On the Relics of Saints*, however, is quite narrow: A monastery in Soissons, Saint-Médard, about ten miles from Nogent, claimed to possess among its relics a baby tooth of Christ. Saint-Médard was an ancient church, especially in comparison with Nogent. Founded in the mid–sixth century, it had occasionally played a prominent role in the political and cultural life of France—notably in 833 when Louis the Pious, the son of Charlemagne, was imprisoned there upon being deposed by his children. It was certainly far more important and wealthier than Nogent. For such a venerable institution to make such a patently absurd claim astonished Guibert. The refutation of the monks of Soissons, correspondingly, inspired some of his most caustic rhetoric. On reading the work it is easy to imagine the author trembling with rage as he searches for the right word to describe his adversaries, until finally settling again on some variation of "stupid." The abundance of things needing to be said, as he observes, left him speechless.

This book falls into four parts. In the first one, Guibert starts to address the supposed tooth of Christ, but he becomes distracted by all of the other abuses associated with relic cults. The range and furor of his invective have led some readers to find in these passages hints of modernity, as if Guibert were a Counter-Reformation apologist or a proto-modern mind. But Guibert is a product of his age, albeit a curious and unusual product. He is not a critic of the miraculous in principle. He in fact relates several wondrous stories in the course of his argumentative presentation. What disturbs him are pointless wonderworks perpetrated through obvious fraud and spread by clerics mainly anxious to collect cash. In the second book Guibert once again starts to discuss the tooth of Christ, but this time he becomes sidetracked with a meditation on the problem of Christological relics in general, and in particular how such relics could exist after the establishment of the Eucharist. Finally, in the third book, he fully treats and debunks the tooth of Christ at Soissons, leaving the way open in the fourth and final book to meditate upon the true rewards of

Christianity: eternal spiritual life and peaceful contemplation, achieved through the mind and not through physical objects.

The arguments in *On the Relics of Saints* are thus in part historical but mainly theological. Relics serve as memorials to the saints. They are physical reminders of the lives lived by holy men. Not necessary for salvation, they are nonetheless useful. To borrow language from Guibert's moral theology, they are good "first steps" on the path to conversion. But Christ has no need for physical memorials, because through the Eucharist he established a direct point of contact with all believers who have access to a priest. Physical relics—such as the supposed tooth of Christ, or the umbilical cord or the foreskin, which other communities claimed to possess—were all useless. But worse than useless, they contradicted scripture. For did not Christ say, "The poor you will always have with you, but me you will not always have"?[5] By making this pronouncement, he demonstrated unequivocally that after the resurrection his body would leave the earth in its entirety. The monks of Saint-Médard, who claimed to possess a part of this body, were making a mockery of the words of the gospel, undermining the purpose of the Eucharist, and calling into question all of the promises that Christ had made about the salvation of the world.

This argument leads Guibert to define, eventually, Christ's body as being, like the Trinity, both tripartite and unified. There is a principal body, or a historical body, which Christ inhabited during his earthly life. There is the vicarial or figural body, which he makes available to us through the Eucharist. And then there is the impassible body in heaven, sitting at the right hand of the Father. The historical body gave us an earthly point of contact, a beginning point for the process of conversion and salvation. The vicarial body provides fodder for contemplation: If believers can learn to see in the bread and wine the true body of Christ, then they will have begun to ascend great contemplative heights. The heavenly body, of course, is the end point of conversion—the divine vision that the elect shall share through eternity. It is a bold and even elegant eucharistic, theological argument, and Guibert no doubt hoped his ideas would win for him general recognition and perhaps even fame—the old demon of "earthly glory," which he believed himself to have conquered in book 1 of the *Monodies*, thus continued to haunt him.

But the Eucharist, like the Trinity, was a dangerous topic to write on. The doctrine in the early 1100s was still very much in the process of definition and redefinition. The famous heretic Berengar of Tours (ca. 1010–1088) had attacked the predominant "realist" doctrine, arguing that the host could not be wholly and entirely the body of Christ. Christ had pronounced at the Last Supper, "This is my body." If *this*, which is to say "the bread," ceased to exist altogether and became entirely "the body," then the predicate in the sentence would have destroyed the subject—a grammatical impossibility in a sentence with a linking verb. If Christ said, "This (bread) is my body," then the bread must continue to exist, after some fashion. Lanfranc of Bec (ca. 1000–1089), who actually makes a brief appearance in *On the Relics of Saints*, defended orthodoxy against Berengar, and in doing so helped to create the doctrine of transubstantiation. The substance of the bread and wine changed into the body and blood of Christ, but the external "accidents," which determine appearance but not reality, remained the same.[6] In 1079 Pope Gregory VII condemned Berengar's position as heretical, and Lanfranc's analysis became the accepted one, although no one, including perhaps Lanfranc, quite yet understood it. The doctrine of the Eucharist, of course, would never be settled to everyone's satisfaction. But in Guibert's day the situation for serious intellectuals was perhaps at its most difficult. To understand transubstantiation required a familiarity with basic Aristotelian concepts and vocabulary, a background that few people (and Guibert was not one of them) possessed. In effect, everyone knew what he was supposed to believe, but nobody knew why it was true.

Guibert probably hoped that, like his teacher St. Anselm of Bec, his arguments could carry the day based on their rationality and elegance. But clearly his audience was not as welcoming of his ideas as he had hoped. The most troublesome point concerned not the mechanics of the Real Presence, but rather the question of what happened if one of the damned participated in the Eucharist. It was a topic that had been aired two years earlier in 1117, indirectly, by a monk named Rupert of Deutz. In one of his exegetical-theological works, he had argued that Judas had not received the Real Presence at the Last Supper—not for any theological reasons, but simply because he had left the table before Christ had established the sacraments. (The four gospels, in fact, are unclear on this point.) Rupert tells us that he nearly lost his "license for writing" because of this argument, but was saved at the last moment when someone discovered a passage from St. Hilary of Poitiers that supported his position. Rupert survived to write another day, and intellectual circles in northern France continued to argue about the questions he had raised: Did Judas receive the sacrament, and, more broadly, could a condemned sinner ever partake of the true body of Christ?

One of these churchmen, a monk named Siegfried, wrote a letter to Guibert asking for his thoughts. Guibert responded with a short response called "On the Handful of Bread Given to Judas." He treads a very fine line in this letter, saying that a certain handful of bread, which Christ gave to Judas, as reported in the gospel of John, was not a sacrament, because Christ handed it to him before he had pronounced, "This is my body." Guibert also concludes that Judas was present at the Last Supper. But he does not ever specify whether Judas, during the Last Supper, did in fact receive the Real Presence.

When Guibert returned to the topic of the Eucharist in *On the Relics of Saints*, he found himself drawn irresistibly back to this question. Teasing out his actual opinion from the text of *On the Relics of Saints*, however, is almost impossible without consulting the original manuscript. Since I have written about this topic at some length elsewhere, I will only summarize my conclusions here.[7] In the initial draft of book 2 of *On the Relics of Saints*, Guibert argued that the Eucharist did indeed contain the true body of Christ, and that each morsel of the Eucharist contained that body perfectly and in its entirety. If an unworthy priest performed the Eucharist, he could nonetheless, despite his moral status, successfully and fully create the sacraments for his congregants. But if one of the damned attempted to participate in the Mass, he or she would receive only ordinary bread from the priest's hand. In this way, Christ's body would be protected from the polluted bodies of nonbelievers. He would also be protected from the indignity of, for example, being eaten by mice or dogs, if careless priests dropped some of the sacramental bread onto the floor.

The argument, however, did not pass theological muster. It was not fitting that the identity and existence of the sacraments should be dependent upon the virtue of the person who received it. To attribute such mutability to the gifts of God was heretical. Guibert tried to defend his position for a time, introducing at least two new pages of arguments into his text, but eventually—probably upon seeing the book *On the Truth of Christ's Body and Blood in the Eucharist* by Guitmund of Aversa—he was forced to recant. Rather than destroy his old arguments, however, he instead pretended that he had never made them in the first place. By making a few careful changes to his text, he could create the impression than an unnamed "adversary" had proposed these ideas, and that Guibert was demonstrating their falsity. "But let no one bear it amiss if I seem to argue for a while from the perspective of someone who thinks otherwise," he writes over a couple of erased lines at the beginning of this section on unworthy communicants. At the end, he writes, again over an erasure, "Against these things, less temperately asserted, I shall respond with briefer— because they are more temperate—arguments." He then inserted into the text a short and, I think, wholly unconvincing refutation.

The net result is that book 2 of *On the Relics of Saints* is a difficult and at times incoherent piece of work. It does, however, introduce readers into the rough-and-tumble world of twelfth-century theology, whose bitter debates would go on to inform the character and structure of the medieval and the modern university. It also helps to explain why such a dynamic and original treatment of the problem of saints' relics has never been widely available to a general audience until now.

FACING ONE'S DEMONS

The final book of *On the Relics of Saints*, like the final book of the *Monodies*, radically changes tone. It becomes a beautifully realized, elegantly presented commentary on the contemplative experience, built around a meditation concerning the world of spirits, or, as Guibert prefers, "the inner world." In essence, he wants to understand what heaven is like, and in order to get a sense of heaven and of God, he chooses to focus on their opposite, demons and hell—something nearer to hand and of which he has had more experience. The devil and his servants, Guibert concludes, are inhabitants of the inner world. They do not have "fleshy" bodies. "Indeed, the nature of demons is exceedingly fine-honed with an inborn alacrity, and on account of the discernment required to see them, or more accurately, on account of their nimble spiritual power, no matter how much they wander through this outer world, the inner world more properly fits their mode of existence."

Life, for Guibert, is a series of struggles against these airy creatures, fought on the battlegrounds of the mind. Indeed, Guibert is at his most eloquent when he describes these awesome struggles of the human psyche, filled as it was with "ethereal spirits ordered like armies into divisions. The mind indeed is called nothing other than *the house of God and the gate of heaven*, which God inhabits and rules, which he unlocks in order to allow entry to spiritual and heavenly sights."[8] The demons that Guibert faces so often in his *Monodies* are surely products of this spiritual conflict, suprarational phenomena rather than supernatural. Seen from this perspective, the otherworldly battles that he describes would not be all that far removed from the modern concept of "facing your demons." Temptation and sin exist in the mind. Through proper meditation, through the careful ordering of one's thoughts, they can be overcome.

This sort of economy for salvation leaves little room for physical, tangible demons. Sin originates from a failure of the faculty of reason to maintain a proper balance, not primarily from the work of the devil or his servants. When Guibert speaks of demons in the abstract (primarily in exegetical works), he tends to place them in apposition to vices ("motions of the mind toward earthly things"), and he usually focuses on wicked thoughts themselves rather than on their possible origins. In his lengthy *Moral Commentary on Genesis*, he addresses the mechanics of demonology only once—in a commentary on Genesis 26:18, an otherwise unremarkable passage where Isaac digs anew wells that had been dug first by his father, Abraham, but that the Philistines had subsequently filled with rocks. The Philistines in this instance are demons. Drunk with pride and overcome with envy, they fill up wells created by "Affection and certain interior motions that serve Reason effectively," blocking up their perceptivity with "great rocks of care." Or else these wells are "the recognition and understanding of virtue" from which we draw "life-giving water," sealed up by demons with a "barricade of earthiness."[9]

But this intellectual perspective seems at odds with the actual tales of the supernatural that permeate the *Monodies*, clustering especially around the chapters at the end of each of the three books. To all appearances the stories are randomly selected and carelessly arranged—like the Romanesque gargoyles that would have decorated the churches of Guibert's world, they peer menacingly out of the dark corners and dead ends of the author's imagination. To take a few examples: A demon with hunched shoulders paces a dormitory and observes the sleeping entourage of the bishop of Beauvais, before commenting about how one virtuous youth in particular torments him. Demons disguised as dogs attack a serving woman who had hidden ill-gotten loot in a baby's crib. A demon convinces a pilgrim to Compostella to castrate himself and cut his own throat. And a monk studies the black arts with a Jew and then takes a mistress, whom he transforms into a dog. How are we to reconcile these passages with the sophisticated psychological observations and the remarkable historical analysis that characterizes other sections of the *Monodies*? How can they be reconciled with the thoughtful and at times brilliant mind that constructed book 4 of *On the Relics of Saints*?

We probably cannot, in fact, reconcile them, and that is not a bad thing. Guibert tried to understand and to exorcise his demons, but he did not succeed. It is not even clear that he wanted to exorcise them. Intellectually he could comprehend how demons fit into the spiritual universe, but emotionally he wished to keep them real and in his world. To illustrate this point we ought to consider another of Guibert's treatises, *Against the Judaizer and the Jews*, a short book in which he engaged in theological debate against certain unnamed Jewish adversaries. As part of his presentation, he defended the Christian doctrine of the Incarnation. Jews found absurd the idea that God would mix his own essence with human corruption. A similar Jewish polemic seems to have inspired Guibert's old teacher St. Anselm of Bec to write the *Cur Deus homo*, or "Why the God-Man." Based on Guibert's diction within his own treatise, he knew of Anselm's book and its methods, innovative in part because, as far as sin and salvation were concerned, Anselm took Satan out of the equation. The traditional school of Christian thought held that the devil, due to original sin, had gained rights over the souls of man. In order to ransom a lost humanity from the thrall of Satan, God had become man and lived a sinless life. The devil nonetheless still tried to claim Christ's unblemished soul and in doing so broke the terms of his contract, thus enabling all of humanity to be saved. Anselm refused to believe that Satan, who embodies injustice, could ever hold rights over man. God did not need to "break the devil's contract" because the devil, as a lawless being, was not entitled to contractual protections. But if the devil were truly powerless, why would there be a need for the Incarnation? How does one explain the Incarnation without appeal to the rights of the devil?

The answer, in Anselm's economy of salvation, is that the Incarnation occurred not to save man from the devil but to reconcile man to God. Only God could redeem man and create reconciliation, but justice dictated that he ought not to do it. Man ought to reconcile himself to God, but he lacked the ability to do so. The only being, therefore, who could and should bring about this reconciliation was someone who was both God (who could do it) and man (who ought to do it)—to wit, the *Deus homo* of Anselm's title, "the God-man." It is an elegant argument and, after the *Proslogion*, perhaps Anselm's greatest intellectual achievement. But Guibert preferred the older school of thought, and he continued to defend it in *Against the Judaizer and the Jews*. Christ became man to ransom a sinful humanity. The devil had powers, claims that could be broken only through a legal process mixed with divine chicanery, a debt to be paid with blood alone. Thus, when choosing between his beloved teacher and his own demons, Guibert preferred his demons.

This conflict, between a fear of demonic power and a desire to minimize it, is the central drama of Guibert's life. He wished to control his demons, to deny them authority and to admit their reality. He may have failed to strike a balance among these impulses, but his heartfelt depiction of the process makes his *Monodies* a true classic of literature. These demons that Guibert could not control were the essential tragedy of his life. They were products of his mind, as his moral theology demanded, but they were no less terrifyingly real because of it.

Was Guibert the identifiable neurotic that some commentators have believed him to be? The description is not entirely inappropriate. The roots of the adult trauma, so readily apparent in the *Monodies* and *On the Relics of Saints*, can likely be traced back to his childhood, to the early death of his father, to the abuses inflicted on him by his surrogate father, Solomon, and to the conduct of his mother—that she continued to live outside the walls of his monastery at Saint-Germer, that she seemed to enjoy free access to the church while he was a monk there, that she adopted a notoriously ill-tempered child in penance for her dead husband's sexual transgressions, and that she regularly prophesied to Guibert that he would be a failure. All of this could only have intensified his mental anguish.

But the central tragedy in the *Monodies* is that Guibert the character never reaches the destination that Guibert the theologian predicted for him. Human life was a pilgrimage, as any student of St. Augustine would have known. The journey was long and full of frustration. "I confess to your greatness, God," he writes at the beginning of the *Monodies*, "my departures from you, caused by countless errors, and the frequent returns you inspired, from my inner wretchedness back to you." The Christian life was an elaborate journey, but, like the famous labyrinth in Chartres Cathedral, it had no dead ends and only one conclusion: peace, contemplation, and perfect understanding. The old Guibert had witnessed the destruction of a city, had failed as a monastic leader to keep his monks in line and his own demons at bay, and had, as a theologian, been forced to recant the higher truths he once believed he had discovered. This Guibert must have believed that the end point of his journey would not be the heavenly understanding he had so earnestly sought. Instead, as he moved farther into the darker corners of his thoughts, he would come face-to-face not with God in heaven but with one of the gargoyles or grotesqueries that inhabited the capitals and corridors of the dimly lit Romanesque churches, a world of perpetual twilight whose boundaries had defined most of his adult life.

PREVIOUS TRANSLATIONS AND THE CURRENT VERSION

Three major English-language translations of Guibert's *Monodies* appeared in the twentieth century. The first, by C. C. Swinton Bland, published in 1925 under the title *The Autobiography of Guibert, Abbot of Nogent-sous-Coucy*,[10] is problematic, being both inaccurate and stylistically awkward, to the point of impenetrability. It remains a popular translation, though, for two reasons. First, like a lot of older and unreadable translations of medieval primary sources, it has been made available on the Internet. Second, John Benton used a revised version of Swinton Bland's translation for a later version of the *Monodies*, published under the title *Self and Society in Medieval France: The Memoirs of Abbot Guibert of Nogent (1064–ca.*

1125).[11] In terms of quality of translation, Benton eliminated many of the obvious errors from Swinton Bland's text, but he preserved its archaic and impenetrable tone. The general impression that readers carry away from Benton's Guibert is one of a man not completely in control of his diction or his mind.

Such a reading dovetails nicely with Benton's general presentation of Guibert's character. He offers in his introduction a subtle reading of Guibert's life, using primarily Freudian methodology. Guibert's domineering mother and his absentee father helped to create in him powerful Oedipal desires. When neither his mother nor his teacher returned this love, he turned his affection inward and developed a narcissistic personality disorder. "When we try to use him as a window onto medieval life," Benton concludes damningly, "we look through the eyes of a disturbed man."[12] It is wonderful rhetoric and wonderful analysis, and it has continued to shape academic reaction to Guibert long after psychohistory faded in popularity and long after we should have realized the folly of applying psychoanalytic methods to someone who never underwent analysis.

The more recent translation by Paul J. Archambault, titled *A Monk's Confession: The Memoirs of Guibert of Nogent*,[13] represents an enormous advance in quality and accuracy over the Swinton Bland/Benton text. This is in part because Archambault had a superior edition of the *Monodies* to work from, published by Edmond-René Labande, with facing French translation and titled simply *Autobiographie*.[14] Based on the work of earlier printed versions of the *Monodies*, the advice of numerous colleagues, and his own good judgment, Labande was able to make numerous revisions and improvements to the existing Latin text. It served as the base text for Archambault's translation and for the current translation as well.

Labande's edition, however, while a great improvement over previous editions, is not perfect. After its publication (and before the publication of *A Monk's Confession*), François Dolbeau discovered two previously unknown, incomplete transcriptions of the *Monodies*. Variations between these manuscripts and the previously established editions enabled Dolbeau to suggest several crucial changes to book 3 of the text, in some cases clearing up errors or points of confusion noted by Benton and Archambault.[15] In the current translation we have adopted many, though not all, of the revisions proposed by Dolbeau and have highlighted in the endnotes those occasions when revisions have substantially changed accepted readings of the text. We have also noticed other apparent errors in the Latin text and have again explained those revisions in endnotes. Finally, Professor McAlhany, thanks to his background in classical Latin, has been able to draw out several—by twelfth-century standards—archaic idioms that distinguish Guibert's language from many of his peers', again clarifying points of confusion in earlier translations. These revisions alone should justify the publication of a new version of the *Monodies*.

Beyond specific points of meaning, we have also attempted to inject a tone into this translation that will separate it from its predecessors. The most fundamental principle of our work has been to recognize that Guibert himself, as described above, was a psychological theorist. He had his own vocabulary and his own system of beliefs—a point that Benton, in *Self and Society*, not only did not recognize but also actively denied.[16] In my earlier writings on Guibert, I have analyzed the details of this system, and it is the current translators' hope that a proper recognition of Guibert's own beliefs will move this version of the *Monodies* closer to Guibert's original meaning than previous versions of the text have managed to do.

Finally, as a longtime student of Guibert's work, I also can say with some confidence that Professor McAlhany (who undertook the lion's share of translator's duties) has moved closer in English to capturing the tone and texture of Guibert's Latin than had previously seemed possible. Guibert is a difficult writer. This difficulty, combined with frequent errors in the Latin editions of his work, has led some scholars to dismiss him as a bad writer. With Labande's edition of the *Monodies*, however, and more important, with the prolific editorial work of R. B. C. Huygens, Latinists have begun to appreciate the craftsmanship and quality of Guibert's language. Stylistically, he goes against the grain of his peers, particularly the circle of writers who worked in the shadows of St. Anselm. Whereas, for example, Eadmer of Canterbury establishes a pleasantly conversational tone in his presentation of English history, Guibert writes with a fussy, antiquated formality. His would have been the booming, stentorian voice of the past, uncomfortable with the colloquial styles employed by more recent and popular writers, in whose Latin one begins to hear the rhythms of the vernacular. Not as idiomatic as Archambault presents him, not as awkward as Benton pretends, Guibert is a clearheaded writer who presents complicated ideas through complex sentence structures and with unusual words. Professor McAlhany has made this Latin accessible and has captured something of its difficult beauty as well.

The other book included here, *On the Relics of Saints*, has never been fully published in translation.[17] It is readily available in two Latin editions. The first one, by Dom Luc d'Achery, was reprinted in volume 156 of the Patrologia Latina. D'Achery sought to make Guibert's presentation in *On the Relics of Saints* conform to the norms of scholastic argument, and as such he imposed onto it several argumentative divisions wholly unjustified by manuscript evidence. The effect of these divisions was to obscure Guibert's meaning rather than clarify it. The most recent edition by Huygens, published in the Corpus Christianorum Continuatio Mediaevalis, is an admirable example of scholarship and has served as the basis for this translation.[18]

Neither of these two books by Guibert made a notable impact on the world of twelfth-century France. Guibert's exegesis and his crusade chronicle did inspire some interest, but as far as concerns the two books included in this translation, medieval readers were simply not that interested. For students of the Middle Ages, however, they are invaluable. They reveal emotions, ideas, customs, practices, and gossip that might otherwise appear foreign to what we know of the twelfth-century landscape. Through Guibert's eyes we see the king of France curing ailing subjects through the miracle of the royal touch, and we see castellans inflicting unthinkable tortures upon their serfs. We see ghosts walking through Purgatory and demons crawling into bed to molest Christian women. We see the devil disguised as a Scotsman and a peasant boy trying to murder his pregnant lover. Above all, we see Guibert's mind, truly a marvelous and formidable place, full of ethereal spirits ordered like armies into divisions, open to heavenly and earthly vistas, where saints and demons clash and where one soul fruitlessly yet tirelessly seeks an ever elusive peace, sensing that he will never capture it but hoping nonetheless for even a brief glimpse of truth amid the vicious battles of this world.

JAY RUBENSTEIN

NOTES

1. The only complete copy of the *Monodies* is Paris BnF Baluze MS 42; *On the Relics of Saints* survives in Paris BnF *lat.* 2900.
2. Colin Morris, *The Discovery of the Individual, 1050–1200* (New York: Harper & Row, 1972). It has also been termed the time of the "twelfth-century renaissance" and the age of medieval humanism. More recently Rachel Fulton has seen in it the creation of empathy: *From Judgment to Passion: Devotion to Christ and the Virgin Mary, 800–1200* (New York: Columbia University Press, 2002), an idea that seems very consonant with the tone and content of Guibert's *Monodies*.
3. Two dates have been proposed for Guibert's birth: 1053 and 1064. The suggestions, while ingenious, are based on quite slender evidence—chiefly on a passing observation Guibert makes in *Monodies* 1.3 about the size of reeds in his homeland as they appear around the ides of April. As our translation hopefully makes clear, this passage cannot be read with any specificity. Guibert tells us that he was born on the vigil of Easter, and he associated the date of his birth with the ides of April, or April 13—which always falls close enough to Easter to explain why Guibert makes the association. John Benton proposed 1064 based on a phrase in *Monodies* 1.14, where Guibert speaks about his relationship with Bishop Guy of Beauvais, ordained in either 1063 or 1064. Again, as noted in our translation, this passage cannot be read with too much specificity. In

particular, we cannot presume that Guy baptized Guibert. Based on what we know of particular events in Guibert's life, such as when he began his exegetical writings, 1064 does seem closer to the mark than 1053, although we believe that birth date in 1064 would make him a little too young to have begun composing his theological treatises at the time of his entry into Saint-Germer. Therefore, with due humility, we propose an approximate date of ca. 1060.

4. See Carole Straw, *Gregory the Great: Perfection in Imperfection* (Berkeley: University of California Press, 1988). Gregory was perhaps the most influential thinker in the formation of Guibert's thought.

5. Matt. 26:11, Mark 4:7, and John 12:18.

6. The best introduction to this vast topic remains Jean de Montclos, *Lanfranc et Bérenger, la controverse eucharistique du XIe siècle* (Louvain, Belgium: Spicilegium Sacrum Lovaniense, 1971).

7. Jay Rubenstein, *Guibert of Nogent: Portrait of a Medieval Mind* (New York: Routledge, 2002), pp. 132–72.

8. Guibert, *Moral Commentary on Genesis*, published as *Moralia in Genesim* by Migne, *Patrologia latina* 156, col. 216D.

9. This exegesis is based on the *Moral Commentary on Genesis*, cols. 201–2.

10. London and New York: Routledge and E. P. Dutton, 1925.

11. New York: Harper Torchbooks, 1970; reprint, Toronto: University of Toronto Press, 1984.

12. Benton, *Self and Society*, p. 30.

13. University Park, PA: Pennsylvania State University Press, 1995.

14. Paris: Belles Lettres, 1981.

15. It is worth emphasizing that all medieval copies of the *Monodies* have been lost. The base text for all modern versions of Guibert's book, BnF MS Baluze 42, is a seventeenth-century transcription. The article detailing these revisions is François Dolbeau, "Deux nouveaux manuscrits des 'Mémoires' de Guibert de Nogent," *Sacris Erudiri* 26 (1983): pp. 155–176.

16. On p. 91, n. 16 of *Self and Society*, Benton argues that Guibert actually disagreed with Anselm's teachings. He made this argument based on an incomplete reading of the *Moral Commentary on Genesis*.

17. The only complete translation is an MA thesis submitted in 1941 at the University of Washington by Louise Catherine Nash

(Sister Mary Edwardine, OP), "Translation of *De Pignoribus sanctorum* of Guibert of Nogent with Notes and Comments," 148 pp. Book 1 alone appeared in translation in Thomas Head, ed., *Medieval Hagiography: An Anthology* (New York: Routledge, 2001), pp. 399–426.

18. Published as vol. 127 in the series: Turnhout: Brepols, 1993, pp. 79–175.

Suggestions for Further Reading

Abulafia, Anna Sapir. "Theology and the commercial revolution: Guibert of Nogent, St. Anselm and the Jews of northern France." In *Church and City, 1000–1500, Essays in honour of Christopher Brooke*, edited by D. Abulafia, M. Franklin, and M. Rubin. Cambridge: Cambridge University Press, 1992.

Amory, Frederic. "The Confessional Superstructure of Guibert de Nogent's *Vita*." *Classica et Mediaevalia*, 25 (1964): 224–40.

Benton, John. "The Personality of Guibert of Nogent." *Psychoanalytic Review*, 57 (1970/71): 563–86.

———. *Self and Society in Medieval France*. New York: Harper Torchbooks, 1970; reprint, Toronto: University of Toronto Press, 1984.

Blurton, Heather F. "Guibert of Nogent and the Subject of History." *Exemplaria*, 15 (2003): 111–31.

Chaurand, Jacques. *Thomas de Marle, sire de Coucy*. Marle, France: Syndicat d'initiative de Marle, 1963.

Cole, Penny. *The Preaching of the Crusades to the Holy Land*. Cambridge, MA: Medieval Academy of America, 1991.

Coupe, M. D. "The Personality of Guibert de Nogent reconsidered." *Journal of Medieval History*, 9 (1983): 317–29.

Duby, Georges. *The Knight, the Lady, and the Priest*. Translated by Barbara Bray. New York: Pantheon Books, 1983.

Ferguson, Chris D. "Autobiography as therapy: Guibert de Nogent, Peter Abelard, and the making of medieval autobiography." *Journal of Medieval and Renaissance Studies*, 13 (1983): 187–212.

Fuchs, Karin. *Zeichen und Wunder bei Guibert de Nogent: Kommunikation, Deutungen und Funktionalisierungen von Wundererzählungen im 12. Jahrhundert*. Munich: R. Oldenbourg, 2008.

Garand, Monique-Cécile. *Guibert de Nogent et ses secrétaires*. Turnhout, Belgium: Brepols, 1995.

Guth, Klaus. *Guibert von Nogent und die hochmittelalterliche Kritik an der Reliquienverehrung*. Augsburg, Germany: Winnfriedwerkin Komm., 1970.

Huygens, R. B. C. *La tradition manuscrite de Guibert de Nogent*. The Hague, the Netherlands: M. Nijhoff, 1991.

Kaiser, Reinhold. "Das Geld in der Autobiographie des Abtes Guibert von Nogent." *Archiv für Kulturgeschichte*, 69 (1987): 289–314.

Kantor, Jonathan. "A Psychohistorical Source: The *Memoirs* of Guibert of Nogent." *Journal of Medieval History*, 2 (1976): 281–303.

Lapina, Elizabeth. "Anti-Jewish Rhetoric in Guibert of Nogent's *Dei Gesta Per Francos*." *Journal of Medieval History*, 35 (2009): 239–53.

Lemmers, Trudy. "The Crisis of Episcopal Authority in Guibert of Nogent's *Monodiae*." In *Negotiating Secular and Ecclesiastical Power*, edited by Arnoud-Jan A. Bijsterveld, Henrik Bertinus Teunis, and Andrew Wareham. Turnhout, Belgium: Brepols, 1999.

Levine, Robert. "Satiric vulgarity in Guibert of Nogent's *Gesta Dei per Francos*." *Rhetorica*, 7 (1989): 261–73.

Mews, Constant J. "Guibert of Nogent's *Monodiae* (III, 17) in an appendage to the *De haeresibus* of Augustine," *Revue des études Augustiniennes*, 33 (1987): 113–27.

Monod, Bernard. *Le moine Guibert et son temps*. Paris: Hachette, 1905.

Moore, R. I. "Guibert of Nogent and his world." In *Studies in Medieval History Presented to R. H. C. Davis*, edited by H. Mayr-Harting and R. I. Moore. London: Hambledon Press, 1985.

Nortier, Elisabeth. "Guibert de Nogent face à la société chrétienne de son temps (v. 1055–v. 1125)." In *Christianisation et déchristianisation: Actes de la IXe Rencontre d'histoire religieuse, Fontevraud*. Angers, France: Presses de l'université d'Angers, 1986.

Ott, John. "Writing Godfrey of Amiens: Guibert of Nogent and Nicholas of Saint-Crépin between Sanctity, Ideology, and Society." *Mediaeval Studies: an Annual Journal of Scholarship*, 67 (2005): 317–65.

Partner, Nancy. "The Family Romance of Guibert of Nogent: His Story/Her Story." In *Medieval Mothering*, edited by B. Wheeler and N. Parsons. New York: Garland, 1996.

Pelikan, Jaroslav. "A First-generation Anselmian, Guibert of Nogent." In *Continuity and Discontinuity in Church History*, edited by F. F. Church and T. George. Leiden, the Netherlands: Brill, 1979.

Riley-Smith, Jonathan. *The First Crusade and the Idea of Crusading*. London: Athlone, 1986.

Rubenstein, Jay. *Guibert of Nogent: Portrait of a Medieval Mind*. New York: Routledge, 2002.

Southern, R. W. *Saint Anselm, a Portrait in a Landscape*. Cambridge: Cambridge University Press, 1990.

Stock, Brian. *The Implications of Literacy: Written Language and Models of Interpretation in the Eleventh and Twelfth Centuries*. Princeton, NJ: Princeton University Press, 1983.

Swanson, R. N. *The Twelfth-Century Renaissance*. Manchester, England: Manchester University Press, 1999.

Van Engen, John H. *Rupert of Deutz*. Berkeley and Los Angeles: University of California Press, 1983.

Chronology

ca. 1060	Approximate date of Guibert's birth, on the vigil before Easter.
ca. 1060/1061*	Death of Guibert's father.
March 12, 1067*	Guibert's formal education begins.
1073	Gregory VII proclaimed pope, inaugurating a new era of reform with a greater emphasis on eliminating practices such as simony (the purchase of ecclesiastical office) and the enforcement of clerical celibacy.
1074*	Guibert's mother and his teacher, Solomon, abandon him for Saint-Germer.
December 1075*	Abbot Garnier accepts Guibert as a monk at Saint-Germer.
1076–1077*	Guibert's occasional lessons with St. Anselm, then prior of Bec, begin.
1078	Anselm elected abbot of Bec. Guibert writes his first book, *A Little Treatise on Virginity*.
ca. 1083	Guibert begins writing a commentary of the six days of Creation, against the will of his abbot.
1084	Garnier retires as abbot of Saint-Germer. Guibert hastily finishes his commentary and attaches to it a short preacher's manual, *How to Give a Proper Sermon*.

* These dates are approximate, based on the suggested date of Guibert's birth.

ca. 1086	Guibert begins expanding his commentary on Creation in the much longer, much more ambitious *Moral Commentary on Genesis*.
1093	Anselm of Bec becomes archbishop of Canterbury.
November 27, 1095	Urban II preaches the First Crusade at the Council of Clermont.
1096	Peter the Hermit preaches the First Crusade before Guibert of Nogent; pogroms occur in Normandy.
July 15, 1099	The First Crusaders conquer Jerusalem.
1100–1103	Guibert's family aggressively seeks to purchase higher office for him.
1104	Guibert's mother takes the veil while continuing to live in her hermitage outside Saint-Germer.
December 1104	Guibert elected abbot of Nogent-sous-Coucy.
1106	Death of Guibert's mother.
February 1107	Guibert preaches before Pope Paschal II, speaking in defense of Gaudry's election as bishop of Laon.
1107–1108	Guibert exiled for about a year from Nogent, for reasons left unclear. He uses this time in exile to write his crusade chronicle: *The Deeds of God Through the Franks*.
1108	Louis VI succeeds his father, Philip I, as king of France.
1111	Guibert writes his short treatise, *Against the Judaizer and the Jews*. Gérard de Quierzy is murdered in Laon Cathedral. Guibert preaches a sermon of purification and reconciliation.

April 1112	Communal uprising at Laon, leading to the destruction of much of the city.
1113	Bartholomew accedes to the bishopric of Laon; Guibert dedicates his *Moral Commentary on Genesis* to the new bishop, almost thirty years after he began writing it.
1115	Guibert finishes work on his memoirs, or *Monodies*, begun at an uncertain date.
1117	Guibert writes a short theological treatise entitled *The Letter on the Handful of Bread Given to Judas*. It raises certain questions of eucharistic theology that he will revisit in his later treatise on relics. Death of Anselm of Laon.
ca. 1119	Guibert circulates his shorter theological treatises noted above, along with another short book entitled *In Praise of St. Mary*, as a group.
ca. 1120	Guibert writes *On the Relics of Saints*.
1121	Guibert witnesses a charter in the presence of Louis VI. Peter Abelard is convicted of heresy at Soissons and forced to burn his own book; Guibert is a probable witness to the trial.
ca. 1121–1124	Guibert writes his final work, an exegetical commentary called *Tropologies on the Prophets*, dealing with the minor prophets of the Old Testament. He was losing his sight while composing it; the work was never finished.
1125	Probable date of Guibert's death.

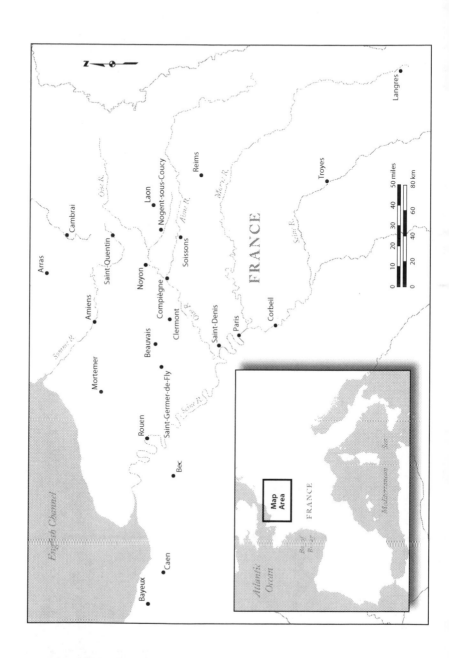

English Channel

Bayeux
Caen
Bec
Rouen
Saint-Germer-de-Fly
Mortemer
Beauvais
Clermont
Saint-Denis
Paris
Corbeil

Arras
Cambrai
Amiens
Saint-Quentin
Noyon
Compiègne
Soissons
Laon
Nogent-sous-Coucy
Reims

Troyes

Langres

Somme R.
Oise R.
Aisne R.
Marne R.
Seine R.
Eure R.
Seine R.

FRANCE

N

0   10   20   30   40   50 miles
0   20   40   60   80 km

Atlantic
Ocean

FRANCE

Mediterranean Sea

Map
Area

MONODIES

BOOK 1

I.

I confess to your greatness, God, my departures from you, caused by countless errors, and the frequent returns you inspired, from my inner wretchedness back to you. I confess the evils of my childhood and youth, still raging within me even as an adult, as well as my inveterate zeal for wickedness, untiring despite my spent and listless flesh. Every time, Lord, I recall my relentless depravities, and how you always granted repentance for them, I marvel at your heart's patience for me: it is beyond comprehension. Repentance and the desire to pray are useless unless instilled with your spirit, Lord, but how will you bear to descend with such kindness into the hearts of sinners, and how will you grant such grace to those who have turned from you, or continue to provoke you?[1]

You know, Father so great, how we carry hearts hardened against those who happen to offend us, and how slow we are to forgive those who, whether once or many times, direct their words or looks against us. But you are not only pious, you are piety itself, or rather the source of piety. If you can reach everyone altogether, then couldn't you provide for an individual? How could you not? When the world stood in ignorance of God, when it lived in shadows and the shadow of death, when it kept a communal silence as the night was driving its course, whose worthy action, whose summons could compel your all-powerful Word to come down from its royal throne?[2] Not even the negligence of all humanity could keep you from showing mercy, so it is no wonder if you are full of mercy for one

individual, even a heinous sinner. I could not say that you
show mercy more easily for one than for all, since in either
case nothing could make it less easy for you. For you, nothing
can be more or less easy. Since you are the source and what-
ever flows from you, you owe to everyone, it is clear that you
do not withhold from individuals what belongs to all.

And so, I always sin and, in my sinning, I always return to
you. A fugitive or deserter from what is pious, when I run back
to piety—does piety lose its essence? When it is buried under
layers of sin, will we find piety something strange? Isn't it said
to you that you will not in your anger withhold your mercies?[3]
The same psalmist also sings that your mercies exist not only
for the present, but for eternity. You know that I do not sin
because I know you are merciful—though I am confident in
stating that you are said to be merciful because if someone
asks for forgiveness, you are there. I do not abuse you in your
mercy when I am driven to sin out of the compulsion to sin. It
would, however, be an abuse, and quite sacrilegious, if I always
found pleasure in excessive sinning because it is so easy to
return to you after sinning. Indeed, I do sin, but when I have
recovered my reason, I am ashamed to have crossed over to my
heart's desires, such that my mind, completely against its will,
lies buried under piles of filth.[4]

But among these daily distresses, what kind of resurrection
could I obtain after a fall? Isn't it much more salubrious to
struggle toward you for a while, to find rest in you even for a
moment, than to forget the remedy completely, and despair of
your grace? And what is despair if not to cast oneself deliber-
ately into the pigsty of utter disgrace? For when the spirit no
longer struggles at all against the flesh, the unfortunate soul
squanders its substance on pleasures. This sinner is engulfed
by a flood, swallowed by the depths: as his thoughts reach the
crest of their debasement, the mouth of the well closes over
him.[5]

Therefore, God of goodness, when I once again was coming
to recognize you after my inner drunkenness, if at times I did
not succeed, I was never entirely without self-knowledge. For
how could I catch a glimmer of understanding of you, if I were

blind to my own self? If, as Jeremiah says, I am clearly a man who sees my own poverty,[6] I should then determine what fulfills this want of mine and seek it out. But on the other hand, if I do not know what good is, how could I know evil, much less condemn it? If I do not know beauty, I never shrink from ugliness. I seek knowledge of you through knowledge of myself, and if I possess knowledge of you, I cannot lack knowledge of myself: therefore, to dispel, through confessions such as these, the darkness of my reason by constant inquiry into your light is a most worthwhile and salutary exercise. Then will my reason, illuminated by an unfailing light, never again be unknown to itself.

II.

And so I must first confess to you the benefits you granted me, so that your servants, God, who read this will fully realize the cruelty of my ingratitude. For if your gifts to me differed in no way from what you shared with others, wouldn't you have surpassed all that I could have possibly deserved? You added many other things still that redound with praise to your name, but nothing to mine, as well as other benefits that I believe must be omitted. If family, fortune, and beauty—I shall pass over whatever else there might be—are granted by your authority, God, good men praise none of these gifts unless those to whom you gave them keep them within the bounds of dignity. Otherwise, they are held in utter contempt because of a flaw they have: they can change. What are such things to me? They may serve the causes of lust and pride simply because they have a certain appearance or name, when they are in fact neutral, and, depending on the habit of mind, can be turned to either good or evil: the greater their inconstancy, the more we distrust them. If no other arguments were made about such things, it would suffice to say that no one creates his family or his appearance, and in these cases especially, no one possesses what he has not received.[7]

There are other things that human effort can sometimes

help to acquire, such as wealth or talent, as Solomon bears witness: "If the iron is blunt, it will be sharpened with great effort." But it only takes a simple statement to quash this entire argument: if reason were not suffused with the light that illuminates every man coming into this world,[8] and if Christ, the key to knowledge, did not open the doors of his teachings, then obviously every teacher would be wasting his breath with useless arguments for deaf ears. Therefore, everyone who has good sense should cease to claim anything for himself except sin. But let us set these matters aside and return to what I began.

I had said, O pious and holy one, that I thanked you for your blessing. And so first and foremost I thank you for the beautiful (but chaste), modest, and extremely reverent mother you gave me. "Beautiful" would have been written in a secular, and rather inept, sense, if infallible chastity's stern face had not reinforced what this empty word intended to express. For example, the poor do not have enough food, so it appears that fasting is forced upon them and is therefore less deserving of praise; and frugality has value only amid abundant wealth. Likewise, the more desirable beauty is, the more we exalt it with all kinds of praise when it holds firm against flatterers.[9]

If Sallust had thought beauty without character praiseworthy, he would not have said of Aurelia Orestilla: "A good man never praised anything about her except her beauty."[10] If he specifies that a good man praised her beauty, but nevertheless says she was shameful in every other respect, I am confident that I can speak for Sallust when I say that she is rightfully praised for a natural gift from God, though the defilements added to her clearly mark her as immoral. In the same way, we praise an idol made of any material as long as its individual parts harmonize with the form, and even though the apostle says that, as far as faith is concerned, no idol exists[11] and nothing is considered more profane, it is not out of place to praise the proper arrangement of its limbs.

Of course, even though ephemeral beauty is changeable due to the inconstancy of our blood, it is impossible to deny that beauty is good in the usual manner of what appears to be good. For if whatever God has established in eternity is beautiful, everything that is temporally attractive is, as it were, a reflection of that eternal beauty. "For the invisible things of God, when understood through what has been created, are made visible," says the apostle. And angels, when they reveal themselves to human sight, always have the brightest faces, as when the wife of Manue said, "A man of God came to me, with the face of an angel." Demons, on the other hand, who are kept under shadows until the day of last judgment, according to the first Peter, usually appear with the blackest of faces, unless they deceitfully disguise themselves as angels of light.[12] There is clearly nothing unjust in this, since they abandoned the glory of their noble compatriots.

Furthermore, the bodies of those of us who are among the elect are said to be configured according to the glory of Christ's body, so that the deformities we contract by accident or natural corruption are remedied after the pattern of the Son of God, transfigured on the mountain.[13] Therefore, if the inner copies of the original are beautiful and good (no matter who makes them visible), their goodness derives from the same source as their beauty, especially when there is nothing discordant in their arrangement. In fact, I recall that St. Augustine himself, in his book *On Christian Doctrine* (if I am not mistaken), said that "he who has a beautiful body and an ugly soul is to be pitied more than if he also had an ugly body."[14] If we are right to lament corrupted beauty, then there must be something good that is debased when vice is added to it, or is enriched by a dignified manner.

And so, thanks be to you, God, who instilled her beauty with virtue. The gravity in her manner conveyed her contempt for all vanity, while the serious look in her eyes, the restraint in her talk, and the unmoving expression on her face did not yield to the charming flattery of admirers. You know, Omnipotent One, how you endowed her from the beginning with the fear of your very name, and with a mind that rebelled against every falsehood. Note that however much chastity she herself possessed, a gift from you, she was equally restrained in criticizing those without it—something you rarely, if ever, find in women of great status. Sometimes household servants or neighbors would spread gossip, but she turned away and took no part in it. She found their whispered rumors just as offensive as if it were her own character they were disparaging. God of truth, you know that no personal bias, such as love for my mother, leads me to say these things, but that it is a subject greater than my words can express, especially since other members of my family are beasts ignorant of God or savage fighters accused of murder—indeed, they shall be banished far from you, unless in your greatness you show mercy to them, as you often do.

But there will be perhaps a more opportune place to discuss her life later in this work; now let us turn to mine.

III.

To be born from this woman, who, to speak as I believe and hope, was most true, was what you granted me, the worst of all her children. I was her last child in two ways: my brothers, who offered better hopes, have died, but I, a life in every way hopeless, have survived. It was as if, after Jesus, the mother of Jesus, and his saints, she was the reason that I, still in the midst of these evils, held on to the hope for salvation promised to all.[15] Indeed, I know, and to disbelieve would be sacrilege, that as lovingly as she treated me, as openly as she promoted me while she was in this world—for mothers are extremely affectionate toward their sons—now in the presence of God she cares for me just as much. From the earliest age, she was filled with the fire of God in Zion,[16] and not even when she slept, to say nothing of when she was awake, did she cease to care for me in her soul. Now, she is overcome by death, the joints of her flesh broken, but I know that in Jerusalem the furnace burns with a force beyond words, especially since there she is filled with God, nor is she unaware of the miseries that torment me. And though she is happy, the farther from the warnings she so often repeated to me, the farther from her habits and from her footsteps she thinks I have strayed, the more she groans for me when I stumble.

Father and Lord God, you know how and of how much evil I am—you gave me my origin from this woman, who is not falsely, but truly good. You also offered me hope in her merits, a hope I would in no way presume to possess if I did not find under your grace at least temporary respite from fear of my sin. At the same time you introduced into my wretched heart something—I don't know if it really is hope, or only the appearance of hope—when by your indulgence I was born and even reborn on the day that is the most holy, the most important, and the most longed for by all Christians.

My mother spent nearly all of Lent suffering from unusually painful birth pangs. She would often remind me of these pains when I lost my way, or headed down a precarious path. Finally, the holy Sabbath, the Easter vigil, dawned. Her agonizing convulsions continued, her torment grew as the hour drew near when it was thought childbirth would naturally occur, but I began to twist around back up into her womb. My father, friends, and relatives had already been worn down with morbid grief for both of us: the child's birth hastens the mother's death, while the child's departure from life, since he could not depart the womb, was providing them all a cause to share their sympathy. On this day, except for the specific solemn office celebrated at this time, the usual ceremonies on behalf of the family were not performed.

A plan arose out of necessity: my father ran to the altar of the Lord's mother. He poured out vows to her, who was and always will be the only virgin who gave birth, and in place of an offering, laid this gift upon the pious mother's altar: if a male child was born, he would be handed over to the clergy to serve God and her; if a child of the lesser sex, she would be committed to a similar vocation.

At once, out came a feeble little thing, like an abortion. The birth had occurred at the right time, but it seemed some worthless creature—the only rejoicing was for the mother's life. This tiny little newborn, so pitiful and so frail, appeared to be stillborn prematurely; the slender reeds growing in that region, right about mid-April, were thicker than its fingers.[17] While I was growing up, I often heard a funny story about that day.

When they were taking me to the life-giving font, a woman rolled me from hand to hand, and said, "You think he's going to live? Nature almost failed to give him any limbs; she gave him more of a rough sketch than a body."

These, my Creator, were all portents of the condition in which I seem to live. Could any sincere service to you be discovered in me, Lord? In regard to you, I possessed nothing real, nothing lasting. Whenever it seemed that I had really performed some good deed, my misguided intention frequently undermined the results. I said to you, God of supreme benevolence, that you bestowed upon me hope, or some semblance of hope, not only when I was born and reborn in the expectation of that joyful day, but also when I was offered to the queen of all things, supreme after God. Lord God, don't I understand, from the faculty of reason you gave me, that for those who live without profit, the day of birth provides nothing more beneficial than does the day of death? If it is true and beyond argument that no one can earn merits before the day of birth, but can do so before the day of his death, then if one has not passed his life in goodness, a glorious day of death, I will declare, offers no more advantages than a glorious day of birth.

For if it is true that he made me, and I did not make myself,[18] and if it is true that I did not determine the day, nor deserve to have it so established, then that day, granted by God, gives me neither hope nor honor, unless my life should follow the religious duties inherent to that day, and vindicate what it portends. My birthday would be splendid because of the feast day on which it occurred, if the virtue that I long for were to govern the motives behind my actions; I would think I had deserved the glory surrounding my arrival into this life, if my mind's perseverance in justice were to ennoble my departure from it. I could be called Peter or Paul, I could be named Rémy or Nicolas, but not even, to speak poetically, would a "name descended from great Julius" benefit me, unless I were to reproduce the original models whose names providence or fortune made for me.[19] Behold, my God, how all the swellings in my spirit are deflated, how the things that I once thought extended the scope of my pride now count for nothing!

Lady, ruler of the earth and heavens second to your only begotten Son, how well those who were compelled to dedicate me to you understood! And how much better I would have understood, if when I became an adult, I had rested my heart upon the foundation of that vow! I do confess that I was given to you as a special gift, and yet I do not deny that often I have, knowing it was sacrilegious, taken myself away from you. Didn't I take myself away from you, when I preferred my rank desires to your sweet fragrance?[20] But even though this wrongdoing so often led me to steal myself away from you, still, because of my dedication at birth, I returned to you with confidence, and through you to the only begotten of you and God the Father. And though I was wasting away from sins repeated a thousand times, your inexhaustible womb continued to give birth to confidence within me, the benefits of your mercies of old reminded me to have hope. But why mercies *of old*? So many times have I experienced, and daily I continue to experience, the constancy of your mercies, so many pitfalls I have avoided because you removed them—there is no need to speak of your mercies "of old," when your endless dispensations reign still. Though recurring sins beget a cruel hardness in my heart, as soon as I return to you, seemingly by a natural instinct, my heart grows soft. When I look at myself, when I consider my troubles, I nearly give up in despair—but then, almost despite myself, I understand that born into my wretched soul is the certainty of finding respite with you. For when I think about it, no matter what evils engulf me, you cannot, if I may speak boldly, fail in your obligation to fulfill my needs.[21] Indeed, I was cast unto you from the womb, and if you do not look after me when I turn away, nor receive me when I turn back, I must attribute to you the just causes of my perdition. You have the ability to do so when you want, and we know the power of the Son flows into the mother: could I demand my salvation from anyone besides you? We share, so to speak, our servile condition, and to you I would shout, "I am yours."[22]

I would gladly share with you an account of these matters elsewhere. Let us turn to other things.

IV.

I had scarcely learned to shake my rattle when you, pious Lord, you who were going to be my father, made me an orphan. Only eight months after I was born, the father of my flesh died. For this, I thank you greatly: there is no question that if he had lived, he would have undermined your plans for me, but you caused him to pass away while still possessed of Christian affection. My looks, as well as a rather quick mind for that young age, suggested that I might be fit for a secular profession, so when the time came to begin studying Latin, he would have undoubtedly broken the vows he made. Your arrangements, good provider, proved salutary for the both of us: I was in no way deprived of the fundamentals of your teachings, and he did not break the promise he had made to you.

His widow now truly belonged to you, and she raised me with great care. When at last she was going to send me to school, she chose the day of the feast of Saint Gregory. She had heard that this servant of yours, Lord, was greatly renowned for his miraculous understanding and distinguished for his boundless wisdom. With the payment of numerous alms, she continually tried to win the intercession of your confessor, hoping that one whom you endowed with intellect would succeed in summoning in me an affection for following that intellect.[23]

And so I was introduced to the study of Latin. I had learned how to form the individual letters as best I could, but I had almost no understanding of how to put the letters together, when my pious mother, eager to educate me, decided to place me with a grammar teacher. Prior to this time, and to some extent even then, grammar teachers were hard to find; there were none in the villages, scarcely any in the cities. Those who could be found knew very little, and could not even compare to the itinerant clerics of today.[24] Thus, the teacher whom my mother chose to entrust with my care had only begun as an old man to study grammar, and since he had imbibed little of this art in his youth, he was all the more uneducated in it. But he was humble enough, and his honesty compensated for his deficiency in the study of Latin.

There were some clerics, known as chaplains, who performed divine offices for the household, and my mother used them as intermediaries to procure this man as my teacher. He already had a position as tutor to one of my young cousins, and was on close terms with some relatives of mine, who had supported him at their court. Nonetheless, when he considered my mother's forceful pleas, adding her honesty and austerity to the scale, he decided on balance, despite his fear of offending those relatives of mine, to accept her offer and enter her household. While he was deliberating, the following vision drove him to his decision.

One night, while he was sleeping in his bedroom—I remember the room, as it was the academic institution for the entire town—he imagined he saw an old man, white-haired and with a demeanor that in every way commanded respect, take me by the hand and lead me to the doorway of his room. When the old man stood at the entrance of the room, he pointed out my teacher's bed to me as I looked on and said, "Go to him, for he will love you greatly." He let go of the hand by which he held me, and when he allowed me to leave, I ran to my teacher and began covering his face with kisses. He woke up, and such great affection for me overcame him that he refused to wait any longer. Casting off any fear of my relatives, to whom both he and his family were completely indebted, he agreed to take up residence in my mother's household.

The boy he had been teaching until then was handsome and from a noble family, but he always avoided the liberal arts, gave up on every subject, and was quite the liar and thief for his age. Supervision did no good at all, and he was rarely in school, but nearly every day he could be found lounging in the vineyards. My teacher had grown weary of the boy's laziness and had become happily acquainted with my mother at just the right time, so once the goal he was seeking became fixed in his mind because of the events in the vision described above, he abandoned his association with the boy along with the masters under whom was living. Still, he would have suffered some punishment when he left, if my mother's prestige as well as her authority had not protected him.

V.

Once he settled in, both his purity in teaching me and his integrity in curbing the recklessness that characterizes youth kept me away from common games, nor did he allow me to go anywhere without his permission, or to take any food except at home. He did not let me accept gifts from anyone, except by his leave, or do anything, whether in speech, judgment, or act, that was not in moderation—it seemed he wanted to make me not a cleric, but a monk. While others my age wandered around wherever they wanted and the reins that ought to be on their abilities at their age slackened, his diligent supervision prevented anything of this sort for me. Wearing my clerical attire, I would sit like some trained animal and watch the crowds play games. Even on Sundays and feast days of the saints, the discipline required by my academic training forced me onward. There was no day, and barely any time, for me to be idle. I was constantly driven to undertake my studies in one and the same way. Moreover, when my teacher accepted me as a student, he was not allowed to teach anyone else.

He kept watch over me in this way, and everyone who took notice thought that all his vigilance greatly honed my meager talents. But everyone's hopes came crashing down—he was completely ignorant of prose and verse composition. Meanwhile, a hailstorm of slaps and blows poured down on me almost every day as he tried to force me to learn what he couldn't teach.

I spent nearly six years with him in this pointless struggle, without receiving any reward worth the time spent. However, every effort he made benefited me, if we consider that his only concern was the basics of decent behavior. Faithfully and lovingly, he instilled in me whatever humility, modesty, and outer decorum I had. But I came to realize he possessed too little judgment and moderation, which became dangerous for me, because under the pretext of my instruction, he never for a moment stopped pressuring me with work. The more any man's nature, to say nothing of a young boy's, is strained beyond its limit through constant intellectual effort, the duller it grows; as the mind burns its energies in unceasing study with greater intensity, the overexertion increasingly saps its strength, until from unyielding rigor it turns slack and grows completely cold.[25]

An intellect still buried within the folds of the body must conduct itself with moderation. For if there is silence at midday in heaven,[26] our gift of contemplation cannot, while we live, remain in a state of unremitting intensity, and so neither, if I may say so, can a mind at work remain steadfast in any kind of thinking. Thus, we believe that when our hearts are intent upon any object, there must be variation in the objects of our intention, so that while we ponder different things in turn, we return refreshed to the one thing to which the soul is most attached, as if we had been given some time for recreation. Allow, then, a nature that sometimes becomes exhausted to have, as a remedy, some variety in its work. Let us remember that God did not create the world uniformly, but rather with days and nights, spring and summer, fall and winter, he let us delight in the changing times and seasons. Everyone, therefore, who has the title of teacher should see how he can moderate his instruction of boys and young men, because we think even those students who display all the seriousness of old men should not be treated any differently.

My teacher had a love for me that was cruel, for his unjust beatings seemed excessively harsh. Still, his efforts were marked by a thorough regard for proper conduct. I was certainly not so deserving of the beatings, because if he actually had possessed the ability to teach what he pretended to know, I was assuredly, for a boy my age, most capable of learning what he would have taught correctly. But since he almost never expressed himself satisfactorily, and what he was trying to express was never clear to him, our lessons wandered aimlessly, banal without being obvious. He could never bring the conversation back around to a conclusion, or even make anything intelligible.

Because of his lack of education, anything he had once learned, as I mentioned, in his old age, and poorly at that, he held onto as irrefutable, and if by some accident he—if I may say so—blurted out anything, he believed the thought to be valid, and would protect and defend it with blows.

Doubtless he could have refrained from such madness. This same learned man says that before nature fully absorbs knowledge, there is no more glory in telling what you know than in remaining silent about what you do not.[27]

He took his cruel revenge on me for not understanding what he did not know, but he obviously should have considered that to demand from a fragile young mind what he had not given it was the greatest evil. Just as rational people can barely, if at all, understand the words of madmen, the sayings of those who do not understand something, but claim they do and try to teach it to others, become less clear by their own attempts to explain it. You will find nothing more difficult than teaching what you do not know—it will be obscure to the speaker, and more obscure to the listener; they might as well be talking to a stone.

I am telling this, my God, not to brand such a good friend with a mark of disgrace, but to make every reader understand that I do not want them to take everything I say for certain, nor to envelop anyone else within my nebulous reasoning. Given that my subject matter is rather meager, I decided to instill it with reason, in the hopes that, even though the one may count for little, and perhaps rightly so, the other might be thought to make it worth the effort.

VI.

Although his severity weighed heavily upon me, at times he made it abundantly clear by everything he did that he had nearly the same love and esteem for me as he did for himself. With watchful concern he hovered over me, looking after my health because others had turned a blind eye, using his great influence to teach me to avoid the decadent behavior of some who took notice of me, and constantly exhorting my mother against the overly elegant appearance of my clothes—indeed, he seemed to take on the role of parent, not pedagogue, and undertook not the protection of my flesh, but the care of my soul. I was listless and rather childish for my age, yet there came upon me a great love for him in return; even though he often furrowed my tender back with welts, I completely forgot his roughness and obeyed him, not out of the fear expected at that age, but from some love planted deep in my heart.

Since my teacher and my mother saw that I was paying them their due deference in equal measure, on many occasions they tested me to see whether I would in any particular situation dare prefer one of them over the other. At last came an opportunity where neither of them took sides about what I ought to do, and thus my trial took place with no risk of an ambiguous outcome. It had happened that I was beaten at school. (The school, however, was nothing more than a room in our house, since my teacher had, for my sake, dismissed from his care the other students whom he had once accepted. My mother in her wisdom demanded as much from him, since she had increased his pay and elevated his position.) I had finished my studies some time around vespers, and had gone to sit at my mother's knee. I had been beaten very severely, even more than I deserved, but when she began to ask, as she usually did, whether I had been beaten that day, I did not want her to think I was telling on my teacher, and flatly denied what had happened. Without asking me, she took off my shirt (which is called a *subucula* or a *camisia*) and saw the bruises on my arms and the welts his lashes had raised all over my back.[28] Pained in her heart that I, at my tender age, had been beaten so savagely, she became agitated and angry, and with grief clouding her eyes, she said, "Never then will you be a cleric! Never again will you be punished so you can learn Latin!" Giving her as reproachful a look as I could, I replied, "Even if I were to die from it first, I will not stop studying Latin, or trying to be a cleric!" She had, in fact, already promised that if I wanted to become a knight, she would provide me with military equipment and weapons when I had reached the proper age.[29]

I scornfully rejected everything she said, but this servant of

yours, God, was so pleased to receive my insults, and so excited
by my contempt, that she revealed to my teacher exactly what I
had said in opposition to her. Both rejoiced at my seemingly
eager aspirations to fulfill my father's vow: I absorbed Latin,
poorly taught though it was, all the more rapidly, and did not
try to extricate myself from ecclesiastical duties. Rather, when-
ever the appointed time came, or anytime it had to be done, I
would have chosen to miss a meal instead of miss any part of
performing my duties at the right place and time. At least that
is how it was then—but you know, my God, how far I later
departed from my intention, and how reluctantly I made my
way to divine services. Even when driven by blows, I would
then only grudgingly consent to attend them. The forces driv-
ing me early in my youth did not, Lord, have their source in
any piety—for these derive from understanding—but were
merely the impulses of a young boy.[30] But once my adolescence
had exhausted itself in bearing the fruits of my inborn wicked-
ness and cast itself into utter shamelessness, my earlier devo-
tion altogether withered away. Although, my God, a good will,
or rather the likeness of a good will, seemed for a moment to
shine forth in me, it soon disappeared behind storm clouds that
rained down thoughts of the worst sort.

VII.

Finally, my mother tried in every way possible to acquire an
ecclesiastical benefice for me. As a result, the first attempt to
place me in an office proved not simply bad, but even wicked.
One of my brothers, a rather young knight garrisoned at the
castle Clermont (the one located between Compiègne and
Beauvais), was expecting money from the lord of the town—
whether it was a loan or a property obligation, I don't know.
The lord kept putting off payment, I think from a lack of funds,
so some of my relatives suggested he grant me a canonry, which
they call a "prebend," of the church there. (Contrary to church
regulations, it was subject to his authority.) Then his dispute
with my brother over repayment would come to an end.[31]

The Apostolic See had at that time delivered a new censure
against married priests, and even the crowds who were deeply
attached to their own clergy seethed with rage against them:
they shouted with fury that the clerics should be stripped of their
ecclesiastical benefices or removed from the church.[32] Among
this mob was one of my father's nephews, a man who outshone
his peers not only in influence but in cleverness. He took such
swinish pleasure in sex that he had no respect whatsoever for
any woman's relations, but from the way he incessantly ranted
and raved against the cleric who held the canonry that I men-
tioned above, you would think that an exceptional sexual purity
drove him to a hatred of such conduct. He was a layman, and
there was no restraining him with laws, but even so, the more
lenient the laws were, the more shamefully he abused them. Nor
indeed could the bonds of marriage constrain him, since he never
let himself get entangled in such snares. As a result, he exuded
the stench of his foul behavior, but because his worldly riches
gave him prominence and protected him, he stubbornly refused
to stop his thunderous denunciations against the clergy for the
impurity that was his own. He thus found a reason to benefit me
at the expense of a priest who was, as they say, well placed.
Because the lord of the town was deeply indebted to him, he had
more than enough influence to compel him to summon me and,
in the cleric's absence and against his wishes, to grant me posses-
sion of the canonry I spoke of. For against all that is just and
right, he was acting as if he were abbot over that church, with
improper authorization of the bishop, and though not a canon
himself, he demanded that canons live canonically![33]

During this time, not only did allegations of marriage
threaten clergymen in the first rank as well as those who held
canonries, but also the purchase of church offices that did not
involve spiritual guidance (such as prebends, cantors, provosts,
and others of this sort) was considered no less a crime. Without
naming the holders of high office who were ordered to shake up
the church's internal affairs and who took the side of the cleric
who had lost his prebend, many of my social peers also began a
campaign of murmurs about simony and excommunication,
which had recently become used more frequently as a penalty.

Now, although this man was a priest with a wife, the threat of expulsion from office could not part him from her. He did, however, cease to celebrate mass. Because he put his own flesh before the divine mysteries, he was justly struck with the punishment he thought he had escaped by forsaking the sacrament. Deprived of his canonry, he had nothing left to restrain him, so he began to celebrate mass as freely he wanted, and even kept his wife. From this seed grew the rumor that daily during the mass, he excommunicated my mother along with her family. But my mother, ever fearful of the divine, worried about the punishments of sin as well as the obstacles that would follow from it: she declined at once this prebend, improperly offered to me, and, in the expectation that some clerics would die, she obtained another one for me from the lord of the castle. And thus we fled weapons of iron and fell upon bow shafts of bronze.[34] For to promise something in the expectation of another's death is no different than to order daily that someone be killed.

Lord my God, I was then enveloped in these awful hopes, and in no way did the promise of your gifts, which I had not yet learned through experience, hold me back. This woman, who belonged to you, did not yet understand the hopes and the assurances she should have had in the nourishment I had from you, nor did she know the gifts borne to me from you. As she was for a time still living in the world, she understood only what was of the world, so it is no surprise that the things which she chose to provide for herself, she also sought for me, who would also, as she thought, seek worldly things.

Later, when she realized the danger threatening her own soul, she drew together all the corners of her heart into a condemnation of her past life, as if to say: "What I do not wish done to me, I shall not do to another."[35] She thought it utter madness to try to do for others what she scorned to do for herself, and considered it an abomination to desire for another, to his own destruction, what she no longer sought to attain. Many people act much differently. We see them cast away all their possessions in a feigned commitment to poverty, but in fact they burn with an excessive ardor not only for their own things, which is bad in itself, but for the possessions of others, which is worse.

VIII.

Since a full account of my own era demands it, I would like to go a little more deeply into the state of religion and the conversions that I saw, which led my mother and many others to take up examples of change for the good. There are ample written accounts of how monastic communities flourished in ancient times. To pass over regions foreign to me, we know that during the reigns of some kings of France the monastic rule was cultivated in various places under different founders. A great mass of people who lived piously poured into some of these houses, and it is a wonder how spaces so cramped could contain such enormous crowds. Some of these, in fact, were influential because of their particular strictness, and to a remarkable degree they restored to the rule many monasteries whose fervor for the order had cooled (Luxeuil in Gaul, for example, and also some in Neustria, now called Normandy). But, to quote a poet who spoke the truth, "it is denied the highest things to stand for long,"[36] and, what is even truer, as that age drove into decline under the reins of iniquity, the love for holy conversion grew cold. The material splendor of some churches slowly faded, and then, since the work of their hands grew soiled, men of good life grew rare.

Thus, in my time, membership in the oldest monasteries drastically declined, but the abundance of resources donated long ago made them content with small communities. Only a few could be found among their members who had renounced the world out of disgust with sin; rather, churches were occupied mostly by those who were handed over by their parents' act of piety, and were nourished in them from their first years.[37] The less fear they had about their own misdeeds, which in their eyes counted for nothing, the more their eagerness to live confined among the monks abated. They would obtain offices or duties that took them outside the walls, whether because the abbots thought it necessary or simply at their pleasure, and, craving to exercise their own will and inexperienced in the liberties of the outside world, they readily found opportunities to dismantle the church's store of funds.[38] Once this money was spent, they still lavished gifts freely . . .[39] And though at that time the monks had little concern for religion, they themselves became all the more valuable because of their rarity.

IX.

The monks were behaving in this manner, and scarcely anyone of any worth joined them, yet a count of the castle of Breteuil, located on the border of Amiens and Beauvais, emerged to awaken the minds of many. He was in the bloom of youth, and he possessed a most charming elegance. The nobility of his family, as well as his remarkably distinguished good looks, gave him prominence, and he was also famed for his other castles and all his riches. Though his mind was built upon a foundation of arrogance and pride, he finally came to his senses, and through contemplation he turned his thoughts back on the wretchedness of his mind's vices, which he had initially pursued in a worldly manner. When he perceived the piteous state of his soul, and because he could do nothing else in this world but condemn and be condemned, defile or be defiled, he began to consider what way of life he should adopt, and over a period of time he had many wide-ranging discussions with men he chose as his accomplices and companions in this great desire. He was named Evrard, a man renowned everywhere among the leading men of France.[40]

Finally, without the knowledge of those whom he would leave behind, he revealed through his actions the purpose behind his lengthy deliberations. He had secretly sought out men whom he formed into a group that would adopt this religious life, and he

fled with them as an exile into some foreign land. Since his
name was completely unknown there, he lived as he pleased. He
set to work making charcoal to help with expenses, selling it as
he wandered through town and country with his companions.
It was then that for the first time he thought he had acquired the
greatest of riches, and was able to observe within him all the
glories of the daughter of the king.[41]

Let me include here the model that he himself followed.
There was before this time a noble young man, Thibaud, whom
everyone today recognizes as a saint—many churches now
standing under his name honor him far and wide. From the
very beginnings of his military training, he had a disdain for
weapons, and slipped away barefoot from his family. He took
up the kind of work I mentioned above,[42] and thus lived for
a time in a state of want, to which he was unaccustomed.
Inspired by his example, Evrard decided to make his living, as
I mentioned, from this lowly occupation.[43]

However, there are no good deeds that do not at some time
provide opportunity for evil. So one day, Evrard was in a vil-
lage about to do some work, when suddenly someone in a pur-
ple cloak stood next to him. He wore silk hose that had been
damaged by rubbing against his shoes, and his hair hung down
in the front like a woman's, reaching the top of his shoulders—
he looked more like a gigolo than an exile. When Evrard asked
in all sincerity who he was, he raised his brow a little, looked
askance, and, without any apparent sense of shame, hesi-
tated to respond. Evrard, made curious by the man's delay,
respectfully pressed him with the question. Finally, he seemed
overcome by Evrard's persistence, and burst out: "I am—but I
ask that you not tell anyone—Evrard, at one time a count of
Breteuil. I was, as you know, once a wealthy man in France,
but chose exile for myself and paid of my own free will the
penalties for my sins." So the well-dressed man spoke. To the
bewilderment of the questioner, this person had unexpectedly
appropriated his own identity. Astonished at the incredible
effrontery of this wicked man, Evrard refused to address his
phantom self, if I may call him that. After he told his companions

about this conversation, he said: "Friends, you should know this life we chose is beneficial for us, but harmful for many others, for you may be sure that many other people are saying what you heard from this man's mouth. If, then, we wish to please God completely, we should avoid anything that provides others with an opportunity for scandal, or rather, for deceit. So let us determine to settle in a place where we can cast off the name of exiles, which we have endured for God, and deprive anyone else of the chance to assume my name." He finished speaking, and they changed their plans: they set out for Marmoutier and once there, taking on the habit of a pure profession, lived out their years as monks.

I have heard that while he lived in the secular world, he had no rivals among the wealthy in his attention to elegant clothes,[44] and furthermore, he had such a furious temper that he seemed easily irritated by anything, even a word, for no reason at all. But later, when he was placed in a monastery, I saw how he treated his flesh with contempt: his servile clothing, the downcast look on his face, his gaunt limbs—it all declared he was not a count, but some rural peasant. And when he was sent into the cities and towns on the abbot's orders, never could he surrender to his own will and allow himself even once to enter the castles he had abandoned. He told me this story himself, as he had great respect for me, even though I was still a young man, and accepted me as a member of his family, when he offered me the singular gift of his love and guidance.

He also had a most agreeable habit: whenever he came upon anyone he knew had a reputation for learning, he made him write down something as best he could, whether prose or verse, in a small book he often carried around with him for just this purpose. Once he had collected the sayings of men famed for their studies, he could then weigh each individual opinion on the basis of what they had written. Although he did not understand anything on his own, from the sure judgment of those to whom he showed these writings, he could soon grasp who had expressed himself, either in prose or poetry, with greater precision on a given topic.

This is a sufficient sketch of the man, once noble, but now

even more so because of his good end. Among the men of our day, it was he who first shone forth gloriously as a model of conversion.

X.

But he who created a Paul from Stephen's prayer spread a more blessed and influential example through another who was more than powerful enough:[45] there was a Simon, son of Count Raoul, and the remarkable fame of his unexpected conversion enriched the religion of our time. Many are still living who recall his deeds, and they are witnesses to Raoul's renown everywhere the Franks ruled, the cities he invaded, the towns he governed with remarkable wisdom. One fact alone can reveal his greatness: he married King Henry's wife, the mother of Philip who was king in his time, after her husband's death.[46]

Young Simon, after his father died, kept possession of his counties only for a short time. Some, in fact, say his father's death was the cause of his speedy conversion. His father's remains had been buried in a town that had come to him by usurpation rather than by inheritance. The son feared this might count against his father's soul, and proposed to move the remains to a town where he had rightfully established his rule. Before moving the body, the remains were uncovered and laid bare before his eyes. When he saw the rotting corpse of his father, once so powerful and fierce, he was moved to contemplate his wretched state, and thereupon all the majesty and glory he once found pleasing, he now began to scorn. Thus he conceived a new will, and finally, burning with desire, he sent away the body that gave him his birth; fleeing his country and his family, he crossed the boundary of the Franks and arrived at Burgundy, near Saint-Oyen in the territory of Jura. I heard, too, that he had been engaged to a young woman from a very noble family, and when she learned that her beloved young man had renounced both her and the world, she could not bear to seem inferior to him. Intending to remain a virgin herself, she joined the crowds of virgins who serve God.

Some time after he undertook the life of a monk, he returned to France. The purity of his talk and the humility of his soul, written clearly on his face, inspired many prominent men and women. At this same time, endless columns of both sexes assembled together to follow his way of life, and the example of his name moved a great many from every quarter to this same decision. Indeed, this man's lesson stirred up a still greater swarm of knightly men.

XI.

One would expect there also to be someone from among the educated who, motivated by the same desire, would gather after him a flock in holy orders. And so there was: not long after that time, a man named Bruno in the city of Reims,[47] both educated in the liberal arts and an instructor of large schools, took the first steps to his conversion, as is known, from the following occasion.[48] A certain Manasses, after the death of the famous archbishop Gervais, used simony to occupy the archbishopric of this city.[49] He was indeed a noble man, but with none of the calm composure that is the particular mark of high birth. His new position produced in him such haughtiness that he seemed to imitate the sovereign kings of foreign peoples, or rather the cruelty of kings. I said "foreign," because the kings of the Franks have always possessed a natural modesty, and in their conduct uphold the saying of the wise man, even if they are unaware of it: "They made you king," he says, "do not exalt yourself, but be among them as one of them."[50]

While Manasses held great affection for soldiers, he neglected the clergy, and reportedly once said: "It would be good to be the archbishop of Reims if I didn't have to sing mass." At that time, Bruno had a very high reputation among the churches of Gaul, and since every decent man abhorred the archbishop's shameful behavior and utterly boorish manners, he left the city, along with some other noblemen among the clergy of Reims, out of hatred for this disgraceful man. Later, after Hugh of

Die—archbishop of Lyon, legate of the Apostolic See, a man famed for his just character—had repeatedly struck Manasses with anathema, and after he had tried to plunder the church treasury with a group of soldiers, he was driven from the position he occupied with such wickedness by the nobility, the clergy, and the burghers. Himself an excommunicate, he went to the excommunicated emperor Henry, but condemned to eternal exile, he wandered from place to place, and finally died without communion.

It is worth relating something that happened during his evil rule in the city. Among the treasures of the church that he had promised to the soldiers who served his tyranny, there was a golden chalice, extremely valuable for two reasons: it was of great size, and it had been gilded with some flakes from the gold, as they claim, the three magi had presented to the Lord.[51] With a set of tongs, the chalice was cut up into parts that he tried to distribute as the payment he had promised, but no one would agree to accept something so holy. At last, a knight who was his benefactor's match in criminality permitted himself to receive a part of the gold—or rather, he greedily snatched it up with contempt for the majesty of the sacrament. He instantly went mad, nor did he spend the salary he had undeservedly claimed, but paid on the spot the penalty for reckless greed.

Bruno, however, once he had abandoned the city, decided to renounce the world as well. Shunning contact with his friends and relations, he set out for the territory of Grenoble. There he chose to live on a steep and rather forbidding promontory, attainable only by a difficult and rarely traveled path (there was a gaping, cragged valley below it), and instituted the way of life described below; his followers still live in this manner today.

The church there is not far from the base of the mountain, occupying a slope with a slight raise. The thirteen monks who are there have a building suitable for monastic life, but do not live together in a cloister as others do. Individual monks have their own cells around the perimeter of the building, and they work, sleep, and eat in these. On Sundays, they receive food from the dispenser—bread and vegetables, which each monk cooks in his cell into a particular kind of porridge. Water for drinking as well as other uses comes from a conduit that runs from a spring; it passes every monk's cell, and water flows into individual rooms through a fixed opening. On Sundays and special feast days, they have fish and cheese (not, I should mention, fish they purchase for themselves, but that they receive as a donation from some good men).

Gold, silver, and church ornaments they accept from no one: nothing is there except a silver chalice. They gather together in the church at different hours than are customary for us. If I'm not mistaken, they hear mass on Sundays and on solemn holy days. They almost never speak—if they need to ask for something, they do so with a sign. Whenever they drink wine, it is so diluted that it has no strength and almost no flavor; it is scarcely anything more than common water. They wear hair shirts against their skin, and the rest of their clothing is very meager. They live under a prior; the bishop of Grenoble, a truly religious man, performs the roles of abbot and treasurer. Although they subject themselves to every kind of poverty, they have accumulated a very valuable library, for the less plentiful their supply of material bread, the more they tirelessly work by that nourishment that does not perish, but lasts for eternity.

What guardians they are of their poverty! In the very year that I am writing, the count of Nevers, a man in every regard both pious and powerful, visited them because of their devotion and the excellent reputation that grew from it, and he strongly warned them to be careful of worldly greed.[52] Upon his return home, he recalled the poverty he had witnessed, but completely forgot the warnings he had given and donated some very valuable silver items, such as cups and plates, to them. The monks, however, had not at all forgotten what he had told them, as he discovered. For not long after he made his intentions known, he received in reply a complete refutation of everything he had said. "We," they said, "choose to keep nothing of worldly wealth, neither for our expenses nor for the adornment of our church. And if we spend nothing on either of these things, what is there that we should receive?" Though ashamed at the offering that belied his own exhortation, the count nevertheless dismissed their refusal, and sent instead cowhides and parchment, which he knew they almost always needed.

This place is called Chartreuse. The land there is little cultivated for crops, but they usually purchase any grain they need with hides from the sheep they raise in great number. There are, moreover, huts at the base of the mountain, and these house more than twenty faithful laymen, who live under their guidance. These monks never for a moment cease to live by their rule, so great is their fervor for the life of contemplation they undertook, nor does it cool over the length of time that they pass in this arduous life.[53]

After this admirable man Bruno had instilled in them through the constant example of his words and deeds the basic habits that I described, he left there on some occasion or another, going either to Apulia or Calabria and establishing there a way of life similar to the previous one. As he conducted himself with great humility and served as a shining beacon of piety in everything he did, the Apostolic See sought to capture him for a bishopric, and even force him into one. Bruno, however, fled from their offer in fear of the secular world, lest he lose what he had tasted of God. He put off accepting such an important office because of its secular, not its divine, aspects.

These are the people who gave rise to the conversions of that time. Men and women continually flocked to them; every rank of society immediately joined them. What could I say about differences in age, when children of ten or eleven years contemplated matters suitable for old men and behaved with much more self-restraint than their tender age should allow? The same thing happened in these conversions as what used to happen with the martyrs of old: weak and delicate bodies possessed a more vigorous faith than those who flourished in the authority that comes with old age and learning.

Since for some monks there were no places except in the oldest monasteries, new ones began to be built everywhere, and large donations were sought for the monks as they flowed in from every direction. Those who did not have the ability to found a monastery of any size provided food and shelter to support the monks—two, four, or however many they could. And suddenly villages and towns, cities and castles, even meadows and fields seemed to seethe with an industrious swarm of monks who spread in every direction. Where once had been the haunts of wild animals and robbers' dens, there now shone forth the name of God and the worship of saints.

The numerous examples all around them aroused a desire in the nobility to accept voluntary poverty. They supported the monasteries they entered with the wealth they now repudiated, and forever exerted themselves in pious pursuits to bring others to this end. In the same vein, distinguished women abandoned marriages to prominent men and kept love of children away from their pious hearts; their wealth they donated to the monasteries and devoted themselves to service to churches. Men or women who could not completely renounce their possessions supported those who did with frequent offerings from their own wealth. They bestowed gifts of the most welcome sort upon many churches and altars and were eager to match, to the extent they could, those who led a life of prayer and piety; it was a life they could not imitate, but they used their own wealth to help others follow it. And so at this time monasteries were thriving, not so much from the sheer number of donations and donors as from the resourcefulness of those who decided to help support the church dwellers in all kinds of ways. Now, however, the increasing iniquity of my contemporaries seems day by day to drag the monasteries down from their once-flourishing state. And still today—it pains me to say—sons take back from these holy sites everything their parents had once donated because of religious desires, or else they never cease in their demands to buy these possessions back, so far have they lapsed from the intentions of their parents.

XII.

At last, after these moral tales I return to you, my God, to tell the conversion of that good woman, my mother. She had just reached marriageable age, when under my grandfather's guidance she

was promised to my father, who was himself still in adoles-
cence. Endowed with a rather attractive face and a serious
countenance that was both natural and becoming, she never-
theless bore from earliest childhood a fear of the name of God.
It was not, in fact, experience that had taught her to abhor sin,
but some dread instilled in her from on high. As she often used
to tell me, her mind had once been deeply immersed in fear of
a sudden death, but now in her old age she grieved that her
soul no longer possessed in its maturity the same goads to
goodness that it once had had in an immature and ignorant
state.[54]

As it happened, from the moment my parents were joined in
lawful union, certain people used witchcraft to loosen their
bond and prevent its consummation. In fact, it was rumored
that the jealousy of my father's stepmother was not without
effect on this marriage: she had many nieces, both beautiful
and from a good family, and she was maneuvering to plant
one of them into my father's bed. When her plans came to
naught, she allegedly turned to the dark arts to shut down any
bedroom activity. My mother had preserved her virginity
intact for seven whole years, a troublesome burden kept
shrouded in silence, until finally my father's relatives prodded
him into revealing the matter.[55] You can imagine all the ways
his family contrived to bring about a divorce, and what pains
they took to persuade my father, a young man with a dull
mind, to become a monk, even though at that time almost no
one talked about the monastic order. Their intentions in this
were not for his salvation, but for his properties, which they
wished to acquire. After their suggestions had no effect on
him, however, they began to harass her, constantly berating
this young girl, in the hopes that, living far from her relatives
and assailed by overbearing strangers, she would leave on her
own without a divorce, once she was worn down by their
insults. But she endured, and calmly withstood their verbal
attacks; whenever any disputes arose, she feigned ignorance.

Moreover, some very wealthy men, realizing she was a
young woman who had taken no part in her conjugal duties,
began to assail her heart. But you, Lord, founder of inner

chastity, you inspired a holiness in her that neither her nature nor her age would have permitted. Because of you, Lord, when she was placed in the fire, she did not burn.[56] You are the reason her morals, though delicate, did not weaken when malicious words rained down on her—in fact, because of you, fuel was added to the furnace, which is to say, external enticements were added to the natural impulses humans feel. And still, no temptations carried this young virgin's soul, ever self-possessed, beyond itself. Were not these works yours alone, Lord? When she was still in the heat of her youth, and continually subject to her conjugal duties, you preserved her for seven full years, and with such self-control that, following the saying of a wise man, even rumor feared to slander her.[57]

God, you know how difficult, or in fact nearly impossible, it would be for chastity to be preserved among women today, though in those days there was such modesty that even rumor could scarcely find fault with anyone's marriage. What a pity! To see how from that time down to our day, modesty and decency among the ranks of virgins has steadily declined, and the restraint married women ought to possess has not only appeared to evaporate, but it has in fact vanished altogether. All their habits can only be described as utter foppery, when there is only witty banter with batting eyes and wagging tongues, their promiscuity on parade. There is nothing not ridiculous in their behavior. The way they dress is completely different from the simplicity of old: sleeves spread wide open, their tunics worn tight, curled toes on shoes from Cordoba— you might see the surrender of all modesty proclaimed everywhere. Every woman thinks she has reached the height of misery if she lacks a reputation among young lovers, and claims for herself the glory of queen and countess, measured only by the number of suitors who surround her.[58]

As God is my witness, there was then a greater sense of shame among men who had married women—they were embarrassed even to be seen in the company of women—than there is now among women who marry men; indeed, their shameful conduct makes them even more boastful and more amorous in public. And why is this, Lord my God, if not because no one blushes at his own wanton frivolity when he sees everyone carrying the same mark of disgrace? And when he realizes he lives according to the same desire nearly everyone feels, how, I ask, could he know shame at a pursuit in which others equally strive? But why do I say, "know shame," when there is only one source of shame for such people—namely, if any of them falls short as an exemplar of lust? No one stops at boasting in private about the number of lovers he has, or a choice beauty that he has seduced; no one is scorned when alone by himself he swells with pride over a lover, but instead he celebrates to universal acclaim the corruption he shares with all.[59] Hear the clamor, as everyone brazenly proclaims in every direction what would instead have been covered in shame and what ought in every way to be suppressed, if there were a conscience aware of chastity's weakened state to censure it. A license for scandalous talk has taken root, and unleashed the soul, but it should be condemned to eternal silence. In this and similar ways, this modern age is corrupted and corrupts, since it contaminates many with diseased ideas, and the infection spreads to others still, for its foulness propagates without end. Holy God, almost nobody heard of anything like this in the time when that servant of yours lived. Instead, a sacrosanct chastity cloaked anything unworthy and crowned all that was innocent.

During those seven years, Lord, her virginity, which you miraculously sustained, labored under countless assaults. There were constant threats to end her marriage to my father and either place her with another husband or force her to move away to a house of one my distant relatives. Though she did at times endure the bitterest struggles in the face of these oppressive demands, she still fought more against both the seductions of her own flesh and any external temptations with a self-control that was extraordinary, but a gift from you nonetheless, my God. I do not mean, God of goodness, that she accomplished this by her virtue, but that the virtue was yours alone. If neither the practice of discretion between spirit and flesh nor any pious intention toward God played any role, but only a concern for decent appearances or avoiding infamy, how was it virtue? Certainly a sense of shame is useful, at least for resisting sin as it draws near. But, just as it is useful before sin, so it is damnable after sin. For anything that blankets the heart in pious shame to prevent it from committing sin is useful for a time, because the fear of God, which seasons ordinary shame with divine salt, can be added to it, and can make what is useful for a time (that is, useful in this world) useful not for a moment, but for eternity. This type of modesty, while it does bring glory, is all the more harmful after sin, to the degree it persists as an obstacle to the remedy of holy confession.[60]

Lord God, your servant, my mother, intended to do nothing contrary to the dignity of the world she lived in. And yet, following the words of Saint Gregory (whom she had never read, nor heard read), she did not remain in that intention, because she later attributed everything she intended to you alone. For this reason, it was to her benefit that she adhered at that time to a worldly form of restraint.

As a result, the witchcraft used, as was all too clear, to break the bonds of natural and lawful intercourse continued for more than seven years. It is easy enough to believe that just as there are tricks that can fool the eyes (so that something seems to come, if I may say so, from nothing, and magicians appear to turn one thing into another), so an even simpler trick can overwhelm these powers aimed at sexual activity. It is such a popular practice that some of the uneducated now know it. And once some old woman finally demolished those evil crafts, my mother performed her bedroom duties as faithfully as she had preserved her long-held virginity under so many verbal assaults.

She was certainly happier at other times! She condemned herself not so much to be in endless misery as to be misery itself, because even though she was good then, and afterward even better, she gave birth to me, forever bad and always growing worse. Nevertheless, you know, Almighty, the purity and holiness with which she raised me to follow you, how much care she took in choosing nurses in my infancy, pedagogues and teachers in my frail childhood. Nor did my little body lack luxurious clothing, whose showiness made me a match for the sons of royalty or nobility. This desire, Lord, you not only gave to my mother, but you also instilled it into others who were much wealthier, and so they provided me with food and clothing not from family obligations as much as from the grace you had offered me.

God, you know how many warnings, how many prayers she daily poured into my ears, that I not give ear to any kind of immorality! Whenever there was time alone free from family cares, she would teach me how and what I should pray to you. You alone know how great were the pains she bore to prevent my unhealthy soul from ruining the healthy beginnings, the brilliant and distinguished youth, which you had given me. From her wish, you had caused me to seethe with unceasing yearning for you, till you could at last furnish my outer splendor with inner virtue or wisdom. And good Lord, good God, if she had foreseen the heap of filth under which I was going to bury those superficial goods that originated from your gifts, with which you had decorated me at her request, what would she have said? What would she have done? How she would have groaned, beyond any consolation! How her mind would have been torn apart! Thanks to you, sweet and gentle provider, you who fashioned each of our hearts! If her eyes so pure had penetrated the recesses of my soul, a view utterly offensive for the pure of sight, it would be a wonder if she had not died at once.

XIII.

Now that I have spent some time on these matters, let me return to some things I passed over. As I was saying, we learned that despite her adherence to the secular world, my mother always maintained a reverence for the name of God. Everyone respected her for the way she supported churches, gave donations to the poor, and made offerings at mass. It is, I know, extremely difficult for me to bring anyone to believe this, hindered as I am by my close relationship to the object of my praise, rendering what I say suspect. Praise of one's own mother may seem a circumspect and insincere way to promote oneself, but it is you, God, who knows her soul, as one who dwells in her soul, whom I dare to call forward as a witness to her excellence in every regard, exactly as I describe her. It is clearer than day that my life strays from the path of all good men, that my pursuits have always been a disgrace in the eyes of anyone with sense, so what use would greatness in the name of a mother, father, or even grandfather be to me, if all its grandeur shrinks down into a wretched offspring?[61] In reproducing their conduct, my will does not correspond to my actions, so if I attribute to myself the praise due to them, the evil would surpass the infamy.

While my mother, then, was still a young woman living with her husband, the following event provided her the greatest incentive to correct her life. In the reign of King Henry, the Franks engaged in a bitter struggle against the Normans and against their Count William (who later conquered the English and the Scots).[62] When the two peoples fought against one another, my father happened to be captured. It had never been this count's habit to offer his captives for ransom, but instead he would condemn them to a life of perpetual imprisonment. When this was made known to his wife (I do not say "mother," since I had not yet been born, nor was I to be until much later), she fainted, nearly dead from her pitiable grief. She took no food or drink, and her utterly hopeless worries denied her any sleep. It was not the size of any ransom that caused her mind to worry; rather, she grieved over a captivity that offered no hope for release.

That same night, a storm arose. Overwhelmed with anxious dread, she was lying secure in her bed, when suddenly the Enemy, who has a habit of plunging into souls lacerated by sorrow, crawled in with her as she lay awake and nearly crushed her to death under his enormous weight. Her breath grew tight, suffocating her; all freedom of movement left her limbs, and she could not utter any sound. Her power to reason was mute but free, so she called upon God, the only help she had. And there, at the head of her bed, some spirit—there was no doubt that it was good—began to shout in a voice as affectionate as it was clear: "Blessed Mary, help!" These words were repeated for a while, and once Mary had heard the words, the good spirit attacked with an intense hostility, as she in her great distress sensed.[63] At this manifestation, the devil, still lying in my mother's bed, rose up, but the spirit blocked his way and grabbed him. Its strength from God, the spirit threw down the devil with a tremendous crash; the heavy blow shook the room, and startled the servants from their slumbers. After the devil had been cast out by divine forces, this pious spirit, who had summoned Mary and expelled the demon, turned to the woman he had rescued and said: "See that you be a good woman!" Bewildered by the sudden noise, the women servants got up together to see how their mistress was. They found her moribund, the blood drained from her face, and all the strength of her tender body spent. They started asking about the noise, and at once heard from her what had caused it, though when they showed up, bringing lamps and talking to her, they could scarcely revive her spirit.

That woman always remembered the last words of her liberator, or rather your words, Lord God, from your messenger, and preserved them in the hope they would be wedded to a greater desire, if God should in the future provide her the opportunity. Once my father died, even though her radiant beauty still cast its glow, she decided to remain a widow. Almost six months old, I would be her only cause for worry.

A single example will suffice to show the tenacity with which she held to her purpose, and the modesty she exemplified. My relatives, envious of my father's properties and possessions, tried to exclude my mother and obtain them all. They set a date to bring the case to trial, and when the day arrived, eminent men took their seats in preparation to hear the arguments. But my mother, knowing full well her in-laws acted out of greed, had withdrawn to a church. Standing before an image of the crucified Lord, she remembered that she ought to pray. Meanwhile, one of my father's relatives, of the same mind as the rest of the family, came to her at their bidding, and began asking her to come hear the decision of the judges, who awaited her. She interrupted him: "I will do nothing about this except in the presence of my Lord." He asked, "Which lord"? She stretched out her hand to the image of the crucified Lord and said, "He is my Lord." Once he heard this, she added, "He is my advocate, I plead my case with him!" Her words embarrassed the man, but he was a very shifty character, so he hid his wickedness behind a forced smile and went back to his accomplices to report what he had heard. Her response filled them with shame as well, and since they realized that in the face of her total honesty their case lacked any justice, they stopped harassing her.

Shortly thereafter, one of the leading men of the country and the province, a nephew of my father who was as powerful as he was greedy, tried to win my mother over with the following speech: "Since, my lady, you lack neither youth nor beauty, you should remarry—you'll be happier for the rest of your life. I'll faithfully raise my uncle's children, and they'll live under my care. All of his property will also fall under my legal control, as is proper." But she replied, "You know your uncle came from a rather distinguished family. He died when God took him away, and Hymenaeus will not,[64] lord, perform his duties for me a second time, unless it happens that a marriage to someone of even nobler birth presents itself." She was being clever when she mentioned finding someone nobler, since she knew it was unlikely, if not impossible. He bristled at the mention of the word "nobler," because she had managed at one stroke to exclude both the noble and the ignoble and dashed their hope that she would remarry. And when he attributed her talk of someone "nobler" to excessive pride, she retorted: "Of course—either nobler or no one." When he understood the intention behind her dignified speech, he abandoned the attempt, and never again sought that she remarry.

And so, with great fear of God, and no less love for all her relatives, especially those in need, she wisely oversaw me and my affairs, and the fidelity she maintained toward her husband while he lived, she continued to practice with redoubled effort in her soul: at his death, she did not divide the former unity of their bodies by the introduction of another's flesh, and nearly every day she had a mass performed for his salvation. And though she was kind to all the poor, out of an abundance of mercy she generously supported a few paupers in particular. The memory of her own sins troubled her deeply; it was as if she were afraid all the world's wickedness had condemned her, and she would suffer the punishment for every sin that had been committed. She was unable to be moderate in her expenses, since thriftiness suited neither her young age nor her elegant and refined habits, but in all other regards, she was remarkable. I have seen with my own eyes and touched with my own hands the coarse hair shirt she wore against her bare skin, even when the outward dress covering it was quite elegant. Not only did she wear it during the day, but also—which was rather extreme for her delicate flesh—she slept in it at night.

Rarely, if ever, did she miss the nightly offices, since at the times set for worship she celebrated together with people of God. In fact, because of the ceaseless dedication of the chaplains her house almost always resounded with praise of God. The name of her dead husband was forever on her lips, to the point she seemed to think of nothing else during prayer, during almsgiving, or even during everyday life. She spoke of him constantly and could not stop herself, for when the heart overflows with love for someone, the tongue will begin to form his name, as if it cannot help but say it.

XIV.

But let us skip over the times when she conducted herself well, though not especially so, and move on to the rest. I had passed almost twelve years, as they tell me, since the death of my father, and during this time as a widow she had taken care of both house and children in the customary manner. At the same time, she had daily conceived in her mind plans that she now hastened to bring to happy fruition. She was carefully weighing both sides of her project, engaged in a discussion about it only with my pedagogue (who had been a schoolmaster, as I mentioned above). At about this time I heard an epileptic, to whom she offered the support of her household, howling one thing or another, and in the midst of his ranting, a demon forced him to cry: "The priests put a cross on her kidneys!"[65] In fact, nothing could be truer—though at that time I had no idea what he meant—for she bore not one, but many crosses. No one was aware of her plan except the pedagogue, but shortly thereafter a steward in her house, who also would soon renounce the world and follow in her conversion, had a dream: he saw her take a husband and celebrate a marriage, and this miraculous event astonished her children, friends, and relatives. The next day, my mother went for a walk in the country with my teacher and the steward, who reported what he had seen. My mother, well versed in such matters, needed no interpreter, but looking back to the teacher silently signaled that this vision was a portent of what they had been discussing: her love for God, and her desire to be joined together with him. She then quickly moved forward on the path she had begun, and no longer able to endure her inner turmoil, she abandoned the life she was living in that town.

Upon her departure, she stopped at an episcopal villa after she had obtained permission to stay there from the lord, Bishop Guy of Beauvais. Guy was a man who possessed all the qualities of royalty, born into a noble family, and to all appearances he was ably suited for the office he held. He had rendered the most distinguished services to the cathedral of Beauvais, including his foundation from the ground up of a church for regular canons, dedicated to Saint Quentin, but then men he himself had educated and promoted, after meeting in secret at the house of the archbishop Hugh of Lyon, legate of the Apostolic See, charged him with simony and other crimes. When summoned, he did not appear, since he was at Cluny, and in his absence from the testimony, he was found guilty.[66] Fearful of the sentence inflicted upon him, he would turn himself over to monastic life there. At this time, he appeared to welcome warmly my mother and my relatives, and singled me out for his care and affection; in particular, he had conferred upon me all the blessings of the sacraments except for the priesthood.[67] And so when friends of my mother asked that he allow her to live for a little while in a house he had built next to the local church, he gladly permitted it. The village itself is called Catenoy, almost two miles distant from our town.

While there she had decided she would move to the monastery at Fly. She had my teacher see to the construction of a small house next to that church, and then she finally left the place where she had been waiting. Though she knew I would suddenly become an orphan and that I had no resources to fall back on—we had, in fact, numerous relatives and in-laws, but none of them would carefully tend to the needs of a boy at that tender age; and even though I had no need of food or clothing, still, a lack of the guidance and discipline necessary for that vulnerable age, care that only women can provide, often troubled me—so even though she knew I would be condemned to such neglect, her fear and her love of you, God, hardened her heart as she passed through the town where I was staying on her way to the monastery. The agony in her heart so pained her, even to glance back at the castle was unbearable torture, for every time she thought about what she had left behind there, the bitterest grief tore her apart.

No wonder if she felt as if her own limbs were being torn from her body! She began in fact to believe—or rather she heard it from others—that she was utterly wicked and cruel. She had barred from her soul, and sent away without any support, a child such as this, so deserving of affection—at least that is what people said, for not only our relatives, but also people outside the family adored me. And you, good God, holy God, in your sweetness, in your charity, you had miraculously hardened her heart, surely the most pious heart in the world, lest it be pious to its own detriment. Any softening would have caused her soul harm, if she had shown any care for the things of this world and put me before her own salvation, neglected God instead of me. But her love was strong as death, because the more closely her love bound her to you, the less troubled she seemed to feel at having cast off what she had once loved.

When she arrived at the monastery, she came upon an old woman in a nun's habit who in her bearing had the appearance of great piety. My mother, with all the submissiveness a student has for a teacher, compelled the woman to live with her. I say "compelled," since once my mother learned of her habits, she spared no effort to cultivate a close relationship with her. Little by little, she began to imitate the old woman's austerity: she started to lead a simple life. She embraced the humblest of foods. She refused the soft mattress of a normal bed, and instead slept content on a block of wood covered with straw. And though she still had the glow of her beauty, unmarked by age, she tried to look older, hoping others would think from her wrinkles that she had already reached her final years. Her flowing tresses, which more than any other feature serves to beautify women, frequently fell under the scissors. She wore drab clothing, draped over her in uncommonly long folds and held together with countless patches, along with a small undyed cloak and shoes riddled with holes beyond repair, for the one whom she was trying to please with her shabby apparel was within her.

Nearly every day she made a new confession of old sins, for she had learned that confession was the beginning of every good thing. Her mind constantly subjected to trial all of her previous deeds: the tribunal of her reason questioned what she had done, thought, and said while she was a virgin in her early years, when she was a married woman, and now when, as a widow, she was more able to follow her inclinations. Once questioned, she brought her actions before a priest, or rather before God through a priest, for judgment. After this, you would have seen her pray in such strident tones, her spirit consumed with such anxiety that she could hardly stop the dreadful groans and tearful words even while she was working. She had learned the seven penitential psalms from that old woman, not by sight but by ear, which she savored (if I may say so) on her lips day and night. Never did the sighs, never did the groans of her sweetly sounding psalmody fail to reach your ears, God.

Occasionally, people from the outside would gather and disturb her cherished solitude. Everyone who knew her, especially noble men and women, thoroughly enjoyed talking with her, since she was extraordinarily charming and pleasant. But once they left, if anything less than true, if any trifling or idle

matter had entered into their conversation, her mind felt inde-
scribable anxieties, until she had reached the familiar waters
of compunction or confession.

But these acts of contrition brought her no assurance and no
peace of mind, no matter how much effort or how much care
she devoted to them. She grieved constantly, tearfully wonder-
ing whether she deserved forgiveness for her sins. And you
know, God, how many were her sins, nor am I unaware of
them. Yet how trifling is their number compared to those who
neither grieve nor sigh! You know, Lord, how far I could gauge
her state of mind, because never did I see her soul's fear of
damnation or love for you grow tepid.

XV.

And what else is there? When she, as I said before, rejected the
world, I had been left alone, without a mother, without a ped-
agogue, without a teacher. Inspired by my mother's love and
counsel, he, the one who second only to her had raised and
educated me so faithfully, followed her example and entered
the monastery at Fly. I thus obtained a corrupt form of free-
dom, and with complete lack of self-restraint I began to abuse
my own authority. I ridiculed the church and shuddered at the
thought of school. I desired the companionship of my cousins,
laymen just beginning their training as knights, and while I
cursed anything that reminded me of the clerical life, I would
promise remission of their sins. Indulging in an unusual
amount of sleep, which was little allowed me before, I began
to waste away. Meanwhile, my "glorious" deeds reached my
mother's ears. From what she heard, she thought my death
imminent, and collapsed, nearly lifeless. To inspire me toward
the priesthood, she had earlier provided me with some elegant
clothes that I used to wear to church, and now I sported them
for wanton behavior not allowed even at that age. I rivaled
older boys in effrontery, without any discretion or moderation
whatsoever.

As strict and disciplined as my life had been before, I was

now just as dissolute, or rather demented. My mother could no longer tolerate the things she heard, so she went to the abbot and asked him and the brothers if my teacher could once again instruct me. Since this abbot had been supported by my grandfather in the past and, in exchange for a benefice, was a dependent of his estate, he readily granted the request.[68] He welcomed my arrival, and after he kindly settled me in, he treated me still more kindly. I call upon you as witness, pious God, who arranged all this, because from the moment I entered the monastery's church and saw the monks sitting together, such a desire for the monastic life was kindled in me that it could not be extinguished, nor could my spirit find rest, until it received the answer to its prayer. While living in the same cloister as the monks, I reflected upon their entire existence and their way of life, and, as wind stokes a fire, my contemplation of them could not but inflame my mind, eager to be like them. Then the abbot began entreating me, with prayers repeated daily, to become a monk, and even though I seethed with boundless desire to do so, no amount of insistent pleading could loosen my tongue to accept the invitation. Now that I am getting older, I find it extremely difficult to keep silent about all that fills my heart, but then as a young boy, I did so with little effort.[69]

At last I disclosed the matter to my mother. She feared it was merely a childish whimsy, and the arguments she used to reject my plan caused me no small regret that I had ever revealed it to her. When I also told my teacher, he drove me still further away from the idea. Deeply irritated at both of their refusals, I decided to turn my thoughts elsewhere and started to act as if I had never wanted any of these things in the first place. I had put off the decision from the Octave of Pentecost up to Christmas Day, while with fervent prayers I continued to hope I could see my plan through. When, Lord, I could no longer endure your inner goading, I cast aside reverence for my mother and fear of my teacher and went to the abbot. He fervently desired this to happen, too, but all his pleas had not been able to draw any promise from my lips. I fell to the ground at his feet and tearfully begged him, in these very words, to "take up a sinner." He happily granted what I asked, and as soon as he could (which was the next day) he brought out for me the proper vestments. As my mother looked upon me from a distance and wept, he put them on me, and commanded that alms be offered on that day.

Because of the stricter rule, my teacher could no longer offer me instruction, but he did make an effort at least to encourage me to study carefully the holy books I was reading. He urged me to reconsider, based on what better scholars said, certain doctrines I did not understand as well, and to compose short pieces in prose and verse. The less attention others paid to my education, the more intently he implored me to work. And, O Lord, true light, I well remember the inestimable generosity you displayed to me then. For as soon as I put on your habit, at your summons, the cloud over my heart seemed to move away, and everything to which I had long been blind during my aimless wanderings now began to take hold of my heart. As well, a tremendous desire for learning suddenly enlivened me: this was my one single pursuit, and if I ever passed a day without any kind of study, I considered it a waste of my life. How often I was thought to be asleep, keeping my tender flesh warm under a blanket, when in fact my spirit was focused on silent recitation or I was reading beneath the covers, in fear that someone would complain!

And you, pious Jesus, you were not unaware that when I did such things, my intention was to win any praise possible, and to achieve greater honor in this present world. I did, to my detriment, have friends who, although they were encouraging me to do good things, repeatedly filled my ears with the fame and glory my writings would bring, and the wealth and power I could attain. Into my unsuspecting heart they introduced hopes worse than any viper's egg,[70] and since I thought everything they promised would soon be fulfilled, they deluded me with expectations of the vainest sort. Everything they said would happen in my old age, I truly believed I would accomplish in my youthful adolescence. To prove their point, they displayed before me my store of knowledge, which thanks to you grew daily, as well as my family and my looks, both considered good for this world. But they did not recall that you forbid ascent to your altar by these steps, since by this way shame shall be exposed. For indeed whoever ascends from another way is a thief and a bandit, and this is shame.[71]

But when I took these first steps, which you inspired, my soul, if it had been wise in a different way, would have been prepared for temptation. And certainly I was something of a wise fool at that time. For though I had only childish fits of joy and anger, would that, Lord, I now feared your judgment, now trembled at even the worst sins, as I then trembled at the least sin, almost no sin at all! I was of course trying to emulate, and as zealously as I could, those whom I saw weeping over the sins they had committed, and nothing pleased my eyes and ears more than whatever had its source in you. Now I comb the scripture for sayings I can flaunt, or rather from the pagans themselves I string together contemptible phrases for my rhetorical blather, but at that time the only things I gathered from my reading were reasons to weep and lament. Any time I found nothing in my reading worthy of reflection, nothing useful for compunction, I thought I had read nothing at all. In my ignorance, I was acting wisely.

But our old enemy, who has learned through long experience to adapt to different states of mind and various ages—it was he who created new battles for my own young mind and body.[72] In my sleep, he often placed before my mind's eye images of the dead, especially those whose death by the sword or some other kind of slaughter I had either seen or heard about. Such awful sights would terrify my spirit, immersed in sleep, and if the vigilance of my oft-mentioned teacher had not fortified me, I could not have stayed in bed at night, nor kept myself from screaming: I could scarcely control my senses. This affliction may seem ridiculous and childish to anyone who has not experienced it, but for those who know its torments, it is so catastrophic that the fear that it inspires, which to some appears easily vanquished, cannot be alleviated, either through one's own reason or through guidance from others. Someone in this state may want to downplay his suffering, but when he slips into even the slightest slumber, his spirit has no power to strike back against such horrid sights. Instead, his

mind, disquieted by grave fears, trembles at the thought of
further sleep, and neither company nor solitude can allay these
passions, since companions cannot hinder the fear, and isola-
tion either makes it worse, or at best does not diminish it.

How differently I acted then, Lord God, from the way I do
now! I used to live with great reverence for your law and a
boundless hatred for all sin, and to drink in everything around
me that could be said, heard, or known of you. I know, heav-
enly Father, that my childish enthusiasms were goading the
devil ferociously, but a little later I would soothe him by aban-
doning all my pious fervor.

Thus one night, after I woke up from my dismal trouble and
as I was lying in bed—it was winter, I think—the lamp next to
me glowed brightly, and I felt more at ease. Suddenly, right
over my head, or so I thought, arose a great clamor of many
voices, though it was the dead of night. It was only the sound
of voices, without words, but the force of this sudden blow
struck hard at my temples and I lost my senses, as if I had
fallen asleep—and I thought I saw a dead man. Someone was
crying out that he had died in the baths. Completely terrified
at this vision, I leapt from my bed, a scream in my throat, and
in that moment I looked back: the lamp had gone out, and
through the darkness of a great shadow I gazed upon a demon
standing near me, in his true form. By this abominable vision I
was almost driven into madness, but the experienced hand of
my teacher, who often stayed up to calm these terrors of mine,
restored me from my agitation and insanity. It did not escape
me even then, my God, in the tender years of my youth, that
the ardor of a good intention burning my soul in no small way
had incited the devil to instigate this wickedness in me. O
pious God, what victories, what crowns of glory I would have
earned, if in this struggle I had firmly stood my ground!

Based on numerous stories I have heard, I gather that
demons are bitterly aggrieved by recent converts, or those who
always hope to convert. I remember an incident from the time
of Guy, bishop of Beauvais, whom I mentioned above.[73] There
was among the squires of his retinue a young man, for whom
the bishop had had a special affection, even more than for his

own peers. The young man was dreadfully ashamed of his sins, and was making every effort possible to escape his secular life, but this unsettling change to something new and unfamiliar was eating away at him. One night, he was to sleep in the bedroom of the bishop, where there was with him a rather pious man named Yves, a resident of Saint-Quentin, if I'm not mistaken, famed for learning; and even more distinguished for his eloquence, a monk of Cluny, who had long carried out the duties of prior under Hugh, abbot of blessed memory. In the room with the bishop were some other men, equally noble and holy, and they all began to fall asleep at the same time. While all the rest slept in the silence of the night, one of the nobles from a nearby town, a very dignified and prudent man, stayed awake. He was thinking about whatever came to mind, and looking all around, when suddenly there appeared before him the tall figure of a demon, its head barely visible, walking forward with hunched shoulders. In this guise, the demon paced up and down the room, looking down at each bed in turn. When the deceiver approached the bed of the young man I mentioned, whom the bishop favored most, he stopped, and turning his gaze down to him as he slept, said, "He vexes me more bitterly than all who sleep here." As he finished, he headed toward the sewer drain and went down into it. The entire time the man was watching this, a great weight pressed down upon him, and he was unable to speak or to move, but as soon as the adversary had left, he was once again able to do both. In the morning, he revealed what he had seen to some sensible men, and when he asked about the young man's condition and his identity, he discovered that his soul was earnestly inclined to attain greater holiness.

If then there is more joy in heaven over the conversion of a single sinner than over ninety-nine righteous men who do not need repentance,[74] there is no doubt that the enemies of the human race are afflicted with the bitterest envy when those who change for the better are snatched away from them. Of course, just as I have taken disastrous steps away from my good beginnings, so, too, this young man. He had received testimony from the demon, but afterward lost his fervor little by little, until he grew cold and turned back to worldly pursuits. Nevertheless, one can believe that the sudden stirring of our good wills would have stung a demon's heart so deeply. And it is no wonder if anybody's abrupt and fleeting desire to repent should pain the devil, when even the perfunctory humility of Ahab, that criminal king, received heaven's notice before man's. The Lord said, if I am not mistaken, to Elijah, "Have you not seen Ahab humble himself before me? Since then he has humbled himself for my sake, I will not bring evils in his days."[75]

XVI.

As my young body steadily grew, my soul, too, tingling with its own cravings and desires, felt the enticement of secular life. I was forever returning to the same thought, turning over and over again in my mind how great a man I could be in this world, and my imagination often went far beyond anything that could possibly be true. But you, God of goodness, who has a care for all, you showed all this to your servant, my mother, and whenever my unstable conscience shifted from one state to another, sane or insane, by your judgment, Lord, an image of it then came to her in a vision.[76] It is said that dreams come from many cares,[77] which is certainly true, yet her cares did not arise from the inner heat sparked by greed, but rather were born of sincere strivings after an inner goodness. She was quite an astute and discriminating interpreter of visions, and thus whenever a troubling one touched her pious mind, whenever she understood that a disturbance in her dream was an omen, she would summon me and examine my studies, reviewing what I was doing alone with myself, how I was spending my time in private. I always obeyed her, and could in no way withhold the understanding I shared with her: my soul seemed attached to her dreams, and everything in them that I recognized, I readily confessed to her. When she warned me to correct my ways, with a sincere desire I promised to do so immediately.

My God, from numerous obscure signs she understood then the condition in which I now suffer, and on many occasions revealed it to me. Every day now within the recesses of my heart I experience everything she believed I had done or would do in my original state,[78] and I observe that it has been fulfilled. The same concerns about me weighed constantly on my teacher's heart as well, and you revealed to his sight through various images, what was happening at that time and what would happen in the future. Each gave, as gifts from God, prophecies of misfortune and success: one to frighten me, so that I might refrain, whether I wanted to or not, from the wickedness hidden within me, but exposed miraculously to those who loved me; the other to encourage me, that I might sometimes rejoice in the promise of a better hope.

At times a spirit of melancholy drifted over me, since I had to endure the intense jealousy of my superiors and peers, and with the support of my relatives, I began to long to move to another monastery. While some in my monastery once saw me as far beneath them in age and education as well as influence and understanding, they realized now, that the gift of him alone, who is the key of all knowledge, had instilled into my senses an appetite for learning, that I had begun to equal them, or, if I may say so, completely surpass them. Their scornful wickedness flared up against me with great fury, and I grew exhausted from the constant debates and controversies—I wished I had never seen Latin, much less learned any of it. They made every effort to disrupt my studies, and many times, seizing on an opportunity from the text itself, they would stir up quarrels through constant questioning. It seemed that the only purpose behind their exertions was to make me shrink away from my eagerness in this study and to shackle my talents. But just as the fuel added to a furnace first seems to extinguish the flame, and then slowly gives it more life, so in the same way the longer my intelligence was enclosed within this struggle, as in an oven, the stronger it grew from its own heat, and the better it became. Examinations in which I was judged to be dull served only to give my intelligence a keener edge, and the difficulties in their objections, which caused me to

ruminate again and again on my conjectures and pore over
different books, gave birth to more ideas and an ability to
respond effectively. And though in this way I became deeply
hateful to them, you know, God, how little, if at all, I hated
them. When they were not able to brand me with disgrace as
they wished, they kept picking away at me and tried to belittle
me as a dilettante.

Even though in midst of such anxieties an abundance of
advantages was being born, during these difficult ordeals my
wearied spirit many times wilted under the endless mental
strain, and since fear filled my heart and my powers of reason-
ing often failed me, I did not consider how this adversity prof-
ited me. Instead, I readily assented to the promptings of my
weak flesh, and arrived at the decision to leave that place,
more because my relatives insistently urged me than because
my abbot kindly gave me permission. I also had my mother's
approval, since she believed this desire came from some pious
intention, as the monastery I wanted to enter next had a repu-
tation for being very devout. As a witness to the evils and
goods in store for me, the following vision came to her.

She dreamed she was in the church of the monastery at Fly,
which is named for St. Germer, and noticed that the inside of
the church was completely deserted. The monks were not
only in tatters, wrapped in coverings far exceeding the size
allowed by the rule, but they were all shrunk down to a cubit
in height, like those commonly called dwarves. But because
where the treasure is, there, too, is the heart,[79] and where the
gaze, there also the love, she anxiously turned her eyes to me.
My stature, she realized, did not surpass the others, nor was I
clothed in garments of any greater dignity, and she began to
lament my condition and this great church's. But then sud-
denly a woman of boundless beauty and nobility advanced
through the middle of the church all the way up to the altar,
preceded by a young girl, whose beauty seemed quite fitting
for her service to the woman she followed. My mother, curi-
ous to know who this woman was, was told that she was the
Lady of Chartres, which she immediately interpreted to mean
that this woman was the mother of God, whose name and

relics there are venerated throughout nearly the entire Latin world.[80] When the woman reached the altar, she bent down on her knees to pray, and the girl who appeared to follow, her noble attendant, did the same behind her. Then she rose up and holding out her hand, spoke with great hostility: "I founded this church—why would I allow it to be deserted?" Then she, the standard-bearer of piety, directed her perfectly serene gaze toward me, and pointed with her radiant right hand. "I brought him here," she said, "and made him a monk; in no way would I allow him to be taken away." Her attendant repeated after her these same words in the same way. The powerful woman had spoken, and no sooner was it said than all the desolation and ruin was completely repaired; everything my mother had seen at first, including our excessively short statures, both the others' and mine, returned to normal by the gracious power and authority of she who commanded it. When my prescient mother relayed the details of this vision to me, I tearfully accepted her powerful words, my spirit filled with remorse. The meaning of this dream, which I sorely needed to hear, caused me to restrain my thoughts from wandering freely, and no longer did I feel the pull of a desire to move to another monastery.

O Lady, mother of the heavenly realm, no matter how repugnant my sins, no matter the innumerable abjurations when I turned away from the love and obedience I owed you, these events and others like them opened the door for my return to you. For in my heart is the constant refrain, that all my acts of wickedness piled together could not bar me from the open shelter of your mercies. As well, I always remember, heavenly Lady, a vision I had one night when I was a young boy who hoped to wear the monastic habit. I was in a church dedicated in your name, with two demons bearing me away. After they had carried me to the top of the basilica, they fled, leaving me unharmed within the walls of the church. I often recall this vision as I reflect upon my incorrigibility, and while I keep committing the same sins, or rather add worse sins to ones that were the worst, I run back to you, most reverent

Lady, not because I mistakenly rely on too great a hope or
some little faith, but only to escape the perils of a lost hope.
Although I always fail because weakness drives me, not
because pride hardens me, I never lose hope for correction.
Indeed, the righteous man falls seven times, and rises again. If
the number seven is taken in its traditional sense to represent
totality,[81] then by whatever kinds of sin anyone falls, as long as
he has the intention to rise back up to righteousness, though
lust of the flesh cause him to slip, and as long as he summons
up the grief characteristic of a sincere penitent, he will never
cease to be called righteous. And why does one cry out to God
to bring us out of our distress, if not because the corruption in
our nature condemns us to obey sin, whether we want to or
not? "I see," says the apostle, "one leading me captive to the
law of sin that is in my limbs; for I do not do the good I want,
but the evil I do not want is what I do." There is a depth to cer-
tain evils, and when an impious man reaches it, he feels con-
tempt, and yet in other depths there is a crying out to God,
and the petitioner does not doubt his voice is heard. When
there is an excess of sin, there is indeed a contempt that comes
from desperation; it can exist in the depth where there is no
substance in which misery does not subsist.[82] Finally the depth
out of which Jeremiah was dragged by a rope made of rags,
and though it . . .[83] nevertheless it has a bottom. For even
though the mind may be cast into a great multitude of sins, it
still possesses within its reason some kind of boundary that
stops it from traveling through an endless abyss without any
recognition of all its iniquity.

XVII.

I had, however, plunged my spirit beyond all limits into writ-
ing poetry, and I set aside every single page of scripture in
favor of such pointless vanity. My inconstancy had already
led me to mimic verses of Ovid and the bucolic poets, and the
way I made a show of arranging the material into epistolary

exchanges was an affectation of their erotic elegance.[84] And so my mind forgot the seriousness it should have had, and once the shame of my monastic calling had been cast away, it took joy in the seductive charms of this diseased freedom. My mind pondered only if anything said in a courtly manner could be put in the words of some poet or another, never considering how much the diligent effort I had to expend in this activity took away from my plan to enter into sacred orders. I was being seized from both directions: the sweet-sounding words I took in from the poets, and then spewed forth myself, ensnared me in their wanton frivolity, and since I kept coming back to them and things like them, all too frequent titillations to my flesh held me captive. Because my spirit, unstable and unaccustomed to any discipline, wore itself away on these things, the only utterance that could pass from my lips came from what these ruminations suggested.

And then this inner madness boiled over. I sank to using some rather obscene words in composing short pieces that possessed little discretion or moderation—or rather, they were devoid of all decency.[85] These pained my teacher once they came to his attention; disgusted with me, he went to bed in a state of irritation, where, drifting off to sleep, the following vision came to him. An older man with the most beautiful head of white hair appeared (it was in fact, if I dare say so, the same man who first brought me to him and promised he would always have love for me),[86] and addressed him sternly. "I want you," he said, "to give me an account of these poems that were composed. But his hand, which did the writing, is not the hand that wrote the poems."[87]

When my teacher told me this, he and I both similarly interpreted the dream. We joyfully lamented, Lord, in our hope in you: on the one hand, we saw your disapproval revealed in this fatherly admonishment, and on the other, we thought that the purpose of this vision was a promise that my frivolous ways would experience a change toward piety. For when that man said that the hand that wrote the words was not the hand of him who did the writing, he evidently meant that the hand would not continue in its disgraceful activity. It was my hand, and it is not my hand, just as we read: "Overthrow the impious, and they will be no more."[88] The hand belonged to me while engaged in vice, but once it was applied to the pursuit of virtue, that unworthy claim to ownership lost its validity.[89]

And yet you know, Lord, and I confess it, that at that time neither fear of you, nor shame at myself, nor respect for this holy vision made me behave with any more self-restraint. Indeed, I did not refrain at all in my inner life from the scandalous indecencies of my trifling compositions. In secret I composed the same poems, not daring to show them to any, or scarcely any, of my companions, and yet I often used to recite them to whom I could, under the name of a false author, and took joy in the praise they received from those who shared religious vows with me. I thought it would be inappropriate to admit that the poems were mine, and since their author could not profit from the fruits of their praise, all that was left to rejoice in were the fruits—or rather the disgrace—of sin. But when you wished, Father, you punished my behavior: misfortunes rose against me from this activity, and you fettered my wandering spirit with great adversity and overwhelmed me with bodily infirmity. A sword then reached to my soul, as distress came upon my judgment.[90]

Since the punishment for sin had granted understanding to the hearer,[91] what little interest I had in this useless pursuit finally withered away. Still, I could not bear to be idle and almost out of necessity, my empty fantasies set aside, I took up spiritual matters and passed on to more beneficial studies. Though late in coming, I now began to thirst for what good teachers had once instilled in me: to apply myself to commentary on scripture, to pore over the writings of Gregory—more than anywhere else, the place to find the keys to this practice— and to grasp the meaning of the words of the prophets or the gospel, following the methods of earlier authors, in their allegorical, moral, and also anagogic senses. In these matters, the one who most inspired me was Anselm, abbot of Bec, later archbishop of Canterbury. From the transalpine region known

as Aosta, he was a man without peer in learning, and in his
life completely devout. When he was still the prior of this mon-
astery, he made my acquaintance, and even though I was still
a young boy, tender in age and understanding, he offered to
make every effort to teach me how I should conduct my inner
self, and how I should consult the laws of reason to govern my
young flesh. Both before and after he became abbot, his piety
and learning made him a welcome visitor to the monastery at
Fly, where I was. He unstintingly favored me with the gifts of
his erudition, and worked at it so diligently that I seemed to be
the one and only reason for his frequent visits to us.

By dividing the mind into a three- or four-part scheme, he
taught me to treat all the transactions of the internal mystery
under the categories of affection, will, reason, and intellect.
Many people, including myself, thought the first two (affec-
tion and will) were one and the same, but he clearly defined
the distinction between them and showed that they were not
identical. However, there are clear arguments to prove that
when either the fourth (intellect) or third (reason) is present,
then the first two are the same. He used this scheme to explain
some chapters from the gospel to me, when he first revealed in
the most lucid manner the difference between willing and
desiring—ideas not his own, but from some books he had,
though they treated these matters less clearly. Then I began to
emulate his thinking in commentaries as much like his as I
could make them, and to concentrate my mental energies on
searching throughout scripture for anything that might agree
on a moral level with these ideas.[92]

It so happened, when I came along with my abbot to a mon-
astery in our province, and suggested to him, as a man of great
piety, that he give a sermon at a gathering of the chapter, he
handed over to me what I sought from him—he both begged
and commanded me to perform in his stead. This was the
same day on which the birth of Mary Magdalene is celebrated;
accordingly, I took my subject matter for the sermon asked of
me from the book of Wisdom, and was satisfied to discuss this
one single verse: "Wisdom conquers evil, it reaches mightily
from one end of the earth to another, and orders all things

gently."[93] I explained it with whatever eloquence I could muster, and the way my sermon conformed to the verse pleased the audience. The prior of the church, who in the range of his knowledge was quite the expert in scripture, benevolently asked me to write something for him that he could use as a subject in some future sermon. Because I knew my abbot, who was present when I spoke, would hardly tolerate anything I wrote, I took a cautious approach: I begged my abbot to grant this request for the sake of the prior, for whom his love was evident, acting as if I spoke on his friend's behalf, and was myself not so eager for the undertaking. Believing that I would write something very brief, he said yes. I seized on his answer as soon as it left his mouth, and began to work on something I had already planned.

This plan was to attempt a moral commentary on the beginning of Genesis, specifically the Hexameron. I prefaced the commentary with a rather short treatise on how to give a proper sermon. After this was finished, I continued with a tropological analysis of the six days, and poured out on the page, albeit in an awkward style, everything that lay within my abilities. As soon as my abbot saw that I was annotating that part of sacred history, he took a less sober view of the project, and sharply warned me to put an end to it. Seeing that the work I had begun would only stick thorns into his eyes,[94] I took precautions to avoid not only him but everyone who could report my work to him, and completed the whole thing in secret. I did not prepare or write drafts of these and other works on tablets, but by composing the commentary as I went along, I put my writing down on the page without change.[95] During this man's abbacy, all my efforts remained cloaked in utter silence, but when he departed, I took the opportunity presented by the vacancy to push forward, and finished the work in a short time.[96] It encompassed ten books, following those four motions of the inner man. In all the books I pursued a moral interpretation, and thus without changing the order of words at all, my beginnings led continuously to the very end. Whether I succeeded at all in this work, I do not know, but I know for a fact that many learned men found it pleasing.

There is one sure benefit this commentary provided me, and not a little one: it freed me from idleness, the minister of my vices.

XVIII.

Since then, I have also written a brief work with chapters on different passages from the Gospels and the Prophets, to which I added some material from Numbers, Joshua, and Judges. I have delayed finishing it even now, for though the material I have at present is completed, at times I think about working on similar passages, if, God providing, life abides in me. In most of these passages, I looked for a tropological meaning, and an allegorical one in a few, following the same practice I used for Genesis. In Genesis, however, my focus was on the moral significance more than anything else, not because there would be insufficient material for interpretation if I at the same time worked on allegorical readings, but because, in my judgment, the moral significance was at this time rather more useful than the allegorical: while faith in God remained undiminished, nearly everyone has debased his habits in all kinds of vice, and I have had neither the freedom nor the will to attempt a work of enormous length.[97]

My mother admired the positive steps I had taken, at least as far as learning was concerned, but fears of the wayward paths that made that time of life treacherous deeply disturbed her. She constantly pestered me to follow her example: though God had provided her with great beauty, she had little regard for anything said in her praise, as if she had no idea she was beautiful, and she cherished her widowhood as if she had always shrunk in horror from the duties of the marriage bed. But you know, Lord, what faith and love she had offered her husband even after his death, how she made offerings nearly every day, uttered tearful prayers, and gave alms generously in her unceasing attempt to release his soul, which she knew was bound up in sin. Then, by God's wondrous dispensation, frequent visions showed her crystal clear images of how he suffered in the expiation for his misdeeds. There is no doubt that this type of vision comes from God, for the splendor of a deceitfully beautiful form can offer nothing but a false sense of security. Only an image of painful punishment—when the dead, or rather angels, who bear the cares of the faithful dead, ask for the remedies through divine worship—gives an incentive to prayer and almsgiving.[98] Sufficient proof that these visions come from God lies in the fact that demons never seek anything to benefit the cause of a person's salvation. These disturbing signs rekindled my good mother's spirit, and the ominous vision of her former husband's inner torments inflamed her to work constantly as his intercessor.

One of these visions occurred on a Sunday night after matins, in summer, when she had lain down upon the narrow bench that served as her bed, and soon felt sleep overcome her. She had the sensation that her soul was leaving her body and that she was being led through a colonnade. As she passed through it, she slowly approached the opening of a well. Now she was right next to it, and men of ghostly form leapt out from its depths. Their hair appeared worm-eaten, and they tried to grab her and pull her in. She was trembling in fear, woefully unsettled by their attack, when suddenly a voice burst out from behind her: "Don't touch her!" The ghosts leapt back into the well, driven away by this forbidding voice. (I failed to mention that while she was passing through the colonnade, sensing that she was departing her human form, the one thing she asked of God was to be allowed to return to her body.) And so, freed from the inhabitants of the well, she stood at its edge, and suddenly realized that my father was standing by her, looking just as he did as a young man.[99] She turned to him and meekly asked if he was Evrard (that was what he had been named), but he denied it.

It should not seem strange for a spirit to deny the name it once had as a man, for a spirit must answer another spirit only in ways that are congruent to its spiritual state. It is ridiculous to think that spirits know one another by their names; otherwise, in our future life we would rarely know anyone besides our friends and family. Obviously, spirits do not need names, since all their vision, or rather the knowledge that comes from their vision, is internal.[100] And so even though he denied he was named Evrard, she nonetheless recognized him and asked him where he resided. He pointed as if not far from them lay a street where he dwelled. She also asked how he was, and he uncovered his arms and his sides, revealing that they were lacerated and crisscrossed with wounds; she stared in horror, shaken to her bones. The visible shape of a young boy was also there, shrieking so loudly that it caused her great distress as she watched him. Moved by the boy's cries, she asked her husband's spirit: "How, my lord, can you endure this infant's wailings?" He replied, "Whether I want to or not, I endure."

The meaning of the infant's weeping and the cuts on the spirit's arms and sides is as follows: during my father's youth, certain people had used witchcraft to prevent him from having legitimate intercourse with my mother. So a group of iniquitous advisors approached him and filled his childish mind with wicked suggestions, urging him to find out whether he could have sex with other women. Like a young man, he obeyed them, and after an ill-considered coupling, he had a child from some woman or other. The child died almost immediately, unbaptized. The lacerations on the spirit's side signified the breaking of his marriage vow; that awful shrieking was the destruction of the infant born in sin. God of unending goodness, such were your retributions against his soul—the soul of a sinner, but living in faith. Now let us return to the account of her vision.

When she asked him whether prayer, almsgiving, or sacrifice brought any relief to him—he was aware that she often did these things for him—he nodded, and then added: "But there is a woman, Liutgarde, who lives among you." My mother understood that his intention in naming this woman was to ask her, too, to remember him in her prayers. This Liutgarde was, in fact, a woman poor in spirit who lived a simple life for God, contrary to the practices of that age.[101]

As she finished talking with my father, she looked back at the well. Above it was a table, where she saw a man dining named Renaud,[102] a knight, and one of the most respected among his companions. On that very day—a Sunday, as I have said—his own kinsmen in an act of treachery killed him after dinner at Beauvais. He was at that very dinner, bent down on his knees with his neck stuck out; there was a pile of wood, and with puffing cheeks he tried to kindle a fire. This vision came to her in the morning, and he, soon to descend into the fires justly kindled by his deeds, died that afternoon. She also saw at this same dinner a man who was trying to help Renaud, but who was to die long afterward: it was my brother, swearing horrible oaths by the Lord's body and blood. There can be no mistake that by swearing falsely and taking the holy name of God and his sacred mysteries in vain, he deserved both the place and type of his punishments. She also saw in this same series of visions the old woman who, as I mentioned above, had joined her at the beginning of her conversion. She was indeed a woman who always covered the surface of her body with many crosses, but against the appetite for empty (as they call it) glory, she was less cautious. This very woman she saw being carried away by two of the blackest spirits, her image but a shadow. While this woman was still alive and they were living together, they used to talk about the state of their souls and what would happen when they died. At some point they had promised each other that whoever died first would, by the grace of God, appear to the survivor and show what kind of condition she was in, whether good or bad.[103] They confirmed their promise with a prayer, earnestly imploring God that after one of them had died, the other be allowed to reveal in a vision of some sort the nature of her fortune or misfortune. The old woman, when she was about to die, also had a vision in which she saw herself: deprived of her body, she was heading toward a temple with others like her, and as she went, she seemed to carry a cross on her shoulders. Upon reaching that temple with her company, she was forced to remain outside, and the doors were barred shut. When at last she died, she appeared, covered in a foul stench, to someone else. She thanked this person profusely for the prayers that would rescue her from the stink and the suffering. And what is more, as she lay dying, she saw standing at the foot of her bed a horrid-looking demon with revoltingly enormous eyes. However, she repeatedly called upon the holy sacraments for the demon to depart from her in disgrace, without claiming anything from her, and by this frightful oath she drove him back.

My mother thus gathered the truth from correspondences between her vision and actual events, and in particular the foreboding oracle of the soldier who was murdered shortly after she had seen him at the place of punishment in hell that he had won for himself. So when she interpreted the cries of the infant, whose existence had not been unknown to her, she felt not the slightest doubt as to what they meant and turned all her efforts toward bringing aid to my father. Opposing like with like, she decided to adopt and raise an infant child, an orphan only a few months old. But the devil hates a pious intention as much as a faithful deed. While the infant would be completely calm all day long, by turns playing and napping, during the night his frenzied screaming and crying aggravated my mother and all her servants—it was nearly impossible for anyone to sleep in the same room. From my mother I heard that nurses were hired to keep shaking a rattle all through the night for this boy, whose ill temper was not his own, but from an instigator within. This clever womanly trick, however, had no success in overcoming the boy's assailant.

The pious woman suffered boundless distress. None of the measures she employed during this constant nighttime wailing could soothe her throbbing temples, nor could she find any sleep at all for her wearied head in its torment, while the outward furor from the boy's inner distress and the enemy who disturbs all were both present. But even though she passed many sleepless nights in this way, never was she found remiss in the nightly divine offices. She knew these torments were expiating her husband's suffering as seen in her vision, and she endured them happily, because, as it seemed to her (and is, in fact, the case), by suffering together with him, she also alleviated his anguish. She never shut the child out of the house, and never did her care for him diminish. On the contrary, realizing that the devil, to undermine her zeal, blazed up against her with ever greater ferocity, she chose to meet any difficulties she faced with a still steadier spirit. For the more she experienced through the child's irritation its instigator, the more her doubts turned to the certainty that the agonizing cries around her husband's soul were subsiding.

XIX.

There were many other things, Lord God, you revealed to her, your servant, and to my teacher, whom you had provided specifically for me. In some of these shone clearly the promise of good hope, and though it would be ascribed to boastfulness if I should write them down, still today I await their fulfillment under the guidance of your most indulgent mother, sweet Jesus, for whose sake I had been cast out of my mother's womb. Other things had been revealed to them when I was still just a young boy, and now I miraculously find them happening in my adulthood. But in any case, my fervent desires were stoked into flame. Just as you had introduced into my heart, as kindling for the fire, some little learning, and had given me a worldly appearance that was quite suitable for someone born into a good rank of society, so, too, did my spirit, as well as some of my friends (who were not, in this way, good ones), wickedly suggest to me that a promotion into some office would serve me well in this world. But I know, Lord, that in your law you had forbidden ascent to your altar by these steps: for you had taught that by this way can the shame of a holy leader be revealed.[104] For those who reach positions of spiritual authority by an excessive external display of excellence fall from it in greater shame, because they strove not for things on their level, but for marvels beyond themselves. During the search for an office, undertaken at the instigation of my relatives, rumors that I would obtain such honors frequently reached my ears. There were many who began to flatter me, but guilefully: they wanted to investigate my character for the purpose of completing reports to villainous rivals, or else they thought my aspirations for office would bring favor to themselves, and claiming that the bribes I received would increase their own profits, they were forever seeking out opportunities to better my income.

But as you know, my Creator, it was only your urging, your inspiration, that gave me the strength not to seek from man anything beyond fear of you,[105] or to give audience or agreement to any man who was trying to procure for me an ecclesiastical office, which only you can bestow. And you know, Lord, that in this matter especially, there is nothing I want or would ever want except what I receive or would receive from you. In this as in other things, I want you to be my maker, not to be my own. Otherwise, Israel could not well have rejoiced in its maker.[106]

My God, how great the adversity, how great the envy that oppressed me at that time! My spirit then began to seethe with a secret longing for what was proposed to me from without, as if it were a flight from temptation. But though ambition burned within me, it never boiled with enough strength to pass my tongue. For I was troubled, yet I did not speak.[107] You know, Jesus, that once I stumbled into sin, I ordered someone who was acting as an agent in these matters (but not at my urging) to do quickly what he was going to do.[108] You know, indeed, how it pained me to have said this. For even though there were many occasions when I could have fallen into other kinds of wickedness, I still would have feared to become a buyer, or rather a seller, of doves. It was but one dove, but there are many seats—not one seat—from which these people sell. Indeed, any division in God and the church does not come from him who suffers it. "Let them be one," he said, "just as we, too, are one," and "Though there are divisions among gifts of grace, it is still the same spirit, dividing them for each individual as it chooses." Also the following verses: "The throne of God"— not "thrones"—"is forever and ever" and "One of the fruits of your body I will set on your throne."[109] All the things that are one in God are therefore made separate through the misguided intentions of man.

Reflecting upon this, in full awareness of the unity of head and body, I certainly did not want to make any claims to privilege for the body: anything that intrudes upon the head from elsewhere can only be in discord with it, and, as is clear to everyone, the head cannot have an awareness of anything that is not counted as part of the body. Indeed, those who will say, "Did we not prophesy in your name, and cast out the demons?", are, if I may say so, apostates most of all, and not members joined to the body. Thus when they hear "I do not know you," it is as if he were to say, "I do not feel they belong to me, because they do not live from me."[110]

There was a hope, silly though it was, that I could alleviate my self-loathing, and I began to pray to you, God, that if these dealings on my behalf ever came to pass, it would only happen through your authority. It sickened me when people told me about how my relatives were making inquiries on my behalf, while others were chosen purely by God's influence, without the intervention of any carnal agent. My relatives' concern in this business was in fact not for my interests as much as for their own. They never discussed anything about it with me, since they obviously wanted to avoid angering my youthful spirit. Finally, God willed that I be deluded no longer. He inspired those acting on my behalf, for the salvation of their souls, to move to other places, and monks of some monasteries who were working to get me elected as their abbot were forced to direct their efforts elsewhere.

I give thanks to you, God, that my childish intentions completely withered away, and that I found it no longer agreeable to yearn for worldly honor. It was at that time, my Father, that you gave me a scourging and you struck me down, my God, corrector of my vain desires. You made me aware again, and thus you confined me within myself; my mind as yet wandering never took flight, but from its depths aspired only to a sincere humility of thought. Then for the first time, Lord, I began to experience that pleasant solitude of mind where you frequently abide and to deliver my inner fervor over to the mother of the heavenly realm, Mary, mother of God, my sole recourse in every time of need. As a result, I took the most affectionate pleasure in being insignificant, a higher position and a great name to cast a shadow in the world I found utterly repellent.[111]

It was then, too, from the taste I had of you within me that I first learned what unity of the will and what purity of the will were, and what unyielding attention to perpetual poverty meant. Could I describe, Lord, how fleeting that paradise was, how short the calm, how brief and uncertain the sensation of such great sweetness?[112]

Only for a few months did I savor it. For but a little while had your good spirit led me onto level ground,[113] resided in my reason, which was enlightened for a moment, and then suddenly—as if you said, "When you wanted it, I did not; now you do not, and it offends you; whether you want it or not, take it"—it turned out I had been elected by some monks who lived far away and were completely unknown to me. But what was this election? Could I truly declare myself to be outstanding, when by your testimony, God, I was judged to be baser, or rather the vilest, among all who were placed under me? The smattering of learning I had acquired, along with the outer touches of a so-called educated person, rendered my electors blind and bleary-eyed! Good God, what would they have said if they had seen what was inside me then? And how would they have felt, if they had realized what sort of person was now to be their superior? You know, you who from some judgment unknown to me ordained this, how disdainful I was of myself, how revolted that I had turned everything upside down by setting myself above better and more dignified men. Indeed, you know, you who had foreknowledge of my heart and mind, that I never desired anything like this, but still I did not want the disgrace of rejection or refusal. So I begged you from the bottom of my heart to be deprived of the office at the outset, and thus I would neither have to take on an awesome burden that terrified me beyond measure, nor out of weakness fail to recuse myself.

It did not escape you, my God, how my advancement bitterly pained my mother. To others it seemed an honor, but to her an unbearable grief; she wanted nothing of the sort to befall me, and she feared the dangers it presented to my youthful naïveté, especially because I was completely ignorant in worldly affairs—no surprise, for I had thus far concentrated only on literary studies, and had not bothered to learn about business. Nevertheless, she as well as nearly everyone who knew me well told me repeatedly that a promotion of some kind would not be long in coming.

You also know, Lord, how with her inner sight she spoke of the good and bad that would happen to me if I were promoted to any kind of position. Even today I experience these things, and they do not pass unnoticed by me or by others. She also foresaw in numerous visions, where I appeared along with others, what would happen to me long afterward. Some of these events I regard without a doubt as occurring or as having already occurred, while some of the rest I expect no less to occur, but I have deliberately refrained from adding them here. God, what warnings she gave me to keep desires away from my mind, assuring me in no uncertain terms of the misfortunes that arise from adversity, which I have experienced. She sighed in anguish over my incautious youth, and she reined in my mind as it roamed along various paths of thought.[114] When she made her case, you would have thought her not an uneducated woman (which she was), but a most eloquent bishop.

The monastery to which I was elected abbot is called Nogent; it lies close enough to the border of the Laon diocese that only a rather small but flood-prone river called the Ailette separates this territory from that of Soissons. I will discuss the history of the monastery in this work, if God should grant me his aid.

But since I mentioned that I had first been nurtured at the church at Fly, with God as my father and Saint Germer, its founder, as my protector, it is worth recording some of the events I heard about or saw happen there.

XX.

After the restoration of this church, following its destruction by the Danes, a monk there named Suger, who led a good life and held the office of prior, was overcome by a fatal illness. He was, if I am not mistaken, a brother of that old woman who took the first steps in her conversion together with my mother. As he lay dying, the devil stood next to him with a book in his hand and said, "Take it, read it. Jupiter sends this to you."[115] When he heard this detestable name, he shuddered in fear of the devil, who then added, "Do you love this house of yours?" "I do," he replied. The devil then said, "You should know that once all strict observance of the rule disappears, it will afterward be thrown into utter disorder." Responding with suitably harsh criticisms, he refuted these words of Satan, and the enemy who was present departed. Once the monk reported what he had seen, he went mad and had to be bound in chains, but before he breathed his last, he retuned to his senses, and making a good confession, he died.

We know the devil is a liar, and we believe he is called the father of lies because of his habitual envy, but in any case, may God prevent his words from coming true! Afterward, in fact, the church did well, and continues to do well today.

XXI.

I also saw during my time there a monk who was a former knight, advanced in age and considered simple in his ways. Because he was born in the territory of the Vexin, his abbot had sent him there to dwell in a small dependency of the church. With the permission of his prior, he offered to repair a highway embankment that had collapsed. He finished the job with donations from the faithful, but when the work was near completion, he kept some of the surplus from their generosity for himself. He was in the meantime seized by a fatal illness, yet he still did not reveal in any confession his guilty secret. Brought back to the monastery to which he belonged, he confessed to neither the abbot nor the prior, though he felt dreadful agonies— heralds of death—caused by his crime. Instead, he entrusted the sum of silver to a servant who tended to the ill. And then one stormy night the increasing intensity of his suffering left him senseless; he lay stretched out on the ground as if dead. Summoned by the ringing bell, we were there by him, and performed the psalms, prayers, and rituals proper for the dying. When we had finished, he was placed on a hair shirt, following monastic custom, and as he seemed in his last gasps to be breathing barely at all, we left him. None of us assured him he would live, but we all promised only that his final ablution would come soon, before his death.

As soon as we left, he began to breathe. He summoned the prior (the abbot was away), and informed him of what he had embezzled and to whom he had entrusted it. He spoke, and after he received absolution from the prior, trying for a brief moment to catch his breath, he died. The prior at that time was my teacher, whom I often mention. How great the mercies of the Lord that we are not consumed, and he saves whomever he wills from narrow straits into a broad place![116]

After this man had departed this life, the inquiry into the embezzlement focused exclusively on the servant. He had hidden the money in a bundle in the straw of his young daughter's crib, but at night, when the child was put down to bed, demons in the form of dogs leapt upon her back and her sides; knocking her around from every direction, sometimes taking bites, they drove her to tearful wailing. When both parents asked why she was crying, she replied that she was being eaten by dogs. Her mother, who had been my mother's servant and occasionally her attendant, ran to her mistress (that is, my mother) and told her of the wicked treasure stored in her house, adding that her daughter was in danger of being torn apart by dogs. My mother replied, "You should know that these are demons who are rejoicing over that diabolical money; they regard it as their own, and thus pursue it." Although her husband had so far been uncooperative, even when subjected to extreme harassment—if I can describe legal charges of violence, theft, and fraud as harassment—once he heard this, he readily admitted to the claims made against him; nor did he remain silent afterward about the demonic attacks he had suffered.[117]

We have heard that God "has mercy on whomever he wills," but that he "hardens the heart of whomever he wills" we can gather from what follows.[118] O, the wondrous judgments of God—the one man, whom I have already discussed, had passed his entire life in knightly exercises and disgraceful whoring, but the other, whom I will discuss, had been rather melancholy for a time, but otherwise there was nothing disreputable evident in him. Clearly, the vice of avarice is all the more ruinous to monks, as it is less natural to them, and thus it is difficult to find any other crime where the devil waits in ambush with greater stealth.

XXII.

There was another monk of ours, also an ordained priest, to whom no foolishness could be ascribed beyond an enthusiasm for riding horses. He had received two gold coins from a noble lady, and soon after caught dysentery and stopped at Saint-Quentin in Beauvais. When this became known at Fly, he was carried back to his monastery on the abbot's orders. He was eating a great deal and then immediately evacuating whatever he ate, so his abbot, who was about to move elsewhere, came to talk to him in fear he would die in his absence. But when the abbot arrived, he had already sat down to satisfy the demands of nature, and because he could not approach him once the chamber pot was set in place, the abbot witnessed the terrible sight of him sitting in this strange position. They looked at one another, and the abbot, embarrassed to have met the man in such a place, did not think it permissible, or in fact agreeable, to grant the wretch confession or absolution of his crime. The abbot took his leave, and the man left the chamber pot and went up to his bed as if he were about to get some rest. When he lay down in bed flat on his back, he was suffocated by the devil. You would have seen in horror his throat and jaw pinned to his chest, as if driven by a violent thrust downward. In this way he died without confession, without final unction, and without almsgiving over that accursed bit of money. When the corpse was undressed for bathing, a small pouch was found hanging from his shoulder, hidden under his armpit. The man who discovered the purse angrily flung it to the ground, clapped his hands together, and ran to the monks

to assail their ears with his unbelievable report. They had cer-
tainly never heard of one of their own dying in this way.

They sent after the abbot, who had just begun to take his
lunch at one of his estates two miles beyond Beauvais. The
abbot, however, had already received news of the monk's
death from another messenger who had arrived there, but who
had known nothing and said nothing of the gold coins. And so
when the messenger sent by the brothers had arrived, he con-
sulted with the abbot about what should be done: would the
man be permitted burial among the others when he had so
shamefully cut himself off from their community? The abbot
took counsel with some wise men and ordered that he be bur-
ied in a field, deprived of prayer and psalms, with the money
placed upon his chest. Yet in their private prayers for him his
brothers did not falter, but instead, when they learned that he
was in even more need of their support, they pressed on with
all the more urgency. As a result of his sudden death, the rest
of the monks had more scruples about money. Let us hear how
they were punished besides at other times for other reasons.

XXIII.

Only a few weeks later, it was the vigil for the martyrs Gervasius
and Protasius,[119] and the weather was overcast. A towering storm
cloud rose up in the sky, accompanied by a little thunder and only
intermittent lightning. In the morning, the bell rang for the first
hour right after we got up, and we assembled in the church with
greater haste than usual. After a very brief prayer, we uttered,
"God, come to my aid!", but as we were about to begin the next
lines, a bolt of lightning struck inside the church with a tremen-
dous crash. It first hit the cock atop the tower and the cross with
its pole, either blasting them to bits or burning them to ashes, as
well as crippling the roof beam supporting them, and then, scorch-
ing the shingles until they were no longer affixed to their nails,
entered through the windowpane on the west side of the tower.
Beneath the window stood a figure of the crucified Lord, which
the lightning broke but did not burn—the head was dashed to the

ground, and the right side had split apart—while its right arm along with the arm of the cross were so burned and battered that no one could find any part of that arm except for a thumb. And once the shepherd is struck, the sheep, as it were, are scattered with blows and death.[120] To the right, a blaze of lightning ran down along the stonework across the vaulted arch under which the stricken figure had stood, leaving a forked streak of black, and when it reached the choir, struck two monks standing on either side of the arch. To the left, as it rushed down the other direction, it scraped off the layer of cement covering the steps, but only in places, as if a boulder had rolled down them, and then struck another monk standing there. The first two monks showed no obvious sign of injury, nor did the other one, except that flecks of mortar that had fallen from the vault could be seen on his upturned eyes. It was strange that the men who died remained fixed in their places, but the rest of us, nearly stunned to death by the lightning's violence, had knocked one another flat down on the ground. Some of us who fell, including me, lost all bodily sensation below the waist; others were so badly injured that we immediately gave them unction for fear they would die. The flame came up into robes of some monks, singeing all the hair on their testicles and setting aflame the growth of hair in their armpits (which are called "undergoats") and passed through holes it made at the ends of their stockings and sandals. It is impossible to describe the ferocity with which the judgment of heaven handed down its sentence in that moment: all the winding courses it took in different directions, all the damage it did, what it burned, and what it broke— no one of our generation has heard of anything like it in France.

An hour after this happened, I saw, as God is my witness, the image of the blessed mother of God, which stood beneath the crucifix, with a troubled look on her face, so altered from its usual serenity that she seemed completely transformed. I would not have trusted my own eyes, but I know others noticed it as well. But after we had recovered from the stupor caused by this incident, we made confession and began in our sadness to reflect upon how we had suffered beyond human expression for our sins. Placed by God face-to-face with ourselves, we looked into our consciences, and the moment we recognized the justice of what we had endured, we saw a serene look return to the pious mother's face. The utter shame and anguish that stayed with us for some time exceed all belief.

Only a few years later, the memory of this event had almost completely vanished from everyone's mind, but as a reminder, God struck again as before, except this time no one was hurt. One night, a peacock stopped to rest next to a chimney extending up into one of the rooms, nestling inside the opening while it slept. It was the feast day of the apostle James, as well as a Sunday.[121] During the night there sounded a heavy crash of thunder; lightning ran down the chimney and overturned the fireplace in the room, but the peacock did not move, still resting inside. A monk sleeping below did not even wake up, while a servant was knocked into a stupor, his limbs numbed. According to blessed Augustine, God does not strike mountains or insensible objects without purpose. He does so, rather, that we might consider it when he strikes things that do not sin, as a clear sign of his judgment against those who do; Augustine uses the example of a nurse who strikes the ground with a rod to stop a small child from whining.[122]

In speaking of that earlier misfortune, I neglected to discuss the character of the three monks who were killed. Two were novices who had just completed their eighth month in the monastic life. One of them, beneath a solemn countenance, was not so seemly on the inside, while the other, as far as we know, had nothing contemptible behind his foolish demeanor. The day before they suffered and died, these two conducted themselves along the lines of the difference I just mentioned. The morning when it happened, the one who was foolish on the outside heard the sounds of thunder and began to make some comments in jest, when suddenly the bolt of lightning he ridiculed entered the church and killed him. The third monk was named Robert, but from his honest simplicity was called in the world "Dove." He was at that time a young man with the first growth on his cheeks, known for his complete honesty, and so willing and able to perform duties for the church and the community that nearly every day he served as everyone else's assistant. He was a good student of Latin as well.

That morning, during the hour that harbored destruction for the monastery, he had already gone to sit in the cloister, as he usually did, while I was still getting up. He indicated to me that he was in excruciating pain, especially in his knees, and then he looked up at the turbulent sky from which his death was soon to come. Note that before their downfall those first two were exalted in their hearts, and God's judgment would soon hand them, I believe, a more severe sentence. But in this monk, humility went before glory, and no one could doubt even then that he would be elevated into the heavenly ranks. In fact, someone afterward had a vision of these three traveling together to Saint Peter's in Rome; two were mere shadows, barely visible, but the third was clad in white, and quickly moved along in high spirits, eager as ever.

Some years later, a third punishment befell the monks, who had by now forgotten these events and in their peace of mind had grown lax (I had already left this monastery). One morning, during a raging storm, they had gone in procession to chant the litanies before the high altar, since they did not dare remain in the choir where the lightning first struck. Suddenly, a flame from heaven dropped down and, according to the testimony of eyewitnesses, descended all the way to the base of the altar, and filled the area around it with the foul smell of sulfur. An elder monk had his eyes scarred over; two boys—one of them a converted Jew, but his faith was sincere[123]—had been prostrate with their heads toward the foot of the altar, but were lifted up and thrown away from it. While they were in flight, their feet were turned around toward the altar and their heads toward the wall of the apse, without their realizing it. The bolt of lightning broke into a chest behind the altar, damaging it in places, but only a chasuble, considered quite precious because it was the most valuable of the monastery's treasures, was completely destroyed. What follows is the remarkable explanation for this.

This chasuble in particular had been sought by an English king, nicknamed "the Red" (he was in fact a redhead), a lawless man and a bitter enemy of churches, whom God struck down with an arrow shot by his own lover boy during a hunt.[124] Since he did not want to deplete his own treasury, he sent a monk as his agent in this matter to the abbot of a monastery called Battle Abbey, with the demand that the abbot give fifteen silver marks to the monk. When the abbot refused, the monastery was subjected to the king's violent temper and plundered. The abbot then had no choice but to buy back what was stolen for fifteen marks. The purchase of the chasuble thus involved the crime of sacrilege, or more accurately, sacrilegious men, and there was no less crime in the amount paid. Because of the way it was acquired, in both its purchase and its price, the chasuble was infused throughout with wickedness. In fact, following this transaction the chasuble was delivered, and upon examination its value was judged to be not even half the price paid; the buyer, as was discovered, had been soundly cheated. And so, while all the other church treasures remained untouched, this one was rightfully condemned, though apparently its seller was spared a similar punishment.

Before the lightning strike, however, one monk, with his conscience gnawing at him, had the following vision. A figure of the crucified Lord appeared to descend from the cross, blood dripping from his hands, side, and feet; he walked through the middle of the choir, and was heard to say, "If you all have not confessed, you all will die." Upon awakening, the monk was horrified with himself, but before he confessed, he along with everyone else underwent this perilous ordeal. When he did confess, he disclosed the sign he had received of this just judgment. In remembrance of this unsettling time of crisis, yearly fasts and almsgivings were instituted in perpetuity for the day on which these things first started, and in addition, daily masses for Saint Mary at her altar as well as mass every Sunday for the Lord's nativity before the altar of Saint Michael. But now let us hurry on to other things.

XXIV.

There was a certain monk, ordained as a priest, who in the secular world had once been a chaplain in my mother's house. To the eye, he was devout, but both then as well as later irresistibly drawn to extravagant vices, and no form of human supervision could restrain him. In this same year (four months after the first unfortunate event, to be precise), he began to grow ill. Within two days, he was unexpectedly at the point of death and began to look all around in terror. Asked by those who knew his true character what he saw, he replied, "A house full of barbarous men." Since they understood that the men he saw threatening him were nothing other than demons, they began to encourage him to make the sign of the cross and put his hope in the name of the blessed mother of God. "I would," he said, "have hope and faith in her, if these barons were not attacking me." It is remarkable that he called them "barons," which on the basis of its Greek etymology signifies "weighty."[125] And how awfully weighty these demons were—no act of penance or invocation could have now driven them away! He was then asked what pained him most, and he replied that he felt like a huge iron rod, glowing hot, seared down through his throat and into his chest. The night was extremely calm, when not the slightest breeze could be heard, yet the window shutters of the house began to strike the walls and bang together as if a crowd of people were constantly coming in. The two monks attending to him (the others were sleeping in the house) were greatly disturbed, since they were well aware that such occurrences did not originate from good. He breathed his last speaking the words I recounted. He was, in the end, a man much enslaved to disreputable behavior, and the end he met fit the life he followed.

In the cemetery of this church, a grave was being readied for a monk who had died, but the man to whom this task fell could not remember if he had already put a grave in its spot. He started digging, and when he got deeper, he discovered the kind of wood plank commonly placed on a coffin. When he removed it, he found the coffin was nearly empty, except for a cowl, commonly called a chaperon, with a head inside, and at the foot of the coffin, sandals half-filled with hay (this used to be done at the time of burial so they would stay on the feet better). In the middle of the coffin, however, there was nothing at all. When some people saw this and told us about it, we marveled at the judgment of God, which is beyond comprehension! What events we witness, their meaning hidden in the tiniest details! In this case, what merits the designation "miraculous" is that the head was left behind, but the body carried away to where God was pleased to take it.

I learned of a similar occurrence from the archbishop Manasses, of good memory, who died most faithfully some years before, and the monks of Saint-Rémy in the city of Reims confirmed it.[126] Long ago, a man named Artaud, the archbishop of the city, had been buried near the feet of Saint Rémy, but after a long while, he was exhumed because of the need to alter the buildings. When his tomb was opened, inside was found not even the slightest trace of his physical remains. Of his clothing, only the chasuble remained to be seen, which evidently did not rot away with his body because it lay there without a single mark on it. If his body had in fact putrefied in the coffin, the fluid from the decay would have certainly damaged the chasuble. We see happening in our time what is reported in the writings of Saint Gregory: the judgments of God are renewed against the corpses of the guilty, whose burial in holy places is clearly undeserved.

There is a monastery founded for the virgins of Caen, built on the orders of the English queen Mathilda, the wife of King William, formerly count of Normandy who had conquered the English.[127] A nun there had allowed herself to fall into some shameful sins, nor could any kind of admonishment compel her to confess. She chanced to die while still in this stubborn state of mind, nor did she say anything to her benefit while she was dying. One of her sisters, sleeping one night in the cell where she died, saw in a dream an enormous fire burning in a fireplace in the house. In the middle of the flames was the nun who died. Not only was she set ablaze, but two evil spirits were also striking her from either side with blows from their two hammers. As she looked upon the tremendous tortures suffered by this wretched woman, a spark from the hammer's impact seemed to fly out into her eye, and the burning sensation from the cinder caused her to wake up. And so it happened that she suffered in the flesh what she had seen in the spirit, and her injury provided truthful evidence consistent with the truth of the vision.

XXV.

At Fly there was a monk called Otmund who, while still a cleric, had made numerous offerings to the monastery, until in the end he offered himself. Upon first becoming a monk, he had regrets over this good beginning, and was greatly distressed at what he had done. Yet when God punished him with bodily illness, he came to realize what would bring him closer to salvation, and after recovering adhered to the monastic rule willingly and not because of obligation. He did, however, possess a temper too inclined to anger, so after he had been made custodian, he drove out of the church more roughly than he should have a poor little man who kept bothering him for alms. This happened during the day, and the following night, as he stepped out to open the doors and announce the hour for vigils, there before him was the devil, in the form of the pauper he had rudely thrown out the previous day, and he rushed forward with a rod raised high as if he intended to strike the monk. The custodian had, in fact, already opened the doors in the partition placed between the clergy and the people, and was going to unlock the other doors, through which the people enter. Although the outer doors were barred shut, the devil suddenly jumped out in the middle of the church, acting as if he were going to hit him. Thinking it was the man whom he had shut out the day before, the monk froze in terror, but finally returned to his senses. When he considered that the outer doors had been shut, he at last believed it was the devil, who made clear by this sign his work in man.[128]

One time in the winter, Otmund left his bed to meet the demands of nature, clothed only in a cowl since he was too lazy to dress as he normally would. In those moments, he felt the pangs of a deadly chill, and not long afterward, a swelling in his extremities brought him to the point of death. The mere mention of death troubled him inordinately, and with mournful wailing and incessant cries of "Woe is me!", he arrived at his final hour. He had taken communion and by the grace of God retained it (everything else he vomited back up); the release of his soul was now imminent. All this was happening in the first hour of the night, when the church guardian, a good man, had put himself to bed; suddenly he heard a countless throng of demons assembling in the brothers' cemetery, which was nearby. Although his power of understanding was free to perceive all this, some spiritual force suppressed the movement of his tongue and body as the demons entered the church, passing in front of his bed, then rushed between the choir and the altar and headed for the house where the ill man lay. The guardian was mentally aware that this was happening and, since he well knew that such an army gathered for a death, in spirit he prayed to God to be delivered from them. As the demons reached the cell of the dying monk, now in the throes of death, the brothers standing around him struck the board, as was customary, to summon the others to assemble. As soon as they had gathered there, he died. I have recounted this story not because I believe him to have been lost to that wicked band, but because I would like to remind everyone, including myself, to consider that the prince of the world came to the Son of God, over whom he has no power,[129] and if the devil came to him, how much more to us, over whom his power is nearly complete! For it is certain that the devil's madness is on good terms with our impetuous desires.

I once saw a woman there who was bitterly angry with her young son. From her wicked mouth she hurled many curses at the innocent little child, including a curse of the baptism in which he had been bathed. At once, a demon swept her away into a frenzied madness, and she began to say and do loathsome things. Brought to the church for the brothers to see, through prayer and exorcism she returned to her senses, and learned from her troubles not to curse the sacraments of the Lord.

There also I saw a young girl subject to demonic fits, who was brought before the shrine of Germer the confessor and spent several days there. One day, her parents dragged her to the altar. Standing next to it, she turned her head back to the choir, looked at the young monks standing behind her, and said, "My God, what handsome young men! But there is one

among them who should not at all be living with them." When
we heard this, we were greatly astonished,[130] wondering to
whom her words were directed. Without delay, one of the
monks slipped away and fled. His death revealed the wicked
life he led as a fugitive, his calling abandoned.

XXVI.

Since I have started to discuss demons, it is not, in my judg-
ment, out of place to include here some stories as lessons about
how we can avoid their teachings as well as the schemes of
those who converse with them. In fact, they do not allow any-
one to learn their witchcraft unless they first strip him of all
Christian dignity through execrable sacrilege.

There was a monk who had been raised since his youth in a
certain distinguished monastery, and had learned Latin rather
well. His abbot had installed him in a cell ancillary to the church,
and while staying there, he fell ill. For this reason he took the
opportunity of speaking, to his misfortune, to a Jew who knew
medicine. Their friendly association made them reckless, and
they began to reveal secrets to each other. Intrigued by the evil
arts, once the young monk realized that the Jew knew witch-
craft, he pestered him continually. The Jew agreed and promised
he would serve as the monk's agent with the devil. A place and
date were set for the meeting, and at last, with his negotiator, the
monk stood before the devil and asked to become, with the Jew's
backing, a partner to his teachings. The unspeakably heinous
chairman replied that this could by no means happen unless he
repudiated Christianity and tendered a sacrificial offering to
him.[131] When the monk asked what to offer, the devil answered,
"What is quite delectable in men." "What is that?" "You will
pour a libation of your sperm to me," he said, "and when you
have poured it out for me, you will taste some of it first, as those
offering sacrifice ought to do." What a villainous act! O for
shame—it was a priest from whom this was demanded! Your
enemy of old, Lord, did this as an abominable sacrilege against
your priestly order and against your blessed host! Do not keep

silent, God, nor restrain your vengeance![132] What can I say?
How can I? He did what was asked, the wretch, whom you
had—would that it were only for a time!—deserted, and along
with this disgusting libation came the abandonment of his pro-
fession of faith. A single incident will suffice for me to indicate
what skills he acquired through this horrid transaction.

He had accustomed a nun from a notable family to meet him
regularly, for he lived in his cell with only one fellow monk
who tended to errands outside, leaving him time for his foolish
behavior indoors. One day the monk and the nun were sitting
inside when they saw from a distance his housemate returning
from some business. With no other means of escape open to the
woman, her departure would cross paths with the monk's
return. Observing the alarm in his partner, the newly made
sorcerer said to her, "Go straight out into his path, never look-
ing right or left. Have no fear!" The woman trusted him and
went out, but he stood in the doorway chanting over her what
he had learned, and turned her into an enormous dog. When
she came near the returning monk, he exclaimed, "Such a huge
dog! Where did it come from?" She passed by him in great fear,
and only from the word "dog" did she come to know of her
form as she escaped. Then the monk, when he finally arrived
home, asked where this dog of such unusual size came from.
"It belongs to that neighbor of ours," he said, "Didn't you
already know about it?" Thinking it true, he kept quiet.

This monk led a life without God for a while, until, by God's
grace, he was stricken with a grave illness and confessed, whether
he willed it or not, what he had done. The matter was referred to
the judgment of wise men, particularly Anselm, later archbishop
of Canterbury, at that time abbot of Bec,[133] who punished him
with the harshest punishment possible: the monk was prohibited
from all worship of the divine mysteries as a filthy profaner of
them. And yet even in a state of excommunication, he could
never completely put it out of his mind that he would still be a
bishop. It was surely demons, liars always and on this occasion
too, who held out this hope to him, because a few years later he
died, not only not a bishop, but an ex-priest for all eternity.

Let me include as well the beginning of a similar story, but one with a better conclusion. There was a cleric in the area around Beauvais who made a living as a scribe, and I also knew him because he was hired to work at Fly. In a conversation with another cleric—and sorcerer—at the castle of Breteuil, he heard the following: "If it were to my profit, I could teach you something, and if you were to do it, you would receive daily gifts of money without working for any man." When the scribe asked what he needed to do, the sorcerer replied that he would have to sacrifice to a citizen of the underworld (that is, the devil). "With what animal?" he asked. "A cock," came the reply, "but the egg from which it hatched had to be laid by the hen on a Thursday in March. After you have roasted it, at the first sign of night take it with you just as it was roasted, with the spit still through it, and go with me to the nearest fishpond. But whatever you see, hear, or feel there, do not dare invoke God, Blessed Mary, or any other saints." "Agreed," he said. Then what a miraculous event! At night, they came to the place, carrying with them a fitting sacrifice for such a divinity. The sorcerer called upon a demon by name while his corrupted pupil held onto the cock, and then with a violent burst of wind a demon stood there and snatched it away. The cleric, who was being pulled away, cried out in terror to Saint Mary. When the demon heard the name of this powerful lady, he took his cock and fled, but was unable to carry it away. The next day one of the fishermen found it on an island in the pond. So regal a name, so sweet to your followers, so fearful to the band of evildoers!

Angered at the cleric, the sorcerer asked him why he had summoned this great woman during such business. But the cleric, moved by penitence, went to Lisiard, archdeacon of Beauvais, who was my uncle, a man in every way educated, prudent and well known for his sophistication in such matters. He confessed his deeds, and for his penance humbled himself on Lisiard's instructions with prayer and fasting.

This should be enough of what I saw or heard about in that monastery. But since I spoke above about my election, such as it was, in the beginning of the second book I will discuss the monastery to which I was, at God's direction, appointed, touching on how it was founded and the antiquities it possesses.

BOOK 2

I.

The place is called Nogent, which is "new" as far as the monks' residence there is concerned, but it has been a site of worldly life for a very long time.[1] Even if there were no written tradition to support this belief, a complex of tombs discovered there, of a style that is foreign and not, I think, Christian, furnishes sufficient proof. For a great many ancient sarcophagi surround the church, and are in the church itself; the sheer number of corpses gathered there indicates it was a place of high renown and sought out by many. As the tombs are arranged not according to our custom, but in a circle, with many surrounding one in the center, like a choral roundabout, and vessels were found in them, whose use is unknown in Christian times, we can only conclude that these were pagan tombs, or very ancient tombs of Christians made in a pagan manner. In this monastery, moreover, there are some writings in verse, to which I would give no authority if I did not see still today certain things that give them greater credibility. The history handed down in this text is as follows.

It says that among the English, before the assumption of the incarnate Word into heaven, there was a king. They were not, however, called English, a rather recent name taken from a group of Saxons who would later occupy their land, but were of old called Britons. This king in Britain, an island in the ocean, had received rich sustenance from poetry and philosophy, and in addition, a natural-born goodness led him to perform extensive acts of mercy. Admittedly, the generosity he displayed in feeding the poor arose not out of a respect for God, whom he did not yet know, but from the promptings of an exceptional human kindness that abounded in him. Thus it was only fitting that the gift of a clearer understanding should be added to the deeds performed out of his innate piety.

With expert arguments, he began to ask himself what true divine power he could expect his gods to hold, since they came in so many forms. He wondered what harmony there could possibly be among them in their governance of heaven and earth, since in their marriages, as long as they lasted, there was such obvious cheating and quarreling, and in their dominion over earth, cruel jealousy was so manifest among them— of sons against fathers, and fathers against sons, leading to usurpation, exile, and death.[2] In the tales sung about them, they behaved nearly as badly as mortals. He thus judged it to be the height of madness if rule over earth, not to mention heaven, were ascribed to beings such as this. And who would grant heavenly power to those whose miserable authority could not in ancient times maintain control over the least little part of the earth without committing a disgraceful crime? As he pondered these and similar ideas, he shut out from his heart the images of the divinities he now thought foolish and turned to the worship of an incomprehensible being, who would properly be worshipped without form, who alone governs all in single harmony, whose invisible things he had seen, since now they were understood through what has been created.[3] In the course of his argumentation, which was sound, certain doubts nevertheless caused him to falter, but God, who declares to those of good will what is better, stirred this man with a voice sent from heaven to set out for Jerusalem. There he would learn the proper understanding of God, how the Son of God came forth from God and lived among men for the sake of men, what he came to suffer or what to reveal, whom he left as his successors in exemplifying the divine name. And after he made his journey there, he would also discover witnesses to these great mysteries, namely his mother along with all the apostles.[4]

Once he had received this revelation of the faith, the British king gave up his wealth and his kingdom, and decided he would hasten to ascertain the truth of what he had learned. He prepared a fleet and, leaving his homeland behind, crossed the adjacent sea. Passing through a great expanse of villages and cities, he reached the border of the province of Laon, and then in order to find lodging, he pushed on to the rural village mentioned above, Nogent. It lies beneath a castle called Coucy, recently built, they say, by the peasants of the land, who are extremely proud and wealthy, as a defense against foreign invasions. Thus, nothing about the castle is the least bit ancient. In those days the place we are discussing was surrounded by forests teeming with hunting game, as well as by the Ailette river, mentioned previously, whose usefulness is far greater than its size. In quantity of fish it surpasses better known waters, for it is not, like other rivers, constrained within the course of its banks, but flows outward to form plenty of standing pools of water that are like artificial fishponds. Vineyards cover the slopes of the hills rising all around it, and the ground on both sides, well suited for both Liber and Ceres,[5] is praised for the soil, which produces good crops of all kinds. The lovely meadows stretching far and wide attest to the fertility this little river provides.

An old tradition, shown to be true, holds that there once stood in this place an extremely ancient shrine, not consecrated to the name or honor of any extant god, but dedicated to a woman as yet unborn who would give birth to a god and man. It had thus been devoted to the future mother of the god who would be born. No sensible person thinks this absurd, since those who had worshipped the unknown God at Athens knew full well that this god would be born of a woman,[6] just like the other rank-and-file gods for whose mothers they had names. And if the small shrine was dedicated to the one who would soon be born, his mother would in no way be deprived of the same honor as the mothers of other gods. Therefore, it does not seem incredible that something done over there for one yet to be born could not also be done here for the one still to give birth.

The British king happened to arrive at this place, thankful to

have reached such favorable country, and decided that he and
his followers would rest their bodies wearied by the length of
their journey and for a week revive their exhausted animals
with the rich fodder nearby. They departed, and with vast
tracts of land and sea behind them, they at last entered the
walls of Jerusalem. Only recently the Savior had suffered, risen
from the dead, and ascended to heaven, and the Spirit had just
been given.[7] The king thus found the city divided into conten-
tious factions, some angered at what had been done, others
approving. There was no difficulty in locating those he sought,
as the loud rumors swirling around the event proved to be
ready informants, openly proclaiming who was spreading this
new law. For they no longer hid behind closed doors as they
used to, nor did fear of Jewish opposition prevent them from
giving testimony of their Lord; rather, he could see them stand-
ing out among the people, such that their bearing alone pro-
vided evidence for the authority of their words. Why prolong
the story? He often found Peter with the other eleven among
the crowds, now followed by a large gathering of disciples, and
Mary, the mirror of all our faith and glory, by her presence
there giving testimony of the God incarnate. The British king,
who was soon to offer first fruits to God, called upon them and
the Virgin Mother, and explained the reasons for his journey:

"You see, fathers and lords, that I have come from the far-
thest ends of the earth to hear you. Until now, I ruled the Brit-
ons as the rightful successor of my forebears. From an error
of long standing they believed the sacred rites of old worthy of
respect, and though I long worshipped the same, my sense of
reason has of late led me to abandon them. For I observed that
those on whom antiquity had bestowed the honor of divinity
were the worst of mortals, and concluded that after practicing
their filthy abominations they would have paid the common
debt to nature. Through rational argument I realized that men
who had lived beneath heaven in need of earthly things had
been appointed to heaven based solely on their reputation, and
it is impossible for those who have been nourished in this
world by the temperate skies of heaven and the abundant
riches of earth to create heaven and earth and everything else

that exists in them. Once I had the demolished the arguments for their divinity, I concluded in my mind that if these gods are in the end deprived of divine authority, it is possible and fitting to believe in a single God: the work of creation and rule over it are his alone, and as all things come from him, he alone contains all in himself and governs all. The idea of a single God became solidified in my thoughts, and temples along with the deceitful images in them were cast away in eternal scorn. Now that my heart had been cleansed from the sewer of idolatry, the purity of a religion wholly true shone forth from the heavens. For a divine voice then commanded me to come to this place, where, it promised, by the dispensation of the Son of God who recently suffered I would receive from you the true and only faith. And so I charge you, by the Mother of the Light whom I now see among those present and who was already revealed to me, and by your works, to show me the mysteries of this new rebirth."

When Peter and his blessed companions heard this, as Mary illumined the heavenly gathering, they paid reverence to the magnificent glory of God and his Son made man, for though he had only recently brought salvation to center of the earth,[8] and preachers of his grace had yet to wander abroad, he had spread the fulfillment of his words even into the boundaries of the West with astonishing rapidity. So this man received the teachings of the faith, and then, cleansed in the waters of baptism, took the name of Quilius. At this school and with these teachers he thus confirmed his understanding of the sacrament that he had received, and when he was about to leave them and return to his own land, he asked them with a faithful heart for some tokens of holy relics, particularly those he learned had touched the body of the Savior: he asked for and received part of the chain he knew had bound the Lord to the post; part of the whip an impious hand had wielded to lash his blessed limbs; part of the crown of thorns that encircled his blessed head; from the cross, some of the very wood to which he had been attached; part of the cloak of the Mother of God, which she had been wearing, it is said, when she gave birth to the Lord; and last some of the clothing of all the apostles themselves.[9]

Making arrangements for the return voyage, he packed these relics in a small chest that he carried with him. He passed some distance through the intervening regions until he reached the very village where he had delayed his journey for the sake of rest. Suddenly overcome by unexpected illness, he retired to his bed, where it was revealed to him in a dream that he would reach the end of his earthly life there. He was also told that his remains would dwell in no other place but there, and that he should know, moreover, that the relics he had received from the holy apostles in Jerusalem were to be buried in the same ground. The man woke up, and since the prediction of his death focused his thoughts on one idea, he made the necessary final arrangements for his body in the hope of a glory soon to follow. There he died, repaying in full the deposit committed to him; his body found its final rest in the earth that was his tomb, and there next to him the chest of relics took its place. Then, after a long time, at God's direction the small chest was unearthed. It had by then been covered with a costly layer of gold leaf by some faithful men who used a very old technique, and has thus come down to our day, the sight of it continuing to provide new proof of ancient tales. And this is how, they say, the place had its beginnings.

II.

Aided by the flowering of the Christian religion, an attractive little church there, long ago established in the name of the mother of God, began to shine forth. Situated beneath the walls of Coucy, the castle mentioned above, and surrounded by wealthy villas of ancient memory, the church drew great crowds of worshippers from those who lived nearby. It is also said that while it was still small, it often glowed with divine lights and was frequently honored with miracles; there is certainly nothing wrong in this, since its lowly reputation among men was undeserved. The domains of the castle spread far and wide under prosperous rulers, and the barons of great wealth were given to generosity. Like the sweetest fragrance, its reputation for holiness began to waft out in all directions, and its fame led a gathering of pious men to propose that the church be handed over to monks in order to have divine services performed there regularly. Since from such a beginning there was no expectation of further growth—the monastery's revenue seemed little more than enough to supply the needs of six monks—the church began to be renovated by people who had no experience and little training in building or enlarging anything. Because there was no one with any skill to oversee construction or give instructions, what they made was full of gaps. The same amount of material could have made something more compact, but at the same time more practical and suitable.

In an era with a greater abundance of wealth than now, the little monastery continued to grow from the donations of the barons of the castle, and it had already benefited from the first fruits offered by lords and from gifts given from elsewhere. Both the brothers of the monastery and its patrons decided it would be useful to place Henry, an honorable man who was then abbot of Saint-Rémy and had for some time before that presided over the abbey of Homblières, in charge of this monastery as well.[10] Though not famed for his learning or his birth, he took great care in managing secular affairs, so that he might be equally attentive to the practice of the rule inside the monastery, too. With these three communities in his charge, he used the resources of the two wealthier ones to supply the needs of this third, just beginning to take root. Among the many acts of generosity he performed for this church, he raised a great tribute to pay for its consecration. Hélinand, bishop of Laon, a very wealthy man intensely concerned with the establishment of churches and their adornment, performed the dedication, bestowing privileges on the church, exempting it from most dues, and enriching it with illustrious gifts.[11]

However, after the abbot was slowed by age and had gone blind, he withdrew to the two wealthier abbeys, easier to govern because of their self-sufficiency, and decided to relinquish control of the third, impossible to manage without constant effort. He called an assembly of the monks at the church, where he attempted to hand over its governance to a monk who was his nephew, but without success. Much to his displeasure, the election instead fell to a monk named Godfrey, a young man at the time and a native to the area, who had been a monk at Mont-Saint-Quentin near Pérrone. When the elder abbot saw the electors casting their ballots in another direction, he wisely quit the post he had maintained with such kindness and generous indulgence, and formally conceded it to the man they had elected.[12]

When Godfrey was elected and placed in charge of the monastery, at a time when the common people just as much as the nobles possessed the will and the means to enrich churches, his conduct was marked by great prudence. As a result, numerous gifts of land and revenue poured in to him all at once during the days following upon his election. He knew quite well how to accommodate himself to the ways of worldly men, with whom he was affable and generous, and when lawsuits arose involving secular matters, about which he had acquired some knowledge, he made intense efforts on their behalf. Moreover, at that time, which I described at the beginning of my work, men truly possessed a spirit of giving for the foundation of monasteries, and lavished upon them land and money; indeed, they were happier to spend their wealth on such undertakings than are their sons to pay us lip service in these days. Because the surrounding monasteries had less zeal for religious life than they ought, and because people saw that this abbot together with his monks were deeply committed to its practice, the church allowed his name to shine forth like a flickering candle in the midst of darkness, due to the leader's self-restraint and to his followers' self-constraint at his every command.

Believing simony to be in both name and deed as accursed as filthy profiteering, he forbade anything to do with it, whether buying or selling, from happening in the church, and once the market was shut down, only grace was admitted. Since he was considered more astute in worldly affairs than most of his fellow abbots, and was therefore better known in towns and cities, there was at first talk of transferring him to one of the wealthier abbacies, and then of conferring a bishopric on him. Meanwhile, the bishopric of Amiens had been vacant for nearly

two years. Godfrey had stepped forward to support an arch-
deacon from this city, someone whom many of the people and
clergy favored, but because of his worldly skills and the monas-
tic habit he wore, while working for his choice, he himself was
chosen. When Richard, formerly bishop of Albano, but at that
time a legate of the Apostolic See in France, convened a council
in the city of Troyes, Godfrey was made bishop of the see of
Amiens, and transferred from his native Nogent.

Although he led a life of blessed glory at Nogent, and everyone
treated him with the greatest respect, so that even the bishops
superior to him honored him with special regard—in short,
although from every quarter he was looked upon as a mirror of
perfect piety, he suddenly rose to this position (whether it was
something he desired or he feared, God only knows). I have
learned, however, that "an estate quickly acquired in the begin-
ning will not be blessed in the end."[13] His first steps indeed
attracted the usual sort of praise, and for some years afterward
he also had an esteemed reputation, but now, as one can see,
whatever glory once appeared to burn hot within him did not just
cool. It went cold. In fact, on the first day of his reception within
the city, when he was going to address the people, he stepped up
to a rather high pulpit and declared that he would face up to
arduous difficulties in the same way, because he did not want that
verse of poetry to apply to him from any failings of his own:

Mountains labor, but a ridiculous little mouse will be born.[14]

This saying planted a seed in everyone's mind to keep an eye on
his subsequent deeds, and in fact, as his stature considerably
diminished day by day, it began to make this pledge of his seem
worse and worse. But for now let us be silent about these matters,
since perhaps we will have a place in what follows, when . . .[15]

III.

After my election, as discussed above, I was summoned to the
place Godfrey had left. He had brought it to a suitably

advantageous condition that if he had been able to stay content with what he had, he could have enjoyed a life filled with blessings and perfectly free, beholden to no one. Whether my election happened against God's will or with his support, I do not know, but I can declare one thing for certain: the search for that office occurred without any campaigning or participation on my part, nor was there any political influence from my relatives. From this latter circumstance, things turned out fine, I suppose, but there was a disadvantage to the former, at least somewhat of one, in that none of them came to know me, nor did I know any of them—the reader will perhaps notice the unhealthy consequences. Yet I am not convinced coming to them as a stranger, and they to me, that we would have started any kind of quarrel simply for that reason, though some people perceived it to be the case. This has happened, or can happen, elsewhere, but I cannot infer that is what happened here. For no one doubts that familiar acquaintance usually gives rise to frankness, and frankness quite easily erupts into rudeness. Without question, we tend to show greater reverence to those whom we do not know, though when I entered that place, their inner thoughts were in no way kept hidden from me. Rather, so faithful were their confessions that in opening their minds to me, they became as one with me. Even though I believed I had seen monks in other places, I knew of none comparable to them in this regard.

You know, most merciful God, that it was not out of any arrogance that I began this work, but that I wanted to confess my sins. And I would indeed confess them in all their vivid details, if I did not fear my horrendous deeds would corrupt the minds of many of my readers. I do confess my sins, but it would be more correct to say I confess mercies commensurate not with my sin, but with your inborn grace. And if I happen to speak about someone, I will reveal his behavior as well as its end results in order to demonstrate your judgments. For you know that I take no pleasure in setting down on these pages, devoted to you and your servants, a word that is bitter or resentful, and that I thus decided to weave together my fortunes, good and bad, to serve perhaps as some kind of lesson for others.

On the very day of my installation, while the monks were

preparing to meet me in procession, one of them, who was rather knowledgeable about scripture and curious, I think, how things would turn out with me, opened up a text of the Gospels placed upon the altar for this purpose, intending to take whatever passage first struck his eyes as a prophecy about me. The book was written by a scribe, not page by page, but in columns; his eye landed in the middle of the third column, on the following verse: "Your eye is the lamp of your body."[16] He ordered the deacon who was to carry the Gospels in the procession to keep his finger on the passage he had seen, and immediately after I kissed the silver image affixed on the cover, to open up the book before my eyes, carefully noting where my gaze landed. And so once I had, according to custom, pressed my lips to the cover, he opened the book, and while he tracked the direction of my vision, I did not look at the top of the page, nor at the bottom, but I turned my gaze to that same verse. When the monk who had conjured up this plan saw that what I had unwittingly done had met his purposes, he came to me a few days later and told me both what he had done and how my actions had remarkably matched his.

You know, God, you who light the lamps of all who believe in you,[17] that you granted me the lamp of a good intention, and that the will I had toward these monks, even among the adversities they brought upon me, was still favorable. Though clearly the filth and misery in my heart, as far as I was concerned, was my own doing, it did not escape you how much my mind was directed to the salvation of those whom you placed under me. Even as I ponder my own misfortunes all the more, I am gladdened in equal or greater measure by their good works that they rejoice in. For I know the more grateful I prove myself to be for the zealous efforts made by men of good will, the greater my deliverance will be before the throne of your grace.

After they welcomed me and led me in to the chapter assembly, I gave a sermon on a prophecy of Isaiah—it was the Sunday before Christmas, when he is read—and said:[18]

"The prophet Isaiah says, as you recently heard: 'A man will seize his brother, a servant of his father, saying: You have a cloak, you shall be our ruler, and this heap of ruins is under your hand. And he will answer: I am not a healer, and in my house there is neither bread nor cloak. Do not make me your leader. For Jerusalem is ruined, and Judah has fallen.' *A man* is one who acts as a woman in face of the devil. He 'seizes his brother' when he joins himself to someone born of God. This person should also be *a servant of his father*, because whoever is taken up into a pastoral office should not be found ignorant of the mysteries of the house of God. For one who does not know the sacraments of the church is unworthy of its administration, given that a scribe trained in the kingdom of heaven, even if faithful in keeping its mysteries and wise in dispensing them, cannot be counted as a servant. And how could one who does not know the church govern the church?[19] Thus, he should be *a servant*.

"What does *a cloak* indicate if not the beautiful appearance of outward works? Therefore, the one who has a cloak is asked to be their *ruler* because the person who creates the appearance of being rather strict in word and deed is often chosen for office. Moreover, *ruins* are said to be *under his hand* because anything detrimental found among the followers is counted against the leader. It is as if the man said to his brother: 'To the eye, you seem to conduct yourself well, but take care that you excel with inner virtue, especially since you know you have to uphold the *ruins* of everyone.' Then the prudent reply: '*I am not a healer*, such that I can counter the spreading "ruins" of so many diseases. All of you notice the outer *cloak*, yet it is not *in my house*, because the soul's habit is not the same as the body's.'[20] He also claims he is *not a healer* because the subtlety of discretion renders it difficult to fathom where vice begins and virtue ends. And this could be on account of what he lacks, since there is not in his house any of that *bread* daily sought from God[21]—namely the comfort provided by a spiritual infusion of divine nourishment, or the strengthening in the inner man by that charity without which he can never receive proper guidance. He therefore rightly refuses to be made *leader*, since his mind has not been steeped sufficiently in divine strength. This is because *Jerusalem is ruined*, which means the experience of inner peace has perished, and also *Judah has fallen*, which means that, after loss of inner tranquility, the confession of sins, which puts an end to all evils, has given way to utter hopelessness, and this is a proper reason to refuse pastoral office. For when vices rise up and throw the mind into confusion, it is overrun in disgrace, and when, struck utterly senseless by these vices, the mind loses its ability to govern itself, it does not renounce them through confession. It is proper for someone else to prevent it from ruling others, but more properly it prevents itself."

These sentences, which I have quoted here by way of illustration, on that occasion I expanded on and supported with examples drawn from scripture.

IV.

Since I have neglected for some time to speak of my mother, whom I considered the one and only good among all my worldly possessions, I ought to mention briefly how her good life attained a better end. She had passed, as she herself would often say, into the last few years of her life, but her strength of spirit remained unbroken, and though her slight body began to fail, the devotion to prayer in her soul did not diminish in the least. Unable to sleep because of her weakened lungs, during the night she would repeat in an extraordinary wheeze the "Jesu Domine" a hundred times over, until she was finally overcome by her ailments and took to her bed.[22]

My brother and I, however, were living in Nogent at that time, two years, if I'm not mistaken, before the return to Fly I mentioned above, which I had not in the least expected to do, but which, thanks to the one who uses our evils for good, turned out far more favorably than one could believe. For in her delicate condition, God spared her heart that so loved God a piercing blow it little deserved from the sword of this ignoble return.[23]

In tears, my teacher then stood by her as she was dying, and said, "My lord's sons are far away, and perhaps you will be grieved, and they more so, should they not be here when you die." With a reproachful look in her eyes, she replied, "Even if they were staying in the room next to mine, as they once did, God knows that I would not want either one of them, or any of my relatives, to be present at my death. But there is one whom I await with the strength left in me; only he do I wish to be here!" So she spoke, and on the night, and at the hour, when we celebrate the mass for God's sending of the angel Gabriel to the Virgin, she departed to her mistress whom she had, as I mentioned, always longed for with unbounded love, and who, I am sure, graciously received her.[24]

A few years before she died, she developed an ardent desire to take the sacred veil. I did not agree to this, calling upon the decretal that says, "No bishop should attempt to veil widows."[25] She was capable of living a perfectly chaste life without the outer dress, I said, and long ago Anselm, abbot of Bec, later archbishop of Canterbury, a remarkable man whom I mentioned above, had also forbidden her from this very thing. Nevertheless, she was all the more inflamed, and no argument I presented could deter her, so she prevailed. When, as part of the ceremony, she was providing her justifications for taking the veil before the abbot John, a most reverend man whom she herself had raised as a young boy, at the end she demonstrated that God had inspired her decision in the following way:[26]

She said that in a vision she had seen a lady of great beauty and dignity; gathered around her in abundance were items used in worship. The lady offered her an extremely precious robe, as if entrusting it to her for safekeeping, a deposit to be returned at the proper time. Without hesitation, we all supported her case, especially when we understood she was summoned to his act of devotion by divine signs. For nearly three years she wore this sacred veil in a manner beyond any possible reproach, and she returned it to the lady who first had entrusted it to her on the anniversary of its reception, amid the greatest joy and the happy sounds of the salvific Annunciation.[27]

I commend her soul to all faithful readers, she whom I know excluded no one of faith from her frequent prayers. Let my

words about her be spoken before God, with the true testi-
mony of my heart, having fabricated nothing in any way.

But since I have returned to the church at Fly, I ought to lin-
ger over it for a while before retracing my wandering steps
back to the rocky soil of Laon.

V.

In this monastery there is a monk who was born a Jew but was
rescued from his superstitious beliefs as the campaign to Jeru-
salem first sounded throughout the Latin world. One day at
Rouen, some men who had vowed to undertake the expedition
after accepting the sign of the cross began to complain among
themselves: "Do we need to travel to distant lands in the East
to attack the enemies of God, when there are Jews right before
our eyes, a race that is the greatest enemy of God? We've got it
all backward!" Once they finished talking, they took up their
weapons and rushed into a church.[28] Either by force or by
some ruse, they frightened the Jews into leaving, then put them
all under the sword without regard to sex or age. Those who
agreed to submit to Christian law escaped the sword-point
looming over them. During this massacre, a nobleman took
pity on a little boy he saw, and grabbing him away from there
took him to his mother.

A lady of rather high status, she had formerly been married
to the count of Eu. (There is a castle at Eu, called Treport, over
which rises the abbey of Saint-Michel by the sea.) This excep-
tional woman welcomed the young child, and with laudable
kindness asked him whether he wanted to follow Christian
laws. Since he thought he was destined for the same slaughter
he had seen his fellow tribesmen suffer, he did not refuse her
offer, and after everything necessary for a baptism had been
hastily prepared, he was taken to the font. Following the pre-
scribed prayers, the sacrament was administered, and then
came the point where a candle is lit, and melting wax drops
into the water. One particular drop appeared to fall into this
water and spontaneously changed from a sliver (if I can call it

that) into the shape of a cross so precise that a human hand could not have made anything like it from such scant material. I heard this from the countess, with whom I had such a close and personal relationship that she referred to me only as her son, and the priest, both solemnly invoking the divine name as their witness. I would not have taken this event so seriously unless I had witnessed the young boy's remarkable success for myself.

The name of the countess was Hélisende, and her son, who saved the child from slaughter and received him at the holy font, was William, and he gave this name to the boy. Since he was still young at the time he switched from Hebrew, of which he had only received a smattering, to Latin, it took root in a short time. Hélisende began to worry the boy's original relatives would call him back from his adoptive ones (they had in fact tried on occasion, but had no success with him), so she entered him into the monastic community at Fly. Handed over to the monastic calling, he displayed such a desire for the Christian life, imbibing with an energetic mind anything related to divine learning and enduring with equanimity everything laid upon him for the sake of his training, that the victory he won over his worthless nature and the glory he took in casting aside his former condition commanded the highest respect from all.[29]

In his youth, he had a monk assigned to him as his guardian, who secretly served as his grammar instructor. A very pious man, he believed that this young newcomer was lacking in his knowledge of our religion, so he attempted to educate him, and not in vain. Every day he worked to sharpen the youth's natural cleverness, until even among the flourishing community of educated men there no one else was thought to have attained greater fame for his intelligence. Yet since he was always cheerful and known especially for his modest life, even though much was made of his learning, he was a nobody as far as jealousy or criticism was concerned. To strengthen his as yet unbroken faith, I sent him a short treatise I had written almost four years earlier against the count of Soissons, a Judaizer as well as a heretic.[30] I heard he eagerly embraced it, and as a result made a compilation of arguments for the faith in pious imitation of that little work. And thus the cross that appeared at his baptism was not a fortuitous accident, but a divine work: rightfully so, for it indicated there would be a man, Jewish by birth, who would possess a faith unusual in our day.

At this same place there was a priest, a rather kind and simple man, who had dedicated himself to monastic life together with his son, also a cleric. The son took after his father in every way, but distinguished himself more, because he was of a more vigorous age and had some education. His father, while living in the world, had been as charitable to the poor as his means had allowed. The devil not only resented this man's goodness, but was pained even more by his complete rejection of the world, and thus one night in a vision, while the man, still a novice, was sleeping together with the others, a crowd of demons suddenly stood before his eyes, carrying pouches slung over their haunches in the way Scotsmen usually do.[31] When one of them, who seemed to act as their leader and spokesman, stopped next to him, the rest of the demons approached one by one and halted. The one standing by him said, "Give us charity." The monk replied, "I no longer have anything to give you or anyone else," for he did not forget he was a monk. Then the Scotsman said, "I have never seen a charitable priest." After he said this, he grabbed a stone in fury and hurled it with tremendous force. The man felt so much pain in his heart, where the blow from the demon's insult landed,[32] that for forty days he nearly worried himself to death, as if a Scotsman had actually struck him with a stone.

Some time later he had fully recovered, but the devil resented that he would do further good.[33] So one night the monk, responding to the demands of nature, was sitting alone after everyone else had left, while the devil lay in wait for him. He approached in the guise of a monk with a cowl over his head, and scraped his foot against the latrine floor, as monks usually do when seeking something during the night. Completely terrified, the monk bolted from his spot in fear, and when he rushed to the door, he struck his head against the lintel.[34] Thus the devil brought down the man from the other direction:

powerless against his spirit, he had stopped trying to harm his soul and attacked his body.

There was another man, from a noble family in Beauvais, and wealthy with holdings in the Noyonnais. He was of an advanced age, his body long worn out, but, in what is unhealthy for such men, he had a wife who was still fairly energetic in duties of the marriage bed. Abandoning his wife and the world, he professed monastic vows at Fly. From his seemingly endless tears and constant prayers, never missing an opportunity to hear the word of God, he proved himself worthy of all our admiration. Always eager to strictly follow the monastic rule, he once heard it pronounced in a chapter meeting that no monk should attempt to enter the infirmary without definite cause, and since that is where he lived, he retained this prohibition in his memory. So one morning, while lying in bed with his eyes still shut fast asleep, two demons in the form of those religious men commonly called *deonandi* sat upon a bench placed next to his bed.[35] The old man awoke and, turning his eyes toward the head of the bed, marveled at the strange people sitting there so familiarly. The one who was sitting closer to him did not have his head covered, and his beard did not hang down, but was tucked in. He had red hair, and walked barefoot, as wandering monks usually do. They say there was straw stuck between his toes, as if he had recently walked on some. The other, however, hid behind the first one, so his face could not be made out, but he wore a cloak down to the ankles and a black hood. Taking notice of these two strange persons before him, he reprimanded them in a very hostile way: "You are laypeople and strangers—where did you get so bold as to come here at this hour, where not any monk in this cloister would dare come without reason?" The demon replied, "I had heard, master, there were pious men in this monastery, and I came to learn more of their religion. Please, don't be upset." The monk answered, "Instruction in the religious life or the monastic rule does not happen here in this building, but if you want to be taught, go to those in the cloister: there you will discover the obligations of the rule and the rudiments of the holy life. So depart from here, for there is no question whatsoever that you are not allowed to do what is forbidden even to monks, who are the masters here."

The demon wished to repeat what he had said and stay, but the monk gnashed his teeth in anger and his words thundered at them, forcing them to leave the building. When they had gotten as far as the doorway, they stopped at the threshold, and the one who had led the conversation looked back at the old man and spoke again: "Turn me from your door then! Be sure, you should have been willing to keep me here with you! One of your dependents is guilty of theft, and if he dared deny it, I would have beaten him in a fistfight and brought great profit to you." The old man chuckled when he heard this, and said, "From your tale, I now have clear evidence of danger, since you said you came here for the sake of religion, and now you confess you are a fighter. As befits such deceit, I will neither listen to you nor keep you here."

The old man, however, was extremely irritated that men such as this had been allowed inside the house, so he got out of bed and went out to the porch, where he found some sick brothers who were staying with him there. He bitterly accused them of allowing outsiders such as this to enter, but they were astonished and thought he was delirious—they swore they had seen no one. When he described who they were, how they behaved, and what they had said, and also indicated the time, he learned, based on his own account and others, that he had been tricked by demons. Some demons, in fact, intend only to play pranks, while others have in mind acts of cruelty that usually lead to injury. To illustrate this, I will provide two examples in addition to the one just given.

VI.

At the fortress of Chauny, one of the servants belonging to Wascelin, lord of the place, had the duty of staying awake at nights to guard the castle. In the evening, as the day grew quickly dark, he became afraid he would miss dinner, which was soon. His post was on the other side of the river, so he

shouted for someone to send a boat from the opposite bank.
When no one heard him, he became furious and said: "You
devils, why don't you carry me across?" A devil appeared right
away, saying, "Climb in! I'll carry you." Soon to take a bad
fall, the unlucky man climbed in. Once he had taken him
aboard, in under an hour the devil had carried him to Italy,
and dropped him off within the suburbs of a city called Sutri,
and with such gentleness that he broke his hip.

This city is almost a full day's travel from Rome. His lord,
who had journeyed there to visit the tombs of the apostles, had
left Rome the previous day and rested in Sutri. He arose before
daybreak, as travelers usually do in the winter months, and
when he and his retinue reached the fields outside the city, he
heard the voice of someone moaning not far from the public
road. They searched for him and found him; he was recog-
nized just from his voice, because it was known to his lord.
Asked how he had come there, he claimed he had been at
Chauny in the evening and described how he had fallen as the
devil was transporting him. The lord, more than astonished,
carried the man to the nearest city, and provided him with
some of his own money, so that he could take care of his return
and his injury. He learned a lesson from what happened to
him, and taught others, that you should call upon God, not
demons, for your troubles.

At Saint-Médard there was likewise a man who had the
same duty at his abbey. On the tower gate beside the fish-
pond, he had passed part of the night making noises, as watch-
men often do, with rattles, his mouth, and horns, until at last
he climbed down intending to walk along the edge of the
water. As he was standing there, the images of three women
appeared, one of whom said as he listened, "Let's go in here."
Another answered, "He's poor, he couldn't treat us well." The
third added, "There's a cleric here, Hugh, big and fat, with
plenty of possessions—he could feed us well. It's best to attack
him." As they began to vanish into thin air, the man came to
his senses and understood that these were the three better-
known kinds of fever, who after their ridiculous investigation
had rejected him as a pauper, and went for one whose flesh

and wealth would be nearly impossible to consume. Without waiting until daybreak, he went to the monks he found nearest at hand and after he told them what he had seen and heard, asked that someone be sent to Hugh to learn how he was. This was done, and he was found in the throes of an intense fever.

From this it can be surmised that these kinds of illnesses are administered by demons, in accordance with the judgment of God. Thus, one also reads in the Gospel about the woman who, bound by Satan, remained bent over for seventeen years.[36] In addition, it is said that whoever suffers from epilepsy (the "falling sickness") is cast upon the ground by an unclean spirit, foams at the mouth, hisses through the teeth, and cannot be controlled. This, it is said, can be cured only by prayer and fasting.[37] Job, too, was stricken both within and without— that is, his body and his possessions—by an infestation of demons.

Who can stop a tale once it has started? So let us also add to the text a fourth which comes to mind. There was a cleric staying at Reims, only moderately educated but an expert at painting, who provided a frightening example for our age. At some point, out of fear for the numerous follies he had committed, he became a canon regular at the church of Toussaints at Châlons-sur-Marne. After he lived there for a while, the fervor he had at first grew cooler every day, while the fever of his earlier passions rekindled. He then abandoned the rule to which he had committed himself, and returned to Reims, where he married. After his wife had borne him several children, he was stricken by a heaven-sent disease for his self-correction. However, before he succumbed to his illness, it was his will to follow the crusade to Jerusalem, talk of which at that time had spread far and wide.

Though seriously ill for some time, under increasing distress he returned to his senses. He begged John, abbot of Saint-Nichasius at that time, to come to him, promising to renounce the world and asking to be clothed in the holy habit. The prudent abbot, suspicious from his knowledge of the man's fickleness, did not consent, but while he refused to present the habit which he sought, he nevertheless brought the sick man inside the monastery. When the man sensed that his illness was growing more severe, he approached the abbot and with repeated lamentations obtained a monastic habit from him, seemingly against his will. Happier because he got what he had wanted, in almost no time at all he seemed to grow calmer than before. Then suddenly, motivated by some divine impulse, he summoned the abbot and said, "Father, order your monks to keep careful watch over me. Know for certain that for some days the judgment of God has clearly been hanging over me: if you and your monks are greatly inconvenienced because of me, know that it will not be for long. Please do not be troubled."

Upon hearing this, the abbot instructed that fearless and vigilant men be appointed guardians for him. And without delay an endless swarm of demons rushed against him from every direction, grabbed him, and dragged him on his back along the floor. With a rabid fury they tried to tear the sacred habit off him, while he held on to the cowl with his teeth, and clasped his arms together lest they be torn away. During the night he was utterly overwhelmed by this wretched misery, driven to pitiful wailing, but occasionally during the day, when the demons departed, he was granted a little rest. Then he could be asked in composure how he was enduring his tumultuous condition.

He would talk a great deal about the souls of men whom he knew or whom those present mentioned to him, as if he held them before his eyes. A widow, who feared her husband's soul was in peril but prayed for him very little, heard of this and asked his advice whether she might pray for her husband, and if he knew what her husband was doing. He replied, "Of course. Pray for him with confidence, for he was here a little while ago."[38]

After he suffered these painful torments for several days, at last he was restored to complete peace. For even though there sometimes seemed to be a pause in his suffering, he would soon see emerging from the walls, from the ground, from everywhere throngs of demons that flew at him to tear him apart. The evil spirits were finally removed, when he was granted clemency by divine judgment, so he summoned the abbot and said the following: "My lord, God repays me for my sins. Know then that after this trial, my end will soon follow. Absolve me of my wrongdoing as you are able, and anoint me with holy oil to consummate this remission of sins." The abbot swiftly carried out his task with devotion, which the man received with grateful affection. Cleansed of all contagion by his punishments in this world, he was free and happy when death came and he entered into life.

BOOK 3

I.

Now that I am going to discuss, as I promised, events at Laon, or rather now that I am going to present the tragedy of Laon, I must first say that the origin of all the evil lies, as it seems to me, in the corruption of its bishops. Though this has been going on for a rather long time, for this work it is necessary to trace the thread back to the beginning, which is thought to be Ascelin (also called Adalbero). He was, as I discovered, a native of Lorraine, wealthy, and possessed many estates. After he sold everything and brought enormous sums of money to the see over which he presided, he distinguished his church with splendid adornments and enriched the clergy and the bishop, yet he soiled all these gifts by an act of wickedness surpassing every other. What indeed could be more disgraceful to him, what could be more ignominious, than his betrayal of his lord the king, an innocent boy to whom he had proffered an oath of loyalty, and his diversion of the course of Charlemagne's descendants to a foreign family? A crime he carried out, like Judas, on the day of the Lord's Supper![1] Clearly, when he deposed future kings as well as his present one, he was planning not a temporary change for his benefit, but rather the fulfillment of his own wicked will at the expense of those who are blameless. However, worldly prosperity did not thereby attend the city and its bishop any less, as God delayed his punishment. Passing over the two immediate successors as bishop, Gébuin and Liétry, let us go straight to Hélinand.

II.

Later there was Hélinand, a man of obscure ancestry from an impoverished family, with only the barest education and insignificant social standing. Through his acquaintance with Gautier the Elder, count of Pontoise (Hélinand drew his origins from that county), he came into the favor of Edward, king of England, whose wife, in fact, had developed some kind of connection with the count.[2] Hélinand became the king's chaplain, and since he understood proper French etiquette, the English king frequently used him as an envoy to Henry, king of the Franks. This king was very greedy, and in the habit of selling bishoprics, so Hélinand would ply him with the most lavish gifts to suggest that upon the death of any of the bishops of France, he ought to take on the episcopal insignia as successor.[3] He had, in fact, accumulated enormous piles of money, since he had been installed in the royal chapel at a time when England was flourishing with boundless wealth. What made him the choice for many legations also brought him into King Henry's favor; the king's ear readily caught his hints, and the deed was done. Once he was introduced into Laon, he did not think he could obtain influence through respect for his family or his scholarly learning, but had placed his hopes in the riches he held in vast supplies and the acts of generosity he had learned to distribute shrewdly.

He turned then to the work of adorning and building churches, and though he appeared to be doing many things for God, he still gave the clearest indications that he was using his good deeds only to curry favor and spread his name. By such craftiness, he even attempted to seize the archbishopric of Reims. He did occupy it for two years, after its sizable revenues had fallen into the hands of King Philip, a most venal man in what belonged to God, until he heard from the pope that one who has a wife cannot under any circumstances acquire another.[4] When someone openly asked him why he made such an attempt, he said that he still would not have acted any differently, even if he had been able to become pope.

Whatever kind of man he really was, whether when alone by himself he was ambitious or showed some other human feeling, this one good quality in any case deserves recognition: he used his enormous wealth to advance his see as well as the churches attached to it, he also protected in splendor the privileged status of the church, and it was fitting for him to have stores of wealth from the outside world, so that he could use it to advance splendidly the lordship of his churches.

III.

After Hélinand's tenure, Enguerrand succeeded to the office, and as much as he outshone the previous bishop in both nobility and learning, he was all the more appalling in comparison to him when it came to protecting the rights of the church.[5] The crown had once used force to draw away some of the episcopal revenues from the see, which Hélinand himself through entreaty and gifts had reclaimed from King Philip and guaranteed their return to the church under the seal of a royal charter. But at his accession Enguerrand returned them all to the king, making his introit a funeral dirge, for the church has now been without these funds over the course of three successive bishops, and will perhaps be without them forever.[6] And thus, as it seems to me, he made all the bishops who succeeded him complicit in his simony, since they accepted the office in such subservience to the royal command that they dared not request the restoration of the damnable payment Enguerrand made to become bishop.

He did not have the least bit of desire for God, and any kind of self-restraint or piety was a joke to him: he was publicly regarded as worse than a buffoon or entertainer for his idle chatter and salacious tales. It was during his time in office that the causes leading to the ruin of the city, the churches, and the entire province began to emerge, which also happened to bring about his unhappy end.

He had a very close relative of the same name, Enguerrand of Boves, who was a very giving man, unstinting in his generosity. To churches, at least to those where he had learned that the religious life was followed, he displayed the utmost respect and munificence, but otherwise he gave himself up to love for women. No matter what woman he was with, whether contracted to him legitimately or on temporary loan, he could barely do anything that was not one of her impudent demands. Since he had little luck in his marriage choices, he began to stray toward other men's wives, and secretly acquired as his own the wife of the count of Namur,[7] a relative of his—or, I should say, in secret he seduced her, but openly joined her in matrimony, a union punished by anathema numerous times and condemned in the solemn pronouncements of councils. It is certain that under pressure from the bishop they would have readily renounced their outrageous conduct, if the husband's kinship and the woman's fawning grief had not weakened the bishop's resolve. But his mild treatment gave strong encouragement to their adulterous embraces, and it effectively served as a clandestine absolution for a public coupling that had been openly excommunicated. For shame! Even the ones whom he offered a deceptive promise of absolution never presumed to think their union absolved!

And then, since from the root of a snake comes forth an adder,[8] which is to say, evils that have been encouraged burst forth into something worse, the man who had lost his wife vented his rage in a massacre against the county of Porcien—who could say how many were killed? The wife, in fact, was the daughter of Roger, count of Porcien, his last remaining child after he had disowned his sons and daughters from a wife of far superior standing. This daughter's mother came from a family of modest means, and once his primary heirs had been excluded at the stepmother's urging, he had married her, with his county as dowry, to this man from Lorraine, Godfrey, count of Namur.

While the husband's attentions were focused on some of his enemies in Lorraine, the wife on his orders was staying at the castle of Tournes in Porcien. Of the marital duties her husband owed her, she was getting less than she wanted, and whether she kept herself from going elsewhere can be known from one fact alone: she came to the man she now possessed pregnant from her adulterous sexual intercourse, an immense height of disgrace, visible to all, that she never would have reached unless she had descended down steps of sins committed in secret. This is the story told about her previous wanton affairs by everyone who knows her, though I am ashamed not only to include it, but even to think of it.

Godfrey was a young man, attractive in every respect, but Enguerrand, to whom she had given herself, was very old. A frenzied rage flared up between them, like enemies at war, and any of Enguerrand's allies that the man from Lorraine could capture he would hang on the gallows, have their eyes gouged out, or have their feet cut off. Even today, there is clear visible evidence of this for anyone who visits the county of Porcien. In fact, I heard from someone who was there during this butchery that in a single day around twelve men who had been captured in one of these conflicts were led to the gallows. Some of the leading men of Porcien acted as intermediaries in support of this adulterous emigration, and for this both their lives as well as their deaths earned them infamy. Thus Venus, when the fires of Vulcan failed to kindle her passion, went to Mars— that is, the heat of sexual desire thus boils over into cruelty.[9] Who could tell of all the pillaging and burning carried out on either side and of everything else that such violent disturbances usually bring forth? There was so much that even those who would wish to describe it fall mute.

And this is how the lord bishop "absolved," in a deranged manner, that diabolical union. A great deal could be said about the character of the bishop that should instead be left unsaid, but one thing stands out above the rest: he would repent before God without any awareness of his sin. In the end, he contracted an illness, but the illness did not distract him from any of his foolishness. Enveloped in the cloud of death, he instantly lost his senses and the ability to speak rationally; he took confession, final unction, and communion because others out of concern forced him to, not because he had sincerely asked for them. His tongue and eyes were now rendered nearly useless in death, when the other, Enguerrand, arrived, to whom he was bound by having granted him spurious absolution. The clerics, in order to perform the anointing, had barred him from the house as an excommunicate, but he tearfully appealed to the dying man and said, "Lord bishop, it's Enguerrand, your relative." The bishop, though he did not have the awareness to make confession, receive unction, or partake of communion, put his hand upon the other's neck and drew him close to receive his kiss. Everyone was scandalized at this, and afterward the bishop uttered nothing but delirious ravings until his spirit breathed its last. The woman, for the sake of whose love he had done this, many times told this story publicly as if to prove that while alive Enguerrand had acted wrongly, in dying Enguerrand had drawn a conclusion to their sin. Thus do the heavens reveal the iniquities of some, so that the earth shall rise up against them and they shall offend the very ones they sought to please with their filth.[10]

IV.

After the death of Enguerrand, the church had a vacancy for two years, until we finally assembled to elect a bishop. Among those present was the same Enguerrand who had brought about the appointment of the previous bishop through his intercession with the king, even though this same king had earlier refused the man episcopal office because of his foolish behavior. From what he said, he clearly had in mind a plan to make whoever was elected bishop indebted to him—whose choice of bishop the king and the clergy would favor—and thus disinclined to oppose his marriage. As a result, and to the ruin of the city and the detriment of the entire province, they elected Gaudry, a chancellor of the king of England, of whose abundant wealth in gold and silver they had heard rumor.[11]

Before this election, opposing factions of electors had attempted to elevate to the episcopal see two different archdeacons of the church, named Gautier and Ébal, but both were rejected by the judgment of the Apostolic See: Gautier had always shown himself to be a military man, not a cleric, and the other had less self-restraint than he should when it came to women. Once they had been dismissed, a third, the church cantor,[12] wanted to force himself into the office, so he sought an audience before the court, and under the pretense of pleading for someone else, he used his speech about the bishopric to talk about himself. Why go on? He nourished the king with many gifts, and swelling with confidence he embraced the promise of expected riches. But there would be no riches. He returned home expecting the king's legates to place him in the episcopal see the following Sunday, but God, who sets snares for such people to cast them down when they are lifted up, struck him down in his pride with a fatal illness, and his corpse lay in the church on the very day he thought he would receive his bishop's wages from the clergy and the people. After he was buried there, as it was told to me, his body audibly cracked open, and a foul liquid gushed forth in a flood up to the middle of the choir. But let us return to the point from which we digressed.

As a result of the efforts of Enguerrand and some others who assisted in his wickedness, the clergy elected Gaudry in the false hope of profit, and then, contrary to canon law, petitioned the king of England for him at the court in Rouen. He never had the least doubt of his election, but because he had not been attached by ordination to any church nor admitted to any but the lower sacred orders, he immediately devised a scheme to become a subdeacon and receive a canonry in the church of Rouen, even though up till then he had behaved in every way like a soldier.

Everyone gave their assent to accept him, except for master Anselm, a beacon to all France, or rather the Latin world, of liberal education and gentle manners, who dissented in his election.[13] He knew the man's character based on the sure testimony of others, while we supported this man as a figure unknown to us, although we did so unwillingly. Some of us, of course, found him offensive, but wrongly fearful of others who were our superiors, we yielded to their influence.

Welcomed with an utterly hollow display of pomp, soon after his arrival to the city he asked us to hasten to Rome with him. He decided, in fact, to pay the expenses for the abbot of

Saint-Vincent, Adalbero, a native of Soissons and well edu-
cated; the abbot of Ribemont, who also had some education;
and me as well, their junior in age as well as learning, to
accompany him.[14] We then departed and came to Langres,
where we heard news that the lord pope Paschal had left Rome
some time ago and was near the border of this diocese.[15] After
we had waited in that town for eight days, the lord pope
arrived in Dijon, and the clergy of Laon, a great crowd of
whom the bishop-elect had brought along with him, set out to
meet the pope, and when he was settled in the castle, they
spoke to him on behalf of their bishop-elect. The pope, already
well informed of the matter through numerous reports, prom-
ised that he would do everything in accordance with the
wishes of the petitioners. Their case was that he had been
elected within canon law, excepting some provisions Anselm
had already brought to the pope's ears to block the election.
But when members of the papal court (that is to say, the pope's
close relations) learned of Gaudry's wealth, they were more
than to happy to help and to sing the man's praises. Indeed, it
is customary for men to grow soft at the mention of gold.[16]

The day after the pope was welcomed into the city of Lan-
gres, he held a debate over this election of ours. After I read in
his presence the written report of the election, filled with exag-
gerated praise of the bishop-elect's life and character, we
abbots who were present and some priests of the church who
had accompanied the bishop-elect were summoned by the
pope, and he began to question us from the report I had just
read. There was, moreover, an extensive assemblage of very
distinguished people: bishops from Italy and our country, as
well as cardinals and other highly educated men.

The pope first asked why we had elected a man unknown to
us, and when none of the priests responded (for some of them
barely knew the basics of Latin), he turned to the abbots. I was
sitting between the other two, and while they remained silent
to the question, each of them from either side prodded me to
speak. Timid because of my youth and afraid that in such a
place and on such an important matter I would be branded as
overly bold,[17] I felt almost too embarrassed even to open my

mouth. Moreover, the proceedings were not conducted in my native tongue, but in Latin. So with stammering speech and halting thoughts, I said what I thought would meet the purposes of the questioner. In composition and style, my words fell flat, but they did not deviate in the least from the truth. It is true, I said, that the man was not known to us from personal experience, but we had received reports of his moral integrity from some people of good will.

The pope brought forward the words of the Gospel ("Who saw this," it says, "testified.")[18] in an attempt to undermine this argument, and without explaining further, also objected that a man from a royal court had been elected. Believing any attempt at evasiveness to be useless, I declared at once that I could not counter his argument, which pleased him greatly. (The bishop-elect's education, in fact, was not equal to his office.)[19] When I realized my vague assurances in response to his first question, while most gratifying to the bishop-elect, carried too little weight, I shifted my speech to the church's pressing need and briefly noted that there was no one at Laon suitable for the bishopric. The pope then asked which orders he held, and I replied that he was a subdeacon. He then asked in which church he had served, at which I hesitated in fear of telling a lie, but my fellow abbots pointed out to me it was in the church of Rouen. Still, for the sake of truth, I added that this was recent. Finally, he asked whether his birth was legitimate (the pope had apparently been told that he was illegitimate). On this point I stood more firmly than the others, since I did not have the slightest doubt about it. The pope then asked, "Will you testify to all this?" To which I replied, "I will say nothing about the other points, but this I can in confidence guarantee—he is not illegitimate, not a bastard." The lord pope reviewed these objections in just the way I described, but the reason he did so in order like this was not to prevent the appointment, but because master Anselm was present, who had laid all these charges before him, and would thus have the opportunity, if he wished, to say directly to the man's face what he had told the pope in private.

But this teacher, when he looked deeper into the ambition of the papal officials (not, I mean to say, of the lord pope),

considered it a difficult task to snatch the club from Hercules'
hand.[20] Seeing that the lords were striving for a different out-
come, this scholarly man of letters refrained from speaking in
opposition to the pope and—if I dare speak of trifles—me, and
at that moment all discussion was put to rest. The bishop-elect
was led out into our midst, and the lord pope granted him the
privilege of ordination. The assembly had broken up and the
pope had departed, when a group of cardinals approached me,
and in their various ways eagerly said, "We were very pleased
with your speech." You know, Lord my God, what their plea-
sure was, because it was not the elegance of my speech that
produced it as much as their high hopes of silver coins from
Rouen, with which Gaudry was stuffed when he arrived. For
both I and my fellow abbot, Adalbero of Saint-Vincent, were
carrying his money, twenty pounds each, which might have
filled their maws gaping in expectation. And so the almoners
were only too pleased to aid him.

When they at last went away, one of the lord pope's cham-
berlains, a monk from Cluny named Peter, who had become
acquainted with this man at Rouen while we were petitioning
the king of England for him, approached me in secret and said
the following: "Since the lord pope accepted your testimony
on behalf of the person you want, and gladly listened to you,
you should now suggest to your choice that he obey the com-
mand of the lord pope in all things and serve those around
him, so that the pope might be willing, if there is need, to lis-
ten to you speak another time on behalf of him and others."
Here is the honey smeared on the rim of the poisoned cup![21]
For what could be better than to follow the orders of the pope?
What could be worse than to serve men in order to purchase
the granting of God's grace? All the same, I shuddered with
horror at being the go-between in this business.

When he was consecrated as bishop at Saint-Ruf of Avignon,
the text of the Gospel revealed to him a gloomy prediction: it
was, "A sword will pierce your own soul."[22] At Langres, it is
true, after he had received the pope's blessing and processed to
the altar of the martyr Mamertus, with the clergy singing, "Te

deum laudamus," he opened the text of the Gospels to receive a prophecy. The first verse he came across—"Woman, behold your son."[23]—he appropriated for himself, and then he even bragged about it everywhere.

In his talk and in his behavior, he was remarkably shallow, remarkably unpredictable. He did, to be sure, consider it a pleasure to speak of military matters, as well as of dogs and falcons, which he had learned about in England. One time, after he had dedicated a church and I along with a young cleric with a good disposition rode next to him, he came upon a peasant holding a lance. The bishop, with the miter he had worn during the ceremony still on his head, snatched away the lance and spurred on his horse as if he intended to run someone through. To which we said, the cleric in our everyday tongue, but I in Latin verse:

They do not go well together, nor do they share the same abode,
Miter and lance.[24]

Meanwhile, that great treasure of English money, goblets, and vessels he had wickedly accumulated soon crumbled to ruins. In fact, I heard from the aforesaid master Anselm, who had accompanied him on a visit to England, that when he had returned there, now as a bishop, numerous claims came forward wherever he turned, for the return of borrowed utensils here, for outstanding loans there. And the teacher understood this to mean that the riches he had shown off had been stolen from others, not acquired by honest means.

V.

About three years into his tenure as bishop he did something that serves as a symbol for all his time in office. One of the leading men of the city, named Gerard, the warden of a convent, was full of energy. Even though in appearance he was short and skinny, the liveliness of his tongue and his mind combined with his keen devotion to military service won him the fear and respect of many throughout the provinces of Soissons, Laon, and Noyon. As much as he was known far and wide for his valor, he was at times all the more savage in his mockery of those around him, delivered in obscene language, yet he would never inflict this upon anyone respectable. And thus it happened that he found it acceptable to slander in private and publicly disdain this countess, about whom I told the story above.[25] This was, however, completely senseless behavior on his part, in that it constituted a revolt against Enguerrand, the woman's captor, who had used his great wealth to elevate Gerard's status. In fact, before Gerard had obtained a wife, he had been shamefully familiar with the woman of whom I speak, and though she had long kept him as a lover, once he took a wife, he reined himself in from her enticements. These women also became opponents, rivaling each other in shameful insults. They were both aware of each other's past indiscretions, and the more intimate their knowledge, the more offensive their talk. And since the countess knew that the abuse hurled at her often came from his mouth, she vented her rage against this husband of the other woman, just as a spurned woman would against her own. More dangerous than any serpent, she became increasingly eager every day for the man's destruction.

But because God places a stumbling block before those who willingly persist in sin,[26] an opportunity to bring about his downfall suddenly presented itself. A quarrel sprung up between Gerard and Gaudry the bishop, and Gerard said some unsuitable things about the bishop and his peers. The bishop endured it quietly, but not patiently. He discussed Gerard's murder with his companions and nearly all the leading men of the city, and after each man offered in turn an oath of mutual assistance in this matter, to which some very rich women added their support, the business was left in the hands of certain conspirators. Following his villainous plan, Gaudry immediately left for the tombs of the apostles, not to seek—as you know, God!—the apostles, but so that it might appear by his absence he had not taken part in such a crime. He set out around the festival of Saint Martin,[27] and when he arrived in

Rome, he remained there until he learned the murder of the man he hated had been carried out, a man who the less hateful he was to all decent people, the more hateful he became to the indecent. It was done in the following way.

On Friday morning in the week of the Epiphany, in the dim early light of dawn he rose from his bed to go to the cathedral dedicated to Blessed Mary.[28] When one of the leading men involved in the conspiracy approached him, Gerard told him of a dream he had had that very night, which he said had struck him with dreadful terror: he vividly saw two bears tearing from his body either his liver or a lung, I don't know which. But oh, what sorrow!—at that time he had been excommunicated! The reason he was denied the sacrament is as follows. A monk living at Barisis-Saint-Armand had taken in two young boys who only knew how to speak German intending to teach them French. Barisis and its dependent estates were under Gerard's advocacy, so when he spotted their elegant appearance, knowing they were not of low birth, he kidnapped them and held them for ransom. In addition to the agreed sum of money, the mother of the boys sent him a fur coat made of ermine, which they call a *reno*. And it was this purple garment he wore for a cloak when he arrived at the cathedral on horseback, along with some fellow riders.

He entered the cathedral and stood before the image of the crucified Lord, while his companions wandered here and there among the various altars of the saints, as the conspirators' servants kept watch, relaying to the bishop's minions in the episcopal residence that Gerard of Quierzy (as he was called, since he was the lord of that castle) had come to the cathedral to pray; Rorigo, the bishop's brother, and the dispenser, named Hugh, from the bishop's court, grabbed their swords and hid them under their cloaks. They passed through the arched walkway encircling the church choir until they reached the spot where he was praying. Gerard was leaning against a column, which they call a "pillar," near the middle of the church, a number of columns away from the pulpit. While it was still the dark of morning and only rarely was anyone to be seen in the vast cathedral, they seized the man from behind as he prayed. He was praying, so the cord of his cloak was tossed over onto his back, and his palms were joined together in prayer before his chest. They pulled his cloak tight from the back, and one of them bound it fast so he could not easily move his hands. As soon as that agent of the bishop held him firm, he said, "I've got you!" Turning his eye back (for he had only one), Gerard replied to him with his usual ferocity: "Get away from here, you filthy letch!" But this man said to Rorigo, "Strike him dead!" Rorigo drew his sword from his left side and wounded him in the narrow area between his forehead and nose. When Gerard realized he had been struck, he said, "Take me where you will." Stabbing him repeatedly, they began to press hard upon him, and when he lost hope in his own strength, he cried, "Blessed Mary, help me!" At these words, he collapsed, suffering his last.

Two archdeacons of the church, Gautier and Guy, were involved in this conspiracy with the bishop. Guy was also the treasurer, with a house near the church, and from this house two servants then rushed out and immediately came there to join in the butchery. For it had been agreed in their sacrilegious oath that if the bishop's officials acted first, help would be forthcoming from this house. In addition to the other wounds, they had slashed through his throat and his legs, and while in the middle of the church he was roaring in extreme agony, the few clerics who were then in the choir, as well as some poor women wandering here and there to offer prayers, were softly murmuring, but paralyzed with dreadful fear, did not dare to grumble an audible protest.

Their business completed, these two most excellent soldiers returned to the episcopal palace. The city's nobles gathered with them, too, thus betraying their own act of betrayal, and the archdeacons joined them as well. A royal provost by the name of Yves, a very capable man, summoned the king's men and the burghers of the abbey of Saint-Jean, whose advocate Gerard had been.[29] The homes of those who took part in the conspiracy, they seized, pillaged and burned, and drove the men from the city. The archdeacons and the nobles accompanied Gerard's killers everywhere they went, thus displaying their loyalty to their absent bishop.

VI.

The bishop, meanwhile, remained in Rome, as if rejoicing in the presence of the lord pope, but was in fact waiting in anticipation, his ears pricked in case any pleasing news from France should reach him. At last, word came that his prayers had been answered—and it did not escape the lord pope that a terrible crime had been committed in this great church. The bishop spoke to the pope and flattered him with gifts to dispel any suspicion of his involvement in this offense. Gaudry then returned from Rome happier than ever.

The church, however, required reconciliation since it had been violated by such an unspeakable deed, and Hubert, bishop of Senlis (himself recently suspended on account of his simony),[30] was summoned by messenger to conduct the ceremony. At the assembly of the people and clergy, a dean of the church (namely, master Anselm) ordered me to give a sermon on this unfortunate event before the people. The substance of my speech was along these lines:[31]

" 'Save me, God, since the waters have entered into my soul; I am stuck in deep mire, and there is no foothold.' Until today you have had evils of every kind, but now a *sword has reached to your soul.*[32] You became *stuck in deep mire* when, as your sins deserved, you fell into the worst of all evils—the loss of all hope. And among these evils *there is no foothold*, because the dignity and power of your church officials and nobles, those to whom you would have run in times of peril, are fallen. And if physical bodies were at times weighed down by these mutual hostilities, still the soul was free, because this church, where the purpose of salvation did dwell, was flourishing inwardly, rejoicing without the slightest stain upon it. Thus *waters* and the *sword enter the soul*, when tribulations and schisms penetrate this inner refuge and pollute its sanctity. But how can this place, which offers no protection to bodies, even those engaged in prayer, now hold any dignity among you, who are ignorant of spiritual matters? God sent against you the wrath of his indignation—indignation and wrath and tribulation, plagues carried by angels of wickedness![33] The wrath of indignation is wrath that is born out of indignation.

"Being indignant, as you know, is something less than being wrathful. Did not God show his indignation at your sinful gains, when outside your city you often suffered pillaging, burning, and murder? Did he not show his wrath when wars from elsewhere were brought within this city, and a hatred for fellow citizens was stirred up among us—lords roused against citizens, citizens against lords, provoking one another's anger, while the abbot's men and the bishop's, enemies who should not be so, unleashed their rage back and forth against one another? But because indignation and wrath caused you to make no correction, he thrust at last upon your stubborn minds *tribulation.* For it was not just any church polluted with Christian blood, nor did the stirrings of war from somewhere else drive fugitives into the church and destroy them, but an utterly spiteful desire, hidden away with criminal forethought, slaughtered a man who was praying before an image of Jesus Christ on the cross. Not, I say, in any church, but in the most illustrious church in France, whose fame spreads beyond the Latin world. And what man? Was it not one who had a distinguished birth to commend him, who, though small in stature, was known to all France for his outstanding courage under arms? The place, the crime, the disgrace were talked of everywhere. If then you do not suffer tribulation in your mind and in the depths of your heart over this wretched business, if you do not feel compassion for such a sanctified place when it is dishonored, know without a doubt that God will *make a path for his anger;*[34] that is, he will make his hidden animosity plain through your destruction. And how can you think God will put off rounding up the cattle—that is, your bodies—when on account of your incorrigibility he will not spare your souls from death? Therefore, as divine vengeance advances against you, step by baneful step, you must know that unless you show yourselves prepared to receive correction under the scourges of God, you will fall into a worse condition still because of the civil wars now brewing among you."

I wove together these ideas and others, and following the clergy's bidding and the people's will, I declared that the bishop I mentioned, who came to reconcile the church, should excommunicate the murderers of that noble man, their supporters and accomplices in this crime, and equally those who defended or sheltered them. Everyone together pronounced them excommunicated, and the ceremony to reconcile the church was performed. In the meantime, this sentence of anathema reached the ears of the archdeacons and nobles, who had abandoned their association with the city. Because of my sermon and my call for excommunication, all those who had been exiled turned their hatred against me, especially the archdeacon Gautier, who burned with an intense loathing against me. It was like hearing a tremendous thunderclap, which, at God's bidding, no lightning strike accompanied: secretly he was against me, but openly respectful.

Let us return to something I passed over. Armed with bulls and rescripts from the pope, the lord bishop returned from Rome. The king, however, believed the bishop was fully complicit in Gerard's murder, a fact he tried to color over by his absence, and the king ordered that all grain, wine, and salt pork be confiscated from the bishop's residence. Nor was the bishop, in Rome at the time, unaware of the confiscation or the reason for it, so he dispatched a letter to the king, who had decided he should be barred from the episcopal see and deprived of his possessions, and he had other letters sent to fellow bishops and to abbots of his diocese and elsewhere.

At the bridge over the Ailette river, which as I noted above was the border between Laon and Soissons, his archdeacons and nobles, whom we had just excommunicated, hurriedly ran to meet him as he took his first step onto the soil of his own territory. So great was his desire to welcome them with kisses and embraces, that he did not think it all worthwhile to visit the church of Blessed Mary, whom I serve at God's command, even though it was the first church he came across within the borders of his diocese, and right next to it he had a lengthy conversation with the men he considered his only loyal followers. He then departed and enjoyed all their hospitality at Coucy.

When I learned of his behavior, completely disgusted, I avoided his sight entirely and did not greet him at all. After three days, if I'm not mistaken, once he laid to rest the outward signs of his fury against me, though it continued to fume inside him—for his associates had in his presence repeatedly blamed me for the events described above—he commanded that I come to him. When I showed myself there and saw a house full of excommunicates and murderers, I seethed with rage. Showing me the pope's letters, he asked that I not support efforts to have him banished from the church. I promised what help I could, deceitfully—as you know, God—and insincerely. For I saw his true wickedness when he was communicating with those whom his church, which they had thoroughly polluted, had excommunicated: that Enguerrand described above was there sitting next to him, and he received as well affectionate greetings from that countess, who the day before Gerard had died whetted with her own sharp tongue the swords of the two men responsible for his death.

Since on the king's orders he was prevented from coming into the city, he threatened with rash overconfidence to enter it, flanked with military reinforcements, declaring that he would accomplish by force of arms something that was nearly impossible for men like Caesar and Augustus. He gathered together a band of knights, and then with a complete lack of self-restraint, as was usual with him, he used up most all the supplies he had raked together. In the end, after he and so many helpers had accomplished nothing beyond the ridiculous, he and his fellow conspirators in the murder of Gerard (that is, the nobles of the city along with both archdeacons), through intermediaries, heaped bribes on King Louis, son of King Philip, and came to terms with him.

He thus entered the city, and gathered an assembly at Saint-Nicholas-aux-Bois. During the mass he conducted there, he declared he would excommunicate those who had punished the conspirators in Gerard's murder with confiscation of their property and expulsion from the city. When I heard this, I whispered into the ear of one of my fellow abbots sitting next to me: "Listen to this—it's preposterous: he ought to excommunicate those who polluted his church with this horrendous outrage, but he himself is taking revenge on those who seized the murderers' property and justly punished them in retribution for their crime!" The bishop, who feared every good conscience, saw me murmuring and assumed I was talking about him. "What are you saying, lord abbot?" he asked. Then Gautier the archdeacon broke in before I could say anything, "Continue, lord, what you started," he said. "The lord abbot was talking about something else."

Though the clergy and people expressed their abhorrence at the decision, he nonetheless excommunicated those who caused harm to his fellow conscripts in sacrilegious butchery. For some time, then, the city and the diocese had a dispute with the bishop, because he had considerably delayed the excommunication of Gerard's killers. Finally, since he knew everyone suspected him and thought him all but accursed, he excommunicated the perpetrators of the crime and those privy to it. However, he had promised a great deal of money to everyone who had supported both him and his accomplices in this assassination by interceding with the king (namely, the king's courtiers), and when he started to renege on his promises, who could say how much abuse he took in public? For none of those who took his side in this matter dared enter the royal court until he had, with a hefty payment in gold and silver, redeemed them from the death penalty for the murder charged to them. And yet he, whom the pope had excused, could not even be accused by the church.

VII.

Some time later, after he had departed for the once friendly environment of England, to request money from the English king he had served, Gautier and Guy along with the nobles of the city began to plot. Such perverse madness had long ago taken root in this city that no fear of God or any lord could be found there, and the public domains were embroiled in rapine and murder according to each man's power or desire. To start from the top of their pestilence, whenever a king happened to arrive there, whose stern regal bearing ought to have commanded respect, from his own possessions a shameful fine would first be exacted: when his horses were led to water, whether in the morning or evening, his grooms were beaten and his horses stolen.[35] Even the clergy were regularly subjected to such contemptible treatment, and neither their persons nor their possessions were spared, but, I could say, "as with the people, so with the priest."[36] And what could I say about the common people? No peasant would come into the city, and anyone who approached without a sure guarantee of his safety was either jailed and held for ransom or else on a false charge was carried into court for no good reason.

Let me give one example, so completely heathen, that if it happened among barbarians or Scythians, it would be taken as certain proof that they had no laws. On the Sabbath, peasants from different areas in the countryside came there for the market, and the inhabitants of the city would offer for sale vegetables, wheat, and other produce, carrying them around the marketplace in jars or shallow baskets or something else. They would offer such things to a peasant looking to buy something, and when he promised to purchase it at an agreed-upon price, the seller would say, "Follow me to my house, and you can see the rest of the produce I'll sell you, and once you've seen it, you can take it." The peasant would follow him, and when they came to the storage bin, the trusty seller would hold the lid open and say, "Stick your head and arms in the bin so you can see that all this is no different from what I offered you in the market." When the buyer stood up on his toes and, leaning over with his stomach against the edge, put his head and shoulders down together into the bin, the good seller would lift up the unsuspecting man by the ankles and quickly throw him in, closing the lid over him as he fell. He would keep him in this prison of sorts until a ransom was paid for him.

This story and similar ones happened in the city. Noblemen and their servants committed open acts of theft, or rather banditry, and anyone traveling at night received no promise of safety—the only thing left for him was to be mugged, kidnapped, or murdered.

In consideration of this, the clergy, including the archdeacons, and the nobles, who were always on the lookout for opportunities to get money out of the people, through their intermediaries gave them the option to obtain permission to form a commune, if they should pay a fitting price. "Commune," however, was a new name, and the worst possible one, for what it was:[37] all those in a servile condition would pay their usual debt of servitude to the lords once a year, and if contrary to the terms of the agreement they were in any way delinquent, they would make regular payments as compensation; payment of all other taxes normally inflicted on serfs of all types would be canceled. The people welcomed this opportunity to pay their own ransom, and handed over enormous piles of money to clog so many greedily gaping maws. Showered with such money, they became more peaceful, and gave their firm oath that they would faithfully keep to their bargain.[38]

After the clergy, nobles, and people pledged their mutual assistance, the bishop returned from England with a large sum of money, and angered at those responsible for this revolution, he kept away from the city for some time. Despite this, quarrels full of praise and glory arose between him and archdeacon Gautier, his accomplice. The archdeacon made some very disreputable remarks about Gerard's murder to his bishop, and though I do not know what the bishop did about this with others, I do know that he complained about him to me: "Lord abbot, if Gautier should happen to make some accusations against me at some council, you wouldn't look upon it favorably, would you? When you left your monks and went over to Fly, wasn't he the one who openly enticed you with flattery while secretly plotting your removal, and warmly supported your case in public while privately provoking me to be against you?"[39] With these remarks he was attempting to win me over against this sinister man, fully aware of the severe gravity of his crime and fearfully anxious about the judgments coming from everybody in every direction.

Though he claimed to have been roused to an unyielding animus against those who had conspired to form the commune together with their supporters, the offer of a large pile of gold and silver suddenly quieted all his histrionics. He swore he would uphold the rights of this commune, in the same way as in the city of Noyon and the town of Saint-Quentin, where there were legitimate charters. The king as well, compelled by gifts from the people, swore to this oath. My God, even after they received so much money from the people, even after they had offered their oaths, who could say how many legal disputes they started in order to subvert what they had sworn to, as they sought to return their serfs, once freed from the yoke of customary demands, back to their original condition? For the bishop and nobles possessed an implacable ill will toward the citizens, and since the bishop did not have the power to revoke French liberties as they do in Normandy or England, forgetting his profession as shepherd to his flock, he wilted in the face of insatiable greed. Anybody among the people brought to trial was treated under the law not as a creature of God, but, if I may call it this, a creature of the court, and he would be drained to the last drop of all that he possessed.

Then, because bribery typically leads to the overthrow of all justice, the minters, knowing that if they sinned in their duties, they could find salvation through pecuniary redemption, debased the currency with so many counterfeits that a great many people were brought to extreme poverty. They minted coins from the cheapest bronze, and by some crooked technique used a tiny amount of silver to make them shinier. What shame! The foolish people were deceived, and in their exchanges with their genuine and counterfeit coins, they took away only slag of the least purity. The lord bishop's tolerance for this practice was rewarded, which hastened the misery of many not only within the province of Laon, but far and wide.[40] Pitifully helpless, and rightly so, to maintain or improve the value of his own store of money, which was so badly debased at his own doing, he decided in an act that was itself utterly debased to use obols from Amiens temporarily as the currency for his city. When these, too, he was entirely unable to hoard, he revived the practice of minting during his tenure, and had the coins stamped with a bishop's crozier to serve as his symbol. Everybody in private rejected these with such loud guffaws that they had less value than any of the debased currency.[41] In the meantime, to promote every issue of these new coins, decrees were circulated that no one mock the worthless impressions of him, providing numerous opportunities to prosecute the people on the grounds they had insulted the office of the bishop. Enormous revenues could thus be extorted from every possible direction.

In addition, there was a monk, thoroughly contemptible in the opinion of all, named Theoderic, a native of Tournai, who brought boundless quantities of raw silver from Flanders. He turned it all into the counterfeit money of Laon, which he scattered everywhere throughout the entire province. By these execrable gifts, he made himself a friend to the greed of wealthy men; he introduced deceit, perjury, and destitution and divested his homeland of truth, justice, and wealth. No enemy action, no pillaging, no burning brought greater harm to this province, as in former times the currency of this city had been welcome even within the walls of Rome.

But since

> Whenever impiety long hidden, but unwilling to be disguised,
> breaks through an artfully contrived cover of modesty,
> it shows through the face like a ray of light through glass,[42]

what he had done darkly to Gerard as if he had not done it, at a later time he did to another Gerard, giving clear proof of his cruelty.

This Gerard was some officer or overseer of peasants who belonged to him, and because he was rather favorably disposed toward Thomas (reputed son of Enguerrand) whom we spoke of above, of all the men we know in this generation the most dissolute, the bishop considered him a bitter enemy in every regard. He seized him and imprisoned him inside the episcopal palace, and then had his Ethiopian tear out the man's eyes.[43] By this deed he openly condemned himself to ignominy, and reopened the wounds he caused for what he had done to the other Gerard. Nor did it escape the clergy or the people that the canons of Toledo, if I'm not mistaken, prohibit bishops, priests, and clerics from capital punishment, death sentences, and mutilation.[44] News of this also reached the king, but I do not know if it went as far as the Apostolic See. I do know, however, that the pope suspended him from his office, and I think he did this for no other reason. But the bishop reached the height of his wickedness when, even though suspended, he dedicated a church. He departed for Rome, where he mollified the lord pope with repeated bribes, and returned to us with his authority restored. And thus God, upon seeing the magistrates and their subordinates share equally in this wickedness by their deeds or their consent to them, was no longer able to withhold his judgments, and allowed at last the evil designs they had conceived to reach the point of widespread fury. By God's vengeance, the bishop plunged headlong from haughty pride and crashed with a horrendous fall.

Near the end of Lent during the holy days of the Lord's Passion, he summoned the nobles and some clerics, having decided it was time to quash the commune he had sworn to along with the king, whose oath he had procured with bribes. He called upon the king for this pious duty, and the day before Good Friday (namely, the Lord's Supper),[45] he instructed the king and all the people to break their oath, which was a noose he had first put around his own neck. This was in fact the day Bishop Ascelin, his predecessor, betrayed his king, as I described above.[46]

For on the day when he ought to have performed the most glorious of all the bishop's duties, the consecration of the oil and the absolution of the people's sins, he was not even spotted entering his church. He was plotting with the king's vassals to have the king break the oath he had sworn and bring the laws of the city back to their former state. But the burghers, fearing their own overthrow, promised the king and his men four hundred pounds, or maybe it was more. The bishop in turn asked the nobles to go with him to speak with the king, and they at the same time promised seven hundred pounds. King Louis, son of Philip, a person of such distinction that the majesty of a king seemed the only thing fitting for him, strong in battle, without patience for lengthy negotiations, intrepid in spirit under adversity—although he was a good man in other respects, in this respect he was not altogether equitable, because, as happened in this case as well as others, he listened too much and gave excessive consideration to base persons corrupted by greed. This brought upon him damaging criticism, and upon many others their ruin.

And thus the king's desires, as I said, tilted toward the larger offer, and when contrary to God he ratified this decision, all their oaths (that is, the bishop's and the nobles') were broken, without any respect for honesty or the sanctity of the holy days. Because he had unjustly thrown the people into turmoil, that night the king, even though he had lodgings prepared elsewhere, was afraid to sleep anywhere except in the episcopal palace. After he departed at the break of dawn, the bishop turned to assure the nobles that they need not worry about having agreed to such a large sum of money, and should be secure in the knowledge that he would pay whatever they had promised. "And if," he said, "I do not do what I promised, hand me over to the royal jail for ransom."

Once the formal agreements to this commune were broken, such furor, such astonishment seized the hearts of the citizens that all craftsmen abandoned their trades, the cobblers and tanners shut their stalls, innkeepers rented no rooms, tavern owners offered nothing for sale, so that their thieving lords could not expect anything to be left over for them. For the bishop and nobles immediately began to take account of everyone's income, and whatever amount could be determined as each individual's contribution to inaugurate the commune was the amount he was required to pay to disband it.

This was done on the day of *Parasceve*, which means "preparation," and on the holy Sabbath—on the days when we receive the body and blood of the Lord—their thoughts were fixed only on homicide on the one side, and perjury on the other. What more? All the designs of the bishop and the nobles during these days were directed toward grinding down the livelihood of those beneath them. But their inferiors, no longer simply angry, but roused to a rabid ferocity, conspired in the death, or rather murder, of the bishop and his accomplices, giving their own oaths in turn. Forty of them swore together, they say, and their plot could not be kept concealed. For word of it reached master Anselm as evening fell that holy Sabbath. He sent a warning to the bishop, who was heading off to bed, not to attend the morning vigil, knowing that if he went he would be killed. But this extraordinarily stupid monster said, "Hah! Could I be killed at the hands of such people?" Although he spoke of them with disdain, he still did not dare arise for morning prayers and enter the church.

The following day, when he was to follow the clergy in procession, he ordered his servants and some soldiers to keep behind him with swords under their clothes. During the procession some small disturbance sprang up, as tends to happen in a crowd, and one of the burghers, thinking the murder plot they had sworn to had been set in motion, emerged from an archway and shouted twice in a loud voice as some kind of signal, "Commune! Commune!" A false alarm, it ceased immediately, but he still brought suspicion onto the opposing faction. When the service of the mass was finished, the bishop called out crowds of peasants from the episcopal estates to man the church towers and ordered them to guard his palace, though it was clear that they, too, were no less bitterly opposed to him, since they knew the piles of money he had promised the king would be drained from their own purses.

On the Monday after Easter,[47] the clerics were about to hold a customary gathering at Saint-Vincent. Since the conspirators realized they had been put under suspicion the previous day, they decided to make their attempt now, and they would have done it if they had realized all the nobles were all gathered together with the bishop. However, they came upon one of the nobles in the area just outside the city, a harmless man who had recently married one of my young cousins, a woman of instinctive modesty, but they did not want to attack him lest they make the others more wary. So when the Tuesday after Easter had come and gone and he felt more secure, the bishop dismissed those he had stationed on the towers and in the palace for his protection and compelled to live there on his own resources.

On that Wednesday, I made my way to him, since by the conflagration he started he had deprived me of my grain supply as well as some shoulders of pork, which are commonly called *bacons*. I urged him to save the city from this terrible storm, but he replied, "What do you think they can accomplish by their unruly behavior? If John, my Moor, dragged by the nose the most powerful man among them, he wouldn't even dare to whimper. Was I the one who forced them yesterday to renounce for as long as I live what they were calling their 'commune'?" I had spoken, and seeing that he turned away in disdain, I refrained from speaking to him further. Still, before I left the city, his inconstancy led to a bitterly acrimonious argument between us, but in the present evils, although many had warned him, he did not take anyone seriously.

VIII.

The next day, Thursday, he was spending the afternoon with archdeacon Gautier discussing how to go about exacting money, when suddenly throughout the city sounds of a disturbance rang out, with people shouting, "Commune!" And through the middle of the church of Notre-Dame, through the same door Gerard's killers had come and gone, an enormous throng of citizens entered the episcopal palace, carrying swords, two-headed axes, bows and hatchets, clubs and lances. Once they realized this was an attempt at revolution, nobles rallied to the bishop from every direction, whom they had sworn to protect in case of such an attack. During this onrush, the castellan Guimar, an older nobleman, very handsome in appearance and innocent in his behavior, was running through the church, armed only with a shield and spear, and as soon as he entered the bishop's courtyard, a certain Raimbert, even though he was his godfather, struck him in the back of the head with a two-headed axe—he was the first to die. Immediately after, Rainier, the man mentioned above whom my sister had recently married, was himself stabbed from behind with a lance as he hurried to enter the episcopal palace. He wanted to go up the steps into the bishop's chapel, but while trying was struck down in front of them, and soon a fire from the palace burned him completely below the groin. Ado the *vidame* was aggressive in battle,[48] but too aggressive in spirit, because his isolation among so many enemies made him ineffective. As he was heading for the bishop's house, he was set upon by the entire mob, but with spear and sword gave such resistance that three of the attackers at once fell at his feet. He then climbed on the dining table in the courtyard, and once his legs, in addition to the other parts of his body, had been wounded, kneeling before his attackers he lashed out this way and that and held them off for some time, until finally someone threw a spear into his exhausted body. Shortly afterward, a fire burned through these halls and reduced him to bare ashes.

The insolent mob, clamoring before the walls of the courtyard, then attacked the bishop. The bishop along with some of his defenders threw stones and shot arrows, fighting back as long as they could. He was always at his most energetic under arms, and as before so now, but because he had in vain taken up a sword he shouldn't, he perished by the sword.[49] Unable to withstand the audacious onslaught of the people, he put on the clothing of one of his attendants and fled into the church cellar. He hid himself in a small storeroom and thought he would not be found once he was shut up inside by a loyal follower who had blocked up the opening. Running here and there, they shouted not, "Where's the bishop?", but "Where's the villain?" They seized one of his young attendants, but because of his loyalty they could not force out of him anything they wanted. Dragging in another, when they asked where their quarry was, they received the answer with a perfidious nod. After entering the cellar and tearing it apart, they at last found him in the following way.

Theudegaud was a thoroughly sinister man, a dependent of the church of Saint-Vincent and long a subordinate and provost of Enguerrand of Coucy in charge of the crossing tolls at the bridge called Sort. He would keep an eye out for when there were only a few travelers, and after he robbed them of all they had, to ensure they did not have an opportunity to prosecute him, he threw them out into the river with lead weights attached to them. God only knows how many times he did this, since there is no one to tell the number of his thefts and robberies, but the unconstrainable, if I can call it that, wickedness in his heart showed on his horrid face. He had fallen into disfavor with Enguerrand and committed himself fully to the commune at Laon. Thus, a man who once spared no monk, no cleric, no pilgrim—indeed no man or woman at all—was in the end the one who would kill the bishop. As a leader and instigator of this criminal undertaking, he spared no effort in tracking down the bishop, whom he hated more than the others.

After they had searched the various containers one by one for him, Theudegaud stopped in front of the cask where the bishop was hiding. He banged on the lid and twice asked, "Who's in there?" Frozen with fear at his knocking, Gaudry could barely open his mouth to say, "A prisoner." The bishop used to call him Isengrin out of mockery for his wolflike appearance (that is what others call wolves), so this criminal man said to him, "Is Lord Isengrin hidden here?" Reviled as a sinner, but still anointed by the Lord, the bishop was dragged by the hair from among the containers, then beaten repeatedly and brought out into the open on the path to the cloister in front of the chaplain Godfrey's house. Even though he begged them for mercy in the most pathetic manner, and swearing on his oath he tried to plead with them—he would never from that day on be their bishop, would give them boundless wealth, would leave the country—their minds were set against him, and they all fell upon him. One man by the name of Bernard, known as de Bruyères, raised up a two-headed axe and savagely dashed the brains out of his holy yet sinful head.

He was slipping from between the hands of those holding him, but before he dropped to the ground, someone struck him from the side through the middle of the nose just under the eyes, and he fell dead. Then they cut off the legs and added many other wounds to the man they had already killed. Theudegaud noticed a ring on the late bishop's finger, but was not able to pull it off easily, so he cut off the finger from the corpse with a knife and stole the ring. Stripped bare, the bishop was thrown into a corner in front of his chaplain's house. My God, who could reveal how many mocking insults passers-by hurled at him as he lay there, how many clumps of mud, how many rocks, how much dirt covered his body!

Before we move on to other matters, I will tell of an occurrence just prior that contributed greatly to his undoing. Two days, if I'm not mistaken, before his death, the leaders of his clergy met in the middle of the church, and complained that the bishop had denounced them before the king during his recent stay in the city, when he said the clerics need not be respected because nearly all of them were descendants of the king's serfs.[50] Faced with this objection, he denied it, saying, "May the holy communion, which I just received from that altar"—he held out his right hand toward it—"bring destruction on me, and I invoke the sword of the Holy Spirit against my soul, if I ever said those things about you to the king." Upon hearing this, some of the clerics were completely astounded and claimed on their oaths that they had heard these things from his own mouth when he said them to the king. Indeed, the volatility of his mind and tongue produced for him this agonizing death.

IX.

Meanwhile, one part of the raging mob headed for the home of Raoul, the bishop's cupbearer and one of Gerard of Quierzy's closest friends. A man of slender build, but with a heroic spirit, he donned a cuirass and a helmet, as well as some light armor, intending to put up a fight, but when he saw their overpowering strength, he feared firebrands would be set and casting aside his arms, offered himself up in the form of a cross naked before their mercy. But God was far from him, and they cruelly slaughtered him as he lay flat on the ground.

Before the butchery of Gerard in the church, Raoul had had the following vision: he saw himself in the church of Blessed Mary, and there men of a twisted mien were gathered. They had set up a traveling show in the church, and were giving a strange performance for some people sitting around in a circle. During this spectacle, some men came out of Guy the treasurer's house, which was next to the church, carrying cups filled with a potion of such an awful stench it was unbearable to anyone who smelled it, and they passed them along the row of spectators. The meaning is clearer than day. Obviously what distinctly appeared to him was a horrid and hateful show given by demons, and the stench of the monstrous crime was wafting through every bit of that house. Indeed, the furious mob first cast firebrands onto that house, and from there the flames leapt onto the church and finally set fire to the episcopal palace.

Gaudry saw yet another harbinger of his future condition. In a vision, he recognized his arms bearer bringing him a message and saying, "Lord, your horse is of an unusually large size in the front, but in the rear so skinny—I have never seen anything like it." He had reached the height of his wealth and great worth earlier, but his abundant riches narrowed down to the poverty of such a dissolute death (for a horse signifies glory in the secular world).[51]

Thus it was the sin of one man that most of all condemned that most glorious church to its miserable downfall, since the fire was seen to creep into the church out of the home of the treasurer, who by simony was also an archdeacon. The church was majestically decorated with tapestries and draperies for the glories of the Easter celebration, and a few of the draperies are believed not to have been given over to flames but were instead ripped down and stolen as the fire spread. Some tapestries, however, succumbed to the flames because it was no easy job for just a handful of men to unhitch the pulleys from their hooks. The altar's gilt panels and the reliquaries of the saints were saved, along with their decorative covering, which is called a *repa*; everything else, I think, was destroyed by fires burning all around. One of the more distinguished clerics had entrenched himself beneath the reliquaries, not daring to leave lest he run into the roaming mobs, but when he sensed the flames beginning to crackle all around him, he ran to the bishop's chair, kicked through the central windowpane above it, and jumped out. The statue of the crucified Lord, splendidly covered in gold and decorated with gems, along with a lapis lazuli vase set before its feet, melted and sunk onto the ground, and it is being replaced only at great expense. After the church

and palace were consumed by the flames—something marvel-
ous to tell and a symbol of God's judgment!—either a piece of
burning wood or a smoldering ember flew over to the convent
and set fire to the church of Saint-Jean. It also reduced to ashes
the churches of Blessed Mary, which is called Profunda, and of
Saint Peter.

As for the wives of the nobles, I have no hesitation in telling
how they behaved during this difficult business. The wife of
the *vidame* Ado, when she saw that at the start of the revolt
her husband took sides with the bishop, believed her death was
imminent. She began to beg his forgiveness for any wrong she
might have ever committed against him, and as they held each
other close for the longest time, wailing and moaning and giv-
ing their final kisses, she said, "Why abandon me to the swords
of the townsmen?" He took his wife by the right hand while
still holding his lance, and when he ordered his steward to
carry his shield behind him, this steward—he was one of the
first traitors—not only did not carry his shield behind him,
but with harsh rebukes stabbed him from the back. He no lon-
ger recognized this man whose serf he had been, though he
had just recently served him dinner. Through the midst of
armed mobs, Ado protected his wife and hid her in the house
of one of the bishop's porters. But when she saw they were
under attack and fires had been set under the buildings, she
turned to flee wherever fate led her. She encountered some of
the women burghers, who grabbed her and beat her with their
fists. Stripped of the valuable clothes she wore, she just barely
made it to Saint-Vincent, dressed in a nun's habit.

My cousin, by contrast, had no concern for household pos-
sessions when her husband departed, but keeping only a cloak
for herself, she climbed the wall surrounding her garden with
a man's agility and leapt down the other side. Some poor woman
took her into her hut, but when a short time later she saw the
flames approaching, she rushed to the door, which the old
woman had bolted shut from the outside, and broke the bolt
with a stone. She then obtained a habit from a nun, a relative of
hers, and disguised herself under the veil, believing she would
find refuge among nuns. But now she saw the flames raging

within the convent, too, so she turned back her steps and went to a house slightly farther away, until the following day her relatives found her after a thorough search. The anguish she initially felt over her fear of dying then changed into more violent grief for her husband.

Some other women, including the wife and daughters of Guimar the castellan, hid themselves away with others in humble places.

When the archdeacon Gautier, who was with the bishop, saw the courtyard under attack, realizing that he had always added fuel to the fire, he jumped out of a window into the bishop's garden. Then, skirting along the wall into the vineyards, he traveled through the wilds with his head covered and hid in the castle of Montaigu.[52] The citizens, when they could not find him, laughed that his fear of them kept him in the sewers.

The wife of Roger, lord of Montaigu, named Armengard, was in the city that day (her husband, in fact, became castellan of the abbey after Gerard). Together with the wife of Raoul the plate bearer, wearing nuns' habits, if I'm not mistaken, she went through the valley of Bibrax to Saint-Vincent. Someone was carrying Raoul's son, about six years old, to safety under a long cloak, but a domestic servant crossed his path, and noticing the man carried something under his clothes, stabbed him at once between his arms.

That day and night clerics and women escaped through the vineyards by a path nestled between two mountain ridges. The men did not shrink from wearing women's clothes, nor the women men's. The fires on both sides had spread far, with winds turning the flames to this area, and the monks feared all their possessions would be burned. So great was the fear of those who had already fled there, it was as if swords were poised upon their necks. The fortunate Guy, archdeacon and treasurer, was absent from this business! Before Easter, he went on a pilgrimage to St. Mary of Vézelay, and the butchers complained bitterly of his absence.[53]

After the bishop and the leaders of the nobles had been killed, they went to attack the homes of others who survived.

The entire night they assaulted the house of William, son of Audouin, who had not agreed with his fellow citizens in Gerard's killing, but had gone with Gerard to the church to pray the morning he was killed. They set upon the structure with fire on one side and hatchets on the other, and chopped away at a wall with axes and pikes, while those inside put up a fierce resistance. At last he was forced to surrender, but by the wondrous judgment of God, though they hated him more than the others, they placed him in shackles, safe and unharmed, and treated the castellan's son the same way.

There was in William's house a young man, also called William, a chamberlain of the bishop, who earned great fame in its defense. When the house was captured, burghers who had taken possession of it asked him if he knew whether the bishop had been killed. (For one group had killed the bishop, while another was attacking the buildings.) He replied he did not know, but while walking around they found the bishop's corpse, and they asked the young man if he could find any distinguishing marks whereby they might identify the corpse lying there as the bishop's. The head and face were so badly mutilated with cuts that he was unrecognizable. The young man replied, "I remember while he was still alive he would often tell a story about military affairs, for which, to his detriment, he had the greatest ardor: he was riding a horse in a mock battle, and during the exercise he made an attack on a soldier. This knight struck him with a lance, and injured that part under his neck which they called the clavicle." They looked for the scar and found it.

When the abbot of Saint-Vincent, Adalbero, heard that the bishop had been killed, he wanted to go there, but was immediately told to his face that if he should interject himself into that raving mob, he would immediately suffer the same kind of violent death.

Those who were present for all these events claim that the daylight continued unbroken to the following day, and no sign of darkness indicated that it was time for sleep. When I objected that this was caused by the brightness of the fires, they argued on their oaths (and which was also true) that the fires had been extinguished or burned themselves out during the day. The fire at the convent, however, was powerful enough to incinerate some of the bodies of the saints.

X.

Almost no one passed by the bishop's corpse as it lay there without casting some insult or curse at it, though no one thought about his burial, so on the following day master Anselm, who during the turmoil of the revolt the previous day kept himself hidden away, poured out prayers before the authors of this tragedy that they allow the man to be buried in some way, especially since he had the title and insignia of bishop. They agreed, though just barely. The bishop had been lying naked on the ground, like a worthless cur, from the evening hours of that Thursday until the third hour of the following day, and at last the magistrate ordered his body to be picked up and taken to Saint-Vincent covered in a cloth. It is impossible to say how much abuse, how many threats were thrown upon the caretakers of this burial, how many curses were hurled like stones at the corpse. Carried into the church, he had no service proper for a Christian—I will not say for a bishop—at his funeral. A shallow grave was dug out to receive him, and the body was squeezed into such a small wooden coffin that his chest and stomach were pressed to the point of splitting open. Even granting the fact that his undertakers were, as I said, terrible, it is clear that everyone present urged them to do these things, so as to treat the miserable corpse as shamefully as they could.

On this day in the church the monks performed none of the divine offices. But why do I say "that day"? Rather for many days, since in their concern for the safety of those fleeing to them, they also feared their own deaths.

Then—it pains me to describe it!—the wife and daughters of Guimar the castellan, a truly noble family, soon after arrived with his body on a two-wheeled cart, pushing it and pulling it all by themselves. After him, Rainier was brought in by some peasant and a noble young girl, a relative of his, and he, too, in a pitiful manner: his lower half had been picked up somewhere and placed over the axle between the two wheels of a wagon, while the upper part still sizzled at the hips from the fires. About these two a good word was found, as it says in the book of Kings,[54] so that everyone of good sense grieved at their deaths. Except for their association with Gerard's killers, there was nothing of evil in them, and thus they were buried with far more compassion than their bishop. Only the smallest of the *vidame* Ado's remains were found after these many days of discord and fire, and these were kept tied up in a tiny bundle until the day Raoul, archbishop of Reims, came to reconcile the church. Solemn mass for the bishop and his accomplices was first performed only then, when he came to Saint-Vincent several days after their deaths. Raoul the plate bearer's elderly mother carried him in along with his young son on the same day as the others; he was buried somehow, with the son laid to rest upon his father's chest.

The venerable and wise archbishop, after he had moved some of the bodies of the dead into a better place, performed divine offices for them all among the extreme grieving of their friends and relatives, and during the mass he gave a sermon about those accursed communes where, contrary to what is just and right, servants violently tear themselves away from their lords.

" 'Let servants,' the apostle said, 'be subject to their lords in complete fear.'[55] And let servants not complain of their lord's severity or greed, but let them heed the rest of the verse: 'And not only to the good and gentle, but even to the ill-tempered.' It is clear in reliable canons that they are subject to anathema who on religious grounds instruct servants to disobey their lords, or to escape from them in any way, much less to resist. And there is further proof of this: no one is admitted to the clergy or the holy orders or monastic life unless he is exempt from servitude; but once admitted, he can in no way be held against the demands of the lords."

He argued this matter many times at the royal court, and often in different assemblies elsewhere. I got ahead of myself in speaking of all this, but now let us return to the order of the story.[56]

XI.

When the citizens considered the enormity and horror of crimes they had committed, they shrunk in dreadful fear of the king's judgment. They should have sought their remedy in him, but instead added one wound onto another when they charged Thomas, the reputed son of Enguerrand of Coucy who held the castle of Marle, with gathering forces to defend them against an attack by the king's men.[57] A robber of paupers and pilgrims to Jerusalem from his early adolescence, he became established through incestuous marriages, and his goal in attaining more power seemed to be the destruction of countless men. His cruelty was unheard of in our day—some who are also thought cruel were gentler in slaughtering cattle than he in slaughtering men. For he did not simply put to the sword those convicted of a crime, as is supposed to happen, but he completely butchered them with horrific torture. When he held any captives for ransom, he would hang them, sometimes with his own hand, by their testicles, and when these were torn away from their bodies, as happened frequently, their vital organs would burst out at almost the same time. Others he would hang by the thumbs or genitals, then place a stone over their shoulders to weigh them down, while he walked back and forth underneath them, and when he could not force out of them a possession that they could not possibly own, in a frenzy he beat them over their entire body with a stick until they promised anything that would satisfy him, or died from their torture. No one could say how many perished from starvation, disease, or torture while chained in his prison.

Two years before, when he went off to Mont Soissons to give aid to someone against some peasants, he saw three of them in a cavern, and coming up to the mouth of it with his lance, he thrust it and drove it through the mouth of one of the peasants. He drew the tip of the lance all the way back from the anus, covered in entrails. Why go on endlessly? The other two in there died at his hands.

One of his captives was once too wounded to continue marching. He asked the man why he didn't walk faster, but he was unable to respond. "Stay there," Thomas said, "I'll make it so you have some trouble going faster." Dismounting from his horse, he chopped off both the man's feet with a sword, because of which the man in fact died. It is pointless for me to continue describing deaths such as this, since there remains just as much of an opportunity to tell of it elsewhere. Let me return to the matter at hand.

For some time, Thomas harbored and supported Gerard's killers while they were under excommunication, and he cultivated the friendship of no one who was not a complete criminal. The saying of Sallust fits him better than Catiline: "He was evil and cruel for nothing."[58] Because of his record of wicked deeds, the citizens turned to him, and after praying that he come to them and protect them against the king, they at last welcomed his arrival in the city. After he heard their prayers, he consulted with his men as to what he needed to do, and they responded unanimously that his forces were not sufficient to hold a city of such size against the king. He did not dare to divulge this response to the frenzied citizens as long as he was in their city, but told them they would march out into the fields and there he would reveal his plan. When they were about a mile outside the walls, he began to speak, "Since this city is a capital of the kingdom, I cannot hold it against the king. But if you fear the king's arms, follow me to my territory and have me as your guardian and ally!" He completely unsettled them with this speech, and then frantic from fear of the crime they had committed and believing the king would soon have their heads, a countless mob fled with him. But Theudegaud, the bishop's killer—the man who with sword in hand had searched the rafters and cellars of Saint-Vincent and the deepest recesses of the cloister looking for fugitives to kill, who would show off the bishop's ring on his finger and swear he was bishop—he and his accomplices did not dare return to the city, but followed Thomas almost empty-handed. Thomas did release William, Audouin's son, and other captives in the city, since William had taken no part in Gerard's betrayal.

With the speed of Pegasus, rumor spread that the city was emptied of its inhabitants, which in turn roused the neighboring peasants and townsmen. Every rural dweller then rushed into the deserted city and, with no one to prevent them, took possession of fully furnished homes. Citizens, especially if they were wealthy, presented themselves in the guise of paupers, since they did not want to draw the eyes of the nobles to themselves.

At that time, the illegitimate and incestuous wife of the aforesaid Enguerrand began,[59] under an appearance of chastity, to spurn him, but really it was because of his old age and weight. Still, she could not go without her customary enjoyment of lovers. There was an extremely suitable young man she loved, but Enguerrand kept her away from any conversation with him, until she finally drove her husband crazy with her tantalizing allurements. He invited the young man and set him up in their house, and as a cover for the wicked love affair, he gave him their own young little daughter in marriage. He also made the young man guardian of their estate instead of Thomas, for whom Enguerrand, though said to be his father, had an incurable hatred and whom he wished to disinherit altogether. The young man was in Coucy at that time and made all sorts of proclamations that he would be Thomas' enemy, and though he lacked the financial means for such daring undertakings, by good fortune he experienced the following success.

When Enguerrand and Guy (this was the young man's name) heard that Thomas had left the city and the people followed him, they went to Laon and found there homes without people but filled with riches of every kind. There was such abundance in the homes (whose previous guardians had watched over them so carefully and had prevented massive losses to swindlers and thieves) that any effort to stop this young man would have been in vain, nor would he ever suffer from any want his entire life. Who could tell, or who could in the telling make anyone believe, how much money, how many clothes, how many foods of every type were found there? For when the groups from the fields and the suburbs, as well as people from Montaigu and Pierrepont, and La Fère, too,[60] all came here, before the men from Coucy, it would be a wonder to tell what the earlier men discovered and what they took away, when our more recent arrivals, although they came later, boasted they found every thing untouched and, as it were, untasted. But is there any judgment or moderation among madmen and scoundrels? Wine and wheat had no value, as they could be acquired just by looking around, and since men such as this had no sources of income in that place, they fell to ruin because of their own terrible lust. A quarrel arose among them about the proceeds of their plunder, and the more powerful claimed the right to whatever any of the lesser men had seized. If one man happened upon another two, he was sure to be robbed by them. This is how completely wretched the state of the city was: those who had earlier fled the city plundered and burned the homes of the clergy and nobles they hated, but now the remaining nobles seized from the homes of the exiles all the property and furnishings, down to the hinges, locks, and bolts.

Neither could a monk—not even one—safely enter or leave the city without being either deprived of his horse or stripped of his own clothes. Both the guilty and innocent gathered at Saint-Vincent with all the property they could carry. Lord God, the monks there saw swords drawn against them, by those who wanted not their money as much as their lives! There William, son of Audouin, forgetful of the escape granted to him by God, allowed servants of Guimar and Rainier, nobles who had been killed, to detain and punish one of his close companions, whom he had just promised security of life and limb and bound to himself in faith. After the son of the aforesaid castellan tied him by the feet to a horse's tail, he was dragged a brief distance until his brains spilled out, and then was hanged on the gallows; his name was Robert, nicknamed the Eater, a wealthy and upright man. The *vidame*'s dispenser whom I mentioned above, named Evrard if I'm not mistaken— the servant who betrayed his lord on the very day he had dined with him—was hanged on high. These kinds of death were exacted upon others as well, but it is impossible to sort out all that was done in the rioting or the punishment of the rioters.

However, one should know that Thomas arrived in the city the day after the bishop was murdered, which was Friday, and left on the Sabbath. On that Sunday God then unleashed his punishments for this tremendous crime. These events took place in the year of the Incarnation of the Lord 1112, the sixth day after Easter, April 27.

This bishop was, of course, a man of boundless frivolity, and if he thought of any worldly foolishness, he would let it slip from his tongue without the least hesitation. In fact, I saw him harass my cousin, whom I mentioned before, even though she was recently married in the city and behaved as chastely as possible, and even though I was listening: he said to her that she was "full of shit" and a "peasant," because she avoided the talk and glances of strangers and thus did not throw herself at him the way other women did. As well, I had written a book about the crusade to Jerusalem, which he was impatient to see, but after it was brought to him, he found it thoroughly abhorrent because I had named in the prefatory dedication my lord Lisiard, bishop of Soissons.[61] He then decided that it wasn't worth reading, yet he appreciated my other small works even beyond any value I put on them. And while he seemed to be capable of accumulating wealth, he would spend it all at once on useless things.

But though all these evils had fully ripened during his time in office, it should be recognized that he was not the only one responsible for them. Rather, they grew from the great wickedness of others, or perhaps of the entire populace. For never in all of France had there been crimes such as in Laon. Indeed, right before these events occurred, a priest sitting in his home by the burning coals was struck on the back and killed by a boy whom he considered rather close. The boy took the corpse and hid it in a secluded room that he locked from the outside. Some neighbors asked the boy if his lord had gone away, since they had not seen him for several days, but he lied and said the priest had gone somewhere or another on business. Since it was not possible to remain in the house because of the unusual stench, he gathered together his lord's possessions and placed the corpse facedown on the ashes in the fireplace. There was a piece of equipment hanging overhead, which they call a drying rack, and he threw that on top of him so people would think he had been crushed by its fall. Thus the boy fled with his property.

Deans of the church used to conduct cases involving priests in their diocese shortly before the end of each month. A priest named Burgund, who was overly talkative and rather impulsive, had accused a neighboring priest over some trifling matter, and the dean fined this priest a mere six silver coins for his fault. Exceedingly upset at this penalty, the priest who had lost his coins laid an ambush for Burgund when he returned home at night, and as Burgund climbed the steps to his house holding a lantern, this priest clubbed him from behind on the back of the head. He fell dead at the blow, without any witnesses.

Another priest, who himself detested a priest, ordered one of his attendants to shoot this priest with an arrow as he was conducting mass before the altar. Although the priest did not die from the blow, the instigator and contriver of the deed had the desire to kill, and was not exempted from a charge of murder and a sacrilege unheard of among Christians.

There were reports of other crimes committed at that same time and in the same district, and visions also appeared, presaging the evil I described. Someone saw the moon setting over Laon, which signified that justice in the city would suddenly fall into eclipse. Someone else among us saw three enormous beams set in a row before the knees of the crucified Lord in the church of Notre-Dame, and also saw the place where Gerard died covered with blood. The crucifix symbolized an eminent person of the church, and in fact three beams blocked his way: his corrupt entry into office, the sin he had committed against Gerard, and last his sin against the people, all of which served as the enormous stumbling block to his goal. The spot where Gerard met his end was covered in blood as long as there was no repentance to obliterate the wickedness perpetrated there.

In addition, I learned from the monks of Saint-Vincent that

the sounds of violent commotion were heard, believed to be
from malignant spirits, and the images of fires in the sky
appeared in the city during night hours. Also, some days before
a boy was born there, a twin from the waist up—he had two
heads and two bodies, each with its own arms, down to the
kidneys, and thus split in two above, united in one below. He
was baptized and he died on the third day. There were, in the
end, many visions and abnormal phenomena whose meaning
was not doubted in the least, because they foretold that greatest
of evils to follow.

XII.

A little after the storm had calmed, the clergy began to work,
bit by bit, to restore the church. The intensity of the flames
appeared to have weakened the wall next to where Gerard was
killed more than the rest, so they erected at no little expense
some arches between the middle section, where the fire dam-
age was worse, and the outer structure. One night, there was a
tremendous crash of thunder, and the impact of the thunder-
bolt caused such a violent rattling that the arches affixed to
the wall broke apart and the wall tilted to one side, making it
necessary to tear it down completely.

O, the wondrous judgment of God! What must be the sever-
ity of your judgment, Lord, against those who inflicted punish-
ment on a man standing before you, praying to you in some
way, if the insensible wall where it happened was not allowed to
escape unharmed! Nor was it an injustice, Lord, that you were
aggrieved at such an injustice. If an enemy of mine cast himself
down before my knees to seek forgiveness and was then killed at
my feet by an enemy of his, all of my animosity for him, because
of the outrage he had committed against me, would at once be
laid to rest. This is the way with us men, but you, God, are the
very source of mercy. If in the reign of Herod you crowned
infants completely ignorant of you simply because you had been
the cause of their destruction, must we think that you would
harden your heart against this man, an undeserving sinner, yes,

but murdered in utter contempt of your name?[62] This is not your way, you who are boundless piety.

Meanwhile, in the customary way, such as it is, for collecting money, they began to carry around the reliquaries and the saints' relics, and so it happened wherever they went, that that holy judge, who punishes some and brings merciful consolation to others, produced numerous miracles. Carried inside a small chest, itself not particularly noteworthy, was a magnificent little reliquary that contained part of the Virgin Mother's cloak, part of the sponge put to the Savior's lips, and part of the true cross (I am not sure if there was any of our Lady's hair). It was made of gold and gemstones, and a verse inscribed in gold told of the mysteries within it.[63]

On their second journey, they went into the district of Tours and arrived at a town called Buzançais, which was under the control of some bandit. They delivered a sermon to the people, and among other things, told of their church's misfortunes. Our clergy sensed that this lord and his garrison harbored evil thoughts at the sermon and that they intended to rob them as they left the castle, putting the one charged with speaking in a tight spot. Even though he had no faith in what he promised, he nevertheless said to the people standing nearby, "If there is anyone ill among you, let him approach the holy relics, and when he drinks from waters the relics have touched, he will immediately be cured." Gladdened at the thought they could catch the clerics as liars from their very own words, the lord and his garrison presented him with a mute and deaf boy around twenty years old.[64] No one could possibly describe the anxiety the clergy felt in their predicament at that moment. As they breathed deeply and offered prayers to the Lady of all and to her only-begotten Son, Lord Jesus, he drank the holy water. The priest nervously asked him a question, to which he gave a clear response—not an answer to what was asked, but an exact echo of the priest's words, since never having heard anything before, he did not know anything to say except what was said. Why prolong the story? In this poor town their hearts at once outdid one another in generosity, and the lord of the town then donated the only horse he had, while the offerings from the rest

nearly exceeded their means. They became such loyal support-
ers of the men they had wanted to betray, who meanwhile tear-
fully praised God their helper, that they handed over the young
man who had been healed to be a constant keeper of the saints'
relics. I saw him in our church in Nogent, dull witted and with-
out the education to talk about or understand anything, but by
his service he proved a faithful herald to this great miracle, and
a short time later died in the course of his duties.

In the city of Anjou there was a woman who had married
when she was still a girl. At this tender age she had placed a
ring on one of her tiny fingers and wore it day and night, irre-
tractably if I can describe it so. As years were added to her
young age, she grew plumper, and flesh protruded from both
sides of the ring, almost completely concealing the metal band.
As a result, she had no hope of ever removing it from her fin-
ger. The holy relics arrived, and after the sermon she came to
make an offering along with the other women. When she
stretched out her hand before the reliquary to deposit the
money she was holding, the ring audibly cracked and dropped
from her hand in front of the relics. When the people, espe-
cially the women, saw how the Virgin Mother had bestowed
such favor upon this woman, which even she herself did not
dare to seek, the offerings of silver coins from the people, and
more so of necklaces and rings from the women, were impos-
sible to count. The district of Tours rejoiced in the fragrant
bouquet of miracles performed by the Lady who is the mistress
of all, while Anjou boasted they truly had the mother of God
close at hand.

Somewhere else—I cannot say exactly in which town it hap-
pened, but it was still in the same diocese—the clergy brought
the relics to a virtuous woman, who had pleaded with all her
might, since she had been ill for the longest time without any
hope of recovery. After she worshipped the relics with a sin-
cere heart and drank the holy water in which they had been
bathed, with Mary as her healer she instantly recovered, and
then honored God's relics with all due offerings. The cleric
carrying the relics had just stepped over the threshold of her
house, when there before him was a boy astride a horse pulling

a carriage, about to block the middle of the lane the cleric had intended to cross. The cleric said to him, "Wait until the relics have passed." Once the carrier of the relics had crossed, the boy spurred on his horse to resume his journey, but he could not budge from the spot. The carrier of the relics looked back and said, "Go in the name of the Lord!" As soon as he said this the horse and carriage moved forward. Behold the power in Mary, and the reverence she commands!

On their third journey, they happened to arrive at a castle in Nesle.[65] Raoul, the lord of the castle, kept a young deaf-mute in his home. They claimed he also possessed knowledge of divination, undoubtedly from demons, and the lord was also said to have great love for him because of this. The holy relics were brought into the castle, and the people honored them with rather scant offerings. This deaf-mute, however, who had already been made aware through signs of the previous deaf-mute's healing and in fact now saw him right there in front of him, gave his shoes to a pauper and followed the holy relics all the way to the monastery at Lihons, with bare feet and a mind filled with devotion. One day while he was napping under the reliquary, the hour for dinner arrived. Most of the clerics went off to eat while a small number remained to keep watch over the relics, and then they, too, went for a short walk outside the church. When they returned they found him lying on the ground in a violent seizure with blood pouring from his mouth and ears in a great stench. At the sight of this the clerics hurriedly brought their colleagues who had gone to eat to see the spectacle of such a miracle. Once the boy had recovered from his spasms, the clerics asked him a question to test whether he was able to speak, and he responded to the questioner by repeating the words he had heard. All raised to heaven the boundless glories of God on high. Who could describe their cries of joy? Then the people of Nesle begged and prayed for them to return to their town, so that they could make full good on what they had failed to offer the relics the first time, and indeed they did so to an exceptional degree. In this case too the Lady shone in her glory, for God her Son brought to fulfillment the gifts of nature he had until that day withheld.

XIII.

Next they intended to head across the sea, and when they came to that mediterranean ocean they embarked on a ship together with some wealthy merchants.[66] Traveling the sea with favorable winds, suddenly they saw bearing down on them the swift galleys of pirates, whose cruelty they feared terribly. The pirates swept the waters with their oars as they advanced, the prows of their ships plowing through the swells, and they were now barely a stadium distant from our ships,[67] to the great dread of the carriers of the relics as well as the laymen on board. Then one of our priests arose from their midst and lifted up the reliquary containing the relics of the Queen of Heaven, forbidding the pirates to approach in the name of the Son and the Mother. At this command, their ships immediately turned to stern, and [were driven off][68] with no less swiftness than they had when they had eagerly sped forward—a cause for praise and glory among all those saved. With abundant thanks to Blessed Mary, the merchants gave many valuable offerings to her.

They reached England successfully, and when they came to the city of Winchester, numerous miracles shone forth there. At Exeter, too, miracles occurred in equal measure, providing the motivation for many offerings. Let me pass over in silence the usual remedies for illnesses, and describe instead the unusual. I will not write an account of their travels, for they themselves have done so, nor will I describe every single event individually, but select those that preach a message.

In nearly every locale they were received with appropriate reverence, but then they came to a village where no priest allowed them shelter in the church, no peasants in their homes. They found two uninhabited buildings there and gathered themselves into one along with all their baggage. The other they used for the holy relics. The wicked people there hardened their hearts to divine matters, and the next day, after the clerics had moved on from the area, with a rumbling of thunder a terrifying bolt of lightning fell from the clouds and destroyed that rural settlement, turning all the dwellings in it into smoldering ash. O wondrous judgment of God! Although those two houses were located in the middle of other houses that were burning, they remained standing, and thus God gave clear proof that those wretched men suffered this fire because of their lack of reverence for the mother of God. But the disgraceful priest, who had increased the savagery among the barbarians he should have instructed, collected his furnishings, rejoicing he had saved them from the heaven-sent fires, and traveled either to a river or the sea intending to cross. There, while trying to transport everything he had collected, he suddenly found it all consumed by lightning. Thus was this wild and undisciplined people taught by its own punishments and made to understand the mysteries of God!

They came to some other town where the proven fame of their miracles excited offerings of every kind for the holy relics. An English man standing in front of the church said to his friend, "Let's go drinking." His friend replied, "I don't have any money," to which the man said, "I'll loan you some." "Where will you get it?" his friend asked. "I was thinking that these clerics—with their lies and magic tricks—get lots of money out of these fools. I'll find some way to collect something out of my own offerings!" So he spoke and went into the church. He approached the raised platform where the relics had been placed, and pretending he wanted to kiss them in veneration, he brought his mouth close. Sticking out his lips, he sucked up some of the silver coins laid there as offerings. He returned to his friend and said, "Come on, let's have a drink together. Now we have enough money for both of us to drink!" His friend asked, "Where did you get it? You didn't have any just now." "I stole it from the money given to those charlatans in the church," he replied, "and carried it away in my mouth." "You did a bad thing, taking it from the saints," his friend said. "Be quiet! Go in this tavern right here." Why prattle on? Their drinking lasted until they nearly brought the sun down to the sea. When evening fell, the one who had stolen the money from the holy altar mounted a mare, and claimed he was going home. But when he came to a nearby wood, he made a noose and hung himself from a tree. Let this be a sufficient selection of the many deeds performed among the English by the Virgin who reigns supreme.

Back at Laon, after they had returned from soliciting money, there was a good-natured cleric who had been given the duty of transporting material for repairing the church roof. He told me that as he was going up the mountain, one of the oxen had given out from exhaustion, and while the cleric was fretting terribly at not finding another ox to take the yoke of the exhausted one, an ox suddenly showed up at a run, as if it came on purpose to help with the work. At a rapid pace, the ox drove the wagon with the others all the way back to the church. The cleric then anxiously worried to whom he should return this unknown ox, but as soon as it was unyoked, it did not wait for anyone to lead it away or to drive it on, but swiftly retraced its steps back to where it had come from.

On the occasion the cleric told me this, he also told another story—how, on the same day that Bishop Gaudry departed for Rome, after arranging for the murder of Gerard, he was standing behind a priest during mass (in fact, a deacon), when suddenly, though the day had been clear and calm without a single gust of wind, a gilded eagle set atop the chest containing the reliquaries popped off and fell, as if from a violent blow. At the time, some men interpreted this event as a sign that an eminent person from that place, namely the bishop, would soon die. But I believe that, while it perhaps had that meaning, it also signified how the fortunes of this city, among all the cities of France the most regal, had fallen, or rather I think they will fall further. For during that crisis in the city I described, the king himself, whose greed had brought it on, did not come back even once. Even the royal provost, fully aware of the wickedness soon to be perpetrated, left the city a few hours before the uprising took hold of it, having first sent ahead his concubine and children. Before he had gone three or four miles, he saw the city engulfed in flames.

XIV.

Once Bishop Gaudry had thus been removed, people began to accost the king's ears with appeals to elect another. They received instead a dean from Orléans with no election. The king's chancellor, named Stephen, who could not be bishop, had been campaigning to get that deanery, so he obtained from the king the bishopric for this man, and he received the deanery of Orléans.[69] As he was presented for consecration, they hunted for a prophetic verse about him, but found only a blank page, as if to say, "I will make no prophecy about him, since almost nothing will be done." In fact, he died a few months later, but he did rebuild some of the episcopal buildings.

At this bishop's death, the current one was elected legitimately and reluctantly; I mean legitimate in the sense that his entry into office involved no venality, nor did he attempt to do anything through simony. Yet the passage of the Gospel in his prophecy had an unpleasant ring, because it was the same as Gaudry's: "A sword will pierce your (that is, his) soul."[70] What the misfortune threatening him is, God shall see.

Before we move on to other matters, I have to mention that Theudegaud, the betrayer and killer of the bishop, was captured by Enguerrand's soldiers two years after the murder and hanged from the gallows. He was seized during Lent, after he had eaten and drunk enough to make almost anyone vomit, then rubbing his belly as he stuck it out boasted in front of some others that—an unspeakable thing to say!—he was filled with the glory of God. Arrested and imprisoned, he begged forgiveness neither from God nor from man; he did not even say anything to anybody when he was led out for punishment, and he died with the same apathetic attitude toward God with which he lived. But now let me return to matters I passed over.

Thomas had harbored, together with that hateful commune, those wicked men who had first murdered Gerard and then the bishop, his lord and relative. Archbishops and bishops throughout France repeatedly struck him with anathema, not only in councils, synods, and royal courts, but also on every Sunday in all parishes and cathedrals, and as his unspeakable villainy spread everywhere. His stepmother, the woman whom Enguerrand had wickedly claimed for himself, with a mind more savage than a wild bear, saw Thomas emerge as her rival, and forced Enguerrand to repudiate his fatherly affection for him as well as the very name of father. Once Enguerrand excluded Thomas from his legal inheritance and became his declared enemy, she used her feminine wiles, to borrow a saying from comedy, to make a madman out of a fool.[71] His mind, steeped in evils that every day exercised a little more power over him, finally erupted into such madness that he claimed it was just and right for him to believe slaughtering men was no different from beasts. Since that woman had had him unjustly disinherited, as things stood, he and his accomplices believed they could justly engage in an orgy of killing. Always with new schemes, that utterly savage woman would every day procure enemies she could expose him to for his destruction. He, on the other hand, never rested from seeking vengeance against Enguerrand through constant pillaging, burning, and murder.

In our generation I have seen no other two people, united in one purpose, who have caused so many of the evils that we have witnessed. If he was the furnace, we could call her the fuel. On both sides their character was such that even though they freely indulged in sexual activities with all and sundry, nevertheless, if they encountered any obstacle, their ferocity would not lessen, but rather intensify. For just as the laws of marriage never held her back, so his individual wives could not keep him from acting shamefully with prostitutes or jealously coveting the flesh of other women. What more can I say? She would rile him up every day by devising some new scheme, and he could not sate his rabid fury with the murder of innocents—even when in one day he tore out the eyes of ten men, who died instantly—until out of mutual exhaustion they would call a temporary truce. But soon after she would open up the old wounds and they would rise up again in mutual killings.

While the province of Laon suffered the convulsions from their malignant spite, at God's judgment a calamity was brought upon Amiens. After the fatal events of Laon's downfall, the people of Amiens enticed the king with money to form a commune, which the bishop, under no compulsion to do so, should not have supported, especially since no one was pressing him to nor were the wretched deaths of his fellow bishop and the conflict among the accursed burghers unknown to him.[72] As soon as Enguerrand, the count of the city, saw that the long-standing rights of his office were being rescinded because the burghers had sworn to this commune, he advanced upon them as rebels with what forces he could muster. There to support him were Adam (this was in fact his name) and the garrison of the tower he commanded, and when the inhabitants of the city had repulsed Enguerrand, he withdrew from the city to the tower. They pressed the count hard with unrelenting assaults, and called upon Thomas to swear to the commune as if he were the lord dearer to them. Thus they roused a son against his presumed parent. In fact, Thomas considered his mother utterly scandalous, and therefore always lacked any affection for his father.[73] Enguerrand, meanwhile, realizing that the butchers and innkeepers were mocking the "weightiness" of his age, summoned Thomas and made a treaty with him, and also instilled in the stepmother, upon swearing countless oaths, a new love for him. She, of course, served herself well in this, and exacted from him no little weight in treasure for renewing the peace.

Once Thomas had exhausted most of his own vast store of treasure, he promised Enguerrand military assistance against the burghers, whom the bishop supported together with the *vidame*. Thomas and Adam, who was in command of the tower, thus began a vigorous attack on the *vidame* and burghers, and then, accusing the bishop and the clergy of being in league with the burghers, Thomas plundered the church of its wealth. In one of the church manors, he established a stronghold from which he then annihilated the rest of the church holdings with burning and plunder. From one of them he took away captives in large numbers as well as a vast sum of money, and he burned to death the rest of the people (or at least the greater part of them), a mixture of different ages and both sexes, by setting fire to the church where they had fled. Among the captives was a hermit who had come to the village to buy bread. After his capture, he was led before Thomas. The feast of Saint Martin was close at hand—the following day, in fact—and as he tearfully and disconsolately explained to

Thomas what his profession was and why he had come there, and asked him to have pity on him at least out of respect for Saint Martin, Thomas drew his sword from its sheath and drove it through his heart and innards, saying, "In the name of Saint Martin, take that!"

On the same occasion he also imprisoned a leper. When the colony of lepers in the province heard of this, they besieged the tyrant's doors with pleas that he return their fellow leper to them, but he threatened to burn them alive if they did not leave. They fled in terror, and once they were safe and all of them from the area had gathered, they called upon God to take vengeance on him. Raising up their voices in unison they cursed Thomas. The leper, however, ended his days in punishment and prison. A pregnant woman put in jail at the same time also died there.

When some of his captives were marching on their journey a little slowly, he ordered the area beneath their necks, which they call the clavicle, to be punctured, and had a rope run through this hole in five or six of them, if I'm not mistaken, and in this way they marched on in painful torment. Shortly afterward, they died in custody. Why drag the story out? In that incident he alone killed thirty men with his sword.

Seeing that Thomas had placed himself in grave danger, his stepmother, in her eagerness to destroy him, commanded the *vidame* to keep a careful watch for his departure. One night, as Thomas was heading somewhere, the *vidame* surrounded him in an ambush; his limbs covered in wounds, he also took a foot soldier's lance to the back of the knee. Injured all over, but most grievously in his knee, he was forced, whether he wanted to or not, to leave off what he had started.

The bishop, however, before his church had suffered all this devastation, was about to conduct mass on a feast day. Without realizing it, a pious priest, at least in appearance, performed the sacrament before him with water alone, and after him, the same thing also happened to the bishop. When he took a sip, and realized it was nothing but water, he said, "Know for certain that a great evil threatens this church." The priest's misfortune, which had happened first, only reinforced these words.

The bishop, unable to please anyone, had realized that neither the clergy nor the people welcomed his presence, so he took one of our monks as a companion and without consulting anyone gave written notice of divorce, if I can call it that, to his clergy and people. He returned the ring and sandals of his office to the archbishop of Reims, and sent a message to both parties that he was going into exile and would never again be a bishop. He thus became an ex-bishop, but when he reached Cluny, on his own accord he became a bishop again and consecrated the altar there. He next went to Chartreuse, described in the beginning of this work, and there lived in a cell outside the convent, keeping with him six silver marks from his travel money. After two months, he was called back not by any of his people, but by the archbishop, and there was no reason for him to delay his return, since he had knowingly set aside the silver marks for this purpose.[74] The clergy and people, however, received him not without some sorrow, since in his absence they had not busied themselves with electing another while equally rejecting him, for he had excited a mob he could not calm down.

Thomas, now powerless to act because of the injury mentioned above, was carried back to his home. Meanwhile, Adam's son Alleaume, a very handsome boy, had become engaged to Thomas' daughter, so this shameful concubine of Enguerrand,[75] now that she had weakened Thomas, prepared to turn her weapons against Adam and his tower. He, however, had remained till then steadfast in his loyalty to Enguerrand against the burghers. She therefore bribed the king to surround the tower with a siege. But it is well known that Adam had paid homage to the king, nor had he defected from him, and the king had received him in his fealty.[76]

No one, not even those whose lives were endangered during this time, could count how many burghers were murdered at the hands of the tower guards—a great many before the siege but afterward even more so. The inhabitants of the city did nothing actively, only passively suffered. As everyone knows, Godfrey could have easily prevented this at the beginning, before the evil spread, if he had not feared the *vidame*, who always had the utmost contempt for him. It was plainly his character to respect only those who spoke ill of him, and to treat well only those who treated him badly. Since from his fear of being bitten by this one man, he eagerly tried to please him, knowing full well he was an utterly perfidious man, at God's just judgment he was torn to pieces by everyone, and by him most of all.

Thomas was unable to bring relief to the tower, into which he had sent his daughter and the more trustworthy of his soldiers. Moreover, because he had done such evil deeds everywhere, the archbishops and bishops, when granted a hearing before the king on behalf of the churches, said they would not perform God's offices in his kingdom unless he brought vengeance against Thomas. For at the same time that plague of a man was supporting the burghers against Enguerrand, the aforesaid Gautier,[77] who together with his fellow archdeacon Guy were the only ones left of Gerard's betrayers, had gone around the middle of Lent to speak to that noble counselor of Enguerrand's.[78] She was his half sister by the same mother, and he had also helped to concoct this adulterous marriage. When Thomas learned of this, he hurriedly sent a message with an order for a certain Robert, the worst sort of criminal (just the kind of servant he liked), that with as many men as possible he watch for Gautier to return from Amiens and that he kill him. Keeping a lookout from no place except the promontory of Laon, Robert went with his men along the bend in the road that descends the mountain and met him in his path. Gautier had sent his escort on ahead, and now followed them from behind, riding a mule toward the city. When they caught sight of him alone, they struck him down savagely with their swords, and at his death, they gleefully returned to Thomas with the mule.

When the king's ears were assailed with these and similarly mournful laments from the churches, during the Lenten season after the archdeacon's murder he mustered an army against Thomas and attacked the strongholds he had erected in the domains of the abbey of Saint-Jean. The king did not enjoy wholehearted support from the knights, who were also few in number, but he had an altogether endless column of light-armed foot soldiers. Upon hearing about the assembly of this force, Thomas ranted foolish nonsense, still lying completely helpless in his bed. He spat back most foully the king's warnings to tear down his unauthorized fortifications, and he hissed at the numerous offers of assistance from his relatives. Then the archbishop and the bishops, mounting a high platform, summoned the people and made a call to arms because of these troubles: they absolved them of their sins, and calling it an act of repentance, commanded them to make a charge on the castle (called Crécy), assured about the salvation of their souls.[79] The daring with which they made their assault was indeed miraculous. The fortifications, however, were remarkably solid, such that many came to see their entire effort as absurd. Those inside the castle were fully committed to its defense, yet when the king captured the first palisade, he stood at the castle gate and called up a warning to the garrison to surrender the tower to him. When they said they would not, he stretched out his hand and swore he would not eat until it was taken. Nevertheless, that day he called off the attack. He returned the next day to resume the battle, but hardly a single one of his knights wanted to take up arms with him. After he accused them of open rebellion, he called on the foot soldiers and was the first to attack the palisade and then began to make for the interior.[80] He immediately broke through to the inside and found an enormous quantity of food. The defenders were captured and the fort torn down.

Not far from here Thomas had established another fortified castle, called Nouvion; its keys were handed over to the king, and the inhabitants fled. Some of the captives were hanged on the gallows at Crécy, to terrify their supporters; some were killed elsewhere. As for the attackers, I do not know of any who were killed except for one soldier. Thomas, however, was safely ensconced at Marle; by purchasing his redemption from the king and the king's men as well as agreeing to pay for the damages he had done to the churches, he restored himself to peaceful relations with the one and to communion with the other. Thus this most haughty and depraved of men was punished by a band of the most impoverished, whom he had often punished in scorn.

It must not be left unsaid that when the king arrived in Laon with his army, the mild weather turned completely stormy. Then the archbishop said before them, "We pray to God, that if he wills what we propose, he grant us good weather!" As soon as he uttered the prayer, the weather again became clear and sunny.

Godfrey returned from Chartreuse on Palm Sunday,[81] and began to spread ideas far different from what he had learned there. He chastised the king, and on a day for celebration and worship, attempted to incite him and the people against the inhabitants of the tower—he delivered not a sermon of God but a Catilinarian,[82] promising the kingdom of heaven for those who perished in the attack on the tower. The next day enormous siege towers were arrayed before the wall of Castillon (this was its name) and manned with soldiers. The tower inhabitants, however, had hidden themselves behind a bastion wall, so as not to betray their presence. As for the bishop, he had departed barefoot for Saint-Acheul, since at that time no one would pay any heed to him about this. Meanwhile, the people in the tower allowed the attackers to approach the walls and move up the siege towers. When these were in place, Aleran, a man who was very experienced in these matters, set opposite them two catapults he had constructed, and assigned about eighty women to launch the stones he had piled up while the soldiers inside fought with swords at close quarters against those coming from outside.[83] On equal footing with the men, the women defended their fortifications with the courage of Achilles, and launching stones from their catapult battered down both siege towers. Though a feverish barrage of missiles, it was reported, wounded the eighty women, they also injured the king with a blow to his armored chest. Of those who were struck by an arrow, only one escaped. Rohard, the bishop's nephew, told me these details.

Seeing they were being overwhelmed, the soldiers hanging onto the siege towers turned to flight, and the rest followed without delay. A little while after the attackers had withdrawn, the tower inhabitants rushed out and dismantled the siege-towers, gathering the building materials for their own use as their former attackers looked on from a distance, not daring to approach within roughly three miles. When the king realized the place was impregnable, he called off the attack and ordered a blockade until hunger drove them to surrender. It has continued to this day, and there is no telling the number of burghers alone who perish nearly every day. Adam, however, taking up a position beyond the areas around the city, harried both Enguerrand and the *vidame* with frequent attacks. If distress gives understanding to the hearer,[84] then he would know that, although it was Thomas who suffered defeat, not every case has two equal sides, nor do God's judgments evenly balance out for everyone so as to permit a bishop to incite men to murder.

XV.

Before I fall to describing events nearby—I intend to speak also of some inhabitants of Soissons—it must be acknowledged that the people of Laon do more abominable deeds than the people in all the other provinces of France. For after having murdered priests, a bishop, and an archdeacon, most recently they also murdered a most resourceful woman of illustrious birth, an abbess of Saint-Jean and a benefactress of her church named Rainsende. Her own servant, a native of Laon, killed her. She suffered what she did for her faith in her church. And what of the church itself—need I mention it was not untouched by acts of sacrilege? But because the queen of all did not allow these deeds to go unpunished, I will tell of them next, as appropriate.

Some of those whom they call sextons, rather lowly dependents who guard the treasures of the church, began to pilfer the vessels used in divine worship and to shift the blame onto the clergy who were their masters (they were obviously laymen). Whoever was involved in the first theft, the second time Anselm, a savage peasant born from the common people of the city, absconded with crosses, chalices, and other gold pieces before matins during Christmas week. Some time later he offered to sell a small lump of stolen gold to a merchant in Soissons and revealed to him the sacrilegious theft he had committed. He received an oath from the merchant not to betray him, but in the meantime the merchant heard that those guilty of the theft had been excommunicated throughout the parishes of Soissons. Once he became aware of this, he came to Laon and revealed the matter to a cleric. Why say more? Anselm was accused, but he denied it. The merchant, on the other hand, offered sureties and called him out to a duel, nor did Anselm decline. It was a Sunday, and spurred on by the clergy, they fought until the thief's challenger fell beaten. There are two apparent explanations for this: either the one who broke his oath and betrayed the thief did not act rightly or, more likely, he bound himself to a completely illegitimate law. There is certainly no canon that agrees with this law.[85]

Feeling more secure because of his victory, Anselm broke out into a third sacrilege, and by some trick that cannot be described he broke into the treasure chest and carried off gold and gems in even greater quantity. For this theft, the ordeal of the holy water was performed.[86] Plunged into it with the other sextons, he floated on the surface and was convicted, and along with him others involved in the first crime, some of whom were hanged on the gallows, while others were spared. When he was dragged to the gallows with the rest, he promised he would talk, but once released he refused. The second time he was led to the gallows, he swore he would reveal the matter. Released again, he said, "I won't do anything without a reward." "You will be hanged," they replied. "And you will have nothing," he said. All the while he was heaping endless abuse on the castellan Nicholas, the son of Guimar,[87] a young man of great fame, who was handling the proceedings. The bishop and master Anselm conferred as to what should be done. "It is better," they said," to give him money than to lose so much gold." They made an agreement with him for around five hundred sous, and receiving their guarantees, he returned much of the gold he had hidden in his vineyard.

He had, in fact, promised to leave the country, for which the bishop had granted him a grace period of three days. Intending to slip away secretly during this time, he reconnoitered all the exits of the city, but no matter what direction he looked, he saw images of broad rivers that made it impossible to take a step outside. These waters flowing invisibly through his imagination were forcing him to leave openly without any profit from his theft, and when the three days was up, raving like a lunatic, he said he was unwilling to depart. As the bishop now began to press him harder, like someone out of his senses he began to mutter that he still knew some things that he had put off telling. When the bishop learned of this from the *vidame*, he took the opportunity to withhold the sous he had planned to give Anselm and imprisoned him, since he had sworn he knew nothing more. Under torture he confessed he had in his possession cut gems, and leading them to the spot, pointed them out perched under a rock in a linen cloth. In addition to these, he had also taken the holy reliquaries, and had not been able to sleep the whole time he had had them, for the saints lashed out at his savage mind until horror at his great sacrilege overcame him. He, too, was hanged on high, and placed next to his fathers, who were clearly demons.[88]

XVI.

Now, to direct my pen to what I had promised, Count Jean of Soissons was a skilled military strategist, eager for peace, but his only intention was to benefit himself. The villainy he had inherited from his father and grandfather always turned back to the destruction of the mother church. By the same token, his mother once ordered a deacon's tongue ripped from his throat and his eyes gouged out—just one of the wonders she was capable of. No one should be surprised that she possessed the daring to commit murder: once, with the help of a Jew, she poisoned her own brother because she lusted after his estates. For his assistance, the Jew was also killed, consumed by fire. But on the day before she was to observe the first day of the Lenten fast, she had a marvelous feast, and that night, as soon as she began to fall asleep, a paralysis overcame her—she lost the use of her tongue, her entire body was enfeebled, and above all, she no longer had any feelings as far as God was concerned, and lived out her life like a pig. By God's righteous judgment, her own tongue was nearly cut out in an attempt to cure her. She remained in this condition from the beginning of Lent until the octave of Easter, when she ended her days. She and her sons, Count Jean and Bishop Manasses, had their quarrels, but they also possessed a deadly, inborn enmity: in this family everyone hated everyone else. In fact, after his mother had been carried to her tomb, the count himself told me the things I just recounted, even as she was being buried, and he added: "Why should I spend money on her, when she didn't want to spend anything on her own soul?"

One could rightly say to the count, "Your father was an Amorite, you mother a Hittite,"[89] and he not only showed himself to be the son of both his parents but behaved much worse. He was so completely devoted to the falsehoods of Jews and heretics that he would say things about the Savior too horrible for the Jews themselves to speak out of fear of faithful Christians. The book that dean Bernhard asked me to write against him explains how wickedly he set his mouth against heaven.[90] His words are unspeakable for a Christian mouth, abominations from which pious ears shrink, so I will not write them. But even though he praised the Jews, the Jews thought him insane, because while he spoke approvingly of their faith, in his public actions he followed ours.

On Christmas and the Lord's Passion, as well as other holy days, he would make such a public display of humility that you would hardly believe him faithless.[91] One Easter night he went to a church to keep vigil, where he asked a devout cleric to tell him something about the mystery of those days. When the cleric explained the details of Christ's suffering and his resurrection, the count hissed: "What a fable! Empty words!" In response, the priest asked, "If you think what I said is nothing but fable and wind, why are you keeping vigil?" "Pretty women pass the night here," he replied. "I like to keep an eye on them." He did in fact have a young, pretty wife, yet he scorned her and spent his affections on a wrinkled old hag. And though he often kept a bed ready for himself and that hag at some Jew's house, he could never confine himself to the bedsheets; crazed with lust, he would thrust himself at this disgusting wench in some filthy corner of the room or even into a closet.

There's more: one night, after the lights had been put out, he ordered a lowly servant to go sleep with his wife, just so he could hang a charge of adultery on her! But when she felt his body and realized it wasn't the count (he was covered in nasty blisters), she savagely beat this miscreant as much as she could on her own and with the help of her attendants. What else can I say? No holy woman, no nun was spared his abuse, nor did he refrain from openly challenging holy brothers.

The Virgin Mother, queen of all, finally could no longer endure this degenerate's blasphemies. As he returned to his city after campaigning with the king, a massive throng of his fellow demons appeared to him. He arrived home with his hair on end and without his senses. That night, when he spurned his wife and lay down with the old hag, he was also lying ill with a deadly plague. He began to panic and consulted the cleric mentioned above, with whom he conducted vigils, about the appearance of his urine. The cleric began by speaking to him about death, and when he started to discuss the count's soul and his craven deeds, the count interrupted: "Do you want me to spend my money on these lecherous con men, these priests! Not a cent! From keener minds than yours I have learned that all women should be common property. This sin doesn't matter at all!"[92] So he spoke, and thereafter he said and did nothing that was not madness. He tried to kick his wife who stood next to him, but he instead dealt a hard blow to a soldier and knocked him down. Completely mad, his hands were bound to keep him from attacking himself or his relations until he had exhausted himself. Finally, demons wrested away his spirit, an enemy to the Virgin Mother and to God her Son.

XVII.

Since I have in mind heretics whom this unspeakably wicked man cherished—a peasant named Clement lived with his brother Evrard at Bucy, a village close to Soissons. He was commonly regarded as one of the leaders of this heresy, and that most vile count said of him that he had found no one wiser.

This heresy was not one to defend its doctrine openly, but condemned to perpetual whispers it slinked around in secret. Its basic tenets, as is said, are the following: they declare the divine Incarnation of the Virgin's Son an illusion; they consider invalid the baptism of young children without understanding under godparents of any kind; they claim the word of God for themselves, which they do by some long roundabout way of speaking; they abhor the mystery which happens at our altar, and call the mouths of all priests the mouth of hell; and if, as a cover to their heresy, among other people they sometimes receive our sacrament, they consider it a meal and eat no more that day. They make no distinction between holy cemeteries and other land; they condemn marriages, even for procreative sex. And since they are scattered throughout the Latin world, you might very well see men living with women without the name of husband and wife—one individual man does not dwell with one individual woman, but men are known to sleep with men, and women with women, for it is a sacrilege among them for a man to have sex with a woman. They exclude from their diet food that comes from anything born by sexual reproduction.[93]

They hold gatherings in underground chambers or around secret hidden shrines, with both sexes together. Candles are lit, and as some woman reclines under everyone's gaze, allegedly with her buttocks exposed, they present their candles to her from behind. When all of these candles are extinguished, from every side they shout "Chaos!", and each person has sex with whoever comes to hand. If a woman becomes pregnant there, after the birth they return to this very place and start a large fire. Sitting in a circle, they toss the child from hand to hand through the flames until its life is extinguished; it is then reduced to ashes, from which bread is made, and each person receives a portion as their Eucharist. Whoever ingests it almost never comes to his senses again from this heresy. If you read about the heresies examined by Augustine, you will find this one matches the Manicheans more than any other. This heresy started long ago with rather learned men, and what remained of it was abandoned to peasants who boast they maintain the apostolic life, devotedly clinging to their reading of Acts and nothing else.

Lisiard, the lord bishop of Soissons and an illustrious man, compelled these two men to submit to an examination. When the bishop insisted to them that they had held assemblies outside the church and were called heretics by their relatives, Clement answered, "Haven't you read, lord, where it says in the Gospel 'Blessed 'eritics'?"[94] Since he was uneducated, he confused *eritis* with *haeretici* and also believed they were called heretics as if "heirs," undoubtedly of God. During the interrogation into their beliefs, they responded as perfect Christians, but still did not deny their unauthorized assemblies. But because it is characteristic of such men to make denials while always seducing in secret the hearts of the dull witted, they were sentenced to the judgment of exorcised water. As preparations were made, the bishop asked me if I could discreetly draw out their thoughts. I put forward to them the question of infant baptism, and they said, "Who believes and has been baptized will be saved." Since I understood that as far as they were concerned, great wickedness was hidden in a good saying,[95] I asked what they thought about those who are baptized in the faith of others. They replied, "For God's sake, please don't ask us to examine it so deeply!" They did the same for each individual point, adding, "We believe everything you say." Recalling that verse to which the Priscillianists once adhered—"Swear an oath or break one, but don't reveal the secret"[96]—I then said to the bishop, "Since the witnesses who heard them expounding such doctrines are not present, lead them to the ordeal already prepared." There was, in fact, a married woman whom Clement had driven mad over the course of a year, as well as a deacon who had heard other damnable statements from Clement's mouth.

The bishop thus conducted mass and took up the Eucharist in his hands with these words: "Let the body and blood of the Lord examine you today." At the conclusion of the service, this most pious bishop and the archdeacon Peter, a man of

impeccable faith, who scorned the professions of faith they
had made in hopes of avoiding the ordeal, proceeded to the
waters. Pouring forth tears, the bishop sang the litany and
then performed the exorcism, at which Clement and Evrard
gave their oath that never had they believed or taught anything
contrary to our faith. Put in the barrel, Clement floated like a
twig. The entire church erupted in endless rejoicing at the
sight, for their infamy had brought together a crowd of both
sexes such as no one present could ever recall seeing there. The
other heretic confessed his error, but unrepentant was cast
into chains along with his convicted brother. Two other proven
heretics from the village of Dormans came to see the spectacle
and were also arrested. Meanwhile, we set out for a council of
Beauvais to consult with bishops about what ought be done,
but the faithful people, fearing the clergy would prove soft-
hearted, rushed to the jailhouse, seized them, and then outside
the city set fire brands under them and burned them together.
The people possessed a just zeal from God against them, lest
their cancer spread.

XVIII.

At Noyon, there is a parish church that the former bishop Bau-
douin had dedicated in honor of St. Nicaise, whose relics, hav-
ing been returned by the people of Reims, had for some time
reposed there—not, I mean to say, in the church, but in the city.[97]
About five years before, when the feast for the martyr was close
at hand, the priest ordered the obligatory celebrations to be
observed. But on the feast day a poor young girl who lived
alone with her mother took up some sewing work. While using
her hands to align the pieces that needed sewing, she pulled the
thread with her lips and tongue, as seamstresses do, and a
rather thick knot in the thread passed through the tip of her
tongue like some extremely sharp object. There was no possi-
ble way to remove it, for whenever anyone tried to pull it out,
extreme pain would torment the wretched girl. In the midst of
a throng of people, this miserable girl came to the cathedral

with her mother to pray for mercy from the queen of martyrs—
not with words, but in groans, for she could barely speak
because of the thread hanging down through the middle of her
tongue. Why go on? The crowd of people returned home with
tears of compassion after they witnessed this little girl's con-
stant struggle. That day and the following night, she remained
at the church with her mother, steadfast in prayer. She assailed
the Lady of heaven and earth with repeated heartfelt pleas,
and, as the priest Anselm, sacristan of the church, told me, on
the following day while the mother intoned solemn prayers and
her daughter responded in mumbles, miraculously performed
as if they knew Latin, the daughter approached the altar of the
Virgin Mother, tearfully embracing it, and as she kissed it repeat-
edly the thread dropped out.

The clergy and people were summoned to see a spectacle of
such grace, and with boundless praises exalted together with
God the Virgin Mother, who in this event proved herself the
queen of martyrs, because just as she punished on her own a
sin committed against a martyr, so she then appeased her own
anger through his vindication. And no little glory was brought
to the martyr's honor. For in the punishment of this humble
little girl, he made known how implacable his opposition
would be against those whose pride stood opposed to him.
This was told to me in the same church where it happened,
and the aforesaid priest showed me the remarkably thick
thread with the still bloody knot.[98] In our time, a similar thing
happened on the day of Annunciation of Blessed Mary, which
was recorded in writing by Radbod, the bishop of the city.

At this church of Nogent, which I serve at God's command,
a knight had committed an act of plunder by stealing cattle
from the monks. Back at the castle of Chauny, he made a stew
from one of the cows, believing he and his accomplices would
dine on it. As soon as he put some of the meat in his mouth,
divine power struck, and while he chewed his eyes bulged out
of their sockets and his tongue from his mouth. Thus pun-
ished, the rest of the plunder was returned, whether he liked it
or not.

Another warrior was trying to annex to his fishing rights a

section of a nearby river, called the Ailette, which for a long time had belonged to the brothers of this place. After he drove away the monks' fisherman from that part of the river and brought numerous charges in court against the church over this, the all-powerful Lady staggered his limbs with a paralyzing illness. But since he ascribed this to chance and not to divine punishment, the most reverent Virgin stood by him as he was sleeping and gave him several slaps to the face, and not gently. He woke up more sensible because of the beating and came to me barefoot and seeking forgiveness, revealing the animosity that Blessed Mary had directed at him and abandoning the possession he had claimed. One thing I have learned— there was no one hostile to that church who, if he chose to be stubborn, did not clearly come to harm.

At Compiègne a royal provost actively opposed the church of blessed Mary and saints Cornelius and Cyprian. The clergy gathered in the middle of the marketplace and in the name of the great Lady and their patron saints warned him to cease his activity, but showing no deference whatsoever to these holy names, he openly rebuked the clerics, who were visibly distressed, for slandering him. He spoke while on horseback but then fell to the ground, and with a discharge from his bowels spattered with filth the seat of the leather breeches he wore.

And since I have started speaking of the reverence that must be shown to the saints, there is a town in the same district, called Saint-Just, which belongs to the bishop of Beauvais. At the beginning of a revolt there, when every vile and petty vassal raged in a frenzy of monstrous insolence against the burghers, the clergy brought out a chest containing relics of the child martyr Saint Just in an effort to calm the people. Some household servant, who was truly readier to hand than others, went back to block their path and with a complete lack of reverence brought down his sword upon this most holy chest, but in vain. Before anyone could say a word, he fell to the ground, a stinking mess from the filthy outpouring of his bowels like the man above.

A priest was governing the church in a village in the same diocese of Beauvais, but a peasant harried him with a hatred so intense that he tried to consign him to death. Because the peasant could not do so openly, he plotted to destroy him with poison. He cut a toad into pieces and stuffed it into the clay vessel the priest normally used to serve the wine at mass. Vessels made for this purpose usually have a long narrow neck that rises up from a rounded base. When the priest came to mass, he performed the sacred mysteries with now poisoned wine, and when the ceremony was finished, he succumbed to a deathly exhaustion; losing his appetite for food and vomiting up anything he ate or drank, he began to waste away completely. After lying ill in bed for some time, he at last with great difficulty managed to get up and come to church. He had realized that the source of his illness was the drink he had taken from that vessel, so taking hold of it he cut through the neck with a knife and poured out onto the stone floor the remaining liquid—it looked like he was milking a sow's udder filled to bulging with little pieces of toad.[99] The man understood that his vital organs were condemned to death, and while he hopelessly awaited the fate that threatened him, he received this advice from someone: "If you wish to cast out the disease you have contracted, ask someone to bring you dust from the tomb of Marcellus, bishop of Paris, or from his altar, and when you swallow it with some water, have complete faith that you will at once recover your health."[100] He hurriedly had this done, and with great affection for the saint drank down the holy dust. Instantly, he vomited out gobs of countless reptiles with all their accompanying venom, and once all the evil had withdrawn he was cured. No wonder Marcellus could accomplish this now in the presence of God, for when separated from him by the barrier of his flesh, he once performed no lesser deeds in a similar case.

XIX.

I am next going to tell something unheard of in our time, told to me by a pious and truly humble monk named Geoffrey, formerly lord of the castle of Saumur as well as of other castles in

Burgundy.[101] Because his life is recognized for its natural affinity to truth, his character, I believe, vouches for his story, which is as follows:

In the northern parts of the territories neighboring his own, there had been a young man who was closely bound to a woman, not with the love for a wife, as one should be, but with love on loan (to use a phrase from Solinus), as one should not. Eventually he recovered his senses, for a while, and planned to go on a pilgrimage to Saint-James in Galicia. But he added a little leaven to the dough of a pious intention,[102] for on this pilgrimage he carried with him the woman's sash, abusing it to remind him of her, and thus what he offered rightly was not now divided rightly.[103] The devil took the opportunity to attack him during his journey, appearing to him in the guise of the apostle James, and said, "Where are you headed"? "To Saint-James," he replied. "You're not traveling the right way," the devil said. "I am James to whom you are hurrying, but you're carrying with you something that greatly dishonors my honor. Until now you have wallowed in a pigsty of all-consuming fornication, meaning that you merely want to appear penitent. You proclaim you are making your way to my presence, as if it were the first fruit of conversion, but you are still bound up in the sash of that nasty little slut of yours." The man blushed at these accusations, and believing it was truly the apostle, replied, "I know, lord, that in the past and even now have I have done works of the most shameful kind. Tell me, please, what advice will you give to one journeying toward your mercy." "If you wish," said the devil, "to make the fruits of your penance equal to the disgraceful acts you have committed, that member which is the source of your sin—your penis—cut it off in accordance with your faith in me and God, and then your life, which you have lived so poorly, take it away as well by slitting your throat." He spoke, and disappearing from sight left the man in a completely confused state of mind.

At night he came to an inn, and made haste to obey the warnings not, as he thought, of the apostle, but of the devil. As his companions slept, he first cut off his penis, then plunged a knife in his throat. His companions caught the sounds of his dying shriek and the gurgle of gushing blood, and roused from their slumber, they brought in a lantern and saw what had happened to him. They grieved at the sight of their friend's dismal death, unaware of the counsel he had received from the demon. Since they had no idea why this happened to him, they did not then deny him care for his funeral rites, and, something that would have been improper for someone who died in this way, made arrangements to have masses performed for the man who seemed to be their fellow pilgrim.[104] From this faithful outpouring to God, it pleased God to close the wound in his throat and through the apostle to restore life to the dead man. Rising up and, to the indescribable astonishment of all, returned to life, he began to speak. Those present wanted to know his motives for killing himself, and he told them of the devil's appearance under the apostle's name. Asked of the ordeal he underwent during the judgment of his soul because of his suicide, he said:

"I was brought before the throne of God in the presence of the Lady known to all, the mother of God, Virgin Mary, where also my advocate, the holy apostle James, was present. There, in the deliberations before God about what would happen to me, the holy apostle, remembering my intention, though sinful and still corrupt, prayed to that blessed Lady on my behalf, and speaking so sweetly she pronounced my sentence: this wretched man, who had fallen to such ruin at the wickedness of the devil cloaked in the image of a saint, would be pardoned. Thus at God's command I returned to this world to bring about my own correction and to proclaim their message."

Geoffrey was an older man when he told this to me, and said he heard it from someone who saw the man returned to life. And it was also said that a distinct and visible scar remained on his throat, everywhere bearing witness to the miracle. The shearing off of his member left only a little perforation, if I can call it that, for urination.[105]

Here is another well-known story, but I do not know if it has ever been set down in writing. A man of the laity, if I am not mistaken, converted to the rule of monastic life and entered a monastery where he bound himself to the vows of the profession. Believing the observance of the rule there was not as strict as he wished, he obtained permission from the abbot to transfer to another monastery that was supposedly more pious and there led his life as devoutly as one can. After some time he fell ill, and died from his illness; upon departing from the present world, he then fell into a contest between the different powers: the opposing forces, pleading that he had violated the vow of his first profession, repeatedly countered the arguments of the spirits of light, who relied upon the testimony provided by his good action.

The case was brought on appeal to a hearing before Peter, the heavenly gatekeeper, but a dispute of this nature Peter immediately referred to the divine presence. When the matter was reported to him, the Lord said, "Go before Richard the justiciar, and carry out the sentence he hands down." This Richard was extraordinarily capable when it came to his worldly possessions, but even more so in maintaining equity and justice. They came to Richard, the case was stated, Richard produced his verdict: "Because the defendant is bound to the earlier vow, there is clear evidence of a deliberate breach of oath. The demons' case is thus not an unjust one, yet the just actions of the man present them with a serious obstacle. Let my judgment, however, be proclaimed in the name of God: he must return to the world to rectify this matter." A dead man only a day before, he emerged back among the living, called on his abbot, and reported what he had seen. Publicly admitting his guilt for his act of desertion and breach of oath, he returned to his original monastery. Anyone who professes monastic stability in the name of God should understand from this story that he ought to keep his promises to God and the saints, for one should not change monasteries unless his superiors compel him to misconduct.[106]

As it is beneficial on occasion to speak of the character of the dying, at Laon there was a man devoted to collecting interest from any possible source, and in the end proved he had led a life suited to his death. During his final days, he demanded a payment of interest from some poor little woman, though the principal had already been paid. Pleading that his death was at hand, she begged him to remit the interest, which he stubbornly refused to do. Put in difficult straits, the woman borrowed the amount of the interest and brought it to the wretch, all but one silver coin. When she again asked him to remit only this one silver coin, he swore he would not under any circumstances. Why drag out the story? She hunted around for a silver coin, which she was barely able to come by, and paid it to him, now gasping in the final struggle of his spirit and his flesh. The dying man took the coin and placed it in his mouth, and after he swallowed it down as if it were his viaticum, he breathed his last. Under such protection, his soul made its way to the devil where it found lodgings, deservedly banished from holy places.

Let me add something that happened with a man of this sort at Arras. For a long time he had stuffed his purses full with filthy lucre, and when he had finally amassed many mountains of coins, he reached his final hours. Then, in the guise of a man, the devil came to him, leading a black bull before him. Standing at the dying man's bedside, he said, "My lord sends you this bull." The ailing man replied, "I thank my lord for the gift," then said to his wife, "Go make something to eat for the man who brought the bull, but take hold of the bull and keep close watch of it." He spoke, and at once expired.

In the meantime, she went looking for the man to see if he would dine, and fodder was brought out to the bull, but neither could be found. Everyone was struck with wonder and fear, nor did they think that such offers of gifts portended anything good. Funeral arrangements were made, the body was placed upon a bier, and then the procession of clergy arrived at the house to perform the usual offices for the dead. But demons were celebrating funeral rites for their servant, and they raised a ruckus in the air at the clergy's arrival. Even though the weather was perfectly calm, a sudden whirlwind nearly toppled over the front part of the house, which they call a "bargeboard," and lifted up a side of the bier, which was placed out in the open. Let this be enough about men who feed on the poor.

No one should be surprised, however, that these same malignant spirits have a greater ability in our time to play pranks on people or to harm them, especially since everything they do, they do like beasts and not in the name of the Lord. For example, I learned of something that happened not many years ago in the district of the Vexin, when some of its nobles were hunting somewhere in that region. They trapped in its burrow a badger that failed to escape—or rather thought they did, for in fact they had caught a demon—and scooped it up in a sack. Using all their might to pull him out, they noticed it felt heavier than a badger, and when they started to carry it back and as night began to fall, suddenly a voice from a nearby mountain swept through the middle of the forest. "Listen up!" it said, "Listen!" Then more voices from the other side rose up in shouts behind them. Finally one voice broke in: "What is it?" "They're carrying off Caduceus," came the reply. This is perhaps what he was named, and rightly so, for he caused many to fall.[107] At his words, an endless swarm of demons rushed out from every direction as if to snatch him away, and the dense throng seemed to envelop the entire forest in darkness. Tossing aside the devil—not badger—they carried, they fled, driven almost out of their minds. As soon as they arrived home, they died.

In this province, a peasant was returning from work one Saturday evening, barefoot and without covering for his shins, and he sat down on the bank of a river to wash his hands and feet. Then a devil from the depths of the river in which he was bathing his feet bound them together. Realizing he was tied up, the peasant shouted for help to his neighbors, who carried him to a nearby house. These men, an ignorant lot, used every tool they had to see if they could break open his shackles. They struggled in turns for some time with useless prodding and prying, accomplishing nothing, each one frustrated in his attempts: spiritual things can only be achieved by spiritual means.[108] Finally, after days of going round in circles, a stranger joined them, and as they looked on, he rushed to the man in shackles and in a moment released him. He hurried away when it was done, allowing no one to find out who he was.

Stories of demons vying for the love of women, and also

intercourse with them, are amply attested in every place, and I would say more if I were not ashamed to.[109] There are some demons who are savage in their wanton acts of cruelty, while others are satisfied with pranks. But let me now turn my pen to happier subjects.

What I am about to relate I heard very recently from a monk of Monte Cassino. Following the death of Hildebrand, who was called Gregory VII, an abbot of this monastery named Desiderius campaigned for the papacy. Though he was in fact a cardinal of the Roman church, he withdrew a significant amount of treasure from the house of our lord Benedict and used the money to reach the pontifical office.[110] At the first mass he performed at the Apostolic See, when he turned to the people to say, "Peace be with you," he collapsed and seriously injured his head on the stone floor. One night after being carried away from there, as he slept, Saint Benedict appeared to him and said, "How dare a simoniac like you enter upon such an office! And what is more, you committed a detestable sacrilege when like a thief you stole away my property and acquired something with it that you obviously do not deserve! Withdraw from office, and from this disgraceful fall come back a more disciplined man, for if you choose to persist in what you have begun, you will call upon yourself a most shameful death, and soon." Upon hearing this, in fear of the multiple punishments for his twofold sin, especially those threatened on the high authority of so noble and powerful a master, he at once abandoned the see he had not earned and returned to the aforesaid monastery. There, to atone for his excesses, this man who once swelled with extravagant pride led a sober life for an entire year as a lowly porter. He proved his humility by being extremely helpful, and thus earned a second term as abbot.

Far different, however, was the case of a monk at Fleury, as I have heard many times. After first agreeing to pay money to the king of the French, he snatched away the previously mentioned church of our glorious lord Benedict out from under Abbot Abbo, a perfectly saintly and learned man.[111] Abbo had been hounding after him, hoping to seize hold of him like a stray sheep and place him in custody, when by chance he found him in

Orléans. This simoniac, realizing it was Abbo who had arrived, could find nowhere to escape, so he went into the latrines, claiming a pressing weight in his bowels. Abbo came in after him and looked around, but not a person was found anywhere—only his cowl was seen hanging from a hook, for since the man was utterly lost, reverence was owed only to his holy habit.

I even saw Véran, a noble man and a relative of mine, subjected to grievous insults and scornful treatment, and since the king also used his influence to support these efforts, on top of everything else he was deposed as abbot. God, however, usually punishes more severely those who are the first in a criminal undertaking. And I have heard that some years ago when these monks of Fleury strayed far from the monastic rule, our most blessed Father condemned many of them to a shameful death.[112]

XX.

Even now as in former days the most blessed martyr King Edmund is a source of miracles among the English. I say nothing of how his body remains without decay to this day, with fragrant spices not from men, but heaven, and we marvel at the growth of his hair and nails as if he were still living.[113] But it can be said that in his miraculous condition he does not suffer anyone to see him. In my time an abbot of the place wanted to know for himself whether the saint's head, cut off during his martyrdom, was now joined to his body, as was commonly reported. He fasted together with his chaplain, uncovered the body and saw everything I just described: nowhere was the flesh withered, and he looked as if he were sleeping. He submitted everything to examination by sight and touch. One pulled on his head while the other held onto both the feet and pulled, but he discovered the body was intact. The hands of both men soon afterward were permanently enfeebled and wasted away.

Let me tell of yet another wonder. The monks had raised a roebuck in the monastery from the time it was young, and as the frisky animal wandered all through the buildings and even the church itself, it fell and broke a leg. Hobbling along on three hooves, it kept slowly moving forward as best it could; while roaming over the entire monastery, it happened to enter the church and with effort went toward the martyr's tomb. Out of animal inquisitiveness it stopped beneath the tomb, and its leg was then healed. What will the pious martyr do in the case of a human being who seeks him out in faith, when he showed to a beast such spontaneous generosity or, to describe it more correctly, such kingly gentleness?

Saint Swithin in the city of Winchester has also to this day proved himself capable of miracles. Not long ago a monk suffered horrible inflammations on both hands, which were worse than any leper's, and had further lost all use of them. For this reason the monk did not attend vigils at night. The saint took offense, and appeared to him, demanding to know why he was absent from the psalmody. He straightaway explained to the saint that the cause of his absence was the excruciating purulence on his hands. "Hold out your hands," said the saint. When he held them out, the saint squeezed them tight and pulled off like a pair of gloves all his scabrous skin, replacing it with the softer flesh of a young boy.

The arm of the martyr Saint Arnoul used to be kept in the town where I was born. When someone brought it to the area, the townspeople were skeptical, and as a test it was thrown into a fire, but with a sudden leap it escaped the flames. Thereafter, a cousin of mine, who was one of the nobles of the castle, was struck with a very serious malady. The arm of the holy martyr was repeatedly laid upon him, and the disease would change its location at the arm's touch and move to another spot. Wherever the strength of the disease took flight, the holy arm's touch would track it down as it fled, until finally, after chasing the disease around his face and limbs several times, all the disease's virulence maneuvered into the area between the throat and the shoulder blades. The skin swelled up into a little lump like a mouse, and then deflated without any pain. Because of this, every year as long as he lived he provided a lavish feast for all the clergy who attended the saint's festival, and his successors have not ceased to do so even today. A woman—not my grandfather's wife, but a dependent of his who was sufficiently skilled for such worldly employments—covered the arm in the finest gold and gemstones.[114]

Guise is a castle in the district of Laon where there is also said to be an arm of Saint Arnoul. Some thieves robbing the church of its treasure had intended at the same time to steal the arm, but once they had it in their grasp, it forced itself from their hands and could not be carried anywhere. These thieves, arrested with the rest of the items they had carried off, confessed this at the very hour they were to be led to the gallows. There is an area of the gold adorning the arm where no lapidary's skill was able to affix any gemstone—it would drop off as soon as it was set, and though the stone as well as the craftsman would change, both the craftsman and his craft would be foiled.

I am not unaware that the martyr Léger, notable for his miracles, is swift to bring aid. In fact, I still remember perfectly, though I was yet a boy living with my mother, a time during Easter I daily suffered in the throes of violent fever. At the foot of the town was a church dedicated to Saint Léger and Saint Maclou, and in her humble faith my mother furnished it with a continuously burning oil lamp.[115] And though I refused almost any food at all, she summoned two clerics, her chaplain and my teacher, and instructed them to carry me there under their watchful charge (following a corrupt practice of long standing, the church was under her jurisdiction). When the clerics arrived there, they ordered bedding for them and me to be set out before the altar. In the middle of the night the ground inside the church began to quake as if struck by enormous hammers, on several occasions the locks on the chests shook violently, and for some time the sound of flails scraping over a threshing floor could be heard. Awakened by the noise, the clerics became worried that fear would worsen my condition. What more should I say? I caught the sounds of their whispers, but because of their companionship as well as the comforting light from the lamp, I was only a little frightened. Passing the night among these disturbances, I returned to my mother safe and sound, as if I had not endured any difficulties at all, and though just recently even the finest of foods revolted me, I was now found to be eager to eat common fare, and no less so to play ball.

The elder William, king of the English, had a tower constructed at his own expense at the church of the glorious Saint Denis, and how immense it would have been, if it had stood completed![116] The craftsmen, however, did not properly align the structure, and it seemed closer every day to causing its own downfall. Yves, the abbot at that time, and the monks feared the collapse of this new building would inflict damage on the older church—the altar of Saint Edmund was there, as well as altars of other saints—and the following vision came to the troubled abbot. He saw a lady of rather distinguished appearance standing in the middle of the church of Saint-Denis, and she was performing the exorcism of water in the manner of a priest. As he marveled at the woman's command of a ceremony to which she would be unaccustomed, he observed that after she had blessed the water, she sprinkled it around, and after she had sprinkled it around, she turned roundabout and made the sign of the cross wherever she had sprinkled it.

Almost immediately, the tower collapsed, but in its fall harmed no part of the church, for according to the abbot's vision, this woman—blessed among women and blessed the fruit of her womb[117]—had fortified the church with her blessing. Instead, it collapsed in a different direction, burying a man walking along the base. When they realized a man lay entombed beneath all the rubble, for the sake of his spiritual consolation they started to remove the pile of debris covering him. After carrying off mountains of mortar and stone, at last they reached him, and—speak of miracles!—discovered he was just as healthy and full of cheer as if he had been resting at home. Indeed, the stone blocks had fit themselves together in a straight line, one after the other, and made him a little shelter. During his long stay there, as he was trapped, no hunger, no fear, no overbearing smell of quicklime troubled him.

Let me place, then, as the conclusion to my book, along with Denis, lord of all France, the most excellent Mary, patroness of heaven and earth.

ON THE RELICS
OF SAINTS

PROLOGUE

To Odo, lord abbot and father of Saint-Symphorien, Guibert, minister and servant of the mother of God wishes a happy advance in God's service.

Since I have heard such a cacophony of questions about the tooth of the Savior that our neighbors at the church of Saint-Médard claim to possess (for they have done what they can to make it common knowledge), I decided to write down a few things about the topic and to set forth what my mind knew about it, because others have kept silent. I started this subject as the beginning of a little book,[1] but when I had begun to give birth to what I had conceived and had barely filled a whole page, such an abundance of things needing to be said about similar topics flooded over me, that I quickly set aside for a time the material that I had taken up and pursued different but not unrelated issues, giving shape to the first book without having completed the subject that had inspired me to write in the first place. In the next section of the book I touched upon the things that I had first promised to address, but when the topic of the body of the Lord happened to enter my discourse, the tooth that I had started to talk about exited it. Finally, once I had finished up those topics that had flooded into my mind, I completed my task in the third book, but whether I have explained these topics so as to satisfy a prudent reader, I do not know. If I have understood anything, however, in the security of faith I profess that I have understood it through faith alone. If someone has a better understanding, I am willing to listen.[2]

One of my benevolent readers has taken issue with the second book, where I call the mystery of the bread and wine "the vicarial body of Christ." He thinks this phrase inappropriate because when we call something the "vicar," it is generally of less value than that thing whose vicar it is. But if he had paid closer attention to my words—how I frequently distinguish the "personal identity," born of the Virgin, and the "identity of the signified," which exists in the bread and in the chalice— then all his doubt would have been put to rest. And if the Lord's words, commanding that, "it happen in memory of him,"[3] are borne in mind, then no question ever need be raised about "vicarial changes." Who indeed doubts that anything that renews the memory of something represented is the vicar of the thing that it represents? More plainly on this question, the Holy Spirit is called "the pledge" and the Son himself the "reflection of glory" and "figure of the substance," and elsewhere, "the image of God." And certainly I do not see what hinders us from calling "vicar" what he himself calls "daily." It is as if by specifying that the bread is "daily," he was suggesting that we use it in the here and now, so that in eternity he might lead us to the enjoyment of that body sitting at the Father's right hand.[4] Obviously he commands that it happen thus in this world so that we will not be denied in eternity the origin of what we have touched here, if only through its external appearance [*species*]. Therefore I can only think it fitting that the Truth, though itself all encompassing, is stamped with the appearance of this vicar.[5]

I have thus decided, my most beloved of men, to make you the judge of this little work, you whom the keen intensity of a dull wit has never trained to examine the meaning of the letter only. Instead, assiduous contemplation has accustomed you to seek—if I might call it this—the spirit of the letter.[6] Securely then have I chosen you, who, as I expect to learn, makes corrections even to inimical points only out of your customary humility.

Moreover, a certain someone,[7] ready enough to speak but less prudent when it comes to understanding what he has denounced, has objected to me—and you heard him—that I spoke against the book of Wisdom when I said that those who are or will be in hell have impenitent hearts. We can read in that book, "These are the ones whom we mocked—saying and making penance among themselves, their spirits weeping because of their agony."[8] My discourse supposedly contradicts other passages, too, if I'm not mistaken. I recall, however, that in that same book which I named "On the Inner World,"[9] I proved that the minds of people in hell have fallen into diabolical rage and obstinacy. This does not even take into account the conclusions I reached elsewhere through contrasting oppositions, which by themselves show how Christ through kindness unites his heavenly members into one body, so by analogy the devil through rage tears apart those who have been conformed to him and over whom he has been made head. Surely no one doubts that it is absurd and discordant with all reason that someone who has departed this world in malevolence would be able to regain in the next world what he did not care to possess while living in this one?[10] Otherwise the statement of Solomon becomes meaningless: that a tree once cut, whether it falls to the south or to the north, remains motionless in whatever place it lands. Obviously, it would not stay motionless if it shifted, either for good or evil, from the condition that conformed to its head.[11]

But because it would be altogether wrong to contradict the book of Wisdom, let us discuss the penance of the damned, in order that we might recognize their perpetual lack of penance. We ascribe to them the ability to repent in one respect only, although this penance bears no fruit: in the midst of such bitter suffering, they so despise the sins for which they are punished that as soon as they come to understand that their grief is fruitless, because no reasoning can change it, a rage born of hopelessness overwhelms their hearts. They come to hate their existence so much that they do repent, but only because they failed to sin more and indulge more in their beastly pleasures while they were alive. Isaiah agrees with this point when he says, "Terror alone will bring understanding to their ears."[12] What the book of Wisdom calls "penance," the book of Isaiah calls "understanding." And although according to Solomon the damned in hell will have neither reason nor knowledge,[13] nevertheless we do know they are not lacking in "understanding" in this sense alone: that they always discern why they are punished. But in the midst of their suffering, because their discretion bears no fruit, they fall back into the madness of obstinacy and scorn. This is why Job, when he describes the "land of misery and shadows," says, "No order but only eternal horror inhabits the shadow of death."[14] There would in fact be order if he who repented—not only of his deeds but also of his desires—would then desist from the things for which he offers repentance. But there is no order when someone repents, on the one hand, because he suffers for his sins but on the other hand, burns in despair and fury because of his appetite for evil. The phrase "eternal horror" refers to this fury, burning uncontrollably in cruel minds alienated from all hope. We see all this most clearly in the traitor Judas, who repented of his treacherous deed but could not restrain his own hands from destroying himself despite this urge to correct his sins.

Certainly if that person who had wanted to trouble me with such a petty question were here, I would ask him—much more reasonably than he asked me—how he interprets the gospel parable about the foolish maidens, who sought oil from wise maidens and who asked the bridegroom to open the door that was closed to them.[15] No one doubts that after the resurrection (to which this story obviously refers) everyone will be sure about his status, whether he is among the saved or the lost. Scripture often calls everyone's day of death his "day of judgment," inasmuch as, at the moment of our passing, we all receive a sentence, either of salvation or damnation; and no one's future inheritance can be hidden from him, since after the spirit divests itself of its fleshly garment, in no way does it become blind and unable to recognize its own eternal good or evil. If therefore someone who has recently shed his body knows everything about his fate, and if after resurrection, the experience of body and soul makes clearer the general condition of the next life, where false piety and flattery fail—I do not mean these traits do not succeed, but rather that they no

longer exist—how then could such words survive in that place
of verity? For in this world of vanity they could not survive if
declaimed in a wise man's presence. Who indeed in this world,
if he is at all rational, accepts the testimony of another's con-
science when, if he considered it fairly, he would be unable to
do so for his own conscience? Who in the next world would
foolishly seek anything from God or demand anything from
man when in this world he did not know how to judge him-
self? No lies can be spun on his behalf when he stands before
him, before whose judgment all will be laid bare.

This point also is demonstrated elsewhere: "Many will say,
'Lord, have we not prophesied in your name, have we not cast
out demons, have we not performed miracles?' "[16] In that final
judgment will they argue on their own behalf with earnest
protests, as if ignorant of their own deeds and with God as
witness to their hearts? When the letter thus leads us to absur-
dity, we must necessarily pay attention to what other meaning
might lie behind the words. A spirit that sees clearly at that
time of judgment would not say or think something like this,
but these words are instead something that a man in this world
would consider, overly awed by the virtuous deeds of hypo-
crites that seem to be so great, or else something the hypo-
crites themselves would think, blinded by the praise sought
from man, believing that what men celebrate about them will
stand before God. Hence: "Woe to those who desire the day of
the Lord."[17] The blind man expects rewards, and because of
that he judges himself worthy to receive the false praise of mis-
erable men. In this way those who are in hell make penance
among themselves: they cause others, through consideration of
the damned and through the example of their damnation, to
ponder the excellence of the saints and then to repent. If we
were to believe that those who are punished in hell grieve that
the sun of justice does not shine on them, then we make non-
sense of the words of the wise man: "Confession perishes in
death." And of the Psalm: "Who will confess to you in hell?"
And "No one in death remembers you." Also, "When the
impious man comes into the depths of wickedness, he brings

contempt." Where do the saints stand with fortitude, if not in the midst of the adversities of this life? This is where the wicked dismiss their labors, when they say that saints have labored in vain on behalf of God.[18] Let us consider other similar passages in scripture, lest other conflicts occur within them.

BOOK 1

ON SAINTS AND
THEIR RELICS

If it is wrong to err about the general course of everyone's resurrection, how much worse is it to detract somehow from the resurrection of the head of all? Since the outcome of everyone's hope depends upon his example, then doubtless the outcome of the promised resurrection grows doubtful if its possible fulfillment in him who promised it seems in any way unlikely or if in connection with his own resurrection, he seems to have broken any of his promises. For when someone makes a promise that he does not keep, either he stands accused of lying, or else he shows himself unable to do for himself what he has promised to give to others. Since it is horrible even to imagine cheating God by shortchanging his power or branding him as unreliable in his promises, let no one claim for himself, under the name of piety, something that in everyone's reckoning is most certainly impious and confirms attacks against the faith of everyone. If therefore a group were to claim something on its own behalf in order to promote the singular glory of their own church and if by that claim they were to weaken the laws of our entire faith, then this particular honor that they claim is completely detestable, causing everyone to suffer inconstancy and loss of faith. Certainly, if you were to weigh your right arm down with so much gold jewelry that these decorations drained your whole body's strength, then this sort of beauty would be totally useless, because a particular splendor was doing harm to the whole, as happens when a bunch of twigs causes the destruction of the main branch—no, more truly of the whole tree.

So it is with things that are held and taught in the church, which has thus far maintained such remarkable balance that no one in it has dared promulgate anything unless upon careful consideration, through reason and example, it had been found to be harmonious with the Catholic faith. Some things, of course, are held but not taught—such as customs about fasting and psalmody. Although divergent in practice, these customs nevertheless should be in harmony with the sense of our faith. He who differs in practices of fasting and singing is not blameworthy if he does so through some kind of understanding. Otherwise, whoever would follow diverse ascetic and liturgical practices in a similar faith on the basis of some special privilege could be labeled—and rightly so—a schismatic, because he would hold as absolute his own singular privilege. If you sing differently or if you fast differently, it is neither fitting nor appropriate for you rudely to preach or enjoin your customs upon others who follow practices no less praiseworthy. Listen to the apostle: "He who eats, eats for the Lord, and he who does not eat, does not eat for the Lord."[1] The same judgment can easily be passed on similar questions.

Other practices are both held and taught, such as the sacraments of baptism and the Eucharist—elements common to Christianity in such a way that our faith cannot survive without them, each one held constant according to an unchanging authority. A uniform doctrine accompanies them, precedes them, and follows them, everywhere and always. Their prayers take the same form, I say, so that their public form might follow what teachers have taught. In regards to these two sacraments, however, one difference must be noted: without water or blood, it is not possible to be a Christian;[2] without the Eucharist, it is possible, provided one holds steadfastly to his faith. Evidence for this point can be found in the case of many martyrs and hermits. The former group never received the Eucharist and the latter did so once or else rarely; nonetheless, they were made saints, incorporating themselves to Christ through their holy work in lengthy solitude. Similarly we read in various places the lesson that a faith firmly held suffices for salvation, even when all else is lacking. Thus the apostle says, "To him who does not work, his faith is counted toward justice." A greater precedence is given to charity, placed before faith and hope, and it alone is proclaimed, as if by *antonoma-sia*, as a work. "Set the works of our hands over us," scripture says, in reference to the common practices of every good profession. "And direct the work of our hands," that is, teach us the better gifts, the higher path.[3] These two tenets are taught among us and they are held because they are taught.

There exist, on the other hand, certain practices that we hold and that are preached in churches, although they do not figure among the things that we must do for our salvation and without which we cannot live rightly. Many might live out their lives well without receiving any help from these practices, and in fact many do live out their lives well without them. Such is the case with saints' bodies and their relics (that is, things that the saints handled). We ought to revere and honor the relics, both because of the saints' examples and the protection they provide, but we must have truly sound evidence as to the authenticity of these relics, such that someone is called a saint only if there is a sure tradition of antiquity about his saintliness or else if true writings, not mere opinion, confirms it. How do you think a person receives sanction—if I might phrase it thus—when no memorial serves to recall his authority and neither writings nor reliable experience of miracles strengthens his case?[4] I mean writings that actually offer proof! There are to be sure many stories about all of the saints that serve less to commend their reputation than to defame it among unbelievers. But even those that are true are often told in such a ragged and pedestrian style, or—if I may use a poetic expression—in a style that creeps along the ground,[5] that by their awkwardness they defame the saints, and even the least little thing about them seems false.

And how could the tales of such writers, who by their own base crudity place even the truth in doubt, not be assessed as perjuries and lies? And whose reputation do we think is blemished when we see not the lives of certain apostles but rather their nonsense, all sooty and tarnished? What lessons do the spinning of these fables—worse than all the clanking of a wagon—bring to the pious? They suggest instead new possibilities for blasphemy to the wicked! What could one call the

"History of Thomas," a book that Augustine opposes not
once but in many places, except a howling in the ears?[6] Are we
to think either God or the saints (following what Job says)
need others to speak wicked lies on their behalf?[7] The holy
apostles, who cohere to the Godhead as hairs or a beard cohere
to the head, have not altogether escaped such storytelling, and
similarly tall tales about them would disturb the minds of
many, if our own knowledge of them were not decorated by
the Gospel and by their own Acts.

What then can I say about men who have become illustrious
elsewhere through the support of no evidence but who, because
some believe them to have been celebrated in some type of
writing, prove especially elusive? What am I to make of one
whose birth and whose life are known to none, and whose
death is entirely obscure, though because of that death his
praises are sung? And what person would pray to those saints
for help, when he does not know if they have merited anything
from God? Doesn't a man's conscience cause grave offense if it
calls as an intercessor before God someone who in fact offers
no great hope? Surely the keenness of your prayer—more
truly, of your intention—grows dull when you do not know
whether the one you pray to shares anything with God.

I knew some men, for example, who had for the longest time
considered a particular person to be a holy confessor, trans-
lated, so they said, from Britain, until a change crept into their
minds and they venerated him as a martyr.[8] When I asked the
reasons for this transformation, they could tell me nothing
more believable about the man's martyrdom than they had
been able to do concerning his former life as a confessor. As
God is my witness, I have read in a Life of Samson, a saint
famous among the Franks and Bretons, and I read it again to
the revulsion of people who happened to be at hand, about a
certain abbot whom that *lectio* named St. Pyro. His death I
had thought blessed, until I followed up by reading correctly
and found that this monument to sanctity died dead drunk,
after falling into a well.[9] And let us not overlook Lanfranc of
Canterbury, bishop among the English, who raised a question
for his eventual successor, Anselm, then abbot of Bec, about

one of his predecessors, who, bound in chains, was killed because he refused to redeem himself with money.[10]

What can I say about those saints whose end plainly puts them among the damned, or about whom it is uncertain whether their deaths occurred in good or evil circumstances, or about whom there is reason to doubt one way or the other? Sweet Jesus! What kind of saint is it whose death causes doubt? Before I pray to him, then, first I have to wonder about the legitimacy of his sanctity. I dare to describe it as profane, the fact that any people might find homes within the sacred precincts behind the altars, as if upon the highest thrones of the heavenly court, when their history, their birth and life, their days and the character of their death survives in the memory of no living person. Even if the faithful honor such people with the name of "sanctity," the priests—I say this to them with all due respect—do not act with proper discretion when they fail to discipline and correct the rabble, tossed about by the winds of its own opinions. If no one can legitimately achieve high rank without some sort of justification, then are these figures not rashly titled with false—no, truly with sacrilegious— names? They are presented in such a way that they seem superior to all mortal men, but in fact they may very well have been sentenced to reside in places of punishment, or else they may have been led into the damnation of hell and, if they knew their fate and had the ability to ask for help, they would be seeking aid from mortal men, just like the rich man in the parable.[11]

The bishops, the custodians of God's people, ought to look to the good of their own, so that if their followers have zeal for God, it is because the bishops permitted them to have it only according to knowledge. Otherwise, the people would sin by offering, but not dividing, rightly.[12] If the prophet says, "Woe to those who call evil good and good evil,"[13] what greater wickedness can there be than to force upon holy altars such people who perhaps ought to be excluded altogether from holy places? If they, from whose bodies miracles flow after death, have not been, as we read, freed from spiritual punishments (and we have learned by evidence that even the just man can hardly be saved),[14] what can we hope from those whose glorification no sight, no sound, no writing, and no miracles support?

Miracles, if they are to be given any credence, must occur because of a life well lived, from beginning to end. There are some signs, you might say, that are double-edged, such that they are said to supply glories to the right and to the left.[15] He who divided the Red Sea for the children of Israel also divided the Pamphylia for Alexander the Great. Read in Suetonius how Vespasian cured a lame man by touching him with his big toe.[16] Prophetic signs have frequently accompanied the births of outstanding princes, such as the aforesaid Alexander, Julius Caesar, Octavian, and others, and signs have foretold their deaths, as with Charlemagne and his son Louis. Even in our time, at the deaths of the kings of the Lotharingians or the English, and upon the change of kingdoms, we have often seen comets appear.[17]

What about that wonder that our King Louis customarily performs, and which we have witnessed? I have seen crowds of people suffering from scrofula around their throats or elsewhere on their bodies coming to him for his touch, receiving it from him with the sign of the cross, as I stood close by and forbade it. He, however, with his usual generosity beckoned them with a serene hand to approach and humbly made the sign. His father, Philip, used to perform this glorious miracle often, but he lost it—I don't know what faults prevented him. I will pass over the question of how other kings conduct themselves in this affair, except to say that the English king never dares such things.[18]

We know that the gift of miracles is distributed in many ways. Portents pass through some people as if through canals, but the people themselves have no share in these signs, even though through these signs they perform a service for the benefit of others. We can obviously include as examples of this phenomenon the prophecies of Balaam and Caiaphas—the speech of an ass and the vision of an angel—since the sounds they made were not their own.[19] We have seen the dying, regardless of their virtue, foretell many future events and make pronouncements about the character of the world to come, just as we customarily attach value to the words of infants who are otherwise innocent, pronounced by them in a way filled with insight—apparently because of the dullness of their minds—about their own fates and the fates of others. The following example makes the point clearly enough.

Recently, during the Easter season just passed, on Easter day itself, in our neighboring city of Soissons, a woman had brought her baby to church so that it might receive the blessing of communion. As the time for the preparation of the Eucharist approached, the boy, not yet understanding anything around him, was waiting under his mother's care, facing the back of the priest, when he saw in the middle of the altar, where the divine grace reposed, a baby more beautiful than seemed physically possible, held aloft in the hands of the priest. Childish curiosity did not permit him to keep quiet while gazing at the sight, and he shouted to his mother so that the whole church heard, "Lady, lady, don't you see what a beautiful boy the priest is holding over the altar?" His mother turned to look, but saw nothing of this vision. A little later, however, after the elevation, when the priest put down the sacrament and covered it with a linen shroud, the boy shouted again, and said, "Look! He wrapped him in a white blanket!" The child repeated these things so that everyone could hear, and the ones with greater understanding perceived that his boyish innocence had looked with eyes of one kind upon the beautiful boy, but with eyes of another sort attended to the material pallium in which a thing of the intellect was wrapped.

Lo! He who saw these things is now growing up in this world, and we do not believe his chances for the afterlife are any better than the usual ones. We know therefore that what he saw neither increased his merit nor amplified his glory, but instead it added splendor to the faith of those who heard him. And how could we say that he saw it for his own good or his own glory, when we know that he hardly, if at all, remembered what he had seen, since he lacked the necessary sense?

We can find still others who attained similar honors not because of any merits that preceded their experiences and not because of the decree of reason, but it happened unconnected to the recipients' zeal and unrelated to any particular just deed they might have done. A clear example is the Holy Innocents, who suffered and obtained the salvation of God without ever contemplating God or his salvation.[20] The potter has the ability to make a vessel for honor or for shame. Did not Christ himself object, "Can I not do what I wish?" Indeed, "He pities whom he wishes, he hardens whom he wishes."[21]

An example from modern times is ready to hand for this point, too. At the fortified town of Saint-Quentin there was once a young man, bound to the clergy by his parents' decision. He had reached the level of an acolyte, if I'm not mistaken. Standing near the front of the apse—that is, between the apse and the altar—on a particular ceremonial day at the hour of the mass, ready to participate in the office, he was holding the paten and the host that was to be offered. A plaster image hung at the front of the chancel that bore the likeness of the crucified Lord, not far from the tomb of Quentin the martyr. And while he was standing by this image and holding the offering, he said to the image, with words as juvenile as his thoughts, "Lord, do you want some of my bread?" Christ deigned to answer him most clearly, "I will shortly give you some of my bread." A disease struck the boy when he heard these words, and a few days later he divested himself of the human form that he had held so briefly and became a possessor of heavenly robes. Now he is buried before the image that made this promise to him.

I learned this story from a cleric from the same church, and I have seen the tomb and believe the evidence it provides as well. Likewise, the first story I told I heard from my lord Raoul, archbishop of Reims, and the clergy of Soissons also provided witness, along with the clergy and the people of Laon.[22] Seneca says in his book *On Gifts* that he who, in return for another's generosity, makes a payment according to value alone follows the example of merchants, while he who gives freely imitates God.[23] Certainly and securely I say that it is much more natural for God to offer a gift freely than to bestow a gift on someone based on whether he has earned it.

There are some, however, whose faith deserves so much from divine mercy that he whose food is to do the will of his Father imparts to them in particular the power of his salvation,[24] finding them more committed than others to seeking what they had undertaken in faith. From here comes the saying, familiar to many of his followers, "Your faith made you saved."[25] That is to say: "The urgency of your faith so pleases me, that the healing you experience grows from you instead of from me"—shown in our times by a recent, exemplary story.

In the territories around Cambrai and Arras, if I'm not mistaken, a young man and a girl, very closely related to each other, were dwelling under the same roof in the countryside. Their constant proximity in the same house led to familiarity, and familiarity led them to try foolish ideas, until shameful incest suddenly spoiled their poorly guarded proximity. Without delay, upon the fulfillment of their desire, the young girl sensed herself with child, and they began lamenting their disgrace with frequent hushed and tearful exchanges. Fearing the scandalous talk and reproachful looks from their fellow countrymen, they chose to abandon their native soil. The girl, however, frightened of her own crime, rushed to a priest and with tremendous sadness confessed her fault. Shortly thereafter, at night, they both departed from that country, as if exiled to a foreign land. But they had not yet left their fields when they came to the edge of an abandoned, open well. Then the young man said, "Let's sit here and rest by the mouth of the well, where you might lighten the weight of your womb." She believed his lies, and when she had sat next to the mad youth, this worst person imaginable punched her in the stomach and pushed her into the well.

She returned to her senses a little later. She was crying at the pain of so steep a fall, and he began to shout to her, as if trying to find out whether she was alive. Once he had heard the soft sounds of her plaintive voice and realized that she was indeed living, he threw stones at her. The young woman quickly went silent and moved to a far corner of the well, not to rest but to escape the deluge of rocks, and when his wicked ears could detect neither breath nor even a whimper from her, he thought her dead, killed both by the fall and by his rocks. He withdrew and returned home, happier because of his secret crime. As for the girl, talk of her was rare—except that she had run away alone. There, stuck in that hole in the ground, so desperate that she did not expect nourishment even from God, she felt a drop of liquid fall steadily from the earth above her head. She positioned her mouth just below the falling water, and so many and such small drops refreshed her that it seemed to equal the riches of Sardanapalus.[26]

Why do I waste time? She passed almost forty days there and received no other nourishment beyond those drops just described. During this forty-day fast, swineherds and shepherds were leading their animals all around the common grazing lands near the well.[27] While they were wandering about these places, they heard a quietly groaning voice coming up from the depths. Leaning their heads over the well, they learned from the voice that a woman had fallen in, and when they asked who she was, she roared back with a thunderous scream her name and where she came from. Hearing her, the shepherds ran to the nearest village with the speed of Pegasus, saying that they had found the girl believed by all to have perished or to have run off into exile. In no time at all a peasant mob rushed there. A crowd of women flew to her; tender age did not hinder young boys, just as indolence did not hinder old women, but instead every available person hurried to her. One of them was then sent down with ropes to raise the fallen woman and to show her to the expectant crowd. After she had been brought before the people and had described the way she had been saved, rumor of this miracle did not confine itself to that area, but instead this sign, so utterly unheard of in our age, circulated through faraway lands.

See here how strong was faith rooted in penance, how strong was constancy grounded in the desire for improvement! The one who has faith rooted in penance never feels anxiety about his forgiveness, once he has made true confession born out of a yearning for correction. This is the faith that the apostle commends by offering repeated examples drawn from the lives of early patriarchs, listing among them even Rahab and Jephthah, whose justifications for their extreme faith are more obscure than all the others he mentions.[28] The faith of this young woman, however, seems to me exceptional—unshaken in her belief as she turned to God in her need. Faith is so important in the eyes of God that heavenly grace cannot refuse to help even those who have not yet corrected their lives. For this reason the prophets inveigh more than once before God, "Do not delay! Free us for the sake of yourself and for the honor of your name."[29] Thus let me say with more certainty than certainty itself that God, who is piety, cannot stop himself from helping anyone about to become exiled from him, even more swiftly than he aids the just man; for he tempts the just for their own benefit and more quickly to the just he pronounces the judgments they seek.

There are still others who have earned heavenly glories in our day not suddenly and because of faith alone, but because of a long life spent in holy labor. In the church of Cambrai about two years ago there lived a deacon, named Erlebald, who had been the chief guardian of the church and who also in his many sermons, delivered to people everywhere in order to demonstrate the fruit of true confession, told the story that I have just related. He ruined his own body with a burden of heavy asceticism, wasting away in the continuous filth of a hair shirt, which he hardly ever—or never—cleaned. Eventually this garment generated an abundance of worms, and these took root in the shirt and bubbled up like spring water. It was held a wonder that human flesh could bear it, since he never took the hair shirt off, not even when going to bed, and he didn't use a mattress either, but instead of a bed he lay on a bench with hardly any straw for comfort, never sleeping nude. Then as the end of his life approached, his spirit began to suffer from serious demonic disturbances. Demons seemed to drag him through cesspools, and when people saw him and asked the reason behind his suffering, he answered that demons had obviously inflicted it upon him because he had done a less than perfect job of restraining the clergy committed to him. As death approached, although to many, and especially to the bishop, the man's appearance seemed good, when

the bishop asked him how he was, he responded, "For the last
thirty days, I have received punishments through daily lash-
ings of the whip." To which the bishop said, "But you, lord—
whatever for?" And he said, "It is a wonder that you say such
a thing, since you know that a man, although saintly, is sub-
ject to lapses and weaknesses whether he wishes it or not. So
you ought to think about those things that you have confessed
to God and to me, to correct them as you have promised me.
Do not put off correction, since you will benefit from it." Then
on Christmas Day, all his days ended. In time this vision and
the visions of others became widely known, and with all of
them taken together, combined with the general high quality
of Erlebald's life, it seemed possible only to think good things
about him as the celebration of Easter approached.

Now see how in the monastery of Bourbourg, a home to
saintly virgins of admirable religion, there were two young
girls of the purest character. One of them died on the day
before the Lord's resurrection and was called upon by her
friend and bound by many oaths that, God permitting, after
she had set aside the flesh, she would return to her as a spirit
and tell how things were with her, either for good or for ill.
Such a shared love had bound the two of them together that
they knew everything about each other while alive and did not
wish it to be otherwise after death. A few days after the one
girl had passed on and after Easter, the young girl who
remained in this world was going to the dormitory (I don't
know what she intended to do). There before her stood her
beloved companion, looking not in the least deathly or horrid,
but instead with flushed cheeks she appeared pleasing to the
senses.[30] Boundless wonder transfixed the other girl, and with
stammering lips she asked her friend how she was doing. "I
feel happy," she said. "For on Easter day just passed, Erlebald,
deacon of Cambrai and I with him amid great rejoicing of the
heavenly host were received before the face of almighty God."
She spoke and she left, even as she embraced with immense
sadness the one abandoned so swiftly.

That man Erlebald had been in the priesthood, where he
had distinguished himself, and was especially close to me in

friendship because of his abundant knowledge of scripture. I rejoice over his friendship and his final reward, exactly as I ought to do—would that I now might be found as pleasing! His laborious faith proved valuable, making God a debtor to his pious deeds. Although I had heard these things from my lord Barthélemy, bishop of Laon, so many witnesses living near this blessed man came forward immediately after his death to say almost exactly the same things about these events that I cannot now strike them from my memory.

We are reviewing these wonders, however, not so much for the sake of novelty but rather to make clear the reasons why the causes behind miracles can differ so much one from the other. I think therefore I should now add: just as we ought to embrace wholeheartedly things evident and obvious, so ought we to punish with harsh censures things that are not truthful but that are, rather, lies fashioned through various deceits. For he who ascribes to God what God has not even thought about compels God to lie, as much as anyone is capable of doing so. If someone accuses me, a worthless little man, of lying or else charges me with having done something that I did not do, it is for me a cause of revulsion and hatred. What then is more destructive, more distressing, more damnable than he who defiles God, the font of all purity, solely because of his own stinking will's ambitions and desires? For I have seen—and I am ashamed to tell this story—a common boy, the squire of a certain knight, or so they say, who died on an estate near Beauvais two days before Easter. The estate pertained to the rights of a certain extremely well-known abbot. People began to attribute unmerited sanctity to the dead boy because of the holy day when he died. Then after some peasants, desirous of novelty, began to honor him, suddenly all the nearby ignorant country folk carried oblations and candles to his grave. Why go on? The grave was covered with offerings, a house was built to enclose the place, and hordes of pilgrims, from as far away as Brittany (though rustics only—there were no nobles), were drawn there. That ever-so-wise abbot and his religious monks saw it all and encouraged the contrived miracles, seduced by the piles of pilgrims' gifts.

Feigned cases of deafness, pretended bouts of madness, fingers cunningly bent back to the palm, or feet contorted underneath buttocks can capture the avaricious hearts of the common mob, but why would a discreet and wise man, under the appearance of sanctity, make himself the promoter of such events? We have heard how such things are bandied about in repeated whispers, and we have witnessed ridiculous deeds performed during the translation of reliquaries, and we have seen the depths of another's purse daily emptied by the lies of those whom Jerome calls "enraged by the rage of their oratory."[31] We are shaken by such great obfuscation, we are stirred by their adulteration of the divine, such that according to the aforesaid Father Jerome, they triumph by preying on fools, spendthrifts, and plate lickers, they surpass the ravens and the magpies with their ceaseless chatter! But why do I enumerate their crimes? It would demonstrate their error more effectively if I told of something specific.

One particularly famous church set out upon this wayward path recently, and through a spokesman they sought after profits to repair their losses.[32] While this huckster was boasting inappropriately about his relics, he held forth from his neck an amulet and said (I was there in person),[33] "Know this! That this little box contains a piece of the bread that the Lord chewed with his own teeth! And if you doubt this in the slightest, look here! A real hero!" he said. "Right here!" (He was talking about me.) "You bear witness to how terribly well-read he is! He'll stand as my witness, if need be." I confess that I blushed upon hearing him. And if I had not revered the presence of the people whom that man seemed to have as sponsors, I would have had to show him up for the liar that he was. But I respected their peace more than that of the speaker.[34] What can I say? Even monks, let alone clerics, do not restrain themselves from this kind of dirty profit, so that even in my hearing they speak heretical things about our faith. According to Boethius, however, I would rightly be judged a madman were I to dispute with the mad.[35]

So that we might more effectively examine the question before us, however, let us next discuss who exactly is a "saint."

Although we hold the apostles to be saints, as well as those whom the church has convincingly demonstrated to be martyrs, in the case of confessors we must take greater care in reaching a verdict. By their blood alone is the exaltation of martyrs justified, even if we lack sufficient written evidence about them, and we do not inquire in the case of martyrs what sort of life they had earlier led, since blood is enough to purge the oldest sins. Sweet Jesus! Why wouldn't it be enough, since blood is sufficient to wipe sins clean and bring men into the fullness of glory? This expiation of sin—before baptism as well as after baptism—eliminates every fault and brings about a cleansing and purification, or rather more truly it enables perfect illumination! I call something "an expiation" when a righteous cause precedes it. In the canons, for example, we read that if a person is found to have been killed while destroying idols and that he died because of it, he is not considered a martyr because of such a death. It seems like a worthy enough cause, so why isn't he a martyr? Because the intention behind the cause is sometimes corrupt. The Donatists, for example, underwent sufferings not unequal to the martyrs, but because they died alienated from charity, they suffered in vain.[36] Some time ago the zeal of God's people at Soissons caused a couple of remnants left over from the Manicheans to be burned to death, but because these Manicheans lacked a just cause for dying, they only added damnation to bodily punishments. I spoke about these things at greater length in my books of *Monodies*.[37]

If, therefore, such uncertainty exists when we are confirming the sanctity of martyrs, what kind of caution is required for confessors, whose deaths are sometimes known with less certainty? If all the church is in agreement about Martin, Rémy, and similarly well-known figures, what can I say about others whom commoners—envious of these saints just mentioned—create every day in every village and in every town?[38] For when some see that others have such great patrons, they wish that they had equally good ones, and so they invent them. In a similar fashion, after the poets had first circulated their splendid works, every witless person out of jealousy, "learned and unlearned indiscriminately," as Horace says, "wrote their own little poems."[39] The ancients, who created a golden age in their own time, elevated into gods and goddesses the inventors of the arts; their successors so crowded the heavens that their descendants eliminated some gods and the rest whom they had set aside they called "the chosen." When the Jews had been taken to Babylon, the Samaritans created their own gods. "Each people fashioned its particular god: the Babylonians made Succothbenoth for themselves, the Cuthites made Nergel," and others made others still.[40] As a rule, according to Gregory the Great, "when a person in disfavor is sent to intercede, the mind of the person who was angry only becomes angrier still."[41] But all deny that they have chosen patrons who might be in disfavor. Just let them explain to me how they believe that their patron might protect them when they don't know anything about him! The only thing you can learn about him is a name. But if the clergy keeps silent, then old women and flocks of vile little ladies will chatter together, telling fictitious stories about their patrons, discussing them over their treadles and weavers' rods. If anyone disagrees with what they say, they will muster in their defense not only their angry reproaches but even their shuttlecocks.

Who, except an utter madman, would call for help from somebody about whom there survives not even a lingering hint as to what sort of person he was? And what is such a prayer worth when all manner of uncertainty gnaws at the mind of the person who prays when he presents to God an advocate whom he does not know? What, I ask, is the advantage of something that is never free of sin? For if you beseech someone without knowing whether he was saintly, then you sin in the very act by which you ought to have sought indulgence. In doing so you offer, but do not divide, rightly.[42] Obviously when your prayers are full of doubt, you do not reconcile yourself to God; rather, you annoy him with the uncertainty you feel about your request, for God will fault a person who sends to him an advocate whom God does not know.

And how could anyone whom you hold suspect speak on your behalf? And if you yourself do not think well of him, how do you imagine that he can benefit you? Ambrose says somewhere, "He to whom I am prepared to entrust myself ought to be above me."[43] Is it not evidence then that you are a complete madman if you call upon someone about whose status you feel uncertain? And why do you beg for him to stand on your behalf before God when you don't know whether he is any better than you? Remember how the Lord commended the virtue of faith as being able to move mountains and in doing so forbade any uncertainty of heart.[44] It is as if he said, "If you set your heart upon something great, whatever it may be, and if you hesitate, even just a little, you will lose it." And it is far more acceptable that everyone should doubt his own virtue than for you to feel hopeless about your patron, upon whom hangs your hope before God. Indeed, you hang onto him because you think less of yourself, but surely you know that if your mediator is a fake, because of him you will lose whatever you could have otherwise gained by your own effort.

But why do I dwell on these things, when the entire holy church is so careful in its pronouncements that it will not even dare to affirm that the body of the Lord's mother has been glorified through physical resurrection, and for this reason: the arguments necessary to demonstrate it are lacking, and—although it is wicked to believe that such a vessel would have been cast down and forced to experience corruption, unrewarded and dishonored, she who after her Son is more splendid than any other creature, because she carried within herself the Lord of Majesty in his entirety, something not permitted even to angels, especially since he is obligated to give back to his mother's body (to which he owes his existence) what is due to his own body, now glorified—we do not dare describe her body as "resuscitated" and can only assert with certainty what is made likely by evidence?[45] Although in other cases reason alone suffices in the discussion of scripture, and although passages drawn from scripture embody reason itself, in this case where the most fitting reason readily suggests that she has been wholly glorified through a resurrected body, since probative evidence is nonetheless lacking, we are free to believe whatever is more glorious about her, but only tacitly, for we can in no way demonstrate its truth completely. Reason in this case, however, is clear beyond question: since many bodies of various holy men are believed to have been resurrected with her Son,[46] then she, whose flesh in no way differs from her Son's—flesh that received no father's incitements in the moment of his conception except those from the Holy Spirit—how under the law of that ancient curse could she return to the dust of the earth, she who was singularly chosen to give birth to the author of our redemption? If I dare to say so, the Son could not escape the punishment of the flesh if he allowed the flesh of his mother to suffer the common lot and conferred to another's flesh what he denied to his mother—indeed, even to his very own flesh.[47] We are not prevented from knowing it through inference, but we are prohibited from asserting it, since proofs are lacking. If we cannot teach the things outlined above about her, whose glory no creature can measure, what ought we to enjoin about those whose salvation and damnation are unknown—except perpetual silence?

About other saints there exist writings worse than doggerel, unfit for the ears of swineherds. Because many attribute the greatest of antiquity to their saints, they seek in modern times to have their biographies written down. I myself have frequently been asked to do so, but given that things right before my eyes can be deceptive, how could I speak truly about something no one has ever seen? If I were to repeat what I have heard said (and I have not only been asked to speak in praise of some extremely ignoble people, but even to extol them before the public), then I, if I were to say the things asked of me, and they, who were encouraging me to say such things—all of us would deserve public censure.

Passing over those whose own obscurity excludes them from consideration, let us touch instead upon those who have a more secure claim to our belief. Even around them, errors are endless. For one group and then another will each claim to possess the same person. To take one example, people at Constantinople say that they have the head of John the Baptist; the monks of Saint-Jean d'Angély affirm that they have it. Could there be anything more ridiculous preached about such a man, other than both groups saying he was two-headed?

All jesting aside, let's examine this in earnest. Since it is clear that the head could not have been copied and that they cannot both possess it, then obviously either the former or the latter have practiced some deception, and if in this matter—a struggle in the name of piety—arrogance and mendacity fight against one another, then each group does things demonic instead of divine. Both the deceivers and the deceived venerate to no good end the thing about which they boast. And if they venerate something unworthily, then the whole chain of people worshipping it become implicated in their deception. For even if it is not the head of John the Baptist but of some other saint, the sin of duplicity is in no way diminished.

But why do I carry on about the head of John, when I have heard similar things in my own days about a countless numbers of saints' bodies? It is well known that my predecessor, the bishop of Amiens, had the body of the martyr Fermin[48]— or so it was thought—translated from one tomb into another, though he found in the tomb no slip of parchment, not even the evidence of a single letter, confirming whose body he had found lying there. (I heard this story from the bishop of Arras and from the bishop of Amiens himself.) To address this matter, the bishop of the city quickly had it inscribed on a lead plaque that Fermin the martyred bishop of Amiens was buried there. And almost immediately thereafter, the same thing happened at the church of Saint-Denis. There the abbot had a fairly lavish shrine built, and when the martyr was raised up and the head and limbs were uncovered, a strip of parchment was discovered in his nostrils, proclaiming that it was the martyr Fermin of Amiens.

Since nothing in this affair supports the Amiens claim, and since whatever evidence does exist by contrast supports the other side, let reason, I say, sit in judgment and pass its verdict. Surely whatever that bishop wrote on the lead plate ought by all rights to be shattered, since no written evidence supports it! And obviously the Saint-Denis monks, who have the support of a written document, can present at least a mumbled case on their own behalf.

Whoever venerates something he does not know is never

free from grave danger, even if that something is actually holy; on the contrary, it normally leads to great sacrilege. For what is more sacrilegious than to honor something as divine when it manifestly is not? Whatever touches upon God is divine, and what could cling to God more closely than those who are united to him in body?

Hear something else that elucidates my complaint and draws a further distinction in the subjects already touched upon. There was a bishop of Bayeux named Odo, the illegitimate son of Count Robert of Normandy and patrilineally brother of William the elder, king of the English,[49] who fervently searched for his saintly predecessor to the bishopric, Exuperius, a man greatly honored, especially at the town of Corbeil.[50] Odo paid a hundred pounds in coins to the guardian of the church where the saint had been taken, intending to remove the body from it, but instead that wickedly clever guardian found the tomb of a peasant named Exuperius, dug him up, and offered him to the bishop. The bishop asked whether these remains brought to him really did belong to Saint Exuperius and even demanded that the guardian give him an oath. "I will swear to you as a solemn oath that this is the body of Exuperius; about his sanctity, however, I will not swear, since that forename has been given to many men judged to have wandered far from sanctity." Tricked by this rogue, the bishop felt more at ease. The townspeople, however, learned about the profit that this custodian had made off of their patron. When summoned before them, he answered, "Look again at the seals on his shrine, and if you find them in any way disturbed, I will pay the penalty."

Just think how much shame this fraudulent episcopal double-dealing brought to all of religion! The peasant Exuperius was profanely promoted—thrust upon a sacred altar of God, a pestilence perhaps never to be removed from it! So many examples of exactly the same thing happening everywhere crowd upon my memory that I do not have the time or the energy to talk about them. There are so many cases of fraud that involve not whole bodies but limbs and pieces of limbs, ordinary bones dispersed everywhere, sold as saints' relics. This practice occurs through men who, according to the apostle, view gain as godliness, since they take what, if they were wise, would be beneficial for their souls' salvation and turn it into shit for their purses.[51]

But all of this business grows out of a wicked common root, since practices such as these deprive bodies of what ought to be the common lot of all humanity. Nothing could be clearer than the fact that man comes from the earth, and that when he has paid his debt through death, he returns to the earth according to the law of original sin. For it is said to him, "You are of the earth, and into the earth you shall go."[52] In pronouncing this verdict on man's present and future, God did not mean: "You are of gold or silver, and into gold or silver you shall return." How can man, I pray, be torn away from his nature—no, more truly, torn away from the commands of God—so that he might then be poured into gold or silver shells, a condition suitable to no creature? If the wise man knew of other containers for human bodies besides the earth, he would not have said, "There is a heavy burden on the sons of Adam, from the day they leave their mother's womb until the day they return into the mother of all."[53] Note how elegantly he says "their mother's" and "mother of all." If I hear "mother" described as the one who supplied her womb and as the one who provides a fixed place that cannot be changed, then consequently this "mother" is the one who gave to mortal men the substance for their existence, but it is also plainly more than a mother. For this mother receives us again, a thing not permitted to ordinary mothers. Whatever sort of sarcophagus you use, hoping to protect yourself from the earth's touch, you will become earth, like it or not. And what is the honor in being enclosed in gold or silver, since it was an ordinary stone that entombed the Son of God? From the beginning of time, even the haughtiest of kings has followed this custom, nor can my memory supply a single example otherwise, and even though they fill their tombs with boundless treasure, I cannot recall ever reading that they exchanged pure marble caskets for gold or silver ones—this would be "to have zeal for God but not according to knowledge."[54] Such a faith, in our time, has brought forth not fruit but rather an unworthy harvest, and it has produced something we know never in the history of the world to have been done anywhere by anyone wishing to display his wealth or piety.

If the bodies of saints had remained in places appropriate to the demands of nature—that is to say, tombs—errors such as the ones I have described would never have occurred. Relic tours happen under a pretext of piety, but because saints' bodies have been ripped out of their graves and carried about in pieces here and there, a nascent wickedness unrecognizably distorts any righteous intention and an all-pervasive greed corrupts what had happened originally with great simplicity. The burial of the dead was for Tobias an act of such merit that Raphael praised it almost exclusively among all his other human deeds and said that these burials had been offered up before the grateful eyes of God.[55] How much wickedness and sin, therefore, must we attribute to those who deprive bodies of their natural debt and instead disturb them under any flimsy pretext? And what flimsier—why don't I just say "what ruder"—occasion is there than that a disciple should set himself above a master?[56] Should the latter be buried behind stone, whereas the former is sealed in gold? Should the latter be wrapped in simple linen, while the former is girded in vestments of silk woven with golden thread? According to the most magnificent Pope Gregory, the men who unwittingly saw the bodies of the apostle Paul and the martyr Laurence received a most severe punishment.[57] What sort of judgment will they receive who, motivated by avarice alone, scatter the restless bodies of saints here and there, turning them into a daily spectacle for, if I may say so, the sole purpose of collecting offerings? They habitually cover the bare bones of saints in little ivory or silver chests and at a specified time and hour uncover them, for a price paid in advance. The spirit of Samuel, who was thriving as a soul with its natural alacrity, lamented his disturbance after being summoned through a medium.[58] Would not physical bones more justly complain of suffering dispersions here, there, and everywhere?

Jacob and Joseph left instructions for their burial,[59] and all saints prepared tombs for themselves, seeing to the work of carrying their bones back to their native soil, almost as though they feared to be damned if not buried in their homes, that is, with their family, which is to say, among their tribe. What else might this mean, except that they placed great importance on having their entire bodies transformed at the glory of resurrection? If no one—that is, no rational person—has hated his own flesh, but rather ministers to its daily needs with servings of food and drink, how much more ought he tend to his body when he receives no pleasure from filling its needs, as we often feel when eating food; and how much more wholeheartedly ought he to do so, when, the course of this "sad service" (as the poet says)[60] exhausted, holding out hope for a better life, free from this present winter and safe from the rainfall of our tumults today, he awaits the command of the archangel to rise? If the apostle calls the people in this condition "the sleeping,"[61] I think it must be wicked to disturb them, especially since during this rest they do not expect anyone to wake them up, except for him who makes the dead live. Let everyone say what he knows. I say confidently that it was pleasing neither to God nor to any of his saints to have a single one of their tombs opened or any of their bodies torn into pieces.

Among the Gentiles, because of their respect for humanity, the duties of washing corpses and of burying the poor, with a funeral bier provided, were performed for all the needy, even though their hope died with the death of the body. But we dig up graves and divide up the limbs of those whom, as copious evidence teaches us, we have angered with all of this moving about. Indeed, when Augusta, the wife of Tiberias—if I'm not mistaken—sought the head of the apostle Paul, Gregory responded that he did not dare get it, recalling the punishments to the gravediggers to which I referred above.[62]

I wish that more saints protected their bodies with the same zeal as does Edmund, a king among the English of no small reputation who is recognized as a martyr.[63] He remains to this day in a condition resembling sleep and does not think it right for anyone to see or touch him. In our own time (I won't bother to go into what we can read in his *Passion*), an abbot of Edmund's church was more curious than proper about whether, as was commonly said, the saint's head had rejoined his body after decapitation. After fasting with another monk, the abbot tried with the monk's assistance to see if the neck adhered to the shoulders, but an infirmity immediately punished his attempts, such that afterward they both lost all ability to use their hands. If every saint's tomb could attain a similar peace, then all the disputes about the disturbance of sacred bodies and about relic exchanges would be silenced, and one group would not be saying that they had the same saint that another group claimed to possess. All the monuments would remain intact, as would be just, and with everyone sleeping undisturbed in the land allotted to them, the scams we have all encountered concerning saints buried in multiple locations would not happen and unworthy men would not hold the places of worthy ones.

Some people have asked me whether relics are harmful to those who venerate them, if they receive honor that belongs to someone else and are not the relics of him whom they are believed to be.[64] I don't think so. For the Lord said about the saints, "Let them be one, even as we are one"[65]—since together they are under Christ, who is their head, as if they shared an identity of body and a unity of spirit with him, adhering to God himself. In the case of the bones of authentic saints, therefore, there can be no error, if some are worshiped as others, since they are all limbs in Christ's body. It does not seem out of place to note that the feast of the Four Crowned Martyrs is a celebration, according to Roman authority, with the names of five other martyrs.[66]

But perhaps someone might ask if God hears every simple person who invokes him by naming as saints those who are not truly saints. To which I must respond: anyone who invokes God uncertainly annoys him, but if he faithfully beseeches the one whom he believes to be a saint but who is not a saint, then he still appeases God. For comparison, let us imagine that someone believes charity is a sin. If he knowingly practices charity, truly based on what his conscience tells him, he commits a sin, even though in another sense what he does is actually good. Thus if someone believes someone is a saint whom he hears called a saint but who is in reality not a saint, if he sincerely and faithfully calls upon that supposed saint, then before God, who is the seed and the fruit of prayer, the intention behind his prayer stands firm and sure, in whatever way his mind in its simplicity seems to err about its intercessor. Because he offers veneration to someone in the belief that it is a good man whom he venerates, he shall not be deprived of a reward from a good man. If you receive a prophet in the name of a prophet—that is, someone who has only the name of a prophet or of a just man without the reality of being one—you will still obtain the honor and the reward of a prophet or a just man, even though that prophet or just man is a fraud who has merely the name or the appearance of those titles.[67] And certainly many men with too little learning often make mistakes in their prayers, but the divine ear measures intentions rather than words. If you hiccup when you are praying, "Let the power of the Holy Spirit be present to us, Lord," and it comes out, "be absent from us," it does not matter: God is not overly concerned with grammar.[68] No voice pierces him, but a heart reaches toward him.

BOOK 2

ON THE BIPARTITE
BODY OF THE LORD

Now that I have explained these things as a preface to my upcoming argument, let me set into the foundation that I have lain a few precious stones of faithful eloquence, polishing and cutting them until we reach the core of that difficult question many have proposed to me. With this goal in mind, I have sorted through all the heaps of gravel in the previous section, in order that I might, God willing, more freely work around and resolve the impediment before us.

When I was discussing what people have been thinking about saints' relics and what they have been doing with them, it lay outside my organizational scheme to mention how certain people in my region claim to possess a tooth belonging to our Savior, which he would have lost naturally when he was nine years old. Still others claim to have the umbilical cord, cut off at birth, or the Lord's foreskin from his circumcision, about which the great Origen says, "There were some who did not blush to write books about the circumcision of the Lord."[1] Passing over these other two relics, we will focus instead on the first one that I mentioned, because it touches us more closely. If we demonstrate its absurdity, then all of the others will be convincingly debunked, too.

Admittedly, one can reasonably argue that something from Christ's body remained in this world, but I wonder what sort of proxy he intended to make available to us through his figural body—I call it "figural" because it occurs in the form of a shadow, on the level of appearance,[2] not because it in any way differs from the powers and the abilities of the "preceding truth" [Christ's body fully realized in heaven]. The "preceding truth" is

also a "personal truth" [Christ in bodily form], which the "sig-
nified truth" [Christ in the Eucharist] refers to and identifies.[3]
What Christ handed down as "having to be done in memory of
him" refers to the undoubted presence of his own true, fully
possessed self.[4] If this presence were anything other than his
true self, it would hold no greater worth than, say, a wedding
ring does for a wife: a ring serves as a proxy for the husband in
the wife's thoughts.

One type of identity created the reason for the other, since
there was a lapse of time between the Virgin birth and the Pas-
sion on the cross, such that, to coin a phrase, the "vicarial iden-
tity" came into existence through the example of his life. What
I call the first and most important body is "the truth," whence
flow the tangible sacraments that we receive. For whatever
truth, granted figurally, the vicarial body contains, it holds that
truth because the first body, from which it was derived, affords
existence to it. Obviously that body is the "principal truth" and
can be called the "principal truth." Nothing about it can be
imagined, as it is beyond what the eyes and the intellect can see
and touch. Although the vicarial body necessarily holds all of
truth, too, it is not the principal body but is rather an inflection
from it. It is the referent and sign of that true body, and it is
always once removed from that body. (Because this vicarial
body is wholly the body that precedes it, I use "sign" not to
refer to a particular thing, but as a figure put forth for the sake
of exterior senses.)[5]

Thus when the psalmist calls the Father the "principal spirit,"
it is not because the structure of the divine essence mandates
that the Father hold authority over the Son and the Holy Spirit.[6]
Rather, it is because the origin of the Son and the Holy Spirit
is drawn from him. When the psalmist speaks of someone as
being "principal," he refers to the last of several persons named,
although when the Son's mouth spoke these three names, the
Father was the first of them.[7] The prophet thus indicates that
nothing comes first and nothing comes last within the Godhead.
Greek foolishness, however, has attempted to conjecture some
kind of original subsisting matter underlying the substances.[8]
But since no element can be made distinct within the divine

being, it seems more appropriate, when we consider divine things, to speak only of its "essence." It is true that some would define the "origin of a substance" as its "subsisting parts," but whoever pays heed to such ideas should be on his guard. How can it happen that God "subsists" or "stands"? The capacity of the human intellect and the limitations of human language do not allow us to speak usefully of God as anything except "essence."

After this digression, I will finally return to a few points that I have so far passed over. The "principal body" established the material for the sacraments that followed it. If some of that principal body remained on the earth while some of it ascended into heaven, why would we need the sacramental guarantee of another body [the vicarial body, or Eucharist] in this life, when obviously it would suffice for us to celebrate this leftover bit from his actual flesh? For our bodily eyes could gaze upon the remnants of the Lord's body that I have mentioned and our fingers touch them without any exercise of the intellect and with no experience of contemplation. There would be no need to try the substance of our faith, as the apostle says, through the stuff of bread and wine, the things actually seen.[9] The mind indeed exercises itself a great deal, moving beyond its established camps, when it learns to gaze upon the invisible through understanding the meaning of the visible. How pleasurable it is, one to be desired with a hot passion, to hold before our eyes, after careful cultivation, without any typology or any intervening veil of meaning, the thing itself, that for which our breast burns and which our heart draws into a close embrace. Furthermore, although God is aware of how visible, sensual things are loved and desired in the judgment of men, it is never appropriate for us, who can always take delight in Christ's own particular body,[10] to grow weary in the face of the impenetrable subtlety required understand it. We should instead take delight in it, veiled in shadow as it is.

Because therefore a small fragment left over from that body—if one can call rightly what surpasses the whole world a "small fragment"—suffices to advance joy and faith throughout the world, why does Lord Jesus give his flesh again in pledge to mortal men through a figural sacrifice? I speak securely when I say that it would have been pointless for him to leave behind this vicarial body as a memorial, if he had also left in the world a gift sufficient to ensure continued mention of him. "As often as you do this," he said, "you do it in memory of me."[11] I want to know how he wishes us to honor his memory, and why he would establish other parts of his body for his followers to celebrate his memory when the smallest particle—I don't speak of many or large pieces, but a single particle—from that body conceived by a Virgin through the Holy Spirit would suffice for a gathering of the whole world. I would interpret the words above as saying, "Since nothing remains in the land that might revivify my memory among you, since your senses don't have access to anything that might revitalize my presence for you intellectually, it is fitting that you have such a gift from me, whereby I might restore myself to you, and in no way diminish among you my presence—a presence that you have loved and that you even now desire." If you study the above-mentioned passage carefully, what else could it mean?

Do we need two bodies to impress his memory upon us? Did he not say to all the apostles (though in fact speaking against Judas alone), "The poor you will always have with you, but me you will not always have"? This pronouncement might seem to contradict another passage: "For I am with you for all your days to the end of the world."[12] The latter statement, however, refers to spiritual protection, inasmuch as he is God, and the former statement to his corporeal presence. But if anyone claims to possess either his tooth or his umbilical cord or, as we read, his foreskin, and if he associates it with this corporeal presence, then he lies. Because Christ says "me you will not always have," the pronouncement encompasses anything connected to his humanity. But perhaps you think that this passage in not meant to encompass small particles of his physical being. If so, then you may not realize how a "part" can take the place of the "whole." It is not only scripture that communicates synecdochally. Even illiterate commoners use this figure of speech in an easily understandable fashion. If by some chance you hurt your foot or your hand or your fingernail and if someone asks you what happened, do you not say, "I've hurt myself"? And what proportion of the whole is a mere fragment of a fingernail? If when injured you do not distinguish between "you" and that smallest part of you that is troubled, then in the same way we must understand the "me" that Christ said we will not always have. If we are accustomed to call our closest friends "half of our souls" and our relatives "our flesh and blood,"[13] then when each of us says "me," what else are we expressing, except the whole of what is in us and what is from us? Certainly if you have your blood let, your hair cut, or your nails clipped, and then someone asks you whose things these were, you respond either that they were yours or that they were from you. If there were some part left over from a field that had been divided or from a hide that had been cut, no one, unless he were mad, would deny that the part that had been cut off was part of that particular field or that particular hide.

Before we proceed to other arguments focused more directly against you, listen to something else related to your case.[14] The Lord says in another passage, "He who eats me lives through me."[15] Note that, similar to what I said about, "*I* am with you" and "you will not always have *me* with you," in this passage the first "me" signifies something different from the second "me." The first "me," that is, means, "He who externally eats, as it were, my flesh and blood lives from it, because he lives from that which illuminates the interior man." Obviously it cannot literally happen that one person would wholly devour another. If we take the part as referring to the whole, though, then it can be understood without difficulty according to the spiritual sense, especially since beliefs about his body dictate that when it is offered in pieces, the whole exists in those pieces. Thus we read about manna in Exodus, that he who gathered more manna did not possess more, and that he who prepared less had no less than anyone else, but that each received as much as he was able to eat.[16] So this sacrament diminishes or grows in accordance with the intellect that seizes it. It diminishes in the presence of a murky

understanding of our faith (although the utility of the sacra-
ment is no less) and it increases in the presence of a more astute
believer, who receives, however, the same quantity of sacred
food needed for salvation as did the simple believer. The suffi-
ciency of this great gift is denied to no one according to the
degree of piety that God has granted him.

As we know, however, every material object can be exam-
ined in terms of greater and lesser, because given the various
sizes of bodies, their qualities cannot all be of equal magnitude:
smaller objects in their slightness cannot contain the same
enormous bulk as do great masses. Yet by the mystical work-
ings of this sacrifice, standards of measure work according to
different laws. For although when the sacrament is broken
into pieces, the pieces possess different sizes, just as is the case
with other objects, nevertheless when measured with the inte-
rior eye, he who takes from the altar everything that has been
prepared there in fact receives no more than he who takes the
least little fragment. If indeed you were to set several loaves of
bread on the altar, would you then believe that each one of
those loaves had become a complete individual body of the
Lord? Does not a greater number of hosts instead—however
many there are—cause the contemplative eye to see in them a
single image?

I also should add in connection with this, although it is not
strictly relevant to my argument, that I have known some peo-
ple who made the following mistake: someone left the sacra-
mental bread in the pyx on the altar without telling the priest
during the celebration of mass, and after the service, he found
the bread still in the box. This case was turned over for judg-
ment to a cleric who was serving at that church, and he settled
the problem in this fashion. What had been in the pyx when it
was on the altar during mass he determined to be a perfected
sacrament ready to be offered to communicants as if it were
the Eucharist. Anyone who doubts that this judgment is ridic-
ulous is stupid.[17] By what reasoning should we believe this
bread to be consecrated, when in fact no one prayed for it,
remembered it, or even knew about it? To be sure, if the priest
failed to notice some bread set under the corporal pallium or a

leftover drop of wine sticking to some part of the chalice, no wise person would think after the performance of the mystery that these bits had anything to do with the sacrament. Nothing at all happens with the host except through the touch of faith of one who prays, and the host truly cannot become holy unless the word of the Lord, which alone makes the sacrament, is spoken over it. This bread carelessly left behind or this drop by chance clinging to a part of the chalice during the mass has the same effect as an unbeliever or a catechumen in church after the Gospel.[18]

But setting these points aside, I will return to the topics with which I began. "He who eats me," he says, "lives through me."[19] If you understand the eating of Christ in such a way that his limbs and pieces of his limbs are passed around to the mouths of those partaking of him—so that, for example, one person gets a finger, another gets a part of a finger and so on and so forth through all the body parts and pieces of parts— then obviously the words of Christ do not agree with this interpretation. Because he says "me," he indicates the entirety of the substance of which he then was—or rather that of which he was according to both of his natures.[20] It is as if he said, "He who eats me, inasmuch as I am man, lives through me, inasmuch as I am God." Indeed he is God in two natures and of two natures: through one he enlivens our mortal self, through the other he enlightens our spiritual self. For this reason, he distributes his body and blood in two parts: first, so that his sacrificial body might lead our bodies into a blessed state, because in their lowliness our bodies need to be freed from physical hardships; and second, so that through his blood he might provide internal light to our souls—just as we read in Leviticus, "The soul of all flesh is in its blood."[21] He makes this point clearer than day because he says nothing about the offering of his body except, "This is my body, which is handed over for you" (and the apostle Paul added that second clause).[22] By contrast, he treats the blood at great length, because he considers the soul more precious than the body. In this way he explains the blood to his listeners: "It is poured forth for many for the remission of sins."[23] If therefore blood is offered for cleansing souls of sin, then obviously there is no sin in the soul except what happens with the soul's desire and consent. Just as a handle can accomplish nothing without an axe, so does a body without a willing soul commit no sin beyond original sin.[24]

If you ask for further examples on this point, similar arguments come readily and plentifully to mind. When John said, "Many (from the Jews) believed in him," he added, "Jesus however did not entrust himself to them." According to Saint Augustine, Jesus did not entrust himself to them, since he does not commend his eucharistic body to an unbaptized person, even if that person does believe. He also said elsewhere, "He who believes in me does not believe in me but in him who sent me"; and again elsewhere, "If you do not eat the flesh of the Son of Man and drink his blood."[25]

Since I have already started talking about the bipartite body of the Lord—that is, what I earlier called "the principal body" from which the later sacraments emanate, and also the "mystical body," which I previously labeled the "figural" body, through which the truth is fashioned, purer than any light, if cloaked in the shadows of bread and wine—I would like to air out these arguments further. Then I will move on to address questions about the Savior's tooth and about the other relics that arise naturally from this discussion. Whether I will be able to clarify these points I do not know.

One might ask whether the body that we take from the altar carries with it the image of the living or the dead Lord. We know, however, that he is alive, that he has always had God dwelling within him, and that he has never lost the name of the Son of God or the reality of that name, not even when he died. When he says that he must be eaten, clearly he means to show us how his person is undivided. He is personally God and man: but how according to reason can God and man be eaten? In the passage where he says, "who eats me," he must have wanted our understanding of it to be tempered thus: "He who eats my flesh and drinks my blood remains in me."[26] What quarrel could men of sound mind stir up about this passage? If God dwelled within the soul of Christ, who would dare to say that that mystery of "the simple creature" (set forth clearly in the divine offices) holds any but a living God? Ought not he, who was born of the Holy Spirit and virginal blood and who manifested the undivided person of God and man— ought not he, in order to reveal himself to us, infuse into the substance of the bread and wine an overflowing surge of all his divinity? If baptismal water not only comes alive through the Spirit but is even called "living water," are we to believe that the fundamental character of the host, changed wholly into something divine through a heavenly presence, then becomes lifeless because God dwells therein? Through the gift of the Spirit, that water, soon to flow into sewers, receives temporarily, or more accurately "momentarily" the power of cleansing sins. This host, either received by the faithful for their salvation or else seized by sinners and the unworthy, always refers to the throne of glory. It is raised up never to fail. I say confidently that it is elevated as the body of him from whom it originated, and it will suffer no indignities and no shameful humiliations because of the acts of wicked men.

If someone partakes of the host worthily, what else happens except that, through the reception of the Lord's flesh, he becomes a limb alongside those who adhere to the highest head?[27] In what other way are we handed over to the body of Jesus except by being drawn into it through communion with his flesh and blood? But if you partake of it wickedly, then you damn yourself utterly, since you will have taken the sacred sacrilegiously. By this act you would scorn and contemn (as much as you can) what you do not recognize as the body of the Lord.[28] Its sacrosanct immunity, however, keeps safe that supreme excellence from all your attempts to harm it.

But let no one bear it amiss if I seem to argue for a while from the perspective of someone who thinks otherwise.[29] I say that the sacrament is thought to exist based on the faith of him who receives it, or else it fails for him who takes it unfaithfully and subjects it to contempt—in the case of the faithful, it would fail either because they do not venerate or honor it, in the case of the unfaithful, because they actively disbelieve it and reject it in their thoughts. For my part, I do not see how the sacrament can be suitable for such minds or bodies. If in the canons of the mass we offer prayers only for those who are orthodox, who cultivate the Catholic faith, and especially who are servants and handmaidens of God (which by itself ought to be enough, never mind that the mass says, "whose faith and devotion are known and recognized among you"), what place does an unbeliever have here, what place does a wicked Christian have? If, O apostles and other saintly disciples, that blood "was poured forth on behalf of you and many others for the remission of sins"[30]—the "many others" here are none other than the elect—then each of the wicked have attained the worst possible result for themselves, taking the sacrament externally, but not receiving the sacramental grace. They take what is visible, but what is invisible and useful and what ought to nourish them for eternal life is instead denied them. And how could such a grace, granted to those preparing for eternal life, adapt itself to someone irremediably damned to the fires of hell? If a catechumen of good faith is ordered to abstain from the sacraments because he has not yet been baptized, how can the sacrament be of any possible advantage for someone who approaches it unfaithfully and impudently? Would it not merely increase the burden of his damnation?

Preachers of the gospel were ordered to say, before staying in a home, "Peace to this house." But it was added, "If a son of peace is there, your blessing will rest over that house. If not, it will return to you."[31] If the blessing a preacher gives fruitlessly to a wicked man returns to his store of merits, do you really think that the gift of the sacrament could be locked away in so foul a prison as the body of a wrongful and irrational recipient, or else in the soul of someone who basely handles it? It does not deserve such sordid places! The Holy Spirit of discipline flees the deceitful and does not live in a soul given over to sin; rather it is snatched away at the onset of wickedness.[32] How then does this divine substance—which becomes the body of the Son of God through the plentitude of the same Spirit and through identification with the Person of the Son—how does it enter into a foul heart, whose corrupt habitation the Spirit of discipline does not suffer and is unable to endure?

But someone objects, "If it is not the sacrament and does not have the grace of the sacrament, why is such a person who partakes of it subject to damnation?" To which I answer: if that bread were nothing other than ordinary bread, and if the person who received it were to believe it to be the holy body and if he were to accept it impudently, he would be no less subject to damnation than if it were the true body of Jesus. It strikes me as obscene to think that such a dignity, which is of no benefit to an undeserving recipient (indeed it brings a sentence of damnation because of iniquitous treachery), could be harmed by such usurpation. It pertains in no way to the sacrament's honor if the blight of a corrupt conscience overwhelms this grace that nourishes all that is fine, and if the pitiable man who took it is punished for his presumption.

Do you think that it would be the body of the Lord if an unbeliever took it? Or how is it the body of the Lord for someone who takes it mockingly or ignorantly, someone with no faith in this mystery? And if a boy or a senseless man who does not know whether it is the sacrament partakes of it, are we to think that he has insolently taken the body of our Lord? To this I cannot agree. I say instead—unless someone has a better idea—that a person cannot be thought to have received this body, well or poorly, unless he has first been able to recognize it, at least a little, through faith. Obviously when the naturally simple or the mad commit grave mortal sins, but do so because of their madness or simplicity, no one dares count it to their damnation. Similarly we ought not attribute sin to anyone who commits evil without consciously recognizing it as such.

To be sure, countless bishops and men of secondary office have celebrated mass before the people without believing in the inner truth of these same sacraments. When they performed these rites and did not understand the value of what, to all appearances, they regularly did, do you think, as much as it pertains to them, that they made something heavenly? Not really. The substances of the bread and the wine did not change, at least for them. As they enunciated holy words, there was no faith in their minds to accompany their outward deeds.

Faith alone is what brings about the secret spiritual transformation.[33]

But in this respect this gift from heaven is especially splendid, for it does not abandon the people who receive it, although it does escape their false priests. Thus the same body that is *not* the body among the priests who administer it unfaithfully *is* nonetheless both the sacrament and the sacramental grace for those who accept it faithfully—albeit from an unfaithful priest. For comparison, if a Jew undergoes baptism with a mind bent on financial gain, as so often happens, surely he does not attain remission for his sins? The Holy Spirit, who has the power to sanctify baptism, cannot indulge even the least sin of someone who falsely and malevolently engages with such purity. If in fact the Holy Spirit were able to impart forgiveness to such a man, it would not be an act of power but of impotence, and unjust impotence at that. To be forbearing to the foolish and the impenitent for their crimes, it seems to me, is nothing other than wicked favoritism by being indulgent to the guilty and to the proud. And how would God be God if he remitted without punishment the trespasses of those who persevered in them? To be sure there have been people who falsely asked to receive baptism, and the Holy Spirit no doubt filled the water at the prayers of the priest and made it efficacious. But when these people approached it deceitfully, they found it ineffectual.

Behold, it is clearer than day that where there is no faith, the sacrament that occurs is worthless. And don't let anyone object that any heathen or heretic can perform baptisms. There is one kind of authority in giving and another kind in receiving the profession of the divine name. The ministry of giving and sacrificing is transmitted externally, and the efficient cause goes back to Christ. Of him it is said, "This is he who baptizes," about whom it is also said that he alone sacrifices.[34] Christ retains this singular authority for himself, but he sets in places "givers," that is, the ministers. It is difficult for us, as we wander this world, to recognize genuine confessors. Thus the psalmist says, "He made the waters to stand as if in a flask." If "waters" are spiritual gifts, described elsewhere in the psalms as "the waters of God, like a river filled with waters," that is baptism itself, then surely God can pour it forth or withhold it as he wishes. Based on the intention and merit of the one seeking it, he keeps it or gives it.[35]

To these previous points something no less important can be added. We know, and many canons tell us, that simoniacally ordained bishops and priests receive no sacramental grace from the one who ordains them. We also know that when the ones who have been simoniacally ordained ordain or consecrate someone else, they cannot make or do anything, since they have not received this grace from anyone. A little divine seasoning helps to resolve this dangerous business: if someone who does not know the priest is guilty of simony accepts a sacrament through the laying on of his hands, the heretical poison of simony is removed through the faith of the one who, unaware of this plague, receives the sacrament. In this way the sacrament, which the simoniac himself does not have, becomes valid through the faith alone of the one who receives it, even though it involves the use of powers that the simoniacal priest does not himself possess. On the other hand, let's consider the case of a holy man completely free of the disease of simony. His assistants, archdeacons and deacons, bring him people to be ordained whom they have recruited through simony. Whatever holy and lawful thing the saint gives to them, they obtain nothing, but are like men dead to the light of day, neither seeing nor feeling.

If on account of the enormity of a single sin, God withholds and imparts these sacraments of ordination—so slight in comparison with the divine sacrifice[36]—or else changes his judgments on the basis of the disposition of the recipients, are we to think that the just cannot be separated from the damned in the performance of this holiest of mysteries? I know that the just are made separate, and in this I do not contradict the blessed teacher of the Gentiles, who says, "He who eats and drinks unworthily eats and drinks judgment for himself."[37] That is, in the case of someone who believes in the reality of the holy body and communes with "the ecclesiastical Word"— if I may phrase it thus—but because of a wicked, savage, and

cruel mind does not show due deference to that Person, I wish
to know what useful or holy thing he could bring away from
the altar? Look! Behold the sacrament—not so much received
as insolently and stupidly usurped! At least this much should
be conceded: it is not apparent how such a person could receive
the grace of the sacrament. And if the grace of the sacrament is
lacking, what is the advantage of having taken the sacrament
at all?[38]

The sacrament exists in three parts. It is set forth as a pledge.
It is customarily called a "consecrated thing." And it is accepted
as a mystery. Let it be a consecrated thing! Let it be a mystery!
All of this becomes but a punishment when the sacramental
grace suffers an unworthy recipient. Are we to say that the
majesty of such a gift, which heaven and earth ought to wor-
ship, plunges itself willingly into the rancid, putrid stomach of
a scoundrel, for the sole purpose of burning the miserable
heart of that condemned man? Far be it from the pious soul of
sweet Jesus! In my heart I believe and with my mouth I confess
that any usurper who approaches these holy sacraments re-
ceives his punishment most worthily. But I would never dare
to profess that such dignity and truth could be confined to
places so unspeakable. "Although we knew Jesus according to
the flesh," the apostle says, "we do not now know him." Now
that he has ascended to sit in equality with the Father, must he
return to endure new insults? Must he who once had no place
to rest his head now be compelled to waste away in dissolute
lodgings?[39] I dare say in good faith before God that Lord Jesus
could bear his cross more easily than the foul customs of
human activity. Does a renewed suffering so call him back
that he craves to return and bear anew the errors of our kind?
Perhaps he grows weary of his impassability and bored with
his repose such that he longs to drop back down into his once
customary bodily sufferings!

I really would like someone to explain to me what he means
by, "He who eats me lives through me." What is "to eat," and
what is "me"? "To eat" is equivocal, having positive and nega-
tive connotations. The Lord uses it absolutely; the apostle uses
it conditionally. But what is eaten? "The bread which I give

you is my flesh," he says. And the psalmist says, "Man has eaten the bread of angels."[40] In my opinion "to eat" is nothing other than to exemplify the life of Jesus. This is because he says "me," as if he were saying, "He does not eat me who does not 'concorporate' himself in unity with me." Do not believe me, unless you find the Lord's words to be in harmony with my own. "Give us this day our daily bread," he said. From whose perspective does he say it? Obviously from those who say and are able to say, "Our Father, who art in heaven."[41] Whose father, do you think? It is the Father of the elect, who strive to conform to the customs of God the Father. "Be holy," he said, "as I am holy."[42] These sons of God, I say, shout for "our bread," as if they were saying, "We confess in deed and in truth you are our Father.[43] Give us bread not of outsiders, but only 'our bread.' " Whose prayer is this? It is undoubtedly the prayer of the saved. They are the ones who say, "Your kingdom come," that is, "Let the holy church, the special kingdom of God, come together in unity." Elsewhere he says that his kingdom is not of this world: "If it were from this world, the world would love his kingdom."[44] Who dares to say that this bread, called "the bread of the angels," belongs to even one of the damned? It is conceded only as the lot of the elect. "Who eats me lives through me," means, therefore, "No one communicates with my flesh and blood if my internal inspiration has not first revivified him."

Think if you will what one of the damned might derive from this sacrament, one whose faults the devil nourishes, thus preparing him for death in hellfire. I do not see at all how a man of this sort, whose death is foreknown (which is God's providence alone to discern) could even once in this life worthily participate in this sacrament. Obviously he cannot become one body with that bread, which we receive for eternal life and which is called "the pledge of eternal salvation."[45] I affirm that as much as one of the damned is separated in this world from any participation in the true sacrament, so will he stand separated in the next world, an exile from the grace of the same sacrament. I say—and no wise man can deny that this statement is reasonable—anyone who has worthily partaken of this sacrament once will not in any way be denied the eternal salvation whose most certain pledge this sacrament is. You thus see for whose advantage this food has been given.

If any ambiguity still gnaws at some stubborn mind, read blessed Cyprian's book *On the Fallen*. There, if I'm not mistaken, you will find some who capitulated during the persecution and who tasted a little of the blood of pagan sacrifice. Later after peace had been restored, they mingled freely in churches, as if innocent, with the faithful, and just like the rest they partook of the holy sacrament. Others—I don't know whether they were men or women—carried the sacrament to their homes wrapped in linen cloths, as was then the custom, and hid it in chests in order to preserve it. To make a long story short, when they returned to take the sacrament out, they found it reduced to cinders and ashes. Also, little boys, whose mothers bore them in their arms to take the Eucharist, coughed it up and spat it out after they received it from the hand of the priest, if these children had previously tasted anything of pagan sacrificial blood.[46] Why would the body of the Lord turn to ash? For what reason does his own body deserve punishment, when vengeance is more appropriately due to those who had abandoned his body? Certainly he who elsewhere bestowed so much honor and human care upon his body should never permit it to be reduced to ashes—if, in fact, these hosts were his body.

Tell me this, if anyone is able: why did the Lord when he was about to leave this world make for us a vicarial body whose possession we might enjoy? The answer is obvious: because of the need for common solace, for the sake of his memory, and for exercising the faith. If these three points do provide an explanation, then in their absence, Christ's vicars serve no apparent purpose. When no one receives solace, when Christ's memory is not kept, when he whose faith ought to be exercised does not wish it, there is no sacrament. We see this not only in pagans but also in Christians who have turned away from God, whom the apostle calls worse than infidels.[47] When there is no faith to be aided and no devotion to meditate on the sacrament, I do not know what purpose the vicars of Christ's body would serve. Recognize then that this mystery belongs to the faithful alone, specifically to that part of the faithful that is to be saved. Whoever disrespectfully procures it—both good and evil recipients are capable of this—I do not know whether he takes the actual sacrament. I do know that because he thinks that what he takes is the sacrament, he damns himself.

What about these cases we have heard about: where dogs or mice consume the sacrament, where negligent custodians leave it moldy or decaying, where it suffers various other accidents, or where fire consumes it? Is it appropriate for that sanctified body that mice nibble at it or that dogs lap it up? This body, which the benevolence of our faith has made available to benefit our souls more than our bodies—should it be made freely available to the bellies of mice and dogs? Will we say that the teeth of vile little animals, because of an accident, can chew on what Christian bishops with so much affection and so many tears sacrifice before their pious flocks with Christ himself presiding as high priest? I say, let all saintly people eradicate such a thought from their minds!

It was demonstrated above that God granted this gift for the aid of the true faith. He distributes it by merit of faith alone, and no creature receives nourishment from it unless he is among the faithful. And although this one food does sustain the faith of each true recipient, it is not the sacrament and it does not have the grace of the sacrament when impious souls or brute animals usurp it. If we were to believe otherwise about the mystery of our redemption, then the stuff of our belief would provide our adversaries with material for ridicule. For they who dispute freely about the holy body and who wish it to be a figure and not the truth, because otherwise it would be common to both beasts and men, are able from this argument to sing mocking songs about us. By easy arguments they defeat us, and from the shame alone of our own dull-wittedness they convince us of their case by saying that our sacraments are common to both men and beasts.[48]

The truth of the sacrament can be found, therefore, wherever there is faith. On those occasions when it falls into the possession of animals or suffers some similar misfortune, because it encounters no faith to which it might adhere, it maintains the substance that it previously held, rather than having its singular purity branded with such a stain of indecency. If it remains in the same state of majesty when it burns or decays or is chewed or licked, such glory withdraws, having suffered no misfortune. Though it may seem to have been subjected to these perils, those who were appointed, supposedly, as guardians of the Lord's body and truly betrayed it do not in fact escape from severe spiritual damage, for they have denied it the observance that it merits. It is not a sacrament, passing over into simple provender, but against the people who have received the charge of caring for the sacrament it constitutes a betrayal of the true mystery in its entirety and a crime of dreadful desertion.

I have treated these topics with a longer digression than expected, but now I shall say my final word on this subject: let no one believe that this food, inasmuch as it can be called "supersubstantial," becomes nourishment for any human being, or for any earthborn creature, unless he is one of the faithful and only as long as it leads to eternal life for those predestined to it. If it should happen that an unbeliever or someone altogether unworthy were to approach it, we can think of it as nothing other than pure bread, and it is no shame to repeat this conclusion: because he impudently usurps what does not pertain to him, he is himself consumed in flames. It is in no way fitting to believe that such splendor could subsist in so foul a home. But just as baptism is holy and makes good-natured men holy, so for the wicked, besides their illicit deception, nothing happens beyond a disturbance in the water. I say these things according to my understanding and I speak faithfully with God as my witness. If anyone thinks otherwise, let him reflect so that he might soberly understand.

Against these things, less temperately asserted, I shall respond with briefer—because they are more temperate—arguments.[49] It is indeed true that the Eucharist is properly the proper nourishment of the true faith. But against the argument that, for the unworthy, it is not only not the grace of the sacrament but also not the sacrament itself, I will respond not only with authorities but also, if authority is lacking, with ample reasoning. First of all, it is not fitting for us to ascribe mutability and alterations to such mysteries: if because of one person's worthiness it is something, but on account of another person's unworthiness nothing were to happen—so that what existed for Peter as sacrament and sacramental grace was for Judas at the same moment neither; or so that baptismal water would seem of no special importance because it becomes mixed with groundwater after the performance of the sacraments and then differs in no way from ordinary waters, as if there was something in it that brought it dignity which immediately disappeared along with its indignity, or the wickedness of a wretched little man could suddenly drive out such remarkable eminence.

Surely he who in this world made himself no less real for Judas and his persecutors than for Mary and his followers, who worthily accepted into his discipleship many who would later abandon it, who even now reigns alongside the Father and shares his sun equally with the good and evil, who according to the book of Daniel grants angelic protection to the faithful and the treacherous alike (shown through Michael, the prince of the Hebrews, whom the prince of the Greeks had resisted)—surely we cannot believe that in this time he would deny his sacraments to anyone, especially because this time is the time of mercy, when he keeps his generosity from no one.[50] But if he did make the damned into exiles from this gift now, what judgment could he exact against them, when he had not entrusted this grace to them in the present life?

But if we were to accept this conclusion about the wicked, so that their own wickedness expelled the sacraments, then their minds would need to feel no fear about their own corruption. They would know that, due to their own baseness, the body of the Lord had returned to its previous substance. To clarify, I know of my own weakness and do not know whether I am worthy of love or hatred when I approach the sacraments. What hope, what blessing can I believe that I am about to receive from them, if because of my sins my hopeless mind knows that such a grace has been expelled? And who in the flesh does not sometimes feel doubt as to whether he is one of the elect? As often as the misery of my humanity presses down upon me, will the Lord's body be for me neither the sacrament nor the grace of the sacrament when I approach the Lord's table? Let the wise man reflect on how many unfitting beliefs grow out of this idea and let him know with certainty and without any incorrect interpretation that, according to the apostle, he who eats the body unworthily eats judgment for himself.[51]

Now that I have completed these most difficult inquiries, the cause of endless error, let us conclude with this observation alone: that the sacrament and the grace of the sacrament exist for the worthy, and that for the unworthy only the simple sacrament remains, without the grace of the sacrament. How this simple sacrament might fare in the souls and bodies of the unworthy, only he knows, whose substance cannot wither or decay, no matter where it is divided or whatever happens to it.[52] It is not inappropriate to apply here a parable of Solomon. "Lots are cast into his lap," he says, "but the Lord determines the decision."[53] We can interpret "the lots known to God alone" in no better way than as the distribution of this gift. The lots lie within his lap, because this gift is enclosed together within divine mysteries. They are carefully and beautifully described as "determined by the Lord," because many are thought to receive the sacrament without the grace of the sacrament, but they are nonetheless nourished for eternal life because God has foreseen their eventual improvement. For things often sit differently in God's judgment than in man's presumption, with worthy beginnings changing to shameful ends, and dishonorable conclusions dissipating a good beginning. Heavenly piety, therefore, moderates the decision that careless severity feared not to judge, or rather, to prejudge, for itself. *Lots are cast into his lap*, because he fashions the heart of each man individually, but he makes the works of each of us known, on the level of pure intellect, after we enter into the sanctuary of God. The Holy Spirit's plans work not only for the good of anyone who loves God, but also for the good of

anyone who might now be caught up in sin but who will some-
day love God, even in the reception of this gift, the Eucha-
rist.[54]

Let whoever wishes throw at me those ashes of Cyprian,
from the story that the contentious person raised against me,
or else let someone bring up the visions of that old man, about
whom we read in the *Deeds of the Elders*, who, as the sacra-
ment returned to the altar, saw unworthy recipients tasting
hot coals from an angel. On this question my faith could never
waver.[55] Then if you still have doubts about mice or other ani-
mals, or about some other way in which the host might acci-
dentally be eaten, I do not presume to make any pronouncement
beyond this one: that I do not believe this substance, infused
by God into this form, can for any reason be taken away. Some
have written that our eyes are deceived by the apparent cor-
ruption of this mystery, just as the eyes of Cleopas and Mary
Magdalene were kept for a while from recognizing the Lord.[56]
I do not know if this argument will ever be enough for me and
for many others. This, however, I do know: the part of the sac-
rament contained in its appearance does seem to suffer misfor-
tunes of this kind, but the part that is truth, joined to the
principal body sitting at the right hand of the Father, suffers
no damage. Concerning those accidents, then, that allow the
unfaithful to disparage our mysteries and against which our
authorities provide no defense, let those who are not foolish
keep this passage in mind (it seems almost specially written for
this purpose): set aside the remainder for the fire.[57] Consider it
thus restored to life from the dead, so that you may think of
whatever was there as being in his glorified body; then you
may feel no more horror at the bellies of mice than at the
minds of sinners, which trouble God far more. For whatever
upheavals it may suffer, it is protected from all injury by going
back to its beginning. Nor should we consider someone a her-
etic if he interprets this conclusion more freely than he ought
to do, out of a desire to protect such a grace from consignment
to unworthy places.

But since we have previously touched on the character of the
body made during the mass, I ought to specify that this body

is entirely consonant with the one that co-reigns immortal and incorruptible alongside the Father. On this point I do not want to hear as an objection that when our God and Lord handed down these mysteries, he said, "This is my body, which is given to you," and, "This is my blood, which is poured out for you and for many," as if he taught that what he handed over was bound by the condition in which he then lived. You should recognize that this argument is false, since he was always immortal through unity with the deity. He did not accept death out of any obligation, but he welcomed it deliberately. He handed over sacraments in the same incorrupt state that he revealed himself to Peter, John, and James on the mountain.[58]

But I have heard one of my learned friends stray far from this conclusion, actually saying that the mystery of this body— prepared by the faith of the priest and the people and preceded by the word of God—contains the image of the passible and mortal Christ. It seems appropriate that I treat this argument with a slightly longer discussion and that I show how my friend has understood this question less fully or less astutely than he ought to have done, especially since he is someone of great learning. Indeed, if he were to examine carefully what I briefly outlined above, he would have described the passibility and the mortality of our lord Jesus in very different ways.

If he were to examine with due subtlety the words of the Savior—"No one takes my soul from me, but I lay it down myself"[59]—he would never so wrongheadedly have attributed suffering and death to our Lord. Obviously, the soul of any man can always be snatched away at any time. The possibility of accidentally suffering and dying is ever present for us all. But truly in the case of him about whom scripture often says, "His hour has not yet come,"[60] for whom the events of hours and the hours of events stand ever unchanging, truly he *lays down* his soul. For what he took upon himself and what he created by himself he can send away whenever and however he chooses. From men indeed the soul is torn away, but because he is what he is through himself and because in him nothing happens except what he wishes, he releases it willingly and by his own will. By what necessity indeed would he die, whom the freedom of the second birth of the Holy Spirit accompanied even during his conception in the womb?[61]

It is said that, "He has paid for what he has not taken,"[62] because he, who among all the dead was free, paid the penalty for sins that he did not commit. The necessity of sinning attaches itself to us through the corruption of our nature and thus enjoins upon us the necessity of dying, but he, because he was born through the Holy Spirit and the Holy Virgin and because sin did not blemish him during his life because he did not commit any sins—he was untainted by original sin. How could the law of sin touch him? How was he forced to pay the price of a sinful nature? Because he was known to be blameless in birth and in deed, what exactions could death or passibility rightfully impose upon him? Death is drawn to our humanity through sin. Where there is no sin, the effective cause of death has been demonstrably annulled, for without doubt and with certainty we know that if we remove a cause, we destroy its effect.

If no act of sin had occurred in man's original condition, then no obligation of suffering and death would have followed, and if the horror of lustful disobedience had not destroyed the mind, no aging process would have accompanied the propagation of offspring. What indeed is fresh, what is cheerful, what is whole, when the anxiety born of a gnawing conscience bites at our desires? According to Solomon, "A cheerful mind makes a verdant age."[63] We know that Solomon refers here to that Paradise planted by the Lord at the beginning of time and sowed with the understandings of angels and in the minds of men. But for many of the angels and for every human nature he established places to stand, though soon to vanish, such that no one can boast about the eternal impassibility of his mind and body. How then are we to comprehend the mind and body of the Son of God, since we find in its personal identity not only humanity but also, infused into it corporally, the plentitude of the Godhead, especially given that it can be said of a pure man, even of one who has not yet learned to live without sin, that his life in this world is like the kingdom of God, one of peace and of joy in the Holy Spirit?[64]

The First Man,[65] I say, was, if I dare say it, passible and impassible, mortal and immortal. He was able through sin to succumb to passions and to death because of the abuse of his will. This will was his own, but it was not free. If he had willed to confine himself within the bounds of true liberty and not sin, he undoubtedly would have remained impassible and could not have died. The Second Man, Lord Jesus, succeeded this first one with an almost identical form, endowed with a nature the more impassible as it was freer—truly more inexpressible than the First, because it was born equally of God and man. How indeed could we call him passible, since the absence of sin from both his origin and his deeds made him immune to all the punishments of suffering and death? Because the First Man had the ability to contain his sin and to be impassible and immortal, ought not the Son of God have rendered our fragile substance, now united to him, more impassible and, if I may phrase it thus, more immortal?

Formed without concupiscence within a virginal womb through the Holy Spirit alone, naturally impassible and immortal—thus was he born into the world. I say "impassible and immortal" to show that, just as the First Man through disobedience willingly surrendered himself to suffering and death, so the Second Man, without any obligation and with the goal of restoring justice, allowed himself to suffer pain and death. If he had not suffered man's punishment, which he did not deserve, then he would not have freed those who were liable to those punishments and who deserved to undergo them. You may therefore believe Christ vulnerable and mortal in this way alone: that he wished to suffer and to die for the sake of human redemption. Do not believe that in suffering and dying he fulfilled some debt of nature sprung from the transgression of our first parent. He suffered and died because he willed it, not because the law of Adam obliged him to do so.

How, then, can you impose a likeness to the passible and mortal Christ onto the sacrifice of his holy body and blood when, by the words of his own mouth, you ought to know that he is impassible and immortal. "No one," he says, "ascends into heaven except the Son of Man who is in heaven." And elsewhere, "I am in the Father and the Father is in me." And before departing from this world, he offered many other similar words about his consubstantiality with the Father. If the Son of Man is in heaven and is one with the Father (indeed he says elsewhere, "I am of the heavens,"[66] which means nothing else than, "I am in the principal Spirit, that is the Father"), what passibility, what mortality could you ever hope to ascribe to him? If you can find any place where scripture calls him passible and mortal, it does so for this reason alone: because by the free choice of his will, he offered himself to death. He did not succumb to it.

There is nothing in Christ that is passible and mortal that you ought to conflate with those vivifying sacraments. If you consider it with faithful and not duplicitous intentions, you will discover in him only what is incorruptible and immortal, except that he voluntarily wished to die. Some things we do willingly and freely, other things we are tormented and compelled to do, as if obligated to pay a debt. But about this question, for the wise, I have said enough.

Certain acquaintances have told me that this same friend of mine has grown accustomed to saying that our Lord Jesus is crucified daily on the altar during the creation of the life-giving host. He says this not only while conferring with learned colleagues, as is usual, but also when disputing in the midst of crowds of rude and unlettered folk.[67] We Catholics, and all wise, pious men, ought to censure and curse this idea with all the authority needed to purge our Lord of extreme helplessness and eternal misery. What more pathetic and unworthy thought could we have about God than to believe that he has become eternally wretched for the sake of our beatitude? What greater weakness could we impute to God than that we need his daily sufferings to prop up our own never-ending restoration? Obviously if things stood thus, so that the atrocity of crucifixion daily butchered the author of life, there would be nothing in our heavenly reward so happy, so glorious, that it would not seem worthless as we contemplated this unending calamity inflicted on Christ, the sponsor of our redemption. And who would not conclude that his death was in fact useless, since not a numerous but rather an unspeakably infinite series of vicars would need to repeat it every day? And why are so many sacrifices performed daily in every church, or rather, on every altar? Truly if it stood thus, if our Savior were affixed to as many crosses as there were altars upon which masses were celebrated, we would call him "all-impotent."

But obviously, since nothing in scripture supports this foolishness, universal reason obliterates it. To be sure, the performance of the ecclesiastical ceremony, which occurs as a sacrifice, does refer to the Lord's Passion, and the sacrament does happen, we believe, in commemoration of our Lord. But it is wicked to conclude from these points that he is crucified as often as the mass occurs. Although we often substitute signifiers for the things signified, they are never the same as things that are pronounced in prophetic shadows and that follow forth in truth.[68] For example, in baptism the threefold immersion signifies the three days of the Lord's burial, but we do not say every time someone is baptized, Christ is buried there with him. The host assuredly refreshes our memory through the daily advent of his true presence, but this image of his Passion does not imply further injuries against God, who is never again to die. Truly, "Christ has risen from the dead and will not now die. Death no longer will master him. He died once because he died for sin. He lives because he lives for God."[69] But if "He has risen and is not dead" and if, according to your interpretation, he is also crucified every day on every altar, I wish to know how your prudence understands the apostle's use of the word *once*, and how is sin (that is, the offering made on behalf of sin) said to die? And how does he "live for God" who now suffers thousands of crucifixions repeated throughout the lands?

The apostle Peter treats this question with similar words: "Christ died once on behalf of our sins so that he might bring us to God."[70] If Christ were compelled to undergo so many sufferings and punishments, how could he ever lift anyone up and bring them to God? If in dying once he restores us for eternal salvation, the mystery that celebrates it is worthy and suitable to his divinity. If, however, after his resurrection, he is dead and— if I may put it this way—he executes himself by being sacrificed on one cross after another, then he is a wretched man who clearly cannot give to anyone the beatitude that he lacks.

The apostle says, "For Jesus has not entered into holy places made by hand, which are figures of true things, but into heaven itself, so that he might appear before the face of God on our behalf. And he does not offer himself repeatedly, entering into the sanctuary every year as the high priest does with another's blood. Otherwise he would have suffered of necessity again and again from the beginning of the world. But instead he has now appeared at the end of the world to sacrifice himself for the eradication of sin. And just as it is established that men die once, after which judgment follows, so also was Christ offered once to bear away the sins of many."[71] Look! Now you see clearly—unless sin is blinding your mind's eye—how the apostle's words make nonsense of your errors!

But I wish to ask which testament carries more weight with you—the old or the new? I do not doubt that you would answer "the new." If you believe, however, that the new is more authoritative, why do you drain Christ's death of any significance through these daily crucifixions, such that the yearly entry of the high priest into the sanctuary seems more meaningful because of its rarity, as opposed to the nonstop daily destruction of our Savior? If indeed according to scripture you believed the penalty of his first Passion to have been efficacious, you would never have extended the abuse that he suffered on your behalf—at least, you wouldn't if you were sane—into crucifixions happening in our time.[72]

We celebrate the sacrament with daily enactments, but the crucifixion is not as a result repeated every day for the sake of punishment. We do so because the performance of such a mystery weakens everyday wickedness and its diurnal variety of sins. We do not reenact these events constantly in order to trouble him, who already performed this task; rather, we recall in our feeble memories and renew in our minds the origin of these sacraments. We understand that they have been performed once for the salvation of all, and do not need to be renewed.

I warrant that I should ask you whether that body, which you say is always being crucified, is the same one that was born of the Virgin and that hung on the cross. I know what you will answer: "It is the very same one." If therefore you believe that it is "the very same one" and if you believe that the body prepared on the altar ought to match his passible and mortal body, then I wish you would explain whether that body, which according to you is passible and mortal, is also the body that, as we have learned, sits impassible and immortal at the Father's right hand. If they are not the same, then necessarily our Lord Jesus has two bodies. One will be vulnerable to suffering pain and death; the other one clearly stands upon foundations of incorruptibility. Because you would make the mystery of the sacred bread and the chalice into a weak symbol of corruptible flesh, the indivisible substance of the Savior would be torn asunder into a senseless duality. If it shames you to say this, and if you maintain that there is only one body—passible on the altar and seated by the Father in heavenly glory—beware lest, in the words of the apostle, you do not crucify Christ anew, now made incorruptible and immortal, and that you do not hold him up to public disgrace.[73] Rather, to move closer to the truth, in the eyes of everyone thinking worthy thoughts about God, beware lest you reveal yourself to be ridiculous.

These arguments, I think, should be sufficient for you, if you can somehow correct your mind. But if you delight in your obstinacy, then perhaps you will ridicule my arguments as fables needing to be rejected by the faithful. Let the scale masters who seek to weigh the Lord's condition cease to ask whether this sacrament that happens among us pertains to the passible or impassible Christ,[74] to the living or the dead.

Indeed, they think that the sacrament ought to be understood in no other way except in the condition in which the Lord handed over his body to be eaten. If indeed, they say, he had given these things to the disciples during the dinners he shared with them after the resurrection and if he had said, "This is my body," no one would have understood the term "body" rightly, unless he understood it according to the condition it was in when he spoke those words. You may recall that, during the Last Supper, he said he would not again drink from the fruit of the vine until he was seen drinking it with his apostles in his kingdom—"kingdom" referring to nothing less than the glorification of his body after the Passion. Thus, "The Spirit had not yet been given, since Jesus had not yet been glorified." This was his condition when he spoke these words: "Who eats my flesh and drinks my blood remains in me," and "who eats me lives through me."[75] Let them understand these passages as referring to the living feast he provides us from the altar.

The question about whether the sacrament is the likeness of the dead Jesus is thus resolved, since he who is dead is, in his death, no one other than the Son of God. Before he was born in time, he was described as "slain from the beginning of the world."[76] And he is read to have performed deeds with the fathers, meaning that—if I might phrase it thus—he was before he was. Thus he who was dead was always alive. We ought not seek any distinction between him living and dead. According to Jude the apostle, he led the people a second time from Egypt, and Paul says that Christ in the desert was tempted by the Israelites.[77] This universal profusion of his life-giving divinity is revealed, if nowhere else, in the canon of the mass, which says, "You sanctify, you vivify, you bless, and you stand before us." Through him, omnipotent God renders all things efficacious.

Now I shall set aside these points and return to the topics that I passed over: the Savior's tooth and his umbilical cord. On this subject we must first note what he said about the Holy Spirit: "It is to your advantage that I go. If I do not go away, the Paraclete will not come."[78] These words of the truth, I think, undermine anyone who might claim to possess relics of this sort. For what does he mean by, "If I do not go away"? Obviously, "If I do not withdraw my bodily presence." The Paraclete, therefore, has not come if his presence has not been withdrawn. Unless all of his bodily remnants are taken away, the mind will not be lifted up into contemplative faith. I said above that our Lord wishes to lead us from the principal body to the mystical for the exercise of our faith and from there, as if by certain steps, to educate us in the understanding of divine sagacity. From the clumsiness of external vision to the subtler gaze of the imagination, it is as if he leads us from hemp to linen cloth, raising us from external bodily images to the comprehension of this mystery. Thus promising something—more truly, containing something—for those awakening from tangible carnality, a new image is fashioned. Indeed, when someone rude and ignorant of allegorical forms contemplates these two materials—bread and wine—placed on the altar, and when this person learns to recognize in them the body and blood of Jesus, to what summit of divine courtliness has he arrived?

God commanded this most difficult task upon us so that the world will not lack altogether a part of his first body. As a result, God has three bodies. The first is the one conceived from the Virgin. The second is the one that occurs figurally in the bread and in the chalice. The third is the one that is impassible, or rather, glorified, sitting now at the right hand of the Father. If anyone wishes to dispute this conclusion and say that the same body was born from the Virgin, hung on the cross, and raised up incorruptible to the Father, he is mistaken. Although the same identity of person exists for each body, the essence is very different in each case and according to the qualities of each nature. To wit, no power of death or suffering could hold dominion over his body once it had been glorified.

This is an appropriate place for us to close this little book and to take up a new beginning. We will continue to examine the things that for the moment we have passed over, as well as to treat other subjects that, through God's inspiration, we expect to include. Let us gird ourselves not against those relics, but against blasphemies.

BOOK 3

AGAINST THE MONKS OF SAINT-MÉDARD WHO CLAIM TO HAVE THE TOOTH OF THE SAVIOR

Devotion toward God and his saints is in all ways commendable, but when devotion claims for itself something that reasoned religion does not support, it becomes, for the pious worshipper of the divine, a cause of misery. He might have expected a reward for his devotion but instead receives punishment for a most wicked error. When someone says or practices anything about God that obviously contradicts the testimony of truth, the mind that has so thought inevitably will be proved to have erred, an error made worse by a refusal to accept correction, since the sin occurred under the guise of piety. There is nothing worse than to do evil deeds and consider them, thoughtlessly performed, as if they were in fact good works. When and whence will correction of this error come, since it is not only believed not to be an error, but it is even thought to be grounds for heavenly honor? Normally either fear or shame leads an errant spirit to correct its sins—fear of either God's desertion or ultimate censure, shame from either the gnawing guilt in the conscience or else the timid looks before men because of their talk. When therefore anxious thoughts do not disturb the spirit and one does not feel embarrassed to be seen by others, then there arises no corresponding opportunity to recover one's senses.

And what kind of offense is it when, although founded upon alienation from God and totally opposed to ecclesiastical authorities, something is preached as if it were doctrine, seemingly supported by a singular privilege, and never in any way reproved by the rule of true zeal? In cases where fear motivates the innermost depths of a conscience toward performing some sort of expiation, there is great hope for correction. But a mind is never raised up to correct itself, when its intention wanders from the equilibrium of true belief while under the pretext of cultivating holiness.

This is how our neighbors, the monks of Saint-Médard, have claimed, because of an inveterate falsehood grown strong in the hearts of the simple, that they possess one of the Savior's teeth, lost, as is natural, in his ninth year. With this single shot from a catapult, they knock down the pinnacle and the height of all our hope, and out of a hunger for their own praise, they topple the lofty monuments of the common faith. For when a strong hope fails after avowing its faith, what else happens except that good appetites and practices are cut off at the roots? Suppose the sap of pure belief flowed in me and I sent out tendrils of holy acts in every direction—if the root of hope, which gives moisture to the trunk and branches, dries up, then there would be nothing in the entire structure of the tree that I could expect to provide pleasure or serve toward a practical end. You sow well, and what you have sown grows well, but then hail destroys it all—when you send out the sickle, do you expect to harvest any benefit from it?

I would like to learn from you what you think about the resurrection. Passing over what shall happen at the end of the world, you will not deny that the same Lord, whose tooth you claim to have in your hands, has been resurrected. Assuming you agree, let me ask whether he has been resurrected partly or wholly?[1] If you declare wholly, what will become of the parts that you took for yourself? If partly, how are the promises he made about our own resurrection at all valid? Obviously if one can prove that he has not fulfilled in his own case the promises he made to us and about us, then no small doubt must envelop our own hopes. Following this line of argument, someone will think the response should be, "What can he do for those who will follow him when he has not fulfilled in faith these same promises for himself? He said that not a hair on our head shall perish,[2] and yet he littered the earth with particles of his own body, like some trail of leftovers, and took the rest to heaven—could he declare that he has resurrected himself? If he cannot fulfill these promises in his own case, incapable as he is of collecting his own limbs, how will he gather together our limbs, which human carelessness will have scattered here and there?"

In your wish to exalt your church with pilgrims' riches and to claim that your church is far nobler and grander than others, you have reached the extremes of madness and the depths of a reprobate understanding and—this may be an awful thing to say, but it needs to be said—you are willing to drag into your lies the words not only of the prophets, but even of Lord Jesus himself. If the prophet says, "You will not allow your Holy One to see corruption,"[3] then we have to charge him with lying, and not without cause, since that tooth is undoubtedly subject to perpetual corruption. And what is more exposed to corruption without hope of redemption than your tooth, which has been cast out from the glory of resurrection and incorruptibility?

My God, what misfortune has befallen that tooth! Never will I say that it was procreated in the virgin's womb through the Holy Spirit with the rest of the body, but it must have arrived from somewhere else and adhered to the Lord's jaws, as if grafted on from the shoot of another tree! The tooth is therefore corrupt, since, if I may break down the word itself, when Christ lost it, his *corpus* was *rupt*ured, and after his exaltation, the tooth was left on the earth and condemned to eternal misery, at least until the end of the world when it shall burn with the heavens and the earth. Thus you are charged with making a false claim or lying, and not just any sort of lying—it makes you blasphemers against the divine, or else, should you obstinately persist, renders you heretics against Catholic doctrine.

Have we received a greater cause for hope than the father

and author of our hope, Lord Jesus, received? Are we to believe that he is going to collect our bodies from their dispersion when we now see his own body in a state of ruin? Behold—thanks to you, we are better off than Jesus! A complete regeneration awaits us, but only a partial one has happened for Jesus in such a way that either he will not receive perfection into eternity or else he awaits the common resurrection. Perhaps then Jesus will prepare a place for the return of the tooth, or else he will open wide and at last welcome back into his mouth the wandering tooth, and at the same time a renewed exaltation will occur for the tooth and the umbilical cord and whatever else may be out there, just as there once was a second circumcision![4] Note well, charlatans, how your small fire consumes so much of the verdure of the Christian truth.

If no other evidence beyond the saying of the prophet, quoted above, supported me, it would be appropriate for you to respond at least to that verse, since you have placed yourself in this difficulty, and especially since the most blessed Peter cited the same passage against the Jews in order to defend the Lord's resurrection.[5] Since it is utter insanity to contradict so outstanding a prophet and an apostle of such princely authority, I wonder how you might presume to speak at all, but in fact you clearly do deny such authorities. Admittedly, many other arguments might occur to you that you might use in some way, at least for a moment, to defend your position—but even so your consciences ought to be horrified just to murmur what does not deserve to be said, even against men of far inferior glory.

You say that the tooth shows no sign of corruption, but even if it is not yet corrupt, it plainly will be so. But how could it suffer any worse corruption than being sent to this filth of perpetual despair, after he has raised the rest of his body to exaltation? And how do you dare to make such a ridiculous claim? Since you do not deny that he has risen, how did it happen that he overlooked his own tooth—through some sort of forgetfulness? But if he forgot about it or else willingly left it behind, what will he do at the resurrection? As he reunites the limbs of other bodies, will he depart having lost a piece of himself?[6]

Let us suppose it were possible. Let us presume that you have in fact been enriched by such a gift. I would like you to explain, if you would deign to answer, into whose body that tooth shall rightfully be ceded at the resurrection, as well as other parts of the body—the umbilical cord and all the rest people claim to possess, in addition to the tooth that we are discussing. For obviously what is said about one of these relics will apply to all the others. Where will these remnants from the Lord our Savior go when the final day shall dawn? If they return to their original body, where will it receive them? What places will open up to accept them? Or has the exalted Savior remained up until now toothless, in order to preserve a place for that tooth's return? And could there be a suitable place for such a small tooth in a jaw that is, because it is the Lord's, so manly?

Enough! Where, I ask, is the umbilical cord going to go? Are we to think that the same body will celebrate two exaltations? That is an idea I have never read about, and no evidence supports it. What will you say then, as you watch everything about your claim fail and become laughable? Why do you brand the Lord (I won't even mention the prophets) with the stain of unbelief? If you had him before you, you would hear him say just as the Jews heard, and no more unjustly, "Who of you will accuse me of sin?" He stated that the weakest and most unfeeling part of us will not perish,[7] yet you in your prudence claim for yourself a remnant not from his hair but from his flesh and bones, leading to his own ruin and causing us to distrust all his promises!

Out of this distrust, moreover, the worst possible considerations arise on both sides. For to believe like this, to speak like this, openly calls into doubt the integrity of divine words, and it creates no small mental cloud to engulf the vision of every shortsighted person. If people gather that he has made promises about himself in vain, then they will fear that, in their own cases, too, he cannot fulfill God's promises. If indeed you promise someone abundance when you cannot even provide for your own basic needs, it becomes obvious, because of your own condition, that you cannot carry out those promises you have made. I am speaking of something that could at times cloud feeble or unstable minds, but, as far as I can see, in the case of intelligent people, by God's mercy, they will find what you have said not so much stupefying as stultifying. I will not, however, ascribe this outcome to any caution on your part—you who do not fear, though forbidden by the law, to dig a well to such a depth of wickedness and leave it open for every brute animal to fall in.[8] Even if, on God's authority, no one comes to harm there, even in our time when this teaching is appreciated less, you in your impudence remain guilty, because you have constantly created a danger that might imperil careless people.

But this is the most serious objection I raise against you: although you customarily teach these things in front of everyone, you have never—never, I say!—sought a better judgment through careful analysis, because wiser men would speak against your sign. Wiser men, as you hear every day, reject it. And you have paid no mind to anything in the scripture not in harmony with it. Indeed if you had looked even superficially at the passages about the nature of his and our own resurrection, a spark of the truths I have spoken would have clearly illuminated everything. And what is more insane than to proclaim into the church's ears what cannot stand up to any formal objection? Paul went up to Jerusalem in order to confer with Peter and the other evangelists to make sure he had not run or was running his race in vain,[9] but you in your prudence are ashamed to learn the things that gave him pause! Turn your minds to Horace: "Why," he says, "out of false shame do I prefer to be ignorant rather than to learn?"[10] Are you yourselves really so dull that you cannot understand how one part of his body seems to have traveled to the Father's throne while the other part remains an exile from the body in heaven and continues to be subject to corruption? What reason would allow that such glory hold one part while perpetual misery captures the other?

Even if no authority supported my argument, it ought to suffice that to divide a body so sacred into parts would be intolerable to its majesty. For if at the resurrection uniformity will exist in our own purely human bodies, when we will be so transfigured that all of our limbs together will be glorified and in no single one of them will anything unworthy remain, not

even so much as an atom of our former baseness, what mad-
ness would cause us to believe that there would be anything
unfitting left over in him, who is God and man in one person?
Is one part of him worthy and another part cut away from his
worth? If out of the mouth of the teacher of the Gentiles,
through whom Christ spoke, came the promise that "He will
reform the body of our humility, fashioned to the body of his
exaltation,"[11] how could he, who apparently for no reason left
behind part of his body for the sake of pointless humility and
showed himself unable to pick up what had once belonged to
him—how could he elevate the lowliness of human corruption
to conformity with his own glory?

When you claim for yourself the limbs of God as if they
were a gift of honor and a special privilege for your own
church, take care that by this claim, in which you think you
are fighting for your own honor, you do not (if I may say so)
humiliate God right down to the earth, as you prattle on about
his tooth. If you seek honor from God, what sort of God do
you believe him to be when you seem openly to accuse him of
dishonesty? If this honor of yours redounds to the infamy of
the one whom you desire to honor, what thanks will you give
after you receive your honor? And how is your service rational
if you worship and cause others to worship something that no
justification of the faith supports? The apostle calls a service
"rational" if the mind is freely exercised in taking the truest
account of the reasons for it.[12] For if anyone venerates and
preaches about someone, without knowing the reasons for the
veneration and for the sermons, he will find himself stumbling
or limping along.

And though report of this boast has spread among all,
scarcely anyone of wisdom can be found who supports it, for
reason, as it considers this matter, falters every step of the way,
and hardly anyone except an ignorant fool is convinced. And
when every discerning mind disbelieves this idea, who would
support it except someone impudent or perverse? Shame alone
ought to restrain your boasts, which clearer heads would never
accept as probable. All learned people ascribe your claims to
stupidity.

But if the reasons I have offered prove dissatisfying to some thinkers, look here—I am prepared to argue with myself on your behalf, first to raise objections in support of your claim and then without any deceit to refute the objections in all sincerity.

I think that this is the way your conjectures work, or rather your claim seems to emerge from arguments such as the following (not that I have ever heard any reasoning from you, but I imagined in my own mind what someone might say, or rather bark out, against my little argumentative tract, for I have heard nothing from you worthy of rational reply). I know that you customarily give the following answer to your interrogators: "Wouldn't he as he grew up lose a tooth naturally when he was nine years old?" To this, I do indeed assent, but many other arguments present themselves touching on problems far different from those you mention. In saying this, I fear to disturb the depths of this question, calling to mind the saying of Boethius, "Rightly I am judged mad if I argue against the mad."[13] In a matter where the mind is of greater import than the will, a madman cannot determine for himself how to respond to an argument. Only on this does he fix his desire: to subdue the opinion of the opposing side with endless shouting. It seems honorable to the wicked to intone one absurd thing after another, so that although they cannot prevail through reasoning, at least they can obtain something close to a victory through continual screaming. Enough, then! Let my speech be exercised on your behalf.

If you say that our God and Lord left the mystery that happens at his table for his followers and their followers as a remembrance of him, in order that the consolation that his followers had through sharing his company might in his absence continue as a vicarial gift, then I do not understand why superfluous parts of his body (if I can call them that) ought to be withdrawn because of the routine provision of the mass given for the increase of universal joy.[14] We call the sacrament "routine" since he himself described our bread as "daily." It is called "daily," because it is necessary, according to the apostle, as long as it is "today."[15] But even if it is for the general good to be united to the body of Christ through the sacrament, the glory of the body parts that he lost ought not to be deprived of their majesty. For just as the privileges of individuals do not make a law universal, so universal glory in no way detracts from the exaltation of any particular part.

If the sacrament serves as a visual reminder that Christ suffered for the world (which is a clear image only to the wise),[16] why wouldn't God allow us to have these slices of his flesh— the excesses of his own body, if you will—for the consolation of those for whom he suffered? If blood and water flowed from his side on the cross, perhaps it touched stone or soil.[17] If these were absorbed or rubbed off or in any way destroyed, why don't you think that those parts, which you earlier described as "leftovers," could have been left behind, as if pledges to renew our faith preliminary to the cultivation of a greater privilege?[18] Those sacraments ritually assist us in remembering him, since in receiving them they unite us with Lord Jesus. These things of a "tangible faith" (allow me to call it that) confer invisible rudiments to spirits who possess a lesser understanding.

There are certain steps toward understanding this truth. The visible and tangible tooth and the umbilical cord teach the simple; the mystery that happens on the altar exercises imaginations; then, contemplation focuses on him, who sits at the Father's right hand, as if seeing to the third heaven.[19] Since flesh and blood are not suitable to ordinary hunger and thirst, the Lord changed them into a sacrament appropriate to human use. The sacrament thus reveals something other than flesh or a tooth said to be a remnant of his resurrected body. These remnants of his once visible flesh hint at the truth. The mystery of the signified flesh becomes effective for those who, through experience of it, become incorporated to the divine flesh and live because of it. The tooth and the umbilical cord are acceptable signs, during these difficult times, of the already-accomplished dispensation, while the sacrament fights more generally for the salvation of souls.

But if you think it controversial that a remnant of his body should exist after his resurrection, we must also consider "baptism after baptism" a controversy. For the baptism that

Christ sought seemed more glorious than the one to follow, although a far better one succeeded its predecessor.[20] Thus if Christ, after his resurrection, left behind some things that pertained to him in order to fortify our unstable minds, will he not be able, after the Last Judgment, more gloriously to restore to himself these glorified things?

We likewise say that, although he has been resurrected, the resurrected body has not risen to the immutable glory that it will possess after the Last Judgment. For if it had been wholly exalted, the side that he showed to Thomas would not have remained open, nor would the wounds on his hands and feet have continued to be visible as well.[21] He preserved these sufferings, and carried them to his Father's throne, so that he might on the Day of Judgment show them to those who pierced him and to all the wicked. Since the scar is not yet covered, his (if you'll pardon the phrase) semichanged body has not attained perfect exaltation. And since complete restoration of the corruptible parts has not yet happened, this still unfinished process must somehow still be fulfilled.

What might I say about his restoration? The form of a servant, which the just and the wicked alike shall see at the time of judgment, will afterward be wholly transformed into the image of the divine. Thus: "And crossing over," he says, "he will minister to them."[22] We ought not to understand this "crossing over" in any way except as follows: the ministry of all the human service that will characterize him at first will be refashioned into a condition of divine majesty, or more truly, into dominion. And during this "crossing over" he will provide to his elect a vision that will give them the fullness of contemplation, of which they shall never tire. Because there will be a transformation from the form of a servant into the appearance of divinity, and because the bodily scars will be covered when the authentic metamorphosis occurs, shouldn't we risk saying that he will at that time take back up the remnant we believe that we possess? Since obviously the emptiness of the wounds shall be filled and the surface made level, is it any wonder if an object, which for the time being he has entrusted to us for the solace of our faith, shall be joined to the same body whence it came? Certainly, if all things great and small are possible for God, you cannot think that, for him, closing his open wounds is greater than reincorporating to himself—using the same unknown process by which he will recollect all the scattered body parts—the relics that he provided for human desire out of his natural providence.

The Son of God says that the Father told him about his enemies the Jews: "Do not kill them," he says, "lest my people become forgetful."[23] The presence of the Jews, whom we have before our eyes, makes us remember Christ crucified, and they demonstrate to us the authenticity of the old books written about them and foretelling their misfortunes, as well as the happy turns in our own fortunes. Who then is able to cast doubt on what we say about the tooth, or equally about the umbilical cord? As that mystical body is known to have been established to unite us together with him, so whatever remnant—which is from what we call "the principal body" (which precedes the mystical body not in majesty but in time)[24]—is said to remain on the earth, we know that it serves to reveal to us the dispensation that he undertook and to strengthen those weak in faith.[25]

Now I will answer these arguments. If you believe that something from the principal body of the humanity he once took on survived in order to provide, as it were, proof, then, as a consequence, almost all the Catholic faith's strength would collapse. For if "faith is the substance of hope," and the "proof of things not visible,"[26] how are these things supposed to subsist or exist substantively in the hearts of a hopeful believer, if his understanding of thoughts about the invisible always returns to the visible? "Who indeed hopes for something that he already sees?"[27] If faith and hope exist only because of a desire for contemplative understanding, there must exist an inner acuity that nurtures and advances them. Bodily customs and sensual desires make faith and hope sluggish and cause them to waste away. Faith ought to be something substantial in each person's spirit, so that what the spirit contemplates the mind grasps, as if it were tangible.

Where is the acumen of one's faith directed here? Better yet, what is hoped, what is believed, when the thing hoped for and believed in depends on the sight of material eyes? How is the mind exercised when it exercises its consideration on something that lies beneath its gaze? If he left his bodily relics on the earth for the purpose of implanting belief in the Incarnation more firmly in human hearts, why did he declare that the Paraclete would not come unless he first went away? He said that he was going to withdraw himself in the flesh from his disciples so that a more abundant spirituality might impress itself upon their understanding. Are we to believe that he wished somehow to undermine his own words in this way, desiring, as you claim, to leave some remnant of himself on the earth? Clearly it would contradict his words, if he who said that the Paraclete would not come unless he went away then left among us part of the same body on which the human mind might again focus.[28] To do these things would be, if I may say so, to undo his deeds, were he to withdraw his own body in order to drive us toward spiritual things and then with part of his body withdrawn, to leave another part behind. There is nothing conflicting in the Lord's words, nothing disharmonious. Unchangeable uniformity always clothes all the sayings of the Gospels.

If you next ask about his blood and water and object that they were spilled on the ground, I cannot answer in any way except as follows: no one has established a judgment about the hairs cut from him in his youth as his body grew, where they fell or what they were transformed into (as is the case about the outpouring of blood and water that we have already examined). Don't you agree they were lost? If the tooth that you claim for yourself continues to exist in earthly misery, by what carelessness do you think the rest of his teeth were scattered here and there, which he would have lost according to the same laws of nature? A more favorable wind must have smiled on your tooth. The rest of them (according to the consequences of your argument) have been given over to decay and destruction, but yours sparkles, crowned with gold and precious stones. And isn't it a wonder that—although he lost many of them and they all deserved the same reverence—after the rest disappeared, you alone can boast to have this the only one! If therefore the hair, the teeth, the flow of blood and water, the discharge from the four wounds, which undoubtedly was spilled upon the earth—if these sit idly by, corrupted on the earth until the end of time, I do not see how the truth of the human resurrection and the promise from the Lord's mouth about our conformity to his image can survive free of outrageous fallacy.

And rest assured, I speak more from confidence than from ignorance, because if someone breaks a few of his promises, he calls into doubt whether he will hold true to the rest of his commitments. And if you concede that the body of the one who is author of that promise is a corruptible body, then by the simplest debating point you can strike down whatever he proclaimed as having occurred for himself or as still having to occur in us. There is sure hope of future gifts because of the gifts we have already received, and whoever is deceitful in the preamble to his speech will lose the attention of listeners as he continues. Similarly, we cannot doubt that if someone carries through faithfully what he promised about his own return, he will inspire unhesitating faith in all his words among everyone to whom he offered himself as surety. But if he is seen to waver in carrying out his promises, then his words will completely collapse amid a flood of uncertainty, regardless of the heights to which he had elevated them.

But this next point alone ought to suffice,[29] even if nothing were to appear in answer to the former arguments—that there was no one in the time of the Lord Jesus' childhood who would have taken an interest in collecting what fell from his sacred head, especially since at that time no one thought him any greater than any other young man. And who would there have been to handle human relics, since whatever remained of the body after death the Jews held as most impure? And what do they consider more impure than touching the bones of a dead man? On every occasion when they touched a body, they were commanded to sleep for a while outside the camps and to offer waters of purification.[30] Beyond the tablets of the law and the rod of Aaron, we know of nothing that they accepted as a memorial of their ancestors. Who then would decide to preserve those things associated with that boy, whom they deemed worthy of nothing beyond ordinary regard?

But let us consider the possibility that the blessed Virgin Mother could have preserved it, as if she had wished superstitiously to pass it down for future generations to worship, just as they say that some of her hallowed milk is preserved in a crystal dove near us at Laon. How far this strays from the truth and even from any appearance of truth the simplest argument can demonstrate. She would not have preserved those things. During Jesus' childhood there was not enough time for pleasure or security that she might place any importance on keeping souvenirs. How much would she concern herself about bringing forth milk for future generations when she was hardly able to hide in her native land, hardly able to live? And who can find any indication of such arrogance in her blessed life or in her beloved manner, from whose mouth nothing was heard except a handmaid's humility? This stuff would not have lasted under any custodianship even for a few years, much less many ages. More likely, natural instability would have caused the curdled milk to evaporate.

But enough. And anyway, what examples, from our more recent age, concerning the collection of relics were available to her mind, thoroughly mature and desirous of no praise? Why would she be the first to begin a practice that she had never seen happen and had not heard of being done—the very image of boastfulness?[31] And if because of the Spirit by which she had conceived her child, it was impossible for her not to have known that he to whom she had given birth through faith was to fill the whole world with his dispensation, why would she preserve a little tooth and the umbilical cord and the rest? In the light of her Son's exaltation she would have considered them (if according to ancient custom they could have been preserved) of no greater magnitude than a lantern under the noonday sun. We know more certainly than certainty itself that the Lady of the ages would never have wasted her time on such trifles—for trifles they plainly are—if he who proclaimed himself

God and man to the world, fully supported in faith by wonders, had desired to be worshiped through bits and pieces of this sort, useful for absolutely nothing. If she did not do it, who did? There was no one at that time who appreciated such things, let alone who held them dear to his heart.

But let us set these matters aside and return to the original proposition. If you say that the Lord's body was not completely transformed after the resurrection and was not yet fully exalted because he had not yet covered the openings of his wounds, you demonstrate in this, I think, the undoubted stupidity of your minds. If he was not wholly exalted because he did not cover his wounds, then he was not even a little, much less wholly, transformed or glorified, because he showed no signs of transformation or glorification to his disciples after the resurrection. He seemed to have changed in no way the outward appearance to which they had grown accustomed. Since he showed them nothing of his new glory after his physical return, some might say that he merited nothing greater from the Father in his resurrection than he had previously held. Even at the hour of his ascension into heaven he revealed nothing new externally that had not been there before his death. If indeed he had presented himself in some new and more splendid fashion, they would have never believed that his flesh had been revived but rather (as they would have assumed) that he was someone else, or that he was a spirit. For this reason, "Fear not, I am he," and, "A spirit does not have flesh and bones as you see me to have."[32]

It was appropriate that he continue to appear with the same outward appearance to ordinary people, lest his unfamiliar brilliance cause weaker minds to form strange and spurious ideas. What is the wonder if he who remained (apparently willingly) wounded in his shadowy form after receiving glory, uncovered and showed them the holes from the nails? And to whom did he show them? First to the apostles and afterward to Thomas—thus to each one who doubted, and then once more. See if he showed a scar as a proof to the two pilgrims at Emmaus, or at the many other gatherings of people during forty days, or to the women grasping his feet, or to anyone else

when he revealed his Passion.[33] Why else did he display the
scars from his wounds except to show his identity, not accord-
ing to his face but according to the more recent signs of his
death? What would those wounds preserved after the resur-
rection show if they were preserved even today? Are they there
to remind the Father, like some forgetful man, of the dispensa-
tion undertaken for men? Enough! Obviously his flesh alone,
sitting at the Father's right hand without wounds, suffices to
remind him, who attends to other things.

But you object that even on Judgment Day the wicked and
the impious will see him as they pierced him. But he didn't say
that they would see his bloody side or his bloody hands and
feet—only that they would see him "whom they pierced." If
you were to see someone whom you had injured but who bore
no mark of the injury that you had caused, would you not
upon seeing him immediately remember the deed that you had
done against him? And what purpose would the wound in his
side serve? What purpose would the nail marks on his hands
and feet serve, when the sign of the Son of Man shall appear?
Will the horror of the five wounds be appropriate on the throne
of glory? And when he was eating and drinking with his dis-
ciples and handling his food, are we to think that pus was
flowing from his gaping sores? Oh, endless stupidity! He fre-
quently shared meals with his followers, not out of necessity
but out of charity, to show that he had truly taken up the flesh.
He entered their room with the doors locked not according to
nature but by power alone,[34] for bones and the substance of
flesh do not penetrate the barriers of walls, and physical mat-
ter does not naturally endure a celestial abode, and this we
attribute entirely to the miracle of his resurrection. He said
that he was about to go away when the two men mentioned
above compelled him to stay.[35] If anyone doubted him, was he
not able at that time to offer evidence of the Passion, recently
enacted, and thus prove to them his nature and his identity?
Did not the transfiguration on the mountain before Peter,
James, and John serve as a preparation, so that he might dem-
onstrate the condition in which he would exist after the resur-
rection, and that he avoided showing after his own resurrection

on account of the weakness of those who saw him? It is as if he were saying, "It is not fitting that upon my resurrection I show you the clarity of my changed body; indeed, your understanding would not be suitable for seeing it. I thus present to you this form only, so that you might learn to consider and cultivate the splendor of its glorious nature, although I have covered it in a humbler, since more hidden, appearance."

Now, about the transformation of his appearance from that of a servant into that of a divinity: if you interpret this to mean that his outward appearance will be changed and then, while the scars are being covered over, the tooth and the umbilical cord and whatever other remnants will be reattached to him like a branch grafted onto its old trunk, we see clearly that, if this is so, there will have been two resurrections of Christ, and he will be twice changed. If such an error takes root concerning the head, why should anyone believe anything about the resurrection of the limbs? We understand that Christ's transition from one form into another means only that after death has been swallowed up in victory and after the wicked man along with his wickedness has been driven away—that is, when the foolish, wicked man is separated from the anger of God's face as his heart approaches, lest he see his glory—then only the elect will be admitted to behold the glory of his divine vision. This is why he said when Judas left: "Now the Son of man is exalted."[36]

Thus he crosses over to his exaltation when he makes us (that is, the elect) cross from the form of a servant, which is common to the just and the unjust, to the eternal vision of him. In this transition he ministers to the elect, satisfying them with his vision after disowning the wicked. Christ makes the transition when, after Judgment Day, he no longer allows the wicked to contemplate his form as a servant and opens himself to the gaze of the elect. Better still, he causes the elect to make the transition toward seeing him.[37]

Now that we have said these things against the defenders of this proposition, let us consider how in the church of Saint-Médard they boast about the priceless miracles connected to their tooth. First, if I am not mistaken, and what first comes to mind, is this: the chaplains of the emperor Louis the Pious discussed the tooth in his presence. While they were opposing the monks' claim, arguing that nothing from that body that sprang from the womb of the Virgin could have remained on this earth, the time for mass arrived. Then, during the ceremony, the reliquary is said to have hung in the air above the altar—this, they say among themselves and to others, proves their case.[38]

But what, I ask, is their case? What heavenly voice, I ask, which angel, I pray, pronounced this to be the Savior's tooth, which he lost as a child? But why do I ask for an angel or a voice? If the thrones and dominions[39] asserted this, the minds of none of the faithful, the minds of no one who has knowledge of the faith, ought in any way to agree with it! As we have said above and have repeated a thousand times, if he stated that not one hair of our head shall fall, but then left some remnant of himself on the earth, then he causes those who believe in him not to believe in his doctrine but to despair because of his own example. And certainly he will never collect anew the ashes of martyrs or their bones scattered through the whole world if he is allowing his own remains to rot away here and there after his resurrection.

Consider how silly that miracle was, since one cannot decide what purpose the "hanging" served.[40] The reliquary fluttered up from the altar into the air. By raising itself from the sacred to the (if I may say so) "unsacred," it apparently showed itself unable to tolerate the holiness of the altar. And if we choose to focus on the word itself—that is, "to hang"—the hanging seems ambiguous. But why do I say "ambiguous," since properly speaking something is ambiguous when it is able both to be and not to be. This, simply, cannot be, not at all, unless God, who is truth, wished to corrupt himself. This miracle is of such inept absurdity that it does not even successfully make an argument. It is stupidly written. He who repeats it is more stupid still.

There follow other matters no less dubious. I call them "dubious" because they are silent when it comes to proof. For sometimes an event, which is referred to as a miracle, could be holy for some other reason, but the event described here could not be, and even if it were, the evidence of this sort of favor cannot be used to prove that the tooth was the Lord's. So let us believe that the tooth belonged to some saint, and perhaps by his merits this sort of thing is granted. Even if it were in fact no saint's, the faith of those who believe in it could still cause it to fulfill their hopes. For many things can happen not so much by the merits of the thing through which the request is made, as much as by the merits of him on whose behalf it is raised.[41]

This sort of thing happened some years ago in the city of Luna.[42] The faithful people there were celebrating the vigils before Christmas, when a pirate fleet slipped into the port, named for Venus, planning to sack the city in a sudden attack, while the people were carrying out divine services at night. As the prows of their swiftly moving galleys cut through the salty shallows, in the cathedral church a boy climbed the pulpit to give the first or second reading of the night. For the opening of the benediction, he said: "Be consoled, my people, be consoled."[43] Then from his mouth the Holy Spirit, barely distinguishable from the boy, interrupted with "*Salandrae!* Pirate ships at the port of Venus!" (They call their ships *salandrae* from the verb to leap, *salire*.) When everyone ordered the boy to repeat the words exactly, not in a murmur but in a loud voice, he said the same thing several times. Then the church deacon, understanding the meaning of what was said, roused the people to arms and ordered them to head to the port of Venus. There, as the huge fleet was driving onto shore, the crowd, armed by God, went out to resist it and without delay fortified the city that was to be attacked, and scattered the enemy. So just as this sign had nothing to do with the merits of the boy who spoke the words, so something often is done not by the one from whom it is thought to arise. Instead, the fruit of the favor runs over to him who deserved to receive it.

The authority for the miracles at Saint-Médard, by contrast, seems rather slight, proven only by an unworthy and tawdry text. For their book, which makes a case for the miracles associated with that tooth and with the saints there, tells of a certain monk who was accustomed to gratify himself with some whore of a woman.[44] One night as he traveled to her, it happened that he had to swim across a nearby river, and while braving the waves he drowned under the weight of his own sin. On the abbot's judgment, he was denied burial in the brothers' cemetery. But, as that book tells, one of the saints there, it says, appeared to the abbot and said to him, reportedly, "Carry him to the others, because he died in obedience to you." What obedience, I ask? Had the abbot ordered him to enter the dangerous river so he could have sex with a shameless woman? Obviously until then he had obeyed the abbot in some way or another, but in this matter we cannot say "he obeyed." "Obedience" can only be understood in a positive sense—unless you are deliberately misusing the term. So in what kind of obedience did he die? If there is any doubt about the meaning of *obedience*, hear what the apostle said of the Son of God: "From what he suffered he learned obedience."[45]

Anything connected to these stories could be considered irrational, and thereby unworthy of any faith and approbation. And of course we know that this tooth, adorned from old with gems and pearls from pilgrim shores, has been accepted because of tradition. What is concealed in the same reliquary has been proven not by those who knew it firsthand. Only the report of their successors has confirmed it. So let them venerate what is to them unknown in two ways: enclosed in gold and gemstones it is completely hidden from view, and what that treasure chest is thought to contain cannot possibly exist.

It will be imputed to Mary that she alone could have preserved what they claim to possess. If so, how did she, who knew from God about the nature of her Son—that it would excel that of any angel or human being—how did she, who beyond everything that exists, second only to her Son, was imbued with the Holy Spirit—how did the details of the resurrection escape her? If they did escape her, certainly it would have been fitting for him to appear to her first after his resurrection, in order to build faith that it had occurred. But why would he appear to her, who undoubtedly knew, before he had suffered and rose again, that he would in fact be resurrected? As we know, she had heard these words: "A sword will pierce your very soul."[46] She stored in her heart these events and the words of those who spoke about him, because she thought no one faithful enough to be entrusted with such a matter, and so it was not at all incongruous that she kept secret her understanding and discoveries. Because therefore neither she, who was not ignorant of his future condition, nor anyone else who might have distinguished him from the common mass of humanity, would have preserved these relics for later generations, whatever anyone dared to take from such a body must be considered superfluous. The saying of the apostle is proven as true as it is brief, that the same body was announced by the angels, proclaimed to the world, and taken up in glory.[47]

We likewise are finished with the rest—because, if the canons caution against counting anyone among the martyrs who dies while smashing idols, lest one be drawn into some error[48]—so no one, even someone who bears a good outward appearance, should be considered a saint, unless proven in some way by divine revelation. Learn how profane it is to seek profit from carrying around the saints or showing their bones, if you wish to rate the saints and avarice equally!

Book 4

ON THE INNER WORLD

No gaze directed to the outer world can capture the state of the inner world, nor can any act of imagination conceive of it. It can be reached, of course, only through the faculty of contemplation, for only the keen insight of intellectual understanding—that one eye, no doubt, that single hair of the neck, by which the bride in the Song of Solomon pleased the groom most of all, that is to say, a singularly and indivisibly focused concentration of thought—can penetrate to that place where there is no physical matter to be found, nor anything subject to sense perception.[1] Just as we are not able to catch sight of the inner world through tangible objects, so in contemplating this inner world, we are unable to perceive material bodies that occupy space or perceive spaces occupied by material bodies. For comparison, if in looking upon the page you direct your attention to the meaning of the ideas, you will examine the letters and their meaning with one set of eyes, but with another you contemplate what reason alone can gather. The power of imagination,[2] by contrast, can never attain this place, because in that place, where neither the temporal world nor physical matter bound to the temporal world can intrude, the mind refuses all entry to things seen or seeable in the outer world. The faculty of imagination takes in only visible forms and their essential decrepitude, and forever impatient of slender subtleties it grows fat as it recalls familiar everyday objects. But if the mind wishes to strive after anything possessing the appearance of a higher truth, it can do so only after casting out that crowd of images from the outside world and focusing on the discernment of objects through the intellect. We are thus commanded to pray to the Father with the door closed, and this is the way to the first and second and third heaven, of which the apostle spoke.[3] When, therefore, spiritual perception advances in this manner, as if to some ethereal heaven, alone and unaccompanied by any earthly thing, it interprets spiritual things according to spiritual criteria and examines the incorporeal images of the inner world with the acute discernment of the intellect.

But the accounts of holy visions in the Old and New Testament seem to present a serious obstacle to my argument, since they describe in connection to this exalted visionary state only visual images of corporeal objects. For example, when Ezekiel, in his vision of God, saw a stormy north wind, a great cloud and flashing fire, brightness all around, four animals with a four-fold appearance, when he also saw the building on the mountain being measured, he seems only to have seen visual representations of corporeal entities, similar to objects he had previously experienced. There he saw thresholds, doors, vestibules and windows, there a man with the appearance of bronze, there a measuring reed and linen cord.[4] Why go on? There he gazed upon physical bodies or the likenesses of physical bodies, and he did not view anything that was not a re-creation in every detail of visible forms from the present world. Isaiah, Jeremiah, Daniel, and all the other prophets to whom God made himself recognizable express themselves in this way, not with truth but with signs and figures, when they declare they have seen the throne of God and compare its appearance to sapphire and topaz.[5] When the prophets convey the divine form as fire or else arrange it in the shape of a human being with individual limbs, this does not reflect the true unity of an omnipotent God, even though we try to comprehend something concerning his boundless essence by thinking of it in terms of a physical body.[6] There is indeed nothing in these scriptural passages that accords strictly with his pure and eternal essence, but there is, hidden behind these figurative and puzzling expressions, if not a literal exposition of his nature, an allegorical lesson about "his limbs."[7]

All of these passages occur, then, according to signs and figures, and among the authors of the Old Testament no credible expression of God's essential being can be found except "I am who I am" and "He it is who sent me to you."[8] All the other words and deeds used to describe him are reminiscent of everyday human experience and accord with our own emotions and behaviors, at least according to those sentiments that are not sinful.

Such is the case in the writings of the ancients, where we recognize that nearly everything happens figuratively, and we have the apostle as witness to this.[9] But even in the New Testament meaning is expressed in ways not altogether different from the Old Testament. The descriptions in the Apocalypse seemingly resemble visible forms in the external world. See how in the book on the Lord's day the prophet saw a form that seemed to be physically contained. But note carefully what he says: "I was in spirit."[10] What does "I was in spirit" mean? Namely, that he was contemplating "spiritual matter," for if what is spiritual had not been visible to him, he would not have been "in spirit." If then the only things visible to him were spiritual, why was he only able to speak about them as if they were physical bodies held before his eyes? Notice how he applies human concepts to the description of the divine—the double-edged sword, the lamp stands and the stars, and (returning to personal appearance) hair white as wool, and feet made of brass.[11] Pore over the entire volume, nowhere will you find anything not spoken of in human terms, nowhere is anything expressed about the substance, or even the essence, of God. Everything in the book is cloaked under a veil of allegories, and the language of shadows obscures its message about the condition of the holy church. And though he who saw all this was said to have been "in spirit," he spoke of nothing except through corporeal and corruptible images, hiding whatever spiritual sense lies within the words.

Those who move from seeing the present world to gazing upon the inner world, therefore, report that they saw nothing there different from what they were accustomed to seeing in this world. One might as a result believe that the same forms which define our experiences exist also in the spiritual world, in both heaven and in hell. If such a uniformity of appearance ("species") did exist (and I do not at all believe that it does!), then there would be no separation and no difference between the body and spirit; in fact, to put it succinctly, spirituality itself would not be anything. For if there is no degree of difference from one world to the next, if one passes from one world to the other as if from one body to another, then there would never be any movement from this present good, whatever it may be, to something better. God has established good things, but they exist through images. We make use of these images until we are granted enjoyment of those other things, called eternal in comparison with the transitory nature of what we have now. We draw similar conclusions from the writings of blessed Pope Gregory, where everyone who was snatched from this exterior world and taken into the inner world recalls encountering nothing except objects similar to what he normally saw here.[12] For if the visionaries talked of bridges, rivers, and sulfurous odors, and also of pleasant fields and homes built with gold bricks, they did so to draw analogies between the inner world and our present condition.

And you should not believe these things appeared in this way only to the people described in the *Dialogues*, but it is true of all the accounts of visions I remember having both read and heard about. What about Bede, for example, who, when he set down in his *History of the English People* the revelations manifested on occasion to his countrymen, fearful in some cases and glorious in others, spoke of nothing that was not completely in accord with our own experience? For they saw mountains and castles, stormy weather and lead coffins for the damned, broken legs of those condemned to suffering, foul-smelling places prepared for torture and punishment, the genitals of a prince gnawed away daily by some animal, as well as mountains of money, cloaks and silk garments, sumptuously woven tunics, furnishings of many kinds—all set before men who to pervert justice had gladly accepted bribes, thus giving evidence of the way that they had corrupted trials.[13] We have contemporary examples, too, since even today if someone has a vision about the condition of souls, it occurs exactly in the manner I have just described.

But in connection with this subject, why does it appear that

Lord Jesus himself only threatens physical punishments? When
he orders a man's hands and feet to be bound and commands
him to be thrown into the outer darkness, and then goes on to
proclaim that there will be wailing and gnashing of teeth,[14]
what does he show us except familiar punishments? Of course,
if we think that the souls of criminals or sinners suffer the same
kind of physical punishment as did their bodies, we do not
rightly compare, according to the apostle, spiritual things to
the spiritual,[15] yet I will nonetheless give ample proof of this
with the following example: Take a man caught in an endless
craving for profit, who to obtain his desires has eagerly dedi-
cated himself to the cruelest works—he tortures himself with
so much hunger, so many sleepless nights, and such constant
toil, that anyone in a similar condition, enduring such torments
against his will, would certainly bring a swift end to his life.
The same point is made clearly in the suffering of captives,
crucified for their money: we see them tortured with horrific
acts of butchery—hanged from their thumbs and genitals,
their teeth pulled out with forceps, fingernails pressed under a
board until they shatter, heels covered in salt and rubbed with
a goat's tongue[16]—and all this they endure with an equanim-
ity, or rather with a cheerfulness of heart, to such an extent
that you could believe their spirits, exulting in some hidden
corner, are soothed by the hope of hidden treasure. And I have
seen firsthand someone who extinguishes a torch of no small
size, glowing hot from its flames, by licking it with his tongue,
in return for his effort asking only for a coin. If then, as the
body suffers in tremendous misery, the soul, intoxicated at the
joy of a hidden hope, finds relief from this same difficulty, we
may conclude—in the same way that the flesh suffers in distress
while the soul remains to an extent free from its disturbances—
the body can be completely untroubled while the simple idea of
unhappiness torments the soul. Comparing in this way physical
bodies to physical things and spirits to the spiritual, as I pro-
posed, we see that each one without connection to the other
takes up crosses proper to its own place and time.

  We see this point especially clearly in the case of holy mar-
tyrs, who rejoiced inwardly at the sufferings of the exterior

man, but we see it equally well from the other direction, in the case of men who are consumed with bitter melancholy: their broken hearts, it is evident, suffer numerous torments while the body, as is clear from examples, is outwardly calm. Among hypocrites, you see how in their greed for empty glory they consider fasts, suffering from cold weather, and spending all day in church followed by sleepless nights as if in wakeful prayer to be mere trifles; likewise the sweet expectation of heaven in the minds of saints makes the daily mortifications of their flesh brief and momentary. Let us accept as fact, then, that just as external punishments are known to turn our frail bodies into corpses, so internally we are either nourished by a cheerfulness of spirit or tormented by the mind's latent vices.

Having made this distinction between spirits and bodies in my argument, let me now address two themes: how the torments of the soul can be considered as something distinct from the pains of the body and why the Lord and every saint has described—I will not say understood—the state of the soul in fleshly terms. To follow up on what I just said, if one wishes, in fact, to discuss this type of understanding, the thoughts of the prophets were far too spiritual in terms of—I will not say what they could have made known to their listeners but rather—what they should have made known to listeners.

Nevertheless, I will say, and I will even say it with certainty, that the prophets could not have made spiritual truth known nor should they have done so. For if they could have, they would have openly proclaimed before the public their incomplete knowledge about the birth of Jesus and the mysteries of the church, if they had actually had permission to express what was only partly clear to them. Whence the saying of the psalmist: "You revealed to me," he said, "the uncertainties and secrets of your wisdom." If these were "uncertain" to him, from whose seed he was to be born, what benefit would there have been in spreading doubtful interpretations?[17] Furthermore, if they were "secret," they should not have been revealed, especially on account of the prophet's uncertainty: for the more secret something is, the more dangerous it is to promulgate, if there is uncertainty. He knew that what was revealed to him was uncertain and secret to others, and for quite worthy purposes decided to keep silent about it. Thus the apostle said, "I heard secret words, which to man it is not permitted to speak."[18] There are two ways we can understand this, as if he said both that a man is not permitted to speak about such things (of course, we usually write without speaking to anyone) and it is not permitted to speak to a man about such things, that is, to explain them to anyone else. Thus the prophets *could not* speak such things simply because they *should not* speak about them. If the prophetic spirit had not restrained them, just as one restrains a horse with reins, then the mystery, which they had conceived in their minds, would not have stayed a mystery. They obviously could not disclose what they held under seal from such a teacher, for if it is not within human discretion, nor within human ability, to contemplate God or the Holy Scripture whenever one wishes, so it was not at all permitted the prophets to understand the future mysteries as much as they wanted—nor were they even allowed to have complete insight into what they were saying.

Of course, visions that come from God often inform us about our future, though we are not able to gather from them how or when events will transpire. In the same way God did not fully touch the prophets' hearts, in that they were given no ability to explain what they had seen. Their incapacity, however, is nothing but an interdiction. And this is why it is said the Lord could not perform a miracle in Capernaum[19]—he "could not" is thus understood to mean that he "should not," for it would be unfitting for him to waste the blessings of his miracles on those he had been unable to bring into his faith. He also forbade pearls to be cast before swine,[20] because the splendor of divine utterance is not suitable for filthy minds.

To pick up the thread of the discussion, everything the prophets not so much understood as much as they expressed in corporeal terms about the nature of God had to be brought down to human understanding, because neither could they find the words to comprehend the form of God's essence, nor, even supposing it were in some way possible to do so, did anyone possess a mind capable of grasping such expressions. And so those who could neither speak about nor hear about the nature of God remained rightly silent about it. But what needed to be said, they expressed in the everyday speech of the people; otherwise they would, like madmen, have faltered in their own utterances. And if they had spoken of anything beyond themselves, just as they themselves could not comprehend their own words, neither could they have found anyone else capable of understanding them. Because of this, on occasion they describe God using comparisons and similes unworthy of him—"a cart loaded down with hay," for example, or "a warrior drunk on wine."[21] They themselves could not have understood their visions unless they had been able to express them with corporeal objects familiar also to us in our own daily experiences, and though these comparisons do not seem appropriate when applied to good men, the prophets did not shrink from using them to describe God. The fact that they made comparisons unworthy of the highest majesty, nevertheless, demonstrates that whatever we hold to be great and noble is still by comparison unworthy of God. This is why in the book of Ezekiel the four bodies that looked very much like strange animals—their four faces more portentous than Janus'—are revealed to signify that we must seek out the intellectual sense if we wish to interpret sights that, to our eyes, are monstrous.[22] If he makes spirits his angels and if there are only spiritual beings in heaven,[23] it is ridiculous to think that physical bodies with such an appearance could be found amid the heavenly beings. Angels, because of their splendor and glory, are very pleasing, while the creatures described by Ezekiel are thoroughly unpleasant in the extreme horror of their hateful appearance, and since a literal interpretation does not suffice, the only other option is to seek the alternative meanings at which they hint. Men thus speak to other men in corporeal terms, because even if they did understand anything at all on the intellectual plane, they still could not express anything that they had understood.

We also must recognize that those who depart into this inner world and then return to us still caught some small glimpse of that eternal gleam that lurks behind these earthly images, even though they were not able to see anything except in terms of what they had experienced in their bodies while among the living. For if they had understood these sights in the way of those who never return to this world, not only the words they used while still in the flesh but even the subtle and acute understanding they possessed while outside the flesh would grow dull and their visions would perish within them— much less would they be able to explain to others what is incomprehensible to themselves. And so when they return from the inner world, they are able to speak to men only in the likenesses of the things they were accustomed to see in the external world, because no saint ever found it possible to explain in speech or writing what he had been able for a brief time, even just a moment, to discover in contemplation of the divine. When therefore in a vision of the glory of the saints they sense a fragrance or hear a choir singing hymns or take in the shining lights, all this is not according to the reality of the spiritual plane but rather according to the characteristics of visible objects with which they are familiar. In visions of this inner world we are shown things that appear beautiful or look valuable or give delight to men, so that we accept the things we usually value most as proof of the glory granted to saints. And thus in the Apocalypse saints are said to be clad in white robes and to carry palms, symbols of victory, and to wear gold crowns, as rulers do.[24] The florid delights and splendors of their appearance are not intended to represent the foolishness of those heretics called Chiliasts, who promise a thousand years of carnal delights after the resurrection, but rather the vision displays an ensemble of images that people customarily find pleasurable and that also demonstrate the glory of those who are saved.[25]

Furthermore, I understand the punishment of the damned to be of the same quality as what I have said about the revelation of those in glory. In scripture their souls are frequently seen burning in fire, whipped with scourges, sunk in stinking waters, as well as suffering the chastisements that the learned Gregory and Bede describe. But these punishments are nothing more than the same ones that we inflict on the bodies of convicted criminals. The damned suffer spiritually, but we recognize their punishments through forms to which long experience has accustomed us. The punishments serve as a warning, since we would otherwise not likely believe the damned to be tortured in such agony. Since, then, we cannot hear spiritual language by which spiritual beings respond to spirits, we use our knowledge of physical bodies, as it were, to tap the sap of our intellect, and we perceive souls as being oppressed in the same way that our bodies suffer torment. Therefore, because we do not believe it possible for unadulterated souls to be subjected to physical punishments, let us turn to the punishments that they can and should suffer.

From the apostle, as I quoted above, spiritual things are to be compared to the spiritual. It would be fairly astonishing if he meant by this that an intangible soul could be afflicted with tangible torments. Yet, to begin with, it might be said that the inner world is called "inner" by the outer world in the same way the apostle said to the Gentiles, "You are called 'the fore-skin' by what is called 'circumcision.'"[26] For my body, which is plainly visible to everyone, has an invisible soul hidden within it, and similarly, this physical creation, which both rational and irrational creatures can see, has a second structure, which only rational beings stripped of their mortality can recognize and touch. No mind occupied by the images of visible things is able to take measure of the soul's condition; it lies open only to minds' eyes freed of the purulence of this world. As an example, I describe a word as "spiritual" because it is produced by the breath as well as by the tongue and teeth (so the apostle, "I will sing praise with the spirit").[27] A word is also, if I may use the term, mental when it is set forth in thought alone, while the lips remain silent. Moreover, a word is intellectual when it is handled through the purest contemplation, without any interior verbal construction. In the same way, this world in which we live can be called visible and figurative, because it stands under our sight and because when are our eyes are idle, the mind can reconstruct its corporeality. The inner world, however, is all the more difficult to penetrate, since nothing is contained there and nothing happens there through bodies, places, or times. To an extent, it is so far removed from our everyday experience that we, who almost never affix our mind's eye to anything beyond what we usually do, must make all the more effort to break through the clouds of our will and thus behold that inner world.

Another question arises from this as to whether the devil and his angels could in general be thought to inhabit the inner world, since the Lord calls him the "prince of this world" in which we live and the apostle "prince of the air," but also prince "of these shadows, the spiritual forces of evil in heaven."[28] And so the question is really whether—given that he is named "of the air" because he dwells within it and wanders invisibly among us—he could also be considered connected to this inner world. I would first reply that however much dignity and purity belongs to that inner world, I would not dare claim that it is not shared in common by both good and evil. Indeed, the nature of demons is exceedingly fine-honed with an inborn alacrity, and on account of the discernment required to see them, or more accurately, on account of their nimble spiritual power, no matter how much they wander through this outer world, the inner world more properly fits their mode of existence. The nature of demons has more in common with the inner world. For if the inner world is spiritual and the devil does not exist in a thick and fleshy body, then we must recognize an identity of substances between the inner world and the devil (excepting the fact that the devil lacks rationality). It is not possible for the devil to exist apart from the inner world.

Until Judgment Day, therefore, the devil will traverse the inner world, because during that time he is God's officer or servant, casting souls into eternal punishment. License is granted to his cruelty to continue in this duty until, when the wheat is separated from the chaff, it shall be judged time to take his power away from him.

Of course I also think that this deadly being and his sinister band are inhabitants of the external world, too. But why do I think so, given that those condemned to punishment in his prisons are so far removed from the environment of the present life that blessed Job describes them as ignorant of whether their children are honored or brought low?[29] It is because the inner world is unlike this exterior world in yet another way: in this one good and evil men are mixed together, but there the blessed and the damned are forever separated from one another. And so after that final day, the devil will no longer have the freedom to spread his plagues wherever he likes, and his accomplices will share in his punishment. No polluted being will any longer be able to pass through the inner world, now made uniformly pure throughout. This is why, when the skies and the lands are made anew, the saints will be able to pass through and dwell in both the inner and the exterior worlds. For when the saints are purged by fire as well as raised to the heavens by the blessed transformation of their bodies, and when this world, or rather the very universe with its inveterate filth is consumed in flames and renewed into an incorruptible state, its environs will become suitable in every way for habitation and inhabitants, and when both the inner and the exterior worlds are cleansed, the mansion and its tenant will flourish together. In the case of the saints, body and soul will rejoice in the glory of a single beatitude, and so, too, the exterior and inner worlds, brought back into a pure unity through the fiery destruction of the one, will provide splendid passageways without any obstacle, allowing saints to triumph everywhere.

Let me return to the discussion I started. If we wish to define as either corporeal or incorporeal those punishments, which I claim the wicked will suffer in the lower world, we can better arrive at an answer by examining the opposite problem: that is, we shall ask whether in the heavenly kingdom the elect will acquire glories that are corporeal or incorporeal. If we think that their glories will be corporeal, so that they attain bodily pleasures, feasts and banquets, we would be explaining nothing at all, or rather we run up against the scripture: "Do not rejoice over the spirits which submit to you, but rejoice that your names are written in heaven." The apostles themselves, as yet still untaught, replied to the Lord: "Lord, show us the Father, and we will be satisfied." And also: "I will see you again and your hearts will rejoice."[30] If the glory of the heavenly denizens lies in such things, what on earth does anyone

seek here? What physical joy is thought to exist in the vision of
God the Father? What about what the psalmist says: "What
is there for me in heaven and what do I desire on earth apart
from you?" "God," he says, "is of my heart and is a part of
me." If therefore he "who sees the Son and believes in him has
eternal life,"[31] and if in heaven and on earth he asks for noth-
ing except to behold God, what place, I ask, is there for bodily
pleasures? There are no examples that would lead anyone to
understand that anything of the flesh exists in heaven, and it
would be astonishing if anyone thought otherwise—he would
seek to find a lie in truth itself.[32] If everything in God's reward
is spiritual, to my mind it follows that what is done in the spir-
itual world by spirits, even things done by malignant spirits—
and this includes punishing the spirits of the corrupt—is also
spiritual. For just as we do not believe that angels become weighed
down by human filth, so we claim it is not possible for souls to be
troubled by bodily punishments.

But, as I said above, we can reach a conclusion better from
the contrary direction. If according to the apostle "the king-
dom of God is not food and drink but peace and joy in the
Holy Spirit,"[33] we can see how drastically different this descrip-
tion is from the eternal disorder and perpetual unrest and
gloom that flourish in hell. "There will be," the Lord says, "in
that place weeping and gnashing of teeth."[34] What is the weep-
ing of souls except a deep and heartfelt sorrow? Only corpo-
real beings shed tears. As for "gnashing," which in a literal
sense applies to teeth, it refers here to those incorporeal souls'
grief, madness, and furor. A human who is said to gnash his
teeth is in a rage, and this is the grief from the misery that
souls have suffered and will suffer for all eternity. There is also
gnashing when the soul, now made a limb of the devil, has
contempt for everything divine, and begins to regret it did not
do even worse things than it did. Thus: "When the impious
man reaches the depth of wickedness, he feels contempt."
"Every tree," he says, "that does not bear good fruit is cut
down and thrown into the fire." That is, cut down from the
ability to sin, which means the same thing as if he were to say,
"bind his hands and feet." To be cast into the fire is to burn

with the constant desire to do evil, and so there is also this passage: "A fire fell from above and they did not see the sun." For if it is the case—and in fact, it is—that in the inner world souls desire, fear, rejoice and grieve,[35] then the impious are never free, not even for a moment, from three of these emotions (for it is never fitting that the impious rejoice). I do not say this merely because the damned are bound by the same passions that once had governed them, but rather because they suffer these passions with a greater furor than ever before, because their sufferings are now more spiritual than they were before. It is not a single passion that burns them, but passions of every sort become within them nothing other than an unquenchable and ever-raging fire.[36]

If someone should object that Saint Gregory says souls are punished with a corporeal fire, let him look closely at what Gregory actually says: "I say the spirit is held in fire, such that it is in the torment of the fire, which it sees and perceives. For it suffers from the fire at the very moment it sees it, and is burned because it sees itself burned."[37] In sum, because the spirit sees that it is condemned, it is consumed by a savage rage in its mind. Consider a man cast into an eternal prison, tormented with a fatal melancholy. This year I saw someone who out of fear of poverty would have hanged himself, if his friends had not saved him: because of his circumstances, in the words of the same blessed pope, he has a spirit in which he will be tortured. But if someone were to object that corporeal fire was the rich man's punishment,[38] I would gladly ask the blessed pope, were he here, if we ought to consider that fire corporeal, as he says, and whether we ought to consider the drop of water and finger and tongue corporeal in the same way. But because I consider it wicked to disagree with such a great teacher and because I do not know how to mix corporeal with spiritual elements in that inner world, which is completely internal, let me commit to God what I have yet to experience: for I am not fighting with anyone, only offering my interpretation with a sincere intention and to the best of my abilities.

As the blessings of the saints, when they attain the vision of God, continue to grow in inestimable sweetness, so the souls of the wicked, united to their head the devil, in the most savage torment burn all the more vehemently with their desire to sin, and their will is in perfect concord with him who feeds on enticing others to sin. And just as the saints, once they have seen the glory of God, are ashamed that they did not expend more labor to acquire it, so do the impious grieve most bitterly, as they come into these tortures, that they were not more enslaved to their wicked wills during their lives. How could it not be so, when it is said of the impious man while he still lives: "Under his tongue there is labor and grief"?[39] *Labor* is the sweat of his efforts to do evil, *grief* that he is not able to carry out all the crimes that he desired. And what can be said about one who becomes incorporated into Satan—how violent in him shall his utterly wicked appetites become? If the blessed burn with eternal ardor for God, the wicked shriek in perpetual rage.[40]

The passage in the Gospel about the rich man and Lazarus applies to my interpretation, which, if it is discussed carefully, sheds light on the condition of the inner world.[41] First, consider what it means that the rich man asks for Lazarus and not himself to be resurrected and sent to his father's house. You will discover that the rich man departed from this life with the worst possible intention, because if resurrected and returned to this world, he had no intention to mend his ways. In fact, he knew for certain that he could never abandon the perversity he held onto even during his torments. And it certainly did not escape him that if he were restored to his previous condition in the world and did not correct his behavior from his earlier pursuits, he would in the end return to the same torments in a damnation one hundred times worse than before. Therefore, he could safely ask that Lazarus be resurrected, since Lazarus, before he had experienced glory, had lived piously in illness and in need. There was therefore no expectation that when he returned to life he would do anything but become better than the good man he already had been. Also relevant to my interpretation is why the rich man—who according to Solomon, as one of the damned, would possess neither wisdom nor knowledge nor reason in hell and certainly would feel driven by the rage of a diabolical intention[42]—would so benevolently ask that his brothers not join him in perdition. If benevolence is a good thing and if it exists amid the tortures of hell, then certainly wisdom and knowledge and reason would also have to exist there, contradicting that saying of Solomon; however, because the Holy Spirit who was in Solomon cannot speak falsehood, it is obvious how pointless this proposition is. It was said above that the wicked in hell will not only not lack carnal desires, but will even burn with perverse loves, and this type of love is what the rich man was thinking of when he feared his brothers' arrival in hell. For he knew the punishment for each of his brothers would be added to his own, and having turned away from God's love in his devotion and care for them, he will burn and rave just as much in their damnation that he sees set forth before him. He therefore feared that Gehanna would be, if I may use the term, quintupled for him, so he prayed that his brothers, at Lazarus' instruction, would be removed from his company.

But somebody still might object that the rich man, because he could not escape punishment by this good deed, must have possessed some degree of goodwill when he expressed a desire for his brothers to live more correctly. To which I reply, there are many instances where we seem to will something, but it is easy to recognize that in fact we really do not. For example, if you suffer from an incurable disease in your finger, and a surgeon advises amputation, you say to yourself that you prefer to have the finger cut off rather than allow the disease to spread and lose your whole hand. The former is better than the latter, though you obviously would choose neither. Such was the will of the rich man, that in willing this he was not truly willing it, but though not truly willing it, he willed it rather than endure an increase in his punishment. Whomever the wicked love instead of God, by a just judgment they envision them tortured before their eyes, and their punishments they always bring back upon themselves.

I do not know what bodies souls have, but in my judgment it is certain that we must understand these words from the Lord's mouth typologically: "Their worm shall not die and their fire shall not be extinguished." If blessed Job, festering and stinking, spoke rightly when he said, "What gnaws at me does not rest,"[43] I do not see how the previous passage can refer to spiritual matters. I have never heard of worms born from a spirit or worms biting a spirit. Since, then, there is a discrepancy in the literal meaning, let us affix in the soul, whose fire is never extinguished as it is consumed with ceaseless anxiety to the point of utterly hopeless misery, spiritual vermin, which is to say the sting of perpetual anguish and eternally fruitless compunction. If you think this constitutes too little of torture and punishment for the damned in hell, do you imagine that anything is worse than being brutalized in endless rabid anger and being forced into conformity with the devil and his angels in utter rage? And clearly they have deserved this madness, since if for them there is never hope of any relief for all eternity, what else is left for them but a furor forever new? If, as the apostle testifies, the gloom of this world is said to "produce death,"[44] where wrathful thoughts and excessive grief drives each person to lay his hands upon himself, think of the bitterness kindled in the enraged minds of men because of their unending death, at peace not even for a single moment. In this life at least the mind is assuaged at times with false hopes; in that place, there is only an internal austerity soothed by no foolish idea; no vain illusion can sneak in to provide these wretched people with even a moment's relief.

Consider as well those who were rescued from hell at the Lord's resurrection. While there, they were "confined to the darkness," though they would have endured only the darkness of tedium.[45] This darkness daily increased because they were for so long deprived of the vision of God, but they still had some hope of attaining it at some time in the future. What deeper darkness could there be, then, than for—I do not say the eyes, but rather—the hearts to become enveloped in a cloud of despair? Let others talk of fires! Let others throw around sulfur! Let them at the same time mix in the scorching winds! I am confident in my opinion that for the damned there is no worse abyss, no death more cruel—a torment more grievous than any torture—than that they lose without hope of recovery such a pious and serene Lord, and as the summit of their misfortune and misery they will never be able to see him anywhere. Indeed they would not be in complete and total darkness if they could hope for some other outcome. For if he "who sees the Son and believes in him has eternal life" and if "this is eternal life, that they know you, God, and Jesus Christ whom you sent,"[46] such that the eternal vision of God is alone sufficient for the blessedness of the saints, who would dare to contest or dispute that the principal, or rather the singular, cause of the calamity of the damned is that they are eternally excluded from the contemplation of God? Nor in any way does it seem absurd—in fact, it is both true and most like the truth—that the deprivation of what provides life for the saints (just as eyes bring light to the body) brings death to the wicked (just as the loss of light creates night).

On a related point, there are some who in their discussion of the soul's form picture it as possessing a human shape. In this opinion I can find no sense; therefore I do not accept it. For if you attribute ears and eyes, nose and lips, chest and stomach, kidneys and ribs, feet and legs to souls, you are making them corporeal. And if they are bodies, how does one body contain another? If souls are contained in bodies like smaller vessels kept inside larger ones, I would like to know how these two bodies fit together so tightly. (I am only arguing against the writings of those who claim souls possess the image of a body, not the authors themselves, for their eminence is such that I consider it rash to refute them.)[47] If a body is inserted into a body, it is necessary that they fit together in such a way that the face is attached to face, hand to hand, and every limb to every other limb, and if, as happens, a part is cut off, two pieces have to be amputated for one. Finally, even if you believe that souls are fashioned in this way, it would be necessary to confine them to a place and dwelling, and you would take away from them everything that makes them spirits and gives them the name "spirit." Will the soul's magnitude be greater than the body's, or will its movement be swifter? One might argue that souls in visions seem to have bodies, but it is easy to demolish the point, because the visionary sees neither a body nor a soul. Rather, only the image of something seen reaches the mind.

These objectors may think to find support for their beliefs because the rich man in hell had a tongue, and Lazarus a finger, but I would like to ask them whether there was water in that spiritual world. If there were, then its inhabitants would have been in need of this material substance. Assume it is so—how was this water so effective at quenching the furnaces of Gehenna? My God! What good could a drop do there, when in vain the Ganges and Indus would flow upon the rich man's tongue? Therefore, we understand that when Lazarus brought a drop of water on the tip of his finger, through even the smallest of intentions he performed for the rich man a service of the tiniest indulgence. This is the little finger the Pharisees and scribes were unwilling to lift to lighten the heavy and unmovable burdens placed on the shoulders of men.[48]

But if they still maintain that the soul has a human image, what will Germanus in his fiery orb, in the passage from blessed Gregory, do for them? Whose side does Scholastica, transformed into a dove, support?[49] This entire controversy thus runs up against one point: that we do not impute to souls the appearance of humanity or of fire or of a dove, but rather we strip them of any corporeality—in fact or in resemblance—and we surrender it all to intellectual subtlety. It is clearly unfitting for someone to argue that a spiritual habitation has corporeal inhabitants. If the words of Lord Jesus are: "my kingdom is not of this world" and "I will not drink the fruit of the vine until I drink it anew in my kingdom," and if we pray daily that his kingdom come,[50] I assert beyond doubt that heaven—the upper part of the threefold structure, which is also called the "throne of God" from its more honorable part—is nothing other than spiritual interiority. And here, as if in a place beyond this world, the Lord says he reigns, because in this world the prince of this air and his followers oppose him, but in the other, he governs all in peace. "After he has handed this kingdom"—that is, those whom he has ruled and rules through charity,—"to God the Father," then God will be "all in all."[51]

Christ also said to the robber: "Today you will be with me"—he does not say "in heaven"—but "in paradise."[52] "Paradise" is where there is a perpetual vision of Christ, and this is nowhere else but the spiritual world. For when he ascended to heaven as his disciples looked on, he did not abandon a lower part to take possession of a higher place,[53] but rather he wished to demonstrate that he was moving to a worthier abode, and in this way he could indicate to less discerning minds that he was sitting beside the Father. But in that inner world there is no height, depth, or any kind of space—it has no time or place at all. Sense perception on its own does not govern reason and intellect. It does not even mix with them—for "a man of the flesh does not perceive the things of God."[54] Reason and intellect, however, not only discern things that are below them, but also reach up into divine things. In the same way, God and the saints, as if intellect and reason, distinguish all corporeal things, but in such a way that nothing corporeal touches upon either of them.

I have carried my interpretations up to this point without the presumption that there are no better ideas, fortifying them not with a curtain wall of words but with faith alone.

Notes

MONODIES: BOOK 1

1. Guibert's sense of self-abnegation certainly seems in these opening passages to cross over into self-loathing. But here and elsewhere he shows himself typical of his age. While he lacks the verbal and emotional subtlety, his argument throughout these chapters is in line with Anselm's presentation in the *Cur Deus homo*, where Anselm argues that the slightest act of sin (disobedience to God) is unforgivable.

2. 1 Cor. 15:34; Job 3:5; Ws. 18:14–15.

3. Ps. 76:10/77:9. The Psalms throughout are cited, where necessary, with two different verses. The first corresponds to the numbering typical of English-language Bibles, the second to the Vulgate Latin Bible.

4. This dense passage, like much of this introductory chapter, grows out of Guibert's psychological system. Sin results when the faculty of reason is overcome by affections. Recovery of reason occurs when the mind's faculties are put back into the right order.

5. Guibert here attempts to invert the fundamental paradox of monastic life—the only way to rise up to heaven is to humiliate oneself. To do so he combines two biblical passages (Ps. 68:16/ 69:15 and Rom. 1:28). The latter is one of his favorites, where Paul speaks of God placing people who do not recognize him into a *reprobum sensum*. Their vision becomes so distorted that they cannot recognize their own sinful condition. They thus sink down into a well while rising to heights of ignorance. Conceptually, Guibert's language is close to a famous tenet of Bernard of Clairvaux's teaching, that human beings live in a *regio dissimilitudinis*, a region of unlikeness, that prevents them from having a clear vision of God.

6. Lam. 3:1.
7. 1 Cor. 4:7.
8. Eccles. 10:10 and John 1:9.
9. Besides indicating Guibert's fundamentally aristocratic world-view, this passage also reveals a key doctrine of his theology—that there is no virtue unless it is born of struggle.
10. Sallust, *Bellum Catilinae* 14.2.
11. 1 Cor. 8:4.
12. Rom 1:20, Judg. 13:6, 2 Pet. 2:17, and 2 Cor. 11:15.
13. Phil. 3:21, and a reference to the transfiguration, when Christ took Peter, James, and John to the top of Mount Tabor and became radiant before them (that is, took on his true divine appearance), and spoke with Elijah and Moses. The story appears in all of the Synoptic Gospels (e.g., Luke 9:28–36).
14. Augustine, *De doctrina Christiana*, 4.28.61.
15. Guibert indicates here that his brothers have preceded him in death, though in *Monodies* 2.4, below, he says that one of his brothers was with him at Nogent at the time of his mother's death.
16. Isa. 31:9.
17. This passage has been used to try to date Guibert's birth to mid-April, on the premise that he was born at the same time these reeds grow. It is apparent, though, that Guibert only comments here on when the reeds appear, not when he did.
18. Ps. 99:3/100:3.
19. Virgil, *Aeneid* 1.288.
20. Guibert's language remains highly technical. The term that we have translated here as "desires" is *voluntates*, the plural for the faculty of "will." As he would have learned from Saint Anselm, and from his own studies, the will is singular when focused on God. When focused on the world, it becomes divided. Though Guibert prefers internal, psychological speculations, he grounds his presentation in sensory perception. A divided will stinks; a unified will is redolent with the perfume of the Virgin.
21. Guibert worries that he is being bold here in suggesting that the Virgin has an obligation to aid him. In the redemptive universe of his teacher, Anselm, only God can redeem sin, but he is not obliged to do so. Only man has that obligation, but he lacks the power to do so. Therefore only a "god-man" (Christ) is able to perform that mission. Guibert suggests here (and in a separate treatise on the Virgin) that her affection for humanity gives her a crucial role in the salvific process.

22. Ps. 119:94/118:94.

23. "Intellect" is another important word in Guibert's moral lexicon. It can also be translated as "understanding," and as such connects to Anselm's famous dictum "faith seeking understanding" (*fides quaerens intellectum*). "Intellect" is thus a type of understanding that pertains to the experience or contemplation of God.

24. In this famous passage, Guibert is perhaps being a better historian than he realized. In describing the dearth of teachers in the later eleventh century, as opposed to the relative abundance in the early twelfth, he is essentially giving a worm's-eye view of the phenomenon historians have called "the twelfth-century renaissance."

25. Elsewhere Guibert names his teacher as Solomon. It is unclear whether the name is an honorific title or an actual name. The portrait of Solomon's teaching is somewhat stylized, being an inverted image of Quintilian's description of what constitutes good teaching (*Institutio oratoria*, 1.3.8–17 and 2.3.11–12). To a degree, though, Solomon's deficiencies are likely a reflection of an older teaching style described by C. Steven Jaeger in *The Envy of Angels: Cathedral Schools and Social Ideals in Medieval Europe, 950–1200* (Philadelphia: University of Pennsylvania Press, 2000)—an emphasis on style, appearance, and manner, with less focus on dialectic than an older Guibert would have preferred. Based on the sophistication of Guibert's Latin, Solomon could not have been quite as ignorant as Guibert portrays him, though certainly by standards of the next generation of teachers, Solomon wasn't very good.

26. Apoc. 8:1, a prophetic passage delightfully turned into a justification for recess.

27. The text of the *Monodies* appears to be faulty here.

28. Corporal punishment was a standard tool of eleventh-century education, particularly in a monastic setting such as the one that Solomon seems to have tried to create for Guibert. Child oblates could be beaten out of custom, not to punish any particular wrong but simply to encourage discipline. Guibert's teacher Saint Anselm advocated a gentler approach to pedagogy, saying that teachers should see themselves as goldsmiths, having to use care and caution when shaping their pupils; described in the biography by Eadmer, *Vita S. Anselmi*, ed. and trans. Sir Richard Southern (Oxford: Clarendon Press, 1972, republished 1996), 1.22, p. 38. Guibert as a writer later in life would seem

to have appreciated this doctrine. As a child, based on how he describes this scene, he apparently accepted the necessity of his own punishment.

29. Guibert's choice here between life either as a scholar or as a knight anticipates by about thirty years the later career of Peter Abelard, who famously observes at the beginning of his *Historia calamitatum* that he chose the lists of Minerva over those of Mars.

30. Again, there is no virtue without struggle. Because passions burn so strongly in the young, it is relatively easy for them to fulfill their religious vows. Guibert urges his readers here to anticipate the pattern of moral advance and decline that will characterize his life and that of every Christian.

31. As Guibert recalls the story, writing in the early twelfth century, it raises for him many problems. First, a castellan exercised control over a prebend whose income and rights ought to pertain to a cathedral canon. This was a clear violation of the ideals of the Gregorian reform, which sought to liberate ecclesiastical authority from secular control. Even more problematic, of course, is that Guibert's family was trying to buy the prebend away from the castellan, violating ecclesiastical injunctions against simony, or trafficking in church offices. The priest, against whom his family campaigns, as described in the next paragraph, is married, thus violating reformers' strictures against celibacy. In other words, every single person in the story is violating the Gregorian reform, and Guibert's family violates one half of the reform, ironically, in the name of enforcing the other half.

32. This passage may be a reference to the Lateran Council of 1059, which did indeed prohibit clerical marriage. More likely, though, Guibert refers to the general atmosphere of the latter eleventh century and the intensified efforts to apply reform principles throughout Europe.

33. Guibert does not intend to indicate, or even imply, that the castellan is serving as a lay abbot. The text merely asserts that the castellan exercised authority over the canons if he were an abbot.

34. Job 20:24. Guibert's mother effectively "put him in the queue" of similarly ambitious young men out to claim benefices from clerics as they died.

35. Tob. 4:16.

36. Lucan, *Pharsalia* 1.70–71.

37. This passage criticizes the common Benedictine practice of accepting child oblates (Guibert thus anticipates the concerns of later twelfth-century monastic reformers). As always, Guibert emphasizes the role of reason and will. Monastic conversion requires a conscious renunciation of one's old life mixed with a willingness to accept a lifelong struggle against sin.

38. There is perhaps a note of self-criticism here. Guibert mentions in his crusade chronicle (7.32) that while a monk at Saint-Germer his duties took him into Beauvais (where he describes how, during the time of the First Crusade, a crowd grew ecstatic thinking it had seen a cross in the clouds). He thus had had the opportunity to administer, or misadminister, church funds.

39. There is apparently a lacuna in the text here.

40. Evrard II of Breteuil, viscount of Chartres, adopted a religious life in 1073 and later (as Guibert describes) joined the monastery of Marmoutiers outside of Tours.

41. Ps. 45:14–15/44:13–14.

42. In other words, making and selling charcoal.

43. Saint Thibaud was from Provins in Champagne. Born in 1017, he converted to the religious life in 1044 and died in 1066, seven years before Evrard's similar conversion.

44. Making Evrard in this respect somewhat like his impersonator. There was in late eleventh-century Europe a growing hostility toward such overly refined clothing and against men wearing their hair long. Much of it was associated with southern France and more especially the Islamic courts in Spain (as below, in *Monodies* 1.12, Guibert references excessively stylish shoes characteristic of Cordoba). Similar fashions at the court of William Rufus in England drew the wrath of Guibert's teacher Anselm, after he had become archbishop.

45. In Acts 7:57–8:1, Stephen the proto-martyr is stoned to death as Saul, who will eventually convert and become the apostle Paul, looks on approvingly. Stephen, in Acts 7:60, prays for God to forgive his killers.

46. Raoul III of Valois in fact repudiated his first wife in order to marry the widowed Queen Anne of Kiev in 1060. The couple was excommunicated by Pope Alexander II on the grounds of incest, because King Henry had been Raoul's cousin.

47. Saint Bruno of Cologne (ca. 1030–1101) is the founder at the church of the Grand Chartreuse and of the Carthusian order, known for its extreme ascetic rigor, for the isolation lived by its

monks (in sharp contrast to the communal ideals of the Rule of Saint Benedict), and for its literary endeavors (at least in terms of book production). Guibert's description here of Bruno's conversion is one of the most important sources available for the order's creation.

48. To take the "first steps [in a] conversion" is for Guibert a technical concept—a moment of self-awareness usually dominated by fear of God, and usually associated with entry into the monastic life. Recent converts usually approach their conversion with a fiery zeal not based on rational understanding, leading to a much more difficult period of advance (and decline) in virtue. Bruno's conversion is not entirely typical, since it begins with a sense of revulsion at the ecclesiastical world that he inhabits.

49. Manasses was archbishop from 1069 to his deposition in 1081. The excommunicated emperor to whom Guibert refers below is Henry IV, by 1081 at war with Pope Gregory VII.

50. Eccles. 32:1. A statement somewhat at odds with Guibert's admiration for other kings, particularly English kings, observable elsewhere in the *Monodies*. One must wonder if Guibert really prefers that a king (for whom a certain degree of cruelty is, as it were, part of the job description) be so modest in demeanor.

51. Guibert expresses some suspicion here of what sounds, on the face of it, an obviously fraudulent claim about relics. It is a theme developed at much further length in *On the Relics of Saints*. It is remarkable that the fake relics are nonetheless effective transmitters of the power of God.

52. William of Nevers participated in the crusade of 1101. In 1115 he was imprisoned by Theobald of Blois (indicating that Guibert was writing sometime before that year). In 1147, one year before his death, he returned to the Grand Chartreuse, where he apparently ended his life as a monk.

53. Again, Guibert makes use of his technical, psychological vocabulary. To obtain contemplation is the final moment of a conversion (begun earlier in Bruno's case with the "first steps" of leaving Reims). Contemplation was a rare gift, one seldom enjoyed for any length of time. The meditative, spiritual feats of the Carthusians, therefore, were in Guibert's eyes extraordinary and extraordinarily admirable.

54. Another common theme in Guibert's moral writings: the beginning of conversion is rooted in fear (and hence in the emotional part of the mind, or the "affections"). Only with experience can conversion become integrated with a Christian's rational facul-

ties. Even though this is a higher stage of Christian development, it often lacks the fervor and power of the first steps toward Christianity.

55. The period of seven years is likely figurative. Guibert perhaps remembers Gen. 29 where Jacob has to labor for periods of seven years to marry Leah and then Rachel. Modern readers are frequently wonderstruck at Guibert's troubled and ambivalent attitude toward sexuality. Having learned of his father's impotence from his mother and other details surrounding the consummation of the marriage, he is perhaps better adjusted than one might expect.

56. Guibert compares his mother to the burning bush seen by Moses, Exod. 3:2.

57. A reference to the short work of Ausonius, *Septem sapientium sententiae*, or "Sayings of the Seven Wise Men." "What is a chaste woman? She about whom rumor fears to lie."

58. It goes without saying that Guibert exaggerates the virtue of a past age to draw unfavorable judgments concerning his own time. In his description of courtly fashion imported from the south and in romantic games and behavioral patterns exhibited by the nobility, however, he is casting an early light on the practices of courtly love.

59. There appears to be an error in the manuscript here. Guibert uses the expression *singulariter apud te intumuisse*, which has led previous translators to read in this passage an awkward address to God. More than likely the passage should read *singulariter apud se intumuisse*, essentially "alone by himself." The passage would be a gloss on Gregory the Great's *Moralia in Iob* 17.4, which reads, *singulariter apud se peritus intumuit.* Cf. 1.2: *apud se tuo dono continens*; 3.2: *qualiscunque . . . apud se extiterit.*

60. A rather dense series of psychological observations that reiterate a common theme in this chapter: the avoidance of sin by itself is not virtue, if performed only out of shame. Guibert, as Peter Abelard after him, would emphasize the importance of "intention" in determining the moral worth of an act. If shame grows from the fear of God, it can be useful. But, Guibert seems to suggest, if a person avoids sin for worldly reasons, it would have been better to commit the sin, since the sin would require confession and self-analysis, rather than to avoid it for secular motives and thus to create an undeserved belief in one's own virtue.

61. The translation here follows the correction of Dachery (rejected by Labande) of *lassitudo* to *latitudo*, because it does in fact better suit the sense of the Latin and is used, for example, in Ambrose's sermon on Ps. 118.

62. Henry I of France reigned from 1031 to 1060. The battle to which Guibert refers here is possibly Mortemer (1054), though we do not have enough specific information (including whether the conflict in which Guibert's father was captured was an actual battle or a simple skirmish) to identify it with certainty.

63. Guibert seems to indicate that an angel or a good spirit calls upon Mary for aid, and that once the good spirit is assured that Mary has heard its prayer, it attacks the devil. These are not metaphorical psychological demons or spirits but genuine supernatural forces.

64. A Greek god of marriage. Guibert shows off his mother's learning, or else just his own.

65. Ps. 7:10/7:9 indicates that God searches out the intentions of man through an examination of the kidneys, making them a seat of conscience. The translation is not as salacious as earlier ones, where the priests were putting a cross "in her loins," but it is, we think, a more accurate reflection of the Latin.

66. Guy was archbishop of Beauvais from 1063 to 1085. As Guibert describes his career, he was a successful and effective "courtier bishop"—an elegant and well-spoken ecclesiastical leader whose career was ended due to the passions of church reform zealots in the final days of Gregory VII's pontificate. He ended his life at the monastery of Cluny. His deposition occurred after the events described here, where Guibert's mother stayed on his estate.

67. John Benton interpreted this passage to mean that Guy had baptized Guibert, which would place Guibert's birth no earlier than 1063. We should be leery, however, of reading "sacraments" as being founded on some sort of specific sacramental doctrine. What Guibert means must remain elusive, beyond suggesting that Guy was intimately involved in his progress in the Christian life.

68. Garnier was abbot of Saint-Germer-de-Fly from 1058 to 1084. The church of Saint-Germer stands today, though it has been rebuilt since Guibert lived there. The precise character of Garnier's connection to Guibert's family is left unclear—or at least Guibert has omitted one or two links in the chain. Presumably, Garnier's family had held land from Guibert's grandfather, or perhaps Garnier himself had, making the abbot favorable toward

bending monastic protocol on behalf of young Guibert and his mother.

69. Guibert has returned to his model of Christian conversion. In the beginning of the process, passions burn more brightly, and some aspects of devotion come more easily, though they are less governed by reason. As he soon makes clear, the intentions that lay behind his *affectus*, or desire, for the monastic life were highly suspect.

70. Isa. 59:5 states that whoever shall eat a viper's egg shall die.

71. Exod. 20:26 and John 10.

72. The imagery that Guibert weaves throughout this passage is subtly militaristic, typical of monastic thought and crucial to Guibert's psychological vision. His mind is literally under attack from demons, the defenses of his soul, like a besieged city, about to collapse due to assaults upon his senses, particularly in this case sight and hearing. The system of demonology here provides a physiological explanation for nightmares: bodily senses serve as a bridge by which demons enter the mind and corrupt its thoughts.

73. Mentioned in the previous chapter.

74. Luke 15:7.

75. 1 Kings 21:29.

76. Guibert's language here has a degree of technical precision: *visionem eiusque species . . . sequebatur*: "the image of each thing followed the vision." The language is Augustinian, used in his sermon 10 on Psalm 149: Patrologia latina 46, col. 844.

77. Eccles. 5:3.

78. The language is suggesting that Guibert is in something of a pre-lapsarian state, since the expression *in primo statu* often refers to the quality of Adam's free will before the fall.

79. Luke 12:34.

80. Chartres Cathedral (dedicated to Our Lady) still contains a fragment of cloth believed to have been worn by the Virgin when she gave birth to Christ. Purportedly brought back from the East by Charlemagne, it was a gift to the cathedral from his grandson, Charles the Bald. Many churches owned relics of the Virgin and could be quite proud of "their" particular Mary.

81. The number seven (mentioned here in reference to Prov. 24:16) is obviously important in Christian thought. It breaks down into three (symbolizing the divine, as in the Trinity) and four (symbolizing the earthly, as in the four corners of the earth). It therefore encompasses, symbolically, everything, as Guibert indicates here.

82. Another passage dense with scriptural reference: Ps. 25:17/24:17; Rom. 7:23, 7:19; Prov. 18:3; Ps. 130:1/129:1, 69:2/68:3, and Ps. 140:10/139:11.

83. Jer. 38:13. There is a lacuna in the text, perhaps of only a few words along the lines of "seems infinitely deep."

84. Ovid (43 BC–AD 17) was one of the most popular classical Latin poets in the Middle Ages, particularly for his *Metamorphoses*, which became the standard sourcebook for classical mythology. He also wrote several works of erotic poetry, most notably the *Ars Amatoria* ("The Art of Love") and the *Amores* ("Loves"); here Guibert seems to have in mind his *Heroides*, a collection of fictional letters in verse from heroines of classical mythology to their lovers (e.g., Penelope to Odysseus), three of which had responses from the men (e.g., Paris to Helen). The most important source of Latin bucolic poetry, itself based on earlier Greek models, was Virgil's *Eclogues*; the bucolic tradition continued in authors such as Calpurnius Siculus (1st c. AD) and Nemesianus (3rd c. AD). Many of these poems present lovesick shepherds vying with one another in the praise of the object of their affections, as well as laments over unrequited passion.

85. Guibert would not be the only eleventh-century writer to indulge in erotic poetry. In particular, his more famous contemporary Baudry of Bourgueil (like Guibert, an eventual historian of the First Crusade) was well known for his somewhat immodest verses.

86. Described in *Monodies* 1.4, above.

87. In his 1111 treatise titled *Against the Judaizer*, Guibert repeats this story in essentially the same terms.

88. Prov. 12:7. The diction, stating that the "hand would not continue in its disgraceful activity," implies that Solomon here scolded Guibert for masturbation as well as the composition of lewd verses.

89. Guibert probably undertook the composition of his *Little Book on Virginity* at this point, since he refers to the vision of Solomon in connection with its composition in the introduction to that book. It was a well-intentioned, if heavy-handed, assignment: instructing a sexually troubled teenager to write a book in praise of virginity.

90. Jer. 4:10.

91. Isa. 28:19.

92. The system Guibert outlines finds echoes in the moral vocabulary of Anselm of Bec, more famous for his theological treatises on the

existence of God (the *Proslogion*) and on the Incarnation (*Cur Deus homo*). But Guibert's description either is based on an earlier version of Anselm's thought, or else it represents Guibert's own deliberate revisions and refinements to Anselm's system—in particular the notion that will and affection can become one unified psychological function, when in the presence of a well-developed faculty of reason, or a higher faculty of intellect or "understanding." Guibert developed this methodology in the course of his commentary on Genesis; at the time he had completed stage one of this process, his interpretation of the Hexameron referred to below, he had not yet formed his final opinion about the role of reason and the distinctions between reason and intellect.

93. Ws. 8:1.

94. Num. 33:55. Abbot Garnier could have had any number of reasons for objecting to Guibert's work. The Hexameron was considered a particularly difficult passage to interpret; for a novice to do so would have bordered on recklessness. Guibert had also implied that he was going to produce a relatively short and discrete work (perhaps a polished version of his sermon presented on the Magdalene's feast day), but instead used his abbot's permission to start a major exegetical project. And finally, to interpret the Hexameron on a purely moral or tropological level would have seemed unusually, perhaps dangerously, innovative.

95. It would become a point of pride for Guibert that as a rule he committed his thoughts directly to parchment without first following the standard practice of composing a rough draft on wax tablets—somewhat akin to completing a crossword puzzle with a ballpoint pen rather than erasable pencil. This sign of literary prowess was, he suggests here, born of necessity, though he intends it to be no less marvelous a feat.

96. Garnier left office in 1084. Guibert did not publish a completed version of his commentary on Genesis until at least 1113, when he dedicated it to Barthélemy, bishop of Laon.

97. The commentary to which Guibert refers here, mixing exegesis of Old Testament history with Gospel passages, has not survived. His observation on the utility of moral commentary was prescient, since the twelfth century proved to be a golden age for tropological exegesis.

98. Guibert touches on a matter here—the suffering of the damned in the afterlife—that he will treat at much greater length in book 4 of *On the Relics of Saints* below.

99. Tradition held that the souls of the dead would appear as they had at the age of thirty, or possibly thirty-three (or else as they would have appeared if they had reached that age).

100. Guibert thus applies to souls in hell or purgatory the same sort of spiritual laws as he imagines pertaining to souls in heaven, as he discusses in book 4 of *On the Relics of Saints*. But however ethereal the soul's existence, Evrard still seems to have lived in something like an ordinary house on an ordinary street, as Guibert reveals in the next sentences.

101. Contemporary sources indicate that masses on behalf of the dead could indeed shorten time spent in the place of purgation, which most Christians must have expected to face after death. Guibert leaves unclear whether the prayers will reduce his father's time of punishment or merely provide momentary relief in its intensity.

102. Quite possibly Renaud de Beauvais, an otherwise obscure veteran of the First Crusade.

103. Such vows were apparently common in Guibert's world. He tells a similar story about two nuns at Bourbourg in book 1 of *On the Relics of Saints*.

104. Exod. 20:26.

105. "Fear" being the first gift of the Holy Spirit and the initial step in Christian conversion.

106. Ps. 149:2.

107. Ps. 77:4/76:5.

108. John 13:27. A reference to Christ's instructions to Judas at the Last Supper.

109. Another rapid-fire compilation of scriptural reference: Matt. 21:12, John 17:21, 1 Cor. 4:11, Heb. 1.8, and Ps. 132:11/131:11.

110. The unity of the head and body is a reference to the unity of the church, of which Christ is the head. Trafficking in ecclesiastical office undermines this bodily unity, as Guibert demonstrates again through a compilation of scriptural references: 1 Cor. 12:12, Col. 1:18, and Matt. 7:22.

111. Cf. Lucan, *Pharsalia* 1.135.

112. In monastic thought, humility is the path to spiritual improvement: to lower oneself in order to advance. Guibert combines this idea with his own moral system, described in *Monodies* 1.17 above, where will and affection unite, enabling reason to grow momentarily strong and advance the journey of Christian conversion.

113. Ps. 143.10/142:10.

114. Guibert's election occurred in 1104, when he would have been around forty-five or fifty years old. One contemporary formula

for "youth" placed it between ages thirty-five and fifty. None-theless, the idea that Guibert seemed too youthful in 1104 to become abbot does strain credulity.

115. Perhaps a reference to Augustine's famous moment of conversion described in his *Confessions*, when he heard a child call out, "Take it and read" (*tolle, lege*). Guibert's diction (*accipe, lege*) is slightly different, perhaps because he is recollecting the passage from memory rather than consulting an actual copy.

116. Lam. 3:22 and Job 36:16.

117. *Vi, clam*, and *precario*, here translated as "violence," "theft," and "fraud," are terms drawn from Roman law. *Vi* ("by force") is a general term for a criminal act, and can refer to any form of theft as a "forcible" act against the rightful owner, not necessarily involving physical violence. *Clam* ("secretly") refers to the act of concealment, when an individual takes possession without the knowledge (and hence permission) of the rightful owner. *Precario* ("by grant") is a form of unlawful possession involving the failure to return an item that has been temporarily loaned.

118. Rom. 9:18.

119. Roman martyrs whose remains were discovered by Saint Ambrose, as famously described in book IX of Augustine's *Confessions*. Their feast day is June 19, placing this story on the night of June 18.

120. Referencing Ps. 70:1/69:2; Zach. 13:7; and Matt. 26:31.

121. July 25. Since this accident occurred during Guibert's later years in the monastery, the likely years (based on the correspondences of July 25 and Sunday) are either 1092 or 1098.

122. Augustine, *Ennarrationes in Psalmos* 250.148.11.

123. Presumably the monk William, described in *Monodies* 2.5 below.

124. William "Rufus" II—successor to William the Conqueror—and his court received criticism from clerical observers for lax morals and their adoption of new fashions perceived as effeminate. His apparent disinterest in marriage has helped secure his reputation among historians for homosexuality.

125. *Baro* (plural: *barones*) is not in fact related to the Greek adjective βαρύς (*barus*), but in the absence of a science of linguistics, etymologies based on obvious resemblance were commonly, and not unreasonably, accepted. The etymology given here is found in Isidore, *Etymologies* 9.4.31.

126. As Guibert's previous editors have noted, Guibert's condemnation of Manasses I of Reims mentioned in *Monodies* 1.11 above makes it likely that he refers here to Manasses II of Reims

(1086–1106), and thus Guibert probably wrote this passage sometime around 1110 or a little later. "Artaud" mentioned in the story would have been archbishop in the mid–tenth century.

127. Dedicated to the Trinity, the nunnery was founded in 1060 along with a church for men (now St. Stephen's), the latter being the special establishment of the duke.

128. Guibert's story inverts the Gospel injunction, "If you did it not for the least of these, you did it not for me." Christ often appears in saints' lives in the guise of a beggar, as he did to Saint Martin of Tours. Guibert, perhaps out of instinctive aristocratic prejudice, has Satan reveal himself through the same means. In general, see Matt. 25:40–45.

129. John 14:30.

130. Matt. 19:25.

131. The meeting is described in the language of commerce and business, lending further anti-Jewish coloring to the passage.

132. Ps. 83:1/82:2.

133. Thus situating the story between Anselm's election as abbot in 1078 and his departure for England in 1092 and his subsequent election as archbishop during that trip in 1093. It is to be regretted that we do not have Anselm's version of this trial.

MONODIES: BOOK 2

1. Its Latin name is *Novigentum*, the first part of which is from *novus*, "new."

2. Criticism of the immoral behavior of pagan gods, while a staple of Christian polemic, also occurs in earlier Greek and Roman writers, some of whom criticized the *Iliad* and *Odyssey* on the same grounds. Although it cannot be certain which gods the British king, given the name Quilius below, worshiped, the behaviors listed here are standard complaints about Zeus'/Jupiter's frequent adultery and quarrels with his wife (and sister) Hera, as well as his violent succession to his father Kronos/Saturn, who had earlier overthrown his own father Ouranos/Uranus.

3. Rom. 1:20.

4. The arguments pondered by the British king bear obvious resemblances to the rhetoric of Augustine in his *City of God*, especially 2.35, where Augustine attacks the morality of Roman gods. In 8.4–11 Augustine acknowledges that Plato and his school came

closest to recognizing the true religion through the application of philosophy alone, much as the king approaches truth here through reason alone, though Augustine stresses Plato's ultimate failure. Perhaps, like the Briton, Plato still required the spark of divine revelation. The word for "successors" in this passage is *vicarii*. It is just possible that Guibert means not "bishops" or other church officials, but rather the Eucharist, which, as he argues in *On the Relics of Saints*, serves as Christ's vicar on earth.

5. Guibert uses the names of the Roman gods who personify grapes (for wine) and grain. Liber is a Latin epithet for Dionysus, and Ceres is the Roman equivalent of Demeter.

6. Paul refers to a statue dedicated to an unknown God while preaching to the men of Athens, in Acts 17:23.

7. The King thus arrives at Jerusalem shortly after the day of Pentecost, when the apostles received the gift of the Holy Spirit.

8. I.e., Jerusalem, considered in both Christian and Jewish traditions to lie at the earth's center, a place that, at the time Guibert wrote, it had begun to occupy on world maps as well.

9. Quilius asks here for secondary, noncorporeal relics, not the physical relics that caused Guibert such consternation (as in *On the Relics of Saints* books 1 and 3, below). The relics of the Passion listed here are fairly standard. It is noteworthy that Guibert claims for his church a fragment of the cloth of the Virgin maintained at Chartres.

10. Henry, abbot of Homblières since 1059 and of Saint-Rémy since 1074, was made abbot of Nogent in 1076.

11. Guibert gives a more measured assessment of Hélinand, suggesting that ulterior motives lay behind his generosity, in *Monodies* 3.2, below.

12. Saint Godfrey (or Geoffrey) of Amiens was elected abbot of Nogent in 1085. As we shall see, he is elected bishop of Amiens in 1104, opening the way for Guibert's promotion.

13. Prov. 20:21.

14. Horace, *Ars Poetica* 139.

15. The surviving text is imperfect here. Given Godfrey's later reputation for sanctity, Guibert's opinion of his character and achievements seems to have been outside the mainstream.

16. Luke 11:34. The scene is perhaps deliberately reminiscent of Augustine's *Confessions* 8.12.29.

17. Ps. 18:28/17:29.

18. Guibert's sermon is a typical example of biblical exegesis, the type of writing that is characteristic of most of his literary output.

He takes here a short passage from the Bible and examines it on a word-by-word basis. Each image or action receives a second (and sometimes third) allegorical meaning beyond the literal. In this passage, for example, *cloak* = outward appearances that can deceive; *house* = body; *Judah* = confession. The ensemble of symbols yields a moral lesson that Christians could apply to their lives. In this case, Guibert reads in the verse a lesson on the perils of leadership.

19. Isa. 3:6–8, John 1:13, Matt. 13:52, Matt. 24:45, and 1 Tim. 3:5.
20. "Habit" in this case is a pun referring to a person's practices and disposition as well as to the garment worn by monks.
21. Luke 11:3.
22. Effectively, she is performing on her own behalf a mass for the dead.
23. The return to Fly seems to have happened in late 1107, which would place the death of Guibert's mother in 1106. The suggestion has been made by Guibert's more recent translator Paul Archambault that this passage refers generically to a brother monk, but given the context, the obvious reading seems also to be the more likely—that one of Guibert's older siblings had joined him as a monk at Saint-Germer, perhaps at the time that the family fortunes had gone into decline around 1104, just before Guibert's election to the abbacy, and had then accompanied him to Nogent. Since this is in fact the first mention of the "ignoble return," we have very good reason to think that book 2 of the *Monodies* is missing a substantial amount of material about the difficult early days of Guibert's abbacy.
24. The annunciation of Gabriel to the Virgin was celebrated daily at vespers, which is to say, sunset.
25. A precise quotation from the Decretals of Ivo of Chartres, 7.55, who in turn cites Gelasius: PL 161, col. 557A, B.
26. John is listed as the abbot of Saint-Germer in the history of the monastery contained in MS BnF *lat.* 13817 from the years 1100 to 1106.
27. It is tempting to read this passage as specifying that Guibert's mother died on the day of the Annunciation. But, as noted above, Guibert is saying only that she died at the hour when the Annunciation would have been daily celebrated.
28. Guibert may use *ecclesia* here to refer to a synagogue, where the crusaders come upon the Jews and decide to kill them. It is possible that he is glossing over some of the action, though, and that the Jews had already sought refuge in a church knowing

what was afoot. Similar scenes would play out in the Rhineland as well, as armies of angry Christians attacked Jews out of a similar religious fervor in 1096. Areas of Europe that had been exposed to the apocalyptic sermons of the famous crusade preacher Peter the Hermit seemed especially likely to engage in extreme anti-Jewish violence.

29. William of Fly in fact produced a handful of works of exegesis, discussed by Gilbert Dahan in his article "Guillaume de Flay et son Commentaire du Livre des Juges," *Recherches Augustiniennes* 13 (1978): 37–104. William L. North is currently preparing an edition of William's commentary on Lamentations, which survives in several manuscript copies dating from the eleventh to the thirteenth century.

30. The book, referred to earlier, is *Against the Judaizer and the Jews*, Guibert's attempt at the popular genre of anti-Jewish polemic. The Judaizer in question is Count Jean of Soissons, described in *Monodies* 3.16 below.

31. In his crusade chronicle Guibert recalls how he even saw Scotsmen traveling through France, anxious to help liberate Jerusalem: *Dei gesta per Francos* 1.1, p. 89, explaining how he was able to conjure this particular image of the demonic.

32. The stone was the insult, reminding the man that, ironically because he had given himself to the religious life, he was no longer able to practice charity as he once had done. Thus the demon's words struck him like a stone.

33. Reading *quin etiam meliora facturus invisus esset* (Ms. *quin eum non . . . inviseret*).

34. The translation here corrects the Latin text in Labande from "insuper liminare" to the far more likely "in superliminare" (see, for example, Exod. 12:7).

35. "Deonandi" may have been a common name, but it does not appear in any other written source. The manuscript is likely faulty. One wonders if it should read *deodandi*, as in "giving to God" (as opposed to "Deonandi"—swimming for God). The word *deodandi* turns up precisely once in the PL: vol. 158, col. 262C, in the first chapter to Anselm's treatise *De Incarnatione Verbi*. Anselm observes that he does not wish to be thought of as presumptive or as a *deodandus*. Schmitt changed this reading to *ridendus*, or "laughable," in his edition. We can only judge from the context here what a *deodandus* might have been—a layman who pretends to be a wandering monk, adopting a guise of asceticism to lend authenticity to his persona.

36. Luke 13:11 (where the number of years is eighteen).
37. Mark 9:17, 29.
38. This man appears, like Guibert's father, to exist in purgatory and in this world simultaneously. It is a sign of just how fluid the boundaries between these worlds were that he could expiate his own sins in purgatory while still alive.

MONODIES: BOOK 3

1. Adalbero was bishop of Laon from 977 to at least 1030, when he disappears from the historical record, and was a prominent figure in the events and negotiations that led to the accession of Hugh Capet to the throne in 987, four years before the political betrayal that Guibert describes. Adalbero was no doubt extraordinarily duplicitous, but Charles of Lorraine, the Carolingian claimant to the throne, was hardly a child. He was brother of Lothar (954–986) and uncle to Louis V (986–987), the last of the Carolingian monarchs. Adalbero seemed to have sided with Charles and his nephew Arnulf, archbishop of Reims, in their attempt to restore the Carolingians to the West Frankish throne. Adalbero, however, eventually betrayed both the Carolingian duke and the archbishop in 991, capturing them while they were staying with him in Laon and thus ending abruptly their challenge to the Capetians. The early eleventh-century historian Adémar of Chabannes places the betrayal on Maundy Thursday, as does Guibert. Richer of Reims, a historian contemporary with the events described, situates it on Palm Sunday. Thanks to Jason Glenn for providing counsel on these topics.

2. Hélinand was bishop of Laon from 1052 to 1098 and was instrumental in the foundation of Guibert's monastery at Nogent. Gautier of Pontoise (or of Mantes) was the nephew of Edward the Confessor.

3. During Henry I's reign (1031–60) the famous Synod of Reims (1049) occurred, where almost all of the bishops in attendance were forced by Pope Leo IX to admit before the body of Saint Rémy to having paid for their offices. The confessions, however, likely point less toward the exceptional corruption of the clergy or to the unusual venality of Henry and more to how accepted the exchange of gifts for high office was in a pre-Gregorian world.

4. Hélinand's wife here is the church at Laon, to which he is already married. Pluralism is thus a form of bigamy. The passage is 1 Tim. 3:2. It is the same passage used to justify clerical celibacy.

5. Enguerrand was bishop of Laon from 1098 to 1104, which means that he died at just about the same time Guibert arrived in Nogent. Guibert notes occasionally in this chapter that he is primarily relaying gossip.

6. The introit is the opening to the mass, performed when the celebrant enters the church.

7. Sibylle de Porcien, whom Guibert never names, and whose background he expands upon below.

8. Isa. 14:29.

9. Guibert provides an allegorical interpretation of a well-known episode from classical mythology, found in book 8 of Homer's *Odyssey*. Vulcan (in Greek, Hephaestus) was a blacksmith, and thus associated with fire. He was lame in one foot, and in physical appearance a stark contrast to his wife, the beautiful goddess of love and desire Venus (Aphrodite). Vulcan suspects his wife's infidelity and forges an invisible set of snares for their bed, in which she and her lover, the god of war Mars (Ares), become entrapped.

10. The passage paraphrases and combines Job 20:27 and Prov. 20:18. Guibert's meaning seems to be that Sibylle sought to clear her reputation and her husband's by telling a story (revealing "their filth") that ultimately served only to condemn them.

11. In this paragraph Guibert both acknowledges and denies his responsibility for Gaudry's election through his choice of verbs. "We convened" to elect a bishop, he says; "they elected" Gaudry, he concludes.

12. Reading *cantor* for *candor* ("bright light") of the manuscripts.

13. Anselm of Laon (d. 1117) was one of the most renowned teachers in Europe. Along with his brother Ralph, he led a school at Laon that began the ambitious project of creating a verse-by-verse commentary of the entire Bible, the foundation for the famous *Glossa ordinaria*. Guibert pays tribute to Anselm and Ralph in his *Moral Commentary on Genesis*. Peter Abelard, by contrast, brutally ridicules Anselm in his *Historia calamitatum*, saying that Anselm lit his candle not to light a room but to fill it with smoke.

14. Adalbero had been abbot of Saint-Vincent de Laon since 1080, one of the more important churches in the city of Laon, where it still stands, having been rebuilt in the eighteenth century.

Saint-Nicolas des Prés sous Ribemont was founded in 1083 and was located about twenty miles north of Laon. The abbot's name referred to here was Mainard.

15. Paschal II (1106–18) presided over the latter, but not final, stages of the Investiture Contest. Despite the venal character of pope and court that Guibert paints here, Paschal is probably best known for offering to surrender all episcopal regalia in Germany to the emperor in return for free elections in 1111. Other ecclesiastics were not as welcoming of this radical compromise, and Henry V imprisoned Paschal for two months, eventually forcing the pope to renounce rights of investiture—a concession that Paschal would shortly thereafter repudiate. These events, however, remained in the future in February 1107 when Guibert traveled with Gaudry's entourage and met up with the papal court.

16. There is an idiom *in coelum laudibus ferre* "to praise to the heavens." Guibert perhaps pointedly omits *in coelum* "to the heavens," here.

17. As noted above, there existed a medieval convention that saw "youth" as a period of life lasting from ages thirty to fifty. Guibert was probably nearing the end of this span in 1107.

18. John 19:35.

19. Other translators have interpreted this passage as commenting on Paschal II's level of education, but a fresh reading of the Latin suggests that Guibert is making concessions about Gaudry's minimal qualifications and venal character.

20. A proverbial saying applied to a task that is extremely difficult or impossible.

21. An apparent reference to Lucretius, *De rerum natura*, 1.936–38 and 4.11–13, where Lucretius describes how a doctor might trick a patient into drinking bitter wormwood by smearing honey around the rim of the cup. The "honey" here is the opportunity to obey the will of the pope, but the cup is full of poison—in this case trafficking in ecclesiastical favors and influence. The reference probably reached Guibert via Quintilian, *Institutio oratoria* 3.1.5, a text he cites elsewhere. Thanks to Gerard Passanante for advice on Lucretius.

22. Luke 2:35. It is unclear why Gaudry would travel to the monastery of Saint-Ruf d'Avignon for consecration, as it would represent a three-hundred-mile detour to the south.

23. John 19:26.

24. Ovid, *Metamorphoses* 2.846. Guibert has substituted the unmetrical *cidaris et lancea* (turban and lance) for *maiestas et amor* (majesty and love) in the original.

25. Sibylle de Porcien, wife of Enguerrand de Boves.

26. Ezek. 3:20 and Heb. 10:26.

27. November 11, 1110 (about three years into Gaudry's tenure, as noted above).

28. The cathedral of Notre-Dame de Laon. The day would be January 13, 1111.

29. The provost was the king's officer in the city of Laon. As is illustrated here, his authority stood in uneasy alliance with the bishop, who held both comital and episcopal authority in Laon.

30. Hubert was bishop of Senlis from 1099 to 1115. He was briefly removed from office because of charges of simony, but was reinstated in 1104.

31. The sermon that Guibert presents is similar to the one he describes himself as giving upon his elevation as abbot: a close exegetical reading of scripture. The method would seem even more inappropriate here, since the message of reconciliation was expected to appeal not just to clergy but to the broader community of Laon.

32. Ps. 69:2/68:2–3, and Jer. 4:10.

33. The entire sentence is a paraphrase of Ps. 78:49/77:49.

34. Ps. 78:50/77:50.

35. Laon was a royal city under the comital rule of a bishop. Guibert's description here, then, is an exaggeration, a distortion, or else evidence of just how low the fortunes of the Capetian kings had fallen in the early twelfth century.

36. Isa. 24:2.

37. The word Guibert uses here is *pessimum*, leading other translators to render this passage as, "commune is a new and evil name." We have read it instead as an example of Guibert's characteristic irony: the name "commune" suggests that it would create community, but in practice, it tears apart the city of Laon, making it "the worst possible name."

38. The description offered here is one of the most important early accounts of a communal movement in France. In effect, burghers in towns pay a head tax in a lump sum in order to exempt themselves from further seigneurial dues, often administered randomly and in ever shifting amounts. Stated more simply, the burghers are paying for the right to be left alone by an erratic aristocracy. Laon thus stands in the vanguard of a wider European movement

toward greater economic and political liberty within urban environments.

39. Obviously, this is another reference (see above, *Monodies* 2.4) to the mysterious circumstances in 1107/08 when Guibert was driven from his monastery—presumably discussed in some now lost section of book 2 of the *Monodies*.

40. By virtue of his office, Gaudry would have exercised direct control over the practices of his mint. The debasement of the currency was, therefore, not something he merely tolerated, but something that he promoted.

41. Guibert seems to be saying that not only has the silver content in the coins been devalued, but also that the minters of Laon have lost the ability to decorate their coins with a figural representation of the bishop.

42. These verses are apparently Guibert's own composition.

43. Described below as a "Moor," he was apparently a dark-skinned slave. Whether he was brought in from Spain or Africa (sometimes called generically in the Middle Ages "Ethiopia") is unclear.

44. It was a well-known and frequently cited law that clerics were not allowed to shed blood.

45. Guibert uses a term for Good Friday derived from Greek, *Parasceve* (παρασκευή).

46. The betrayal of the Carolingians, as described above, *Monodies* 3.1. The date of the meeting Guibert describes is April 18, 1112.

47. April 22, 1112.

48. The *vidame* was a layman charged with defending the temporal domains of a bishop.

49. Matt. 26:52.

50. Constantly evolving definitions of serfdom and freedom, combined with the kind of social mobility that enabled the commune to come into existence in the first place, made it possible to subject extraordinarily prominent families to charges of servile dissent. The most famous such case involved the Erembald clan in Bruges, whose murder of Count Charles the Good led to similarly catastrophic urban violence set, again, against the background of communal politics—described famously by Galbert of Bruges in a narrative that can be usefully compared to Guibert's treatment of the Laon commune.

51. This paragraph seems to interrupt the narrative flow Guibert is establishing (since he discusses Guy the treasurer in the previous paragraph and the following one). As such, it probably rep-

resents a later insertion into the text, highly characteristic of Guibert's work habits.

52. A castle roughly twelve miles from Laon.

53. Vézelay Abbey, dedicated to Saint Mary Magdalene, was one of the most important pilgrimage sites in France, where Saint Bernard would famously preach the Second Crusade. Earlier editions have translated "Versiliacensis" as "Versigny." There are two villages called Versigny within a reasonable distance of Laon; neither one, as far as we can determine, has a reputation as a pilgrimage site, as does Vézelay; and *Versiliacensis* is close to *Verseliacum*, one of the accepted variant spellings of Vézelay.

54. 1 Kings 14:13.

55. 1 Pet. 2:18.

56. Guibert seems to have gotten a little over two years ahead of himself, since the ceremony of reconciliation, performed by Archbishop Raoul of Reims, occurred in September 1114.

57. Guibert's assessment of Thomas de Marle (1078–1130) is echoed in Suger's biography of Louis VI, where Thomas is also described as essentially the worst man who ever lived: *The Deeds of Louis the Fat*, trans. Richard C. Cusimano and John Moorehead (Washington, DC: Catholic University of America Press, 1992), 7, p. 37. There has been some attempt to rehabilitate Thomas' reputation by saying that throughout his life he simply engaged in the accepted practices of seigneurial lordship—which were, and always had been, brutal (Jacques Chaurand, *Thomas de Marle, sire de Coucy* [Marle, France: Syndicat d'initiative de Marle, 1963]). Guibert's reaction, however, seems to have been justified, for Thomas challenged even an eleventh-century sense of propriety. One piece of information Guibert omits here is that Thomas was a hero of the First Crusade. He initially joined the armies of Emicho of Flonheim, known mainly for their vicious attacks on Jewish communities in the Rhineland. Emicho's army was largely wiped out in Hungary, but Thomas managed to complete the pilgrimage and even to perform heroically in the capture of Jerusalem on July 15, 1099. One cannot help but wonder if the extraordinary brutality of the First Crusade affected Thomas' character later in life and thus might help to explain or contextualize the scenes described here.

58. *Bellum Catilinae* 16.3; Guibert changes Sallust's diction slightly, but with no difference in meaning.

59. Described above, *Monodies* 3.3.

60. Like Montaigu, Pierrepont and La Fère are ten to fifteen miles from Laon.

61. The book is the crusade chronicle, the *Deeds of God Through the Franks*, completed around 1108. Guibert's next major work to be published (in the sense of being completed and circulated, with a dedication included) would be his *Moral Commentary on Genesis*, dedicated to Barthélemy, Gaudry's successor as bishop of Laon.

62. The "crown" referred to here is the crown of martyrdom bestowed upon the Holy Innocents, the children whom Herod ordered to be slain in his attempt to kill Christ. The Innocents represent a curious case—Christian martyrs before the crucifixion, who died in ignorance of the faith and yet on behalf of it. Guibert mentions their veneration again in *On the Relics of Saints* 1, below.

63. The picture Guibert paints of the relic tour here is largely positive, and should be compared to the very different (and much more critical) account given in *On the Relics of Saints* 1, below. One might note that all of the relics described here are noncorporeal: that is, they are objects touched by saints but not part of the saints' bodies—except for the Virgin's hair, a relic for which Guibert expresses some muted skepticism. Guibert does not describe here the claim made by the canons' spokesperson (reported in *On the Relics of Saints*) that the reliquary contained a piece of bread from the Last Supper. The canon Herman of Laon, who participated in this tour, also describes the miracles, published in PL 156, cols. 961–1018. Guibert refers to this account in passing below.

64. The story (like the one below concerning the English thief) provides precious evidence that medieval observers could be as skeptical to the reality of miracles as are modern readers.

65. In Picardy, about forty miles northwest of Laon.

66. The English Channel.

67. A stadium is approximately 625 feet.

68. There is a lacuna in the manuscript.

69. Stephen Garlande was a member of one of the most prominent families in the France of Louis VI. Though his relatives on occasion went into rebellion and fell from favor, Stephen still served as Louis' chancellor for much of the king's reign. Alongside Suger of Saint-Denis, he was the most powerful and influential man in France.

70. Luke 2:35. Despite Guibert's pessimism, Barthélemy would enjoy a long tenure as bishop (1113–51). By the time Guibert wrote these words, he had already dedicated his *Moral Commentary on Genesis* to the bishop. Barthélemy's episcopate would also witness (though Guibert would not live to see it) the restoration of the commune at Laon in 1128.

71. Terence, *Eunuchus* 1.254.

72. It will be recalled that the bishop of Amiens was Godfrey, Guibert's saintly and successful predecessor as abbot of Nogent.

73. A reference to Enguerrand's first wife, Ada de Roucy. Guibert indicates that Thomas believed himself to be a bastard, too.

74. Guibert described the extreme austerity of the Grand Chartreuse in *Monodies* 1.11, above. The fact that Godfrey kept some money for future use (in light of the Carthusians' attitude toward gifts, described earlier) provides in Guibert's mind further evidence that Godfrey never intended to give up his office as bishop of Amiens and that he certainly never had any intention of adopting the rigors of the Carthusian life.

75. That is to say, Enguerrand's wife, Sibylle de Porcien.

76. By this point it is difficult to sort out who is opposing whom (or even what Guibert believes about this question). Thomas had earlier renounced his loyalty to the burghers and joined Enguerrand and Sibylle, but Sibylle here brings the king in to fight against Adam, the castellan loyal to Enguerrand. Sibylle's motives are not clear, as Guibert presents them. All that matters in his analysis is that she is the instigator.

77. The archdeacon mentioned above in *Monodies* 3.4 and 3.7, where he is described as more of a warrior than a cleric, as a conspirator against Gerard, and as a man who hated Guibert with a particular passion.

78. Again, Sibylle de Porcien, whom Guibert steadfastly refuses to name.

79. The bishops effectively declare a crusade against Thomas of Marle (himself, as noted earlier, a hero of the crusade), making an attack against him a penitential and meritorious act. Guibert does not note the irony, since he is determined not to mention Thomas' connection to Jerusalem. Crécy is located about ten miles to the north of Laon.

80. Guibert stresses the role of foot soldiers for the sake of irony. Foot soldiers were far poorer than knights and were exactly the type of men whom Thomas had most brutally tortured.

There is poetic justice, therefore, in the fact that they help bring down this worst of all men—a point Guibert will make directly later on.

81. The Sunday before Easter—in this case, April 11, 1115.

82. Catiline was a young and dissolute aristocrat who fomented a revolt in Rome after a failed attempt to win the consulship, the highest office in Rome, in 63 BC. The great statesmen and orator Cicero took credit for preventing the revolt when he was consul, and wrote four speeches attacking him, known as the *Catilinarians*. The episode was treated by the historian Sallust in the *Bellum Catilinae*, from which Guibert quotes several times.

83. Guibert's previous editor no doubt exaggerates when he observes that there was *rien d'exceptionnel* about these eighty women participating in the battle (who are defending the tower, not attacking it, as Archambault reads the passage); *Autobiographie*, p. 414, n. 3. The details of the siege recall stories of the First Crusade. It is possible that Aleran, the engineer experienced in such warfare, accompanied Thomas de Marle on the crusade.

84. Isa. 28:19. In this verse, God warns sinful leaders against having false confidence. Guibert draws a pointed moral from the passage, and from these events. Although Thomas rightly suffered God's judgment, his enemies nonetheless did not act righteously, and bishops in particular overstepped their prerogatives by sanctifying this conflict. The fact that the siege was continuing even as Guibert wrote indicates that our author himself is in no position to sort out the judgments of God.

85. Clerical opposition to trial by combat was growing during Guibert's lifetime. The famous canonist Ivo of Chartres in particular opposed it on the grounds that clerics ought not to be directly involved in the shedding of blood.

86. This ordeal entailed plunging the accused person into cold water. If he sank into the water, the water had accepted him, and he would be declared innocent. If he floated, the water had rejected him, and he would be pronounced guilty. The ordeal by water, unlike the duel, remained canonically acceptable until outlawed by the Fourth Lateran Council in 1215, although clerics did express doubts about its utility. As a procedure, it was employed chiefly when guilt was strongly suspected but evidence was otherwise lacking.

87. Guimar's death is described above in *Monodies* 3.8.

88. Acts 13:36.

89. Ezek. 16:3. The Amorites and Hittites in the Bible were Canaan-
ite tribes against whom the Jews made war. In the symbolic lan-
guage of Guibert's exegesis, the Amorites were "embitterers,"
and the Hittites were "stupefied" or "senseless." Count Jean is
therefore bitter and stupid.

90. The book is *Against the Judaizer and the Jews*, referred to
above in *Monodies* 2.5.

91. In the treatise *Against the Judaizer and the Jews*, Guibert coins
the word *neutericus* to describe Count Jean, since he neither
follows the religion of which he speaks favorably (Judaism) nor
speaks favorably of the religion that he follows (Christianity).

92. The implication is that Count Jean has adopted the heretical
beliefs that Guibert will make reference to directly and in detail
in the next chapter.

93. The heresy as presented here is a mixture of attacks against the
sacramental authority of priests in ceremonies such as baptism
and the Eucharist and of certain dualist ideas associated with
Manichaeism and described by Saint Augustine. Guibert himself
draws attention to this similarity. It is unclear how much, if any,
of this represents Clement's and Evrard's actual beliefs. Probably
Guibert, after gossiping with fellow abbots, has colored an anti-
sacramental doctrine with a lewd and clearly parodic series of
half-formed notions, ceremonies, and sexual practices.

94. John 13:17. The verse, in Latin *beati eritis*, actually means
"You will be blessed."

95. Mark 16:16. The great wickedness that Guibert senses in the
heretics' citation of this passage is that the recipient of baptism
must believe himself to be saved. Because infants do not under-
stand the tenets of Christianity, Clement and Evrard believe,
the ceremony for them is fruitless.

96. Guibert is again drawing on Augustinian writings against her-
esy, showing how dependent upon textual research (as opposed
to actual investigation) contemporary perception of heresy and
unbelief was.

97. The dioceses of Noyon and Tournai were joined at the time of
this story. The bishop (previously misidentified as Hardouin,
because of a defect in the manuscript) was Baudouin I (1044–
68). St. Nicaise was legendary bishop of Reims around the year
400 and was killed by barbarians while defending his church.

98. Stories of this sort are not uncommon in miracle collections, where
saints punish the people attached to their church—effectively, the
saints' serfs—for working and hence seeking profit on a saint's

feast day. The economy of this miracle is slightly more compli-
cated, since it is the Virgin who acts on behalf of Saint Nicaise. It
was also common practice to leave behind at a shrine evidence of
the saint's intervention, in the form of a votive offering. It most
often was a candle, sometimes fashioned in a symbolically mean-
ingful way (a pilgrim with a broken arm, for example, might mea-
sure his arm with a wick and then leave an appropriately sized
candle at the shrine), though it could be something more specific,
as in this case, a bloody piece of knotted thread. Bishop Radbod II
of Tournai, mentioned subsequently, served from 1068 to 1098.

99. Reading *sumen* (udder) for *semen*. As Labande notes in his edi-
tion, the sentence with *semen* makes no real sense. The shape of
the vessel, as described by Guibert, would give it, held upside
down, an udderlike appearance.

100. Saint Marcellus is a bishop of Paris who died in the early fifth
century. The details of his life are almost entirely obscure. His
miracles include driving away a giant serpent, perhaps explain-
ing why a priest would turn to him for assistance with reptilian
poisoning.

101. Geoffrey, a former castellan and nephew of Abbot Hugh of
Cluny (1049–1109), who joined the monastery in 1088.

102. Cf. 1 Cor. 5:6.

103. To divide rightly is to practice discretion. To offer rightly what
is not divided rightly is to perform a good deed but with flawed
intentions or reasoning. Throughout this passage, the devil
speaks as closely to the truth as possible, using some of the
vocabulary from Guibert's own moral system, making the sud-
den use of crude language in the story all the more startling.
This passage is related to a commentary tradition on Cain and
Abel, mentioned again in *On the Relics of Saints* 1, below.

104. As a suicide, the man should have been denied Christian burial.
His friends are treating him instead as a murder victim.

105. A verse version of this story, with considerably fewer embellish-
ments (particularly the details about urination and castration), is
attributed to Guaiferius of Salerno, a monk of Monte Cassino,
published in PL 147, cols. 1286–1288. A later version appears as
chapter 17 in *The Miracles of Saint James*, trans. Thomas F. Cof-
fey, Linda Kay Davidson, and Maryjane Dunn (New York: Ital-
ica Press, 1996), pp. 84–89, attributed, curiously, to Guibert's
teacher Anselm of Bec. According to this last version of the story,
the miracle recipient traveled about the countryside describing
his resurrection and, as proof, showing off his mutilated body,

including the perforation that he subsequently used for urination. The miracle also cites Abbot Hugh as someone who saw the man, making him the likely source for Geoffrey's story.

106. The moral of this story was to become a real point of controversy in the twelfth century, particularly because of the advent of new monastic orders, all of which claimed, in one way or another, that they followed the Benedictine Rule more closely than did their rivals. The Cistercians were especially notorious for receiving other Benedictine monks on the grounds that the austerities practiced in their own communities made their life a higher and more honorable one than was practiced, for example, by Cluniac monks.

107. Guibert connects the Latin verb "to fall," *cadere*, with the name Caduceus (normally, the staff of Mercury—the pagan god here elided, as medieval thinkers often did, with a demon).

108. Cf. 1 Cor. 2:13.

109. Perhaps a reference to the devil's attempt to crawl into bed with Guibert's mother, discussed above, *Monodies* 1.13.

110. Desiderius of Monte Cassino, the church founded by Saint Benedict, was elected pope in May 1086, taking the name Victor III. Despite Guibert's description, he was reportedly reluctant to accept the office and abandoned it almost immediately. Some of the more radical members of the Gregorian party perceived him as too much of a conciliator, and it was, in any case, unsafe for a reforming pope to live in Rome, a city still largely under the control of supporters of the antipope Clement III. Desiderius resumed the papacy under pressure the following year but died four months later on September 16, 1087. The nasty picture Guibert paints of him here reflects Guibert's own distrust of most anyone who managed to attain high ecclesiastical office, but also probably shows dissatisfaction that the monks of Monte Cassino felt with their abbot's indecisive leadership (since he continued to hold abbacy until shortly before his death).

111. Fleury boasted that they had stolen the relics of Saint Benedict, a claim that Monte Cassino disputed. Abbo was a famous and learned tenth century abbot and author who played a role in reforming monasticism in France and in England. He was killed during a riot in 1004 while trying to impose a more rigorous way of life on a monastery in Gascony.

112. We know little about Véran. There was an abbot by that name in 1080. It sounds, based on the general tone of the paragraph, as if Guibert is describing events in the somewhat distant past.

113. Edmund was an Anglo-Saxon king killed by the Vikings in 869 and buried in the church of Bury St. Edmund's. Guibert tells a shorter version of this same story near the end of *De pigneribus* 1. A similar scene would recur in the later twelfth century when Abbot Samson of Bury St. Edmunds, similarly examined the martyr's body, with no apparent consequence; Jocelyn of Brakelond, *Chronicle of Bury St. Edmunds*, trans. Diana Greenaway and Jane Sayers (Oxford: Oxford University Press, 1989), pp. 99–101.

114. It is remarkable that Guibert would celebrate a miracle performed by a dismembered arm covered in gold, as, on both counts, it would seem to violate the principles of proper relic veneration that he lays down in *On the Relics of Saints* 1, below.

115. St. Léger was a seventh-century bishop of Autun. St. Maclou was a sixth-century Welsh or British saint venerated in Brittany as the founder of Saint-Malo (another variation of his name).

116. William the Conqueror (1066–87). The church is Saint-Denis, the abbey to the north of Paris that served as the royal mausoleum for most of the Middle Ages and the Early Modern period.

117. Luke 1:42.

ON THE RELICS OF SAINTS: PROLOGUE

1. Guibert indicates here that he was intending to write a small pamphlet—probably to fill up eight folios or sixteen pages of parchment—but his verbosity soon got the better of him.

2. As the next sentence indicates, one of Guibert's readers did offer an objection.

3. Luke 22:19.

4. Rapid-fire examples of scripture where elements of the Godhead are described in terms of figure and representation: Eph. 1:14, Heb. 1:3, and 2 Cor. 4:4, followed by a reference to the Lord's Prayer (Luke 11:3), "Give us this day our daily bread."

5. This passage is densely theological, where Guibert is answering objections to his eucharistic theology in book 2, below, where he interprets the Eucharist as the vicarial body. The attempt at an Aristotelian vocabulary (substance and species) is awkward. The translation leaves some of the difficulty in place.

6. This passage contains a little "conceptual wordplay." Christian thought traditionally cast in opposition the concepts of "letter" and "spirit," the former referring to external, literal meaning

(also, "Jewish" meaning or interpretation) and the latter to the true, internal meaning.

7. The manuscript is damaged here. Guibert calls this unnamed adversary something presumably unflattering, but we shall never know what.

8. Ws. 5:3.

9. A reference to book 4 below.

10. A true sense of repentance is a gift or a reward. If one refuses that gift in life, Guibert argues, one obviously will not receive that gift after death.

11. Eccle. 11:3.

12. Isa. 28:19.

13. Eccles. 9:10.

14. Job 10:22.

15. Matt. 25:1–11.

16. Matt. 7:22.

17. Amos 5:18.

18. Eccles. 17:26, Ps. 6:5/6:6, Prov. 18:3, Ws. 5:1, and Job 9:29.

ON THE RELICS OF SAINTS: BOOK 1

1. Rom. 14:16.

2. That is, without the water of baptism or the blood of martyrdom, which had the same cleansing effect as did baptismal waters.

3. Quoting Rom. 4:5, 1 Cor. 13:13, and Ps. 90:17/89:17.

4. Guibert puns here with the verb *sancire*, which means "to authorize." It is to some degree a verbal necessity, since the vocabulary for what we would call "canonization" was still in flux in the early twelfth century.

5. Horace, *Ars poetica* 28.

6. A reference to the Gospel of Thomas, an early Christian Coptic text to which Augustine refers. It is doubtful that Guibert would have been at all familiar with the book, outside of Augustine's commentary.

7. Job 13:7.

8. The two classic types of saint are martyrs (who die for the faith) and confessors (who suffer for the faith).

9. Saint Samson of Dol is a fifth-century saint and a patron of Brittany. A *lectio* refers to a sacred text read daily within a

monastery. Pyro appears as a character from the Life of Sam-
son, chapters 20 and 24, BHL 7478.

10. The well-known story of Saint Anselm's debate with Lanfranc
about the possible sanctity of Lanfranc's predecessor Elphege,
killed by Vikings, appears in Eadmer's *Vita Anselmi* 1.30. Lan-
franc suggested that Elphege, who died while protecting the
wealth of his church from Vikings, was a good man, but was
not necessarily a martyr, since martyrs die while confessing
the faith. Anselm's arguments convinced Lanfranc to recognize
Elphege's cult.

11. 2 Pet. 2:4 and Luke 16:19–25. The story of the rich man in the
parable will take on a very important role in book 4 of this
treatise, below.

12. This is one of the more complicated passages in the text with a
somewhat elusive meaning. It is unclear from Guibert's sentence
structure whether he places "custodians of God's people" in
apposition to bishops or whether they constitute a separate
group, such as priests, as Huygens suggests in his edition. Gui-
bert also alludes to two biblical passages. The first, Rom. 10:2,
suggests that a zeal for God ought to be built on knowledge.
The second is a reference to a commentary tradition on Cain
and Abel. Cain in his sin neither offered nor divided his sacri-
fices as he ought to have done. The language is close (but not
identical) to Gen. 4:7. The interpretation goes back at least to
Tertullian. Guibert uses similar language in his *Moralia in Gen-
esim*, commenting on Gen. 22:6. "Division" refers to the prac-
tice of discretion. If one performs spiritual offices correctly, but
without proper discretion, then the ceremonies are mere hollow
forms.

13. Isa. 5:20.

14. 1 Pet. 4:18.

15. That is, as the following analysis makes clear, the performance
of miracles by itself is no sure sign of sanctity. Rather, God
allows miracles sometimes to occur in the name of unworthy or
unbelieving men.

16. The Alexander of medieval legend did at times appear semi-
divine. Guibert refers here to how the seas receded to allow his
army entry into Pamphylia at Mount Climax. Suetonius reports
in *Vespasian* 8 that the emperor performed two miracles—
healing a blind man with his own saliva and a lame man by
touching him with the heel of his foot.

17. On this last point, Guibert probably has in mind 1066, when Halley's comet returned, thus seeming to announce the Norman Conquest.

18. This well-known passage about Louis VI and his father, Philip, is one of the earliest and most detailed descriptions of the Capetian miracle, famously studied by Marc Bloch in *The Royal Touch: Monarchy and Miracles in France and England*, trans. J. E. Anderson (London: Routledge, 1973). Guibert indicates that he has seen the miracle performed, and also professes some skepticism about whether it is appropriate for a king to do such things, mixing saintly and political roles in such a way. The fact that the English kings do not attempt such things is thus not necessarily a criticism or a statement of French patriotism. There were in fact traditions that King Edward the Confessor performed miracles, though not necessarily touching, for the King's Evil. According to the Miracles of Saint Frideswide of Oxford, Henry II, around 1180, was attempting to cure scrofula.

19. Num. 22:22–30, when Balaam's ass sees an angel of the Lord, tries to avoid it, and ultimately speaks to Balaam to reprove him; and John 11:49–52, when the high priest Caiaphas pronounces upon the sacrificial character of the death of Christ.

20. The Holy Innocents, as noted above, were the Jewish children ordered slain by Herod. They were regarded as saints, even though they performed no good deeds and even though they were born before the time of Christ, thus having no faith or grace of baptism, either.

21. Rapid-fire biblical quotations: Rom. 9:21, Matt. 20:15, and Rom. 9:18. The gist of the argument Guibert intends readers to draw from them is again that miracles and visions are value-neutral. They are tools of God and do not necessarily reveal anything about the moral character of the recipient of the vision.

22. Raoul was archbishop of Reims from 1108 to 1124. He would appear to be Guibert's most reliable source for the story about the child seeing the baby Jesus in the host.

23. Seneca, *De beneficiis* 3.15.4.

24. That is to say, Christ; John 4:34.

25. Mark 10:52.

26. The mythical last king of Assyria, whose wealth was legendary (later to be celebrated by nineteenth-century Romantics and in a painting by Delacroix).

27. It almost goes without saying that the number forty here is symbolic, inspired by the many forty-day periods in the Bible (the flood of Noah, Moses' forty days atop Mount Sinai, forty years of wandering in the desert before reaching the promised land, Christ's forty days in the wilderness), and by the Lenten fast.

28. The passage to which Guibert refers appears to be Heb. 11:31–34. Rahab was a prostitute in Jericho who assisted the Israelites with their attack upon the city (Josh. 2:8–24). Jephthah was forced to sacrifice his daughter because of a vow made in the heat of battle (Judg. 11:29–40).

29. The source material for this passage in fact appears twice: Ps. 79:9/78:9 and Dan. 9:19.

30. As always, Guibert is careful in his presentation of ghostly apparitions. What the living young girls see is not the reality of the afterlife, but rather evidence of how God uses physical appearance to convey higher heavenly truths.

31. As Huygens observes in his note on this passage, Guibert refers to a letter of Jerome (*Ep.* 147) by memory without actually having the text before him—a trait, as we have noted, characteristic of Guibert's working methods.

32. The reference, of course, is to the cathedral at Laon, which—as described in *Monodies* 3.12 above—organized a relic tour to raise funds to rebuild the church after its destruction during the communal riots.

33. Guibert describes the object as a *philacterium*, a particular type of reliquary worn around the neck. The term also is associated with Jewish practice—a small container with a fragment of parchment bearing Hebrew scripture worn around the neck during prayer.

34. Guibert perhaps refers to Anselm and Ralph of Laon, the famed schoolmasters to whom he paid tribute in his *Moral Commentary on Genesis*. Anselm similarly at the papal curia kept quiet about Gaudry's lack of qualification for the bishopric of Laon in *Monodies* 3.4.

35. As we shall see in book 2 of this treatise, each fragment of the Eucharist (the reenactment of the Last Supper) contained wholly and perfectly the body of Christ. To claim "an actual piece" of the bread that Christ ate is as theologically irrational as it is historically ludicrous. The Boethius passage is a reference to the possibly spurious *Liber contra Euthychen et Nestorium*.

36. The Donatists were the theological and political adversaries of Saint Augustine. Augustine, in some of his least palatable writ-

ings, argued that persecution of the Donatists was justified, and that if Donatists died on behalf of their faith, they were not in fact martyrs, because their faith was false.

37. *Monodies* 3.17 above. In this sentence and the previous one, we see in Guibert's thought on heresy a more general medieval tendency—to seek for parallels in the writings of Augustine, as if modern heretics were ancient holdovers, rather than to investigate them as products of the twelfth-century world.

38. Guibert refers, of course, to Saint Martin of Tours and Saint Rémy of Reims, perhaps the two most important saints in France.

39. Horace, *Epodes* 2.1.117.

40. 2 Kings 17:29–30.

41. Gregory the Great, *Pastoral Care* 1.10.

42. See above, n. 12.

43. Ambrose, *De officiis* 2.12.62.

44. Mark 11:23.

45. This difficult passage addresses the question of the possible physical resurrection of the Blessed Virgin Mary. Medieval Christians by and large believed that Mary had been bodily taken to heaven in the Assumption, celebrated on August 15. The belief indeed dates as far back as the fourth century in Eastern Christian tradition. As Guibert rightly notes, however, no scriptural passage justifies this tenet of faith, however compelling or fitting the argument may seem. Another student of Anselm of Bec, Eadmer of Canterbury, would use similar arguments to defend an Anglo-Saxon feast day, the celebration of the Immaculate Conception of Mary. Both doctrines have found acceptance in the modern church. Guibert, unlike both Eadmer and his theological successors, at least acknowledges that such reasoning is suggestive, but not compelling.

46. According to Matt. 27:52–53, at the moment of Christ's death, many graves around Jerusalem opened and the dead rose from them and walked into the city.

47. Guibert indeed risks a sensationalist argument here. If Christ did not save his mother's body from corruption at death, then surely Christ, too, would have suffered corruption and would be powerless to save anyone. The arguments throughout this paragraph are reminiscent of those advanced in *Monodies* 2.1, to explain why the ancients would have worshipped the mother of a god yet to be born. The "ancient curse" refers to God's words to Eve at the fall, especially Gen. 3:16.

48. Godfrey of Amiens, Guibert's predecessor as abbot of Nogent, treated above in *Monodies* 2.2 and 3.14. Saint Fermin was a third-century bishop of Toulouse who was martyred while preaching the gospel in Amiens in 303.

49. Odo and William in fact shared a common mother, Herleva (who was never married to Duke Robert I), not a common father.

50. Exuperius is a legendary fourth-century bishop of Bayeux. His life is not well attested. His remains were translated to Corbeil to escape Viking attacks.

51. Guibert combines here scatological rhetoric with references to 1 Tim. 6:5 and Deut. 32:29. Comparisons of money and manure were common in Europe during the Gregorian Reform.

52. Gen. 3:19.

53. The wise man, of course, is Solomon, quoting Ecclus. 40:1.

54. Rom. 10:2, as cited above.

55. Tob. 12:12–15.

56. That is, that saints should set themselves above Christ.

57. In *Ep.* 4.30 Gregory the Great (590–604) refuses the request of the Empress Constantina (d. 605) to send the head or some other body part of the apostle Paul. Gregory describes there the awful power of relics, and advances arguments very similar to Guibert's about the need to honor the integrity of their bodies. Gravediggers who disturbed bones near the tomb of Paul (but not of Paul himself) died shortly thereafter. Those who unintentionally gazed upon the bones of the martyr Laurence died within ten days.

58. 1 Sam. 28:7–25.

59. Gen. 47:29–30 and Gen. 50:23–24.

60. Virgil, *Aeneid* 6.223.

61. 1 Thess. 4:13.

62. Guibert is mistaken: Constantina, mentioned above, was the daughter of the Emperor Tiberias II Constantine (574–582) and the consort of the Emperor Maurice (582–602).

63. Edmund was an Anglo-Saxon king killed by the Vikings in 869 and buried in the church of Bury St. Edmund's. Guibert tells a shorter version of this same story near the end of *De pigneribus* 1. A similar scene would recur in the later twelfth century when Abbot Samson of Bury St. Edmunds, similarly examined the martyr's body, with no apparent consequence; Jocelyn of Brakelond, *Chronicle of Bury St. Edmunds*, trans. Diana Greenaway and Jane Sayers (Oxford: Oxford University Press, 1989), pp. 99–101.

64. This paragraph is a marginal addition to the one surviving manuscript of this text. Given its substance, it seems to be an addition in the truest sense. That is, after completing and presenting his work, Guibert is answering a question raised by a concerned member of his audience. The question would likely have been raised in response to the next paragraph.

65. John 17:22. The Gospel passage refers to believers in general united to Christ in heaven, rather than to a special category of believers who attain the heavenly vision before the general resurrection.

66. The Four Crowned Martyrs were honored on November 8. Two different traditions existed, one honoring four men and one honoring five.

67. Matt. 10:41. This passage in general offers a remarkably clear presentation of the idea that the intention is what makes an act virtuous or sinful—yet another indication of how consonant Guibert's thought was with his more famous contemporary Peter Abelard.

68. The mistake is much easier to imagine in Latin: "be present to" is *assit*, "be absent from" is *absit*.

ON THE RELICS OF SAINTS: BOOK 2

1. Relics of the Lord's circumcision (the holy Prepuce) were somewhat common in medieval Europe, the umbilical cord less so. The quote from Origen has never been identified and is likely an example of Guibert working from a characteristically faulty memory.

2. Guibert's language here is both technical and sparse. The word for appearance is *species*, a crucial term in the still nascent theology of the Eucharist: *species* is what the eye sees, as opposed to the more real, truthful underlying substance. Some liberty has been taken here with the Latin to attempt to clarify Guibert's meaning—that he does not wish to detract from the power of Christ's "figural body," since it is intimately connected with the underlying truth of his heavenly body. Guibert tries to clarify this terminology as his argument develops.

3. This vocabulary used here, which we have sought to clarify through parenthetical expressions in the text, caused one of Guibert's benevolent readers to object, as Guibert mentions in the preface to this work.

4. The quotation refers to Christ's words at the Last Supper; see Luke 22:19. Guibert's word choice here for Christ's Real Presence is *proprietas*, which in medieval law could refer as well to an alod—that is, land held in full ownership without obligation to any lord. The word choice would seem to emphasize the fullness with which Christ inhabits the Eucharist.

5. Some liberties have been taken here with Guibert's pronouns, in order to clarify in English what exactly he is referring to. The complexity in the argument grows out of the theological paradox that is the Eucharist: that this sign of Christ's body and blood is the reality of that body and blood. The sign is removed (or as Guibert delicately phrases it here, the sign is "inflected") from that reality, but it is united with that reality.

6. Ps. 51:12/50:14.

7. Matt. 28:19: "Therefore go and make disciples of all nations, baptizing them in the name of the Father and of the Son and of the Holy Spirit."

8. Perhaps the fundamental division between Greek and Latin orthodoxy grew out of differing interpretations of the Trinity. The most famous point of contention concerned the debate over "filioque," a word added in the Western tradition to the Nicene Creed. As a result, the Holy Spirit proceeded not simply from the Father, but from the Father and the Son. Guibert's contention is that in making this claim, the Greeks have introduced distinctions and temporal points of origin into the unified (and inherently paradoxical) concept of the Trinity. It was a dangerous thing to interpret too freely about the Trinity. In 1121, shortly after Guibert completed this book, Peter Abelard would be put on trial in Soissons for his trinitarian beliefs, resulting in the burning of his book—an event Guibert most likely would have witnessed.

9. Heb. 11:1.

10. Inserting *corpore* with the expression *proprie proprio*. A similar expression occurs in the sermons of Geoffrey of Vendome, PL 157, col. 267D, in reference to the host.

11. A quotation from the mass, deriving ultimately from Luke 22:19 and 1 Cor. 11:25.

12. John 12:8 and Matt. 28:20.

13. Augustine, *Confessions* 4.6.11 (referencing Horace, *Odes* 1.3.8).

14. The "you" in this sentence refers to a monk at Saint-Médard defending the validity of the tooth of Christ. But, as happened in book 1, Guibert begins to lose the thread of the argument

against his adversaries at Saint-Médard and focuses instead here on fine points of eucharistic theology. These passages do relate to his case against the tooth of Christ, but they are not strictly essential for disproving its authenticity.

15. John 6:58.

16. Exod. 16:18.

17. A delightful sentence, though it is not entirely clear that everyone would have agreed readily with Guibert's assessment. As churchmen propagated and enforced the doctrine of the Real Presence more aggressively in the eleventh and twelfth centuries, it led to a wide array of new questions and problems. *The Monastic Constitutions of Lanfranc*, ed. David Knowles (London: T. Nelson, 1951) (Lanfranc being one of the inventors of the doctrine of Transubstantiation) describe not just the elaborate care to be taken in the preparation of the host, but also the strict procedures required if any of it should drop on the ground or otherwise be mishandled. The affected places on the floor, be they stone or wood, shall be taken up and removed. Those responsible for mishandling the host shall be whipped and held to a regime of fasting or further beatings in penance. Seven priests shall also be chosen at random to prostrate themselves and sing penitential psalms on behalf of the community.

18. In antiquity, catechumens, who had expressed interest in Christianity but had not yet accepted it, were required to leave church after the sermon and before the mass. Guibert's point thus seems to be that bread and wine that have not been deliberately blessed by the priest receive no grace and accomplish nothing.

19. John 6:58, as quoted above.

20. The two natures are divine and human, God and man.

21. Lev. 17:14.

22. 1 Cor. 11:24 and Luke 22:19.

23. Matt. 26:28.

24. The vocabulary in this sentence draws on Deut. 19:4-6, a passage that touches on similar issues of sin and intention. If an axe should break apart while a man is chopping wood in such a way that the axe head strikes and kills a neighbor, then that man who wielded the axe can seek shelter in another city and not be subject to the law of vengeance. Where there is no intention, there is no crime or sin.

25. The scriptural passages cited here all come from John: 2:23–24, 12:44, and 6:54, respectively. The Augustine reference is to the *Tractates on the Gospel of John* 11.2–4.

26. John 6:57.
27. Similar to phrasing from book 1, above, describing the apostles, who adhere to the head as if hairs or beards.
28. The language here and elsewhere in this part of the text draws heavily on 1 Cor. 11:26–29.
29. As noted in the introduction, this passage in the original, only surviving manuscript of *De pigneribus*, is written over an erasure. It would seem to have been added later onto an existing argument. In other words, Guibert wrote the pages that follow as his own original contribution to eucharistic debate, not as an attempt to enter the mind of "one who thinks otherwise."
30. Matt. 26:28.
31. Luke 10:5–6.
32. This passage draws heavily on Ws 1:4–5.
33. Guibert moves dangerously close to the Donatist heresy here, suggesting that unworthy priests cannot perform the sacraments required of their offices. The next paragraph, however, saves him from this misstep, at least, by shifting all of his emphasis onto the recipient of the sacrament rather than its conduit, the priest.
34. John 1:33 and Heb. 10:12. Sacramental authority stretched back in a continuous chain of authority to Christ, who passed this grace on by laying hands on his apostles.
35. Ps. 78:13/77:13 and 65:9/64:10. Because it is impossible for us in this life to separate the elect from the damned, to separate true confessors from fictive ones, God has established priests as conduits for sacramental authority, regardless of their meritorious or faulty characters.
36. Despite this protracted excursus on simony, then, Guibert makes plain here that again he considers the key issue at the heart of the Gregorian reform ultimately trifling, at least in comparison with the serious business of the mass.
37. 1 Cor. 11:29.
38. Guibert inadvertently moves closer to the twelfth-century solution to this conundrum: an unworthy communicant can receive the physical body and blood of Christ, but does not receive the blessing or the grace of that sacrament (*res sacramenti*).
39. 2 Cor. 5:16 and Luke 9:58.
40. John 6:58, John 6:52, and Ps. 78:25/77:25.
41. Luke 11:3 and Matt. 6:9.
42. Lev. 11:44.
43. 1 John 3:18.
44. A very rough paraphrase of John 15:19.

45. Eph. 13:14.

46. Cyprian (d. 258) was the archbishop of Carthage. His tenure overlapped with the Decian persecution. Cyprian took a hard line on how to deal with those who had lapsed during this persecution, and his book referred to here is a justification of those policies. Guibert, as usual, works from memory, and as is often the case, his memory is faulty. In the actual stories, a woman left the host in a chest only to find it aflame and impossible to touch. A man who had lapsed found that he could not swallow the host because it tasted like ash. One girl was unable to accept the Eucharist because her nurse had involved her in a pagan ritual, unbeknownst to her mother.

47. 1 Tim. 5:8.

48. The snide opponents referred to here are not Jews and unbelievers, but are rather Christians who contend that the sacrament is a sign and not truth. These hypothetical (though no doubt they were very real opponents whom Guibert was imagining) make the case that unless Christians content themselves with a figural sacramental truth rather than a physical sacramental truth, they will always be vulnerable to the argument from Jews and unbelievers that mice and animals are capable of eating the real, substantive body of Christ.

49. As noted in the introduction, the final lines on this page in the single surviving manuscript of *De pigneribus* are written over an erasure. The text that immediately follows is written in a remarkably different hand on parchment inserted at a later point in preparation of the manuscript. In other words, Guibert begins to retract at this point views of the unnamed adversary, which were, in fact, originally Guibert's own views.

50. This long sentence grows out of a hodgepodge of scriptural reference: John 6:67, Matt. 5:45, Dan. 10:12–21, and Ps. 102:13/101:14. The figure of Michael, mentioned in Daniel, is perhaps the archangel. In this passage he is resisting the prince of the Persians.

51. Eccles. 9:1 and 1 Cor. 11:20.

52. The remainder of this paragraph, in the original manuscript, is a lengthy marginal addition written in very small letters by the hand belonging to Guibert. It is, therefore, an afterthought to this section, which is itself an afterthought to the main book.

53. Prov. 16:33.

54. Rom. 8:28, a verse where Paul speaks about how all things work to the good of those who have been predestined for

salvation—thus fitting into the general theme of predestination that runs throughout this section.

55. "The ashes of Cyprian" is of course a reference to the anecdote discussed above. The story of the old man's vision Guibert probably took from Guitmund of Aversa, a Norman monk turned Italian bishop of the late eleventh century. He wrote one of the most important theological treatises on transubstantiation, which seems to have provided Guibert with the conceptual vocabulary used in his refutation of "the adversary." In this treatise, Guitmund relates an anecdote similar to the one Guibert uses here, attributing it to a book called *The Lives of the Fathers*.

56. Cleopas was a disciple who encountered Christ after the resurrection on the road to Emmaus but did not recognize him; Luke 24:13. Mary Magdalene, in the Gospel of John, encountered Christ at the empty tomb, but again did not recognize him; John 20:14–15. The theological interpretation here is that Christ changed his outer form, his *species*, in order to conceal his identity momentarily from people who knew him well. Thus the Eucharist can similarly change its *species* to appear as ash or coal, even though its substance (already changed by performance of the Eucharist without affecting the *species*) remains the same. The argument again comes from Guitmund of Aversa. Guibert makes immediately clear that he does not completely buy it.

57. Exod. 12:10—dietary regulation for the Passover. Excess food was to be destroyed rather than saved.

58. Another reference to the transfiguration (see above, *Monodies* 1.2). In this context, Guibert uses the story to emphasize that the Eucharist contains the divine body, which Christ as man always possessed.

59. John 10:18.

60. A frequent refrain in the Gospel of John: John 2:4, 7:6, 7:8, 7:30, and 8:20; see also John 13:1, when we read that his hour has indeed come.

61. See John 3:3–8. The first birth is of the flesh, and the second is of the spirit, through baptism. According to traditional theology (and as Guibert goes on to argue), men die because they are born with the blight of original sin. It is for this reason that they have need of the liberty, or immunity, that a second birth in baptism can provide. Christ, however, was born already in possession of that liberty.

62. Ps. 88:5/87:6.

63. Prov. 17:22.

64. A very loose paraphrase of Rom. 14:17 lies behind this passage. The scriptural passage discusses the applicability (and relative unimportance) of dietary laws and is at best only peripherally connected to Guibert's discussion of the purity and impassibility of Christ.

65. That is to say, Adam. Christ is known as the Second Adam. Guibert refers to him here as "the Second Man."

66. John 3:13, 14:10, and 8:23.

67. It is impossible to know the identity of this friend about whom Guibert speaks. It was certainly easy, however, to slip into this sort of error. The learned and urbane poet, historian, and archbishop Baudry of Dol, for example, could not resist writing in his crusade chronicle that Christ was being crucified every day in Jerusalem, as long as the city was in the possession of Muslims (*Historia Ierosolimitana* 4, 13, published in *Recueil des historiens des Croisades Historiens occidentaux* 4, p. 101).

68. Guibert again engages the fundamental trope of biblical exegesis. The literal meanings of the Old Testament are but shadows that the New Testament has fulfilled. But the same sort of allegorical process is at work in Christian ceremonies. The Eucharist thus signifies the Passion but is not the Passion itself. The analysis nonetheless treads close to heresy because of the special place of meaning and significance attributed to the Eucharist. Due to the doctrine of the Real Presence, the host is not a shadow of Christ's body. It does not signify Christ's body. Rather, it *is* Christ's body. If it also signifies the Passion, might a believer not then easily conclude that (on the model of the Real Presence) it was the Passion? This is the sort of misguided idea (with the grotesque consequences that Guibert has outlined here) that the church's fixation on transubstantiation and the Real Presence, starting in the mid–eleventh century, inadvertently created.

69. Rom. 6:9–10.

70. An abridged version of 1 Pet. 3:18.

71. Heb. 9:24–28.

72. The next paragraph is another lengthy marginal addition to the original text. It seems to be a relatively even-tempered summation of the general argument.

73. Heb. 6:6: "they crucify the Son of God again and subject him to public shame."

74. The codicological irregularities that have characterized so much of the past several pages (beginning with Guibert's refutation of the "person who thinks otherwise, and continuing

with his frantic debate against those who believe the living Christ is crucified daily on the altar) finally end here. The next page in the manuscript has been tampered with slightly in order to make it cohere grammatically to this section, but it is readily apparent with the start of the next paragraph that Guibert is referring to a differently worded argument—presumably to a page that ended up on the scriptorium floor.

75. Matt. 26:29, John 7:39, and John 6:57–58.
76. Apoc. 13:8.
77. Jude 5 and 1 Cor. 10:8.
78. John 16:7. "Paraclete" is a term for the Holy Spirit.

ON THE RELICS OF SAINTS: BOOK 3

1. The argument here builds upon the language of book 2 of *On the Relics of Saints*, above. The main points are theological rather than historical. The body of Christ in heaven is resurrected wholly and perfectly. Nothing pertaining to his body that is holy can remain on earth. The promise of perfect bodily resurrection (to be discussed in greater detail in book 4) for all of the saints upon the Day of Judgment would grow suspect if Christ could not fulfill these promises for himself. Historically, of course, a tooth of Christ could survive on the earth (a point that Guibert will address later on). But the theology in this case dictates the course of history and the practice of historical interpretation.

2. Luke 21:18.

3. Ps. 16:10/15:10, where the psalmist rejoices that his soul will not be left in hell and the Holy One (from a Christian interpretive tradition, Christ) shall not decay.

4. Josh. 5:2–9. The Lord ordered Joshua to circumcise a generation of Israelites who had not undergone the ceremony at birth.

5. The prophetic passage is Ps. 16:10/15:10, quoted just above. Peter recalls this verse when addressing a mocking crowd in Jerusalem in Acts 2:27.

6. These arguments again rest on theology. What makes physical relics holy, in Guibert's analysis, is that the saints will one day reclaim them and incorporate them into their perfected heavenly bodies. Saint Anselm taught a similar lesson to his disciple Eadmer, who was once allowed to break off a piece of the body of Saint Prisca. Eadmer was disappointed when he was only able to tear away a small piece, but Anselm assured him that Prisca

would be as grateful to him at the resurrection as if he had been taking care of her entire body; Eadmer, *Vita S. Anselmi*, 2, 55, pp. 132–34.

7. A reference to Luke 21:18, above, stating that "not a hair on your head will perish." The previous reference is to John 8:46.

8. Exod. 21:33.

9. Gal. 2:1–2.

10. *Ars Poetica*, 88.

11. Phil 3:21; the teacher of the Gentiles is Paul.

12. Rom. 12:1.

13. Boethius, *Contra Eutychen*, preface, 31–33; this was one of Guibert's favorite aphorisms; he uses it also in his treatise *Against the Judaizer and the Jews*.

14. Guibert is now speaking in the voice of an imagined monk of Saint-Médard, raising objections to his own theology, as presented in book 2 of *On the Relics of Saints*. The imagined monk even borrows from Guibert's own controversial sacramental language, with his use of "vicarial body."

15. Referencing Luke 11:3 and Heb. 3:13.

16. Guibert again draws on the language of book 2 of *On the Relics of Saints*, recalling that the sacrament exists to train Christians in the art of contemplation ("wisdom/*sapientia*" being an attribute more closely associated with intellect, or contemplative understanding than is "knowledge/*scientia*," generally associated with lower forms of learning).

17. According to John 19:33–34, when Roman soldiers pierced Christ's side on the cross, blood and water flowed from the wound, exegetically representing the Eucharist and baptism.

18. The fictional Saint-Médard monk thus argues that this particular relic of Christ is no different from the other relics Guibert discussed in book 1 of *On the Relics of Saints*. It serves as a preliminary step for the less discerning, of which the higher step is the Eucharist.

19. The third heaven is the apostle Paul's description of the contemplative experience; 2 Cor. 12:2.

20. Jesus accepted baptism from John the Baptist, although John, as he had told his own followers, baptized only with water; the one to follow him, Christ, would baptize with fire and the Holy Spirit. See Matt. 3:11–17.

21. The apostle Thomas demanded to see Christ's wounds before he would fully accept the truth of the resurrection. Hence the expression "doubting Thomas." The figure of the apostle inserting

a finger into Christ's side was a popular subject in medieval art, particularly in Romanesque sculpture; see John 20:24–29.

22. Luke 12:37.

23. Ps. 59:11/58:12. This verse, in Christian thought, served to justify the continuing presence of the Jews in the world. They were a remnant of the past to remind Christians of Christ's sacrifice. According to most traditions, they would be converted at the Day of Judgment.

24. Using again the vocabulary from book 2 of *On the Relics of Saints*, the "principal body" is Christ's historical body, of which the monks of Saint-Médard claim to possess a fragment.

25. Here Guibert finishes speaking in the voice of the monk of Saint-Médard and starts to refute their case.

26. Heb. 11:1, 3.

27. Rom. 8:24.

28. John 16:7.

29. After the theological arguments, Guibert now turns his attention to historical criticism, as if to demonstrate that the tooth is nonsensical according to the dictates of both faith and reason.

30. Num. 19:9 and 31:23.

31. Guibert perhaps forgets here the story of Quilius, in *Monodies* 2.1 above, who received relics from Mary and the apostles shortly after the crucifixion.

32. John 16:20 and Luke 24:39.

33. John 20:24–28, Luke 24:13, Acts 1:3, Matt. 28:9. Paul says in 1 Cor. 15:6 that Christ appeared to more than five hundred people after his resurrection.

34. John 20:26.

35. The pilgrims on the road to Emmaus, described in Luke 24.

36. John 13:31. The previous sentence is an awkward amalgamation of several scriptural passages: 1 Cor. 15:54, Ezek. 33:19, and Ps. 54:22/55:22.

37. Here Guibert has finished his point-by-point debate with the fictitious monk of Saint-Médard.

38. Louis the Pious (778–840) was Charlemagne's son and successor as emperor. As noted in the introduction, after being temporarily deposed by his sons in 833, he was imprisoned in the church of Saint-Médard. Guibert here imagines the emperor's chaplains taking up his own arguments against the relic's authenticity.

39. Col. 1:16; thrones and dominions are two of the traditional nine orders of angels.

40. It is the basic point of Guibert's theology of miracles: miracles do not occur simply for the sake of wonderment but to impart a lesson.

41. This argument builds upon points raised in book 1 of *On the Relics of Saints*—specifically where Guibert suggested that if a believer prayed before false relics, the faith of the prayer alone might lead to a miracle, despite the falsity of the relics.

42. Luna was an Etruscan city largely destroyed by pirate attacks in the eleventh century. Nearby Portovenere still stands on the Ligurian coast of Italy, containing many twelfth-century structures.

43. Isa. 40:1.

44. Guibert refers here to a collection of shrine miracles made at the church of Saint-Médard. Such collections were common in medieval churches that wished to promote the popularity of their saints. The story that Guibert tells here obviously has nothing to do with the tooth of Christ. Rather, he cites a somewhat incoherent miracle as a way of questioning the general integrity of the Saint-Médard community.

45. Heb. 5:8.

46. Luke 2:35. This verse is the basis for much speculation among contemplatives about the interior life of Mary—her awareness of her son's fate and the suffering it caused her. Guibert refers in the next sentence to another verse from the same chapter, Luke 2:19.

47. 1 Tim 3:16.

48. A point discussed in book 1 of *On the Relics of Saints*.

ON THE RELICS OF SAINTS: BOOK 4

1. Song of Sol. 4:9.

2. In modern parlance, of course, "imagination" is the most celebrated of mental faculties. Guibert uses the word differently here. It refers to the way in which the mind interacts with the physical world—literally, the way that it processes "images." To transcend images is to attain a higher faculty, called in Guibert's vocabulary "intellect." An "intellectual" in this sense is not an academically trained person, but rather is someone who has learned to transcend the world and focus on God. To dismiss "imagination" then is not to undervalue creativity but to encourage readers to seek a higher contemplative state of mind.

3. Matt. 6:6 and 2 Cor. 12:2; cf. Apoc. 21.1.
4. Ezek. 1:4–14 and Ezek. 40.
5. Apoc. 21:19–20.
6. Besides God appearing to Moses as a burning bush, he is described in Deut. 4:24 as "a consuming fire." Scripture often uses anthropomorphic language to describe God as well. Heb. 8:14 mentions God's right hand, and Heb. 10:12–13 implies that God has hands and feet. Guibert's argument, throughout book 4, is that human language must speak of God through allegory, since the divine essence transcends human understanding.
7. Since God is incorporeal, he obviously does not possess limbs, or any bodily parts. Passages such as "Now you are the body of Christ, and each one of you is a part of it" (1 Cor. 12:27) therefore exist to teach lessons about the church, how despite the diversity of its members it nonetheless exists and functions as a unified body.
8. Exod. 3:14.
9. 1 Cor. 10:1–11. The "ancients" in this case are the Israelites, whose literal experiences were to be read by Christians allegorically, offering moral lessons to be applied to their own lives.
10. Apoc. 1:10. Most readers of the Apocalypse (or "Revelation"— the last book of the New Testament) would find very little in it redolent of the ordinary, physical world. Guibert's larger point is that human beings (even the prophet John) can only make divine truths comprehensible through tangible allegories.
11. All images from the Apocalypse: Apoc. 1:12–16, 19:15, and 2:18.
12. Guibert refers in a general way to the *Dialogues of Gregory the Great,* a collection of hagiographic and theological texts that includes several visions of the afterlife, described in tangible terms. It is a problem that Gregory himself does not deal with, since he is concerned mainly to explain why God allows some to experience the afterlife (e.g., *Dialogues* 4.36).
13. Bede serves as Guibert's standard against which to judge writings that deal with the miraculous. The final section of *Ecclesiastical History* records a handful of visions of the afterlife: 5.2–14.
14. Matt. 22:13—a parable in which Christ describes how a wealthy man invited to a wedding feast is thrown out because he has not worn a wedding garment.
15. 1 Cor. 2:13.
16. We obviously must take Guibert's use of the first-person verb, "we see," literally, based on his descriptions of torments inflicted

on prisoners by Thomas of Marle. The "goat's tongue" torture, reportedly developed in the Roman Empire, involved having the goat lick a prisoner's heels until it had worn away all the flesh on the feet.

17. Ps. 51:6/50:8. The psalmist is David, from whom Christ would be descended.

18. 2 Cor. 12:4.

19. This is a probable reference to Mark 6:1–5, where Jesus is unable to perform miracles at Nazareth, apart from a few healings. In this famous passage he observes that a prophet is without honor in his home. Guibert, working from memory as always, confuses Nazareth with Capernaum, that in Matt. 4:13 Christ visits upon leaving Nazareth.

20. Matt. 7:6.

21. Amos 2:13; Ps. 78:65/77:65.

22. Ezek. 1:5–6; Janus was a two-faced god. "Intellectual" here again (the word in Latin is *intellectualitas*) refers to the level of meaning that transcends mere human understanding—the ability of the mind in this life to attain a foretaste of the vision of God, which is an experience that, as Guibert has made clear by now, transcends the powers of speech. Guibert is also applying a fundamental concept of medieval biblical exegesis: if a passage makes no sense, or appears to contradict an obvious or crucial truth, then that passage must be interpreted allegorically, and not literally. The monstrous character of the four animals in Ezekiel serves to emphasize the importance of the allegorical truths they represent.

23. Ps.104:4/103:4.

24. Apoc. 7:9, 4:4.

25. Chiliasm was a heresy that grew out of a literal reading of Apoc. 20:1–6, where the prophet speaks of a thousand-year period when Satan will be bound and Christ will rule on earth with saintly judges. The standard Augustinian interpretation of these verses is that the thousand-year period refers to the time of the church before the Last Judgment. Historians routinely discount the importance of millenarianism throughout most of the Middle Ages, but it does seem to be a recurrent theme in the thought of religious dissenters.

26. Eph. 2:11. Guibert here passes over hastily what is a fairly dense analogy. The Jews, he argues, are circumcised in the flesh, by which they imagine they have access to some secret truth, and therefore look upon the Gentile Christians as uncircumcised, as though they do not have access to these truths. The Jews, however,

are imprisoned by literal, external truths and correspondingly lack access to the higher, invisible truths of Christianity. In the same way, Guibert suggests, "interior" could be viewed as a convenient label applied by the exterior world to something to which it has no real access or understanding.

27. 1 Cor. 14:15. The Latin *spiritus* acquires the meaning of "spirit" from its origins as "breath."

28. John 12:31; Eph. 2:2, 6:12.

29. Job 14:21, where Job speaks of the dead generally rather than the damned specifically.

30. Luke 10:20, John 14:8, and John 16:22. All of these verses indicate, if somewhat obliquely, that the joys of heaven will be spiritual.

31. Ps. 73:25–26/72:25–26, and John 6:40.

32. 1 John 2:21.

33. Rom. 14:17. The Vulgate reads "righteousness and peace and joy," which should perhaps be supplied here, since they would parallel the words, "eternal disorder and perpetual unrest and gloom," which follow.

34. Matt. 22:13.

35. A series of rapid-fire references that demonstrates the variety of Guibert's learning: Prov. 18:3, Matt. 3:10, Ps. 58:8/57:9, and Virgil, *Aeneid* 6.733.

36. That next paragraph is the last of the lengthy marginal additions to the text. Guibert probably added a passage, again, to meet objections raised by his first readers, or, rather, the first people to hear him publicly read his arguments. As is apparent from the answer, Guibert was uncomfortable with the direction of the argument and was prepared, if not to concede the point, then at least not to dispute it further.

37. Gregory the Great, *Dialogues* 4.29.

38. Guibert refers here to a parable in Luke 16:19–31. The rich man is condemned to hell, while the poor man Lazarus is taken up into the bosom of Abraham. The rich man asks Abraham to send Lazarus to hell with a drop of water on his finger and thus to soothe his suffering, but Abraham only replies that the rich man is receiving his just deserts, just as Lazarus is receiving his reward in heaven.

39. Ps. 10:27/9:28.

40. The verb here, *stridere*, translated here as "shriek," derives from the same noun, *stridor*, used to communicate gnashing. Here, obviously, there are no symbolic teeth involved, but Guibert

does use the word to refine his earlier arguments. He touched upon these general arguments in the introduction to the text, indicating that they were somewhat controversial among his original readers.

41. This is the same parable of the rich man as discussed above. Guibert mentions it here as though he has not yet raised the topic (and since the paragraph dealing with it is a later addition, at the time he wrote this latter section, he had in fact not dealt with it). Here he discusses the second half of the story only. In brief, the rich man asks Abraham to send the poor man's soul to warn his relatives about hell, lest they suffer his fate, but Abraham responds that his family already has the sayings of Moses and the Prophets, which should count for more than a message from the dead.

42. Eccles. 9:10, cited previously in Guibert's introduction to this treatise.

43. Isa. 66:24 and Job 30:17. The gist of the argument is that Job suffered actual physical punishments, not spiritual ones.

44. 2 Cor. 7:10.

45. According to the legend of the Harrowing of Hell (a popular subject in medieval iconography), Christ, between the crucifixion and the resurrection, went into hell and freed certain virtuous souls (notably, Adam). The doctrine receives only oblique scriptural confirmation.

46. John 6:40 and John 17:3.

47. It is not clear what authorities Guibert has in mind here— perhaps the Patristic theologian Tertullian, who argues in *De anima* 9 that a soul has a body peculiar to itself. As is apparent from Guibert's frequent asides and occasional marginal notes, audiences for twelfth-century theological treatises were armed with an array of Patristic citations, ready to use them to strike down ill-considered or half-formed arguments. The decision Guibert claims here to have taken, to refute writings but not authors, seems an overly fine distinction.

48. Matt. 23:4. A drop of water on the tongue thus is a prayer of indulgence to ease sufferings, like the prayers that Guibert's mother offered for the sake of his father's soul. (See *Monodies* 1.18, above.) In this analysis Guibert somewhat surprisingly does not mention that Lazarus did not in fact place a drop of water on the tongue of the rich man, according to the parable.

49. Two anecdotes from the Life of Saint Benedict, in Gregory the Great, *Dialogues* 2.34–35. In the first one mentioned here,

Benedict saw Bishop Germanus of Capua being carried into heaven in a fiery globe. In the second, he saw his sister Scholastica ascending to heaven in the form of a dove. Guibert rhetorically asks his opponents how we are to interpret these visions if the souls were literal, physical bodies.

50. John 18:36, Matt. 26:19, Mark 13:2, Luke 11:2, and Matt. 6:10.

51. 1 Cor. 15:24, 28. The "threefold structure" mentioned here is the physical world, the spiritual world, and the middle place that man occupies, existing in parallel to the "tripartite" body that Guibert describes above in book 2 of this treatise (the physical body of Christ, the heavenly body of Christ, and the eucharistic body that exists in this world).

52. Luke 23:43. Christ was crucified between two thieves. According to Luke, one of the thieves mocked him, but a good thief (traditionally named "Dimas") was respectful, and Christ promised him that on that day the thief would be with him in paradise.

53. A reference to the ascension of Christ to heaven after the resurrection, described in Acts 1, when his apostles saw him rise into the clouds.

54. 1 Cor. 2:14.

Index